SPORT
IN
CONTEMPORARY
SOCIETY
An Anthology

THIRD EDITION

SPORT IN CONTEMPORARY SOCIETY

An Anthology

D. STANLEY EITZEN
Colorado State University

St. Martin's Press
NEW YORK

Editor: Don Reisman
Project Editor: Laura Ann Starrett
Production Supervisor: Christine Pearson
Graphics: G&H/Soho
Cover Photo: Alan Zinn
Cover Design: Judy Forster

For information, write:
St. Martin's Press, Inc.
175 Fifth Avenue
New York, NY 10010

ISBN: 0-312-00973-9

ACKNOWLEDGMENTS

Janet Lever, "The Paradox of Sport: Integration through Conflict," excerpted from *Soccer Madness*, 1983. Reprinted by permission of the author and The University of Chicago Press. Copyright © 1983.

Richard E. Lapchick, "For the True Believer." Excerpts from *Broken Promises: Racism in American Sports* by Richard E. Lapchick. Reprinted by permission of the author.

Eldon E. Snyder and Elmer A. Spreitzer, "Baseball in Japan" from *Social Aspects of Sport*, Second edition. Copyright © 1983, pp. 53–56. Reprinted by permission of Prentice-Hall, Inc., Englewood Cliffs, New Jersey.

Sandy Padwe, "Drugs in Sports: Symptoms of a Deeper Malaise," *The Nation*, September 27, 1986. Copyright © 1987 by *The Nation*. Reprinted with permission.

John Underwood, "What's Wrong with Organized Youth Sports and What We Should Do about It." *Spoiled Sport: A Fan's Notes on the Troubles of Spectator Sports* by John Underwood. Copyright © 1984 by John Underwood. Reprinted with permission.

Acknowledgments and copyrights are continued at the back of the book on pages 381–382, which constitute an extension of the copyright page.

Preface

Most Americans are at least somewhat interested in sport, and many are downright fanatical about it. They attend games, read the sport pages and sport magazines, and talk endlessly about the subject. But even those fans who astound us with their knowledge of the most obscure facts about sport— who the opposing pitcher was when Don Larsen pitched his perfect no-hit World Series game or how many winning seasons the football team of Slippery Rock has had—do not necessarily *understand* sport.

Do sport buffs know how sport is linked to other institutions of society? Do they understand the role of sport in socializing youngsters in American values? Do they know how much racial discrimination continues to exist in American sport, and why? Do they know how often or how seldom it is really the case that sport enables its participants to rise in the American social structure? Do they know that the assumption that sport builds character is open to serious question? What about the relationship of violence in sport to the structure of society? What about the ways in which sport has perpetuated sex-role stereotypes in society? How do owners, coaches, and other sport authorities exercise power to maintain control over athletes? These are some of the issues this book examines.

There are two fundamental reasons for the ignorance of most Americans about the role of sport in society. First, they have had to rely mainly on sportswriters and sportscasters for their information, and these journalists have usually been little more than describers and cheerleaders. Until recent years journalists have rarely looked critically at sport. Instead, they have perpetuated myths: "Look what baseball did for Jackie Robinson" or "Football helped a whole generation of sons of coal miners escape the mines."

The second reason for our sports illiteracy is that sport has been virtually ignored by American academics. Only in the past twenty years or so have American social scientists and physical educators begun to employ scientific research methods to investigate the social aspects of sport. Previously, as with sports journalism, academic research in the field of sport tended to be biased in support of existing myths. In particular the early research by physical educators was aimed at proving that sports participation builds character. In this limited perspective such phenomena as cheating, violence, and failure were, for the most part, simply ignored.

Today, however, not only academics but also a new breed of sports journalists—though the latter are still a minority—are making insightful analyses of sport's role in society. They are examining the positive *and* the negative consequences of sport. They are substituting facts for myths. Most significantly, they are documenting the reciprocal impact of sport and the various institutions of society: religion, education, politics, and economics. There is no danger that sport will suffer from such examination. On the contrary, sport is revealed as a subject far more complex and far more interesting than most of us have imagined.

This book is a collection of the writings representing this new era of critical appraisal. It includes contributions from both journalists and academics. The overriding criterion for inclusion of a particular article was whether it critically examined the role of sport in society. The praise of sport is not omitted, but such praise, as with condemnation, must be backed by fact, not mythology or dogma. (Occasionally, a dogmatic piece has been included to challenge the critical faculties of the reader.) The selection of each article was also guided by such questions as, Is it interesting? Is it informative? Is it thought-provoking? Does it communicate without the use of unnecessary jargon and sophisticated methodologies?

In short, the selections presented here not only afford the reader an understanding of sport that transcends the still prevalent stereotypes and myths; they also yield fascinating and important insights into the nature of American society. Thus, this book has several groups of potential readers. First, it is intended to be the primary or supplementary textbook for courses in the sociology of sport, sport and society, and foundations of physical education. Second, the book can be used as a supplemental text for sociology courses such as the introduction to sociology, American society, and American institutions. A third audience for this book is general readers who wish to deepen their understanding and appreciation of sport.

The third edition of *Sport in Contemporary Society*, while retaining much of the structure of the earlier editions, has undergone extensive revision. Two parts from the previous edition have been combined, two others have been dropped, and three new parts have been added: "Sport and Deviance," "The Politics of Sport: International Dimensions," and "Sport and Religion." Only nine of the selections from the previous edition have been retained, making it possible to include twenty-six new and more up-to-date essays. The result is a collection of lively and timely essays that will sharpen the reader's analysis and understanding of sport *and* American society.

My choices in these revisions have been guided by the valuable suggestions of my editors, Andrea R. Guidoboni and Don Reisman, and by the comments submitted by individuals who have used or considered using previous editions of *Sport in Contemporary Society*. These reviewers include Peter Adler, Denver University; Alfred Aversa, Jr., Fairleigh Dickinson University; Gerry R. Cox, Fort Hays State University; Martha Cornwell, Union College (Kentucky); Joel Devine, Tulane University; Joseph E. Faulkner, Pennsylvania State University; David M. Furst, San Jose State University; Carl F. Galow, Valparaiso University; Jeffrey Goldstein, Temple University; David A. Gover, Winthrop College; Larry J. Halford, Washburn University; John G. Hanna, University of Southern Maine; Jeanne L. Johnston, Bethany College; Raymond Kasper, Northeastern Illinois University; Michael Malec, Boston College; David Marple, Loyola Marymount University; Richard E. Martin, Butler University; Howard L. Nixon, University of Vermont; Harold L. Ray, Western Michigan University; Ed Rosenberg, La Roche College; and Eric A. Wagner, Ohio University.

My greatest debt is to the authors of the works found in this volume. My thanks to them for their scholarship and, most significant, for their insights that help us to unravel the mysteries of this intriguing and important part of social life.

D. Stanley Eitzen

Contents

SPORT
IN
CONTEMPORARY
SOCIETY
An Anthology

Part One

Toward an Understanding of Sport

The character of American sport has changed dramatically in the twentieth century. Sport was once primarily engaged in by persons who sought the enjoyment of physical activity and competition. Although there are occasions for this level of sport now, sport for the most part has become corrupted. The athlete's pleasure has been superseded by what brings pleasure to fans, parents, sports team owners, alumni, television, and the corporations that buy television advertising. Sport has become spectacle, big business, and an extension of power politics. This shift to what might be dubbed "corporate sport" is seen not only in the professional leagues but also in the Olympic Games, colleges, high schools, and even children's sports. What once was regarded as play has become work. Spontaneity has been replaced by bureaucracy. The goal of pleasure in the physical activity has been displaced by extrinsic rewards, especially money.

The selections chosen for this book examine the current organization of sport critically from a number of perspectives. The three selections in this part serve to raise the reader's consciousness about sport in two ways. They point to the ubiquity of sport in society, the contemporary problems and issues of sport, and to how social scientists study and analyze sport. Thus, they set the stage for the analyses of specific areas of sport found in the subsequent parts of this anthology.

The first selection is taken from sociologist Janet Lever's perceptive analysis of soccer in Brazil, *Soccer Madness*. Lever provides an excellent introduction to the sociology of sport by showing how sport integrates people in societies, communities, and large cities. Lever's functional analysis contrasts sharply with the following selection by Richard E. Lapchick. Lapchick begins with the

1

unifying functions of sport but quickly moves to the problems found within sport—racism, sexism, corruption, commercialization, and dehumanization.

The final selection by sociologist Jay J. Coakley enhances our understanding of sport by elaborating on the two contrasting theoretical approaches—functionalist and conflict—that guide the work of sport sociologists. The understanding of both these perspectives is vitally important to the analyst of society. It is crucial to note that each approach offers significant insights about society. However, the theoretical approach guiding the structure of this book and the choice of selections is the conflict perspective. As I stated in the preface to Eitzen and Sage's *Sociology of North American Sport:*

> [The] goal is to make the reader aware of the positive and negative consequences of the way sport is organized in American society. We are concerned about some of the trends in sport, especially the move away from athlete-oriented activities toward the impersonality of what we term "corporate sport." We are committed to moving sport and society in a more humane direction, and this requires, as a first step, a thorough understanding of the principles that underlie the social structures and processes that create, sustain, and transform the social organizations within the institution of sport.[1]

NOTE

1. D. Stanley Eitzen and George H. Sage, *Sociology of North American Sport,* third edition (Dubuque, Iowa: Wm. C. Brown, 1986), p. xi.

1. *The Paradox of Sport: Integration through Conflict*

JANET LEVER

Sport belongs in the world of play and leisure, yet business elites, mass media, and government and political leaders recognize its potential for making profits, disseminating propaganda, and eliciting pride. Organized sport prevails virtually everywhere and has developed over the past half-century from a relatively minor element of culture into a full-blown social institution.

An indicator of the importance of sport is the sheer amount of time and affect people the world over devote to it. A cynical sport commentator once said, "We all agree to *pretend* sport is important," but judging by the emotional displays of those watching or playing a closely contested match, people are not pretending.

When survey researchers inquire about the appeal of sport, the overwhelming response is that games are entertaining and provide a break from real life. Sport stands apart from routine reality; contests offer excitement and drama because the outcome is uncertain. Luck and injury intervene, so an announcer can justifiably say, "on any given day, any team can beat any other team." The action is live, not scripted. Each contest is unique, unrehearsed, and finite, and the resolution, when it comes, is clear-cut. Unlike the chaos of ordinary life, sport offers us structure, with rituals signaling the beginning, middle, and end. Sport's symmetry gives us a sense of unity and completion within boundaries that are visible and enforced.

Contests can be more engrossing than other forms of entertainment. Unlike other performances, sport lies within the realm of personal experience for most of the audience. Most fans have played the games, are knowledgeable about rules and strategies, and can share the athletes' pleasure in accomplishing difficult physical feats. Fans appreciate both the skills and the human spirit required to excel at the highest levels of competition. Given the violent nature of sport, fans also value the bravery required of their athletes, who are risking injury. Their physical strength, grace, and courage make professional athletes the male sex symbols of society.

The excitement and drama of sports invite active spectators who cheer and shout. Their affection and loyalty make sport a genuine emotional outlet with few equals in the world of adult entertainment. The audience's exuberance

---

SOURCE: Janet Lever, *Soccer Madness* (Chicago: The University of Chicago Press, 1983), pp. 1–21.

after home runs, goals, or touchdowns not only shows appreciation of effort and skill, but is rooted in the fans' personal involvement in a team's fate. Obviously fans prefer the pleasure of winning to the suffering of watching their teams go down in defeat, but even suffering can be appreciated as an indication of loyalty and caring deeply about something. Fans frequently use the word "love" to express feelings toward their teams and favorite players, and the word "hate" to show contempt for select rivals.

When asked why they enjoy sports, people rarely refer to their special relationships with other fans. More often, they see themselves as spectators of an event, not as part of the spectacle. Fans recognize the satisfaction they get from supporting a winner, releasing emotion, and witnessing violence on the field or a skillfully played game. Yet a large part of the euphoria of sport spectacles is created by the mass of humanity that has come together to share an event; many fans report physical responses—chills, flutters, butterflies—at the sight of crowds pouring into the stadium seats before the contest begins. Whether acknowledged or not, camaraderie between fellow fans, be they neighboring strangers in the stadium or friends surrounding a television set or transistor radio, adds to the joys of sport.

THE ROLE OF SPORT IN SOCIETY

Open enjoyment of the game does not negate the serious social consequences attached to widespread fandom. Likewise, speculations on the larger social significance of sport must not deny its sheer entertainment value. Nevertheless, the serious consequences of sport for society remain largely unexamined. Intellectuals, viewing play and games as trivial and inconsequential, feel little need for scientific scrutiny of the light side of life. Journalists and philosophers have contributed interesting speculations more often than social scientists have provided empirical data.

The careful examination of the role of sport in society remains minimal despite growing recognition that avocations, like occupations, are salient bases for identification in modern life. Not only do people devote more time to playing, watching, and discussing sport than to any other organized activity in public life, but the media, big business, and government manipulate that interest in sport to serve their own interests. Organized sport, as a major social institution, has consequences for any society. Sport can be used and sport can be abused. We need better understanding of the phenomenon to make the distinction.

Sport affects society in many ways, but [here we are] devoted to a careful exploration of its most important and universal consequence: *Sport helps complex modern societies cohere.* Creating order amid diversity is a problem that pervades modern thinking. All societies have conflict; cleavages and antagonistic factions are inevitable because of scarcity, injustice, and prejudice.

All societies are also integrated to some degree, or they would cease to exist. Despite hostility and divergent interests, individuals, kin groups, towns, cities, and regions somehow get connected into a single national system. Of course the degree of integration in any society varies; a well-integrated society is one whose members are able to act together to achieve their collectively defined goals.

Sociologists have been justly criticized for their inattention to the central issue: What mechanisms are used to make a society whole? What makes society greater than the arithmetic sum of its parts? Spectator sport is one mechanism that builds people's consciousness of togetherness. Paradoxically, sport helps bring the whole together by emphasizing the conflict between the parts. Sport is the perfect cultural reflection of our Janus-headed existence: it becomes the arena for conflicting interests while cultivating a shared outlook as the basis for order.

Its unique qualities enable sport to accomplish this antilogical feat. According to Anatol Rapoport, the feature distinguishing games from other forms of conflict is that the starting point is not disagreement at all, but rather the agreement of opponents to strive for an incompatible goal—only one opponent can win—within the constraints of understood rules. In other words, conflict is not the means to resolve disagreement, but rather the end in itself. Sport is struggle for the sake of struggle, and it is this unique motive that explains the unifying power of its conflict.

Sport, then, is the play form of conflict. Athletes and teams exist only to be rivals; that is the point of their relationship. In the world of sport, there should be no purpose beyond playing and winning. Unlike rivals in the real world, who have opposing political, economic, or social aims, sport competitors must be protected, not persuaded or eliminated. In fact, a strong opponent is more valued than a weak one.

We tend to think of conflict as a problem that needs to be solved. But in its play form the benefits of conflict are made more apparent. First, conflict is more exciting than harmony. Second, the staging of conflict demands collaboration. Both sides must agree to the same set of rules, standards of acceptable play, and authorities. Cooperation becomes a product of sport rivalry through the desire to test skills, spirit, and the favors of fate. Not even heated rivalries or questionable victories disrupt the relationship, for the structure of sport requires repeated meetings. Only one team can win a single game, but the conflict retains its playfulness because sport as process is not zero-sum. The vanquished today may be the victor tomorrow—or, if not tomorrow, next season; the rankings are momentarily clear-cut, never final.

Besides, sport victories are merely symbolic. Prestige may be gained or lost, but no goods exchange hands and no soldiers are killed or imprisoned. We continue to interact because sporting conflict is materially inconsequential. As columnist Pete Axthelm said after the surprising U.S. victory over the Soviet Union in the 1980 Winter Olympics, "Beyond the happy rhetoric, our hockey triumph didn't validate our system any more than defeats in other years had undermined our way of life."

If sport simply expressed the paradox inherent in all social interaction, it would serve well as an interpretation of our lives. But its utility extends beyond metaphor. Although sports can display contrived conflicts, such contests are usually dull. Spectator sports engross us most—and make their integrative contribution—wherever they dramatize social divisions that are real and meaningful. The "foundation stone" of nearly every variety of spectator sport, according to sportswriter Michael Roberts, is "the linking of the participant's destiny with the fan's, in terms of a common city, nation, race, religion, or institution of higher learning."

The organization of sport determines which loyalties are tapped. U.S. sport teams most often represent schools and cities. The territorial monopoly that limits a city to one team in a league is unknown outside the United States. Cities elsewhere have more than one professional team in a sport, and those teams reflect special characteristics of their fan populations. A few of the most notorious rivalries in the soccer world illustrate the point: in Lima there is racial rivalry between Alianza Lima (blacks and mestizos) and Universitário Lima (white Creole); in Buenos Aires there is ethnic rivalry between Boca Juniors (Italians) and River Plate (English and Spanish); in Rio de Janeiro there is class rivalry between Flamengo (working class) and Fluminense (elite); in Glasgow there is religious rivalry between the Celtics (Roman Catholic) and the Rangers (Protestant). Its teams are less known, but in Tel Aviv there is political rivalry between the Hapoel team, sponsored by the Labor party, and the Maccabi team, sponsored by the party of the moderate right.

If rooting for a sport team or a particular athlete can reinforce one's sense of membership in all these salient status groups, then the scene is set for sport to accomplish its divide-and-integrate role. The Celtic fan may feel his Catholicism most strongly when facing the opposing Protestant Ranger fans, but they are literally standing on the same ground. To be rivals, participants must acknowledge their membership in the same system. The bond between the Celtic and Ranger fans will be further reinforced whenever their athlete-idols join together in a national team to represent Scotland.

Sports contests can symbolically represent any of these groups that claim people's solidarity, but they will arouse the strongest passions where they are linked with the status groups that arouse the most passion. Typically, our strongest sentiments are reserved for our primordial groups, those groups into which we are born, whether they center on language, custom, religion, race, tribe, ethnicity, or locale. Primordial sentiments represent a "consciousness of kind," and that consciousness is pervasive and easily tapped—unlike class consciousness, which usually needs to be cultivated.

The resilience of primordial attachments is seen as most problematic in new and industrializing nations. Anthropologist Clifford Geertz describes this problem as the clash between primordial and civil sentiments. Primordial sentiments are the basis for the cleavages and prejudices that inhibit unified action. Civil sentiments require subordinating obligations to primordial groups for obligations of citizenship. Being a citizen of a respected nation offers a modern basis for personal identity, yet the more traditional bases for a sense of self typically conflict with the state's need for overarching political unity.

For people in developing nations, political unity is essential to achieving their collective goals of a rising standard of living, more effective political order, greater social justice, and a bigger role in the world system. But, as Geertz observes, primordial sentiments become exaggerated during modernization as status groups fear losing power to a new centralized authority or, worse, being dominated by rival primordial groups. Geertz predicts that a more perfect union between multiple groups will be most successful where the goal is the modernization, not the obliteration, of ethnocentricity.

Geertz differs from most other intellectuals in his respect for primordial sentiments. Most think of them as "retrograde" and irrational. Old-fashioned primordial sentiments have been accused of inhibiting class solidarity and getting in the way of progress. But Geertz, seeing them as the roots of personal identification even in modern society, says they remain essential and deserve to be publicly acknowledged.

Typically a hindrance, primordial sentiments can be harnessed to aid national evolution. They are easy to mobilize because they are so apparent and powerful. In fact, Geertz says that universal suffrage makes courting the masses by appealing to their primordial sentiments irresistible to the political factions trying to solidify their power. Geertz's analysis highlights the channeling of ethnic differentiation into "proper" political expression (such as territorial subunits and political parties), but he recognizes that political outlets are not the only way to preserve primordial sentiments while furthering civil unity. He laments that other channels remain obscure.

This [selection] focuses on the case of soccer in Brazil to demonstrate that large-scale organized sport presents an alternative mechanism for using primordial identities to build political unity and allegiance to the modern civil state. Sport's paradoxical ability to reinforce societal cleavages while transcending them makes soccer, Brazil's most popular sport, the perfect means of achieving a more perfect union between multiple groups. Local soccer teams publicly sanction and express the society's deepest primordial sentiments, while the phenomenal success of the national team has enormously heightened all Brazilians' pride in their citizenship. . . .

SPORT: AN EXPRESSION OF SOCIABILITY AND COLLECTIVE SPIRIT

Sport is able to perform its divide-and-unify role on multiple levels. Whether we examine it at the world, national, or local level, spectator sport gives dramatic expression to the strain between groups while affirming the solidarity of the whole. Sport promotes connections from the largest level of universal communication to the smallest level of the momentary bonding of two strangers. Events or sentiments that heighten allegiance at one level usually do so at the cost of diminishing allegiance elsewhere. Sport remarkably builds solidarity in multiple levels simultaneously. Recall those Celtic and Ranger fans who are reinforced in their different Catholic and Protestant identities at the same time as they are reminded of their mutual citizenship in Glasgow, Scotland, and—in the case of international play—the world.

Sport accomplishes this feat by paralleling the intricate weave of government agencies in organizational structure. Small towns, even rural areas, are linked to each other and to big cities for state and regional championships. Major cities are knit together into national leagues and are reminded of one another during regular competitions. Nations that play the same sports are drawn into relationships with one another through continental and worldwide federations that stage international contests between representative teams; nationalistic feelings are fanned while people are simultaneously united into a global folk culture.

While organizations as diverse as the Catholic church, the Lions Club, and professional or scientific societies stretch from local to international levels, sport is different. It provides a common frame of reference, meanings, and rules that transcend cultural, political, and language barriers. Sport provides the excuse for regular and routine meetings, both of administrative representatives around a conference table and of player representatives on the field. Those representatives have agreed on universal standards of performance and scoring to regulate, as far as possible, impartial officiating. In the end, a sport pantheon of stars and a series of special events make up a set of global symbols that constitutes one of the few elements in a folk international culture. High culture—opera, ballet, and the visual arts—also creates international stars, but they unite elites around the world. Only popular culture can promote universal communication and shared experience for the masses. . . .

Let's explore some general attributes of sport that ideally suit it to the task of bringing people together in any society in spite of, sometimes even because of, their differences.

Sport at the Interpersonal Level

Sport has long been recognized as grist for conversation between persons who may have few other interests in common. Sport, like the weather, is a subject the cabby can discuss with his customer in the cashmere coat. Like the weather, the sporting scene can be followed day-by-day or more generally, comparing this "season" with past seasons. The differing evaluations of teams or players and the problematic character of game outcomes can sustain sport conversations a great deal longer than talk about the weather. Clear-cut resolutions in sport contests give debates an empirical edge as opponents contest one another frequently—almost daily in some sports. Sport conversations can have the tone of light-hearted debate or take the form of constructive dialogue, with each party adding to the knowledge of the other: "Who got the most . . . ?" "Well, I read once that . . ." "That's interesting. Did you know that . . . ?" The special significance of officials' calls, complex rules, human error, and historical comparison become the bases of sport talk. The uninterested bystander appropriately fears that the discussion could go on endlessly.

Some argue that sport fandom is a waste of time because, win or lose, the material circumstances of a fan's life do not change one iota (unless he has placed a wager on the outcome). Were we to apply a strict means/ends analysis, we would miss a major appeal of sport. Sport is a play form of association that is appreciated for its lack of consequence. Sociability around sport and game rituals is an end in itself. People talking sport, though they may appear to be arguing, are having fun. It is a pure form of banter. Neither party expects to change the opinion of the other or, more important, to affect the outcome of a single game by his talk. Although both care about the outcome of a game, there is the understanding that, in the "real" scheme of things, which team becomes champion is irrelevant.

The air of unreality is also reflected in the suspension of status differentials between fans in a stadium or sport bar. Fans rarely exchange names or personal information, even though they may talk to each other throughout the game. Neither wealth, occupation, nor formal education counts in this artificial world. Everyone is entitled to a point of view, and one runs little risk of being rebuffed when voicing an opinion. People atuned to a sporting event are expected to talk back. "You're never lonely in the ballpark." Sociability between those in different social positions can be awkward, but fans implicitly agree to focus on the game and not on each other.

In stadium and bar encounters, fans are expected to suspend personal moods and enter the social mood of the crowd; this suspension makes sport good escapist entertainment. Usually that social mood is festive, at least while victory still seems possible. People say there is a party atmosphere. Joining in the expression of group emotion is mandatory; a spectator who remains emotionless in the wake of a tie-breaking run or goal by the home team seems odd. Exley, in *A Fan's Notes*, describes hating the man next to him in the stadium who cheered good play on both sides rather than becoming involved in the fate of one team. As theologian Michael Novak advises, "the mode of observation proper to a sports event is to *participate*—that is, to extend one's own identification to one side, and to absorb with it the blows of fortune." Imagine poor Pope Paul VI's dilemma when, it was reported, he watched the 1970 World Cup final between Brazil—the world's largest Catholic country—and his native Italy and would not allow himself to cheer for either side.

The communion of strangers at a stadium or a sport bar is more than just an inferior substitute for family gatherings. There is a special joy in sharing emotion with strangers. Standing in McSorley's Bar in Greenwich Village during the 1978 baseball World Series, I heard a New York Yankees devotee say, "We're all fans here. We have something in common. We love the team." He embraced total strangers each time a run brought victory closer. It did not matter that many were not native to the city, enthusiastic support of the Yankees declared that they belonged.

Focusing on the game eases social interaction between friends as well as strangers. The simple progress of the game serves as a guide for interaction. The fan who is a student of sport history, performance statistics, or strategies can take pleasure in displaying and exchanging that knowledge. So many aspects of sport are a matter of record that fans can claim to be eyewitnesses to significant events; friends who have witnessed historical moments together feel a special bond.

Sport holds an important place in family life too. The implicit agreement that all fans are peers also suspends normal authority roles. As with social class or race, generational differences too can be put aside, easing talk between a boy and his father. A man's ten-year-old son may be following the teams so closely that he can answer his father's questions about current standings, while the father can reciprocate with his historical perspective. This not only suspends authority, it has the potential to *reverse* it for a brief moment. Since many parents find it difficult to have two-way conversations with their off-spring, such temporary suspension of authority must seem a blessing.

Insofar as teams have long traditions—sometimes stretching back for a century or more—and loyalties are often inherited, sport can also connect a man to his father. Sport roots people not only in places, but also in the past. Christopher Lasch said of "the culture of narcissism": "to live for the moment is the prevailing passion—to live for yourself, not for your predecessors or posterity." Sport is one of the things that help us preserve our sense of historical time. At a minimum, it offers continuity in the personal life of the fan who has favored a team from childhood to adulthood. As another patron of McSorley's Bar commented, "You watch a rookie blossom; you watch him grow up. It's like family."

Sport in the Community

Communal societies, small cities, and towns do not have the integration problems of complex modern societies or metropolises. Nevertheless, they inevitably contain factions that are separated by mild to bitter antagonisms. Even in communities where people know each other, they are usually divided by their kin affiliations and relative social power, and sometimes by race, ethnic, or religious differences too. Sport can serve to dramatize the strain between these factions, but it can also elicit a temporary truce while all parties are reminded of their commonality.

We can look at one of the simplest forms of sport to isolate its elementary ingredients. Anthropologist Clifford Geertz has described cockfighting in Bali. Geertz says the fights absorb the Balinese not because the cocks represent a bet to their supporters, but because they represent competitive status groups and allow them to "allegorically humiliate" one another. Backing a cock with a bet is a way to express allegiance to one's kinsmen or solidarity with one's local village. "Home games," fights between local cocks, exacerbate factions between kin groups, while "away games," between an outsider cock and a local cock, mend ruptures between the villagers. While both assuaging social passions and heightening them, the fights primarily function "in a medium of feathers, blood, crowds, and money, to display them."

Whether sport can perform its dual dividing and unifying roles within the community depends wholly on the organization of its sport. In hundreds of American towns with no professional team to represent them and just one high school each, the school teams serve only to unify the townspeople. Sport teams are usually the community's most visible representative to the outside world; sometimes a team is the *only* collective symbol of the town. By carrying the town's name, the team reaffirms the community's existence against rival towns. People's sentiments toward their communities are strongest when they feel threatened by outsiders, even symbolically via sport challenges. The team's participation in state or regional tournaments lets the townspeople enjoy the feeling of solidarity while providing one of the few occasions for association with neighboring townspeople. . . .

High school and adult amateur sports continue to have a natural place in the organization of small towns. Recently the high school basketball team in Manchester, Vermont, won the state championship for the fifth time. More people attended their final game than had voted in the town's previous elections. Because no one wanted to babysit, the entire town—men, women, teenagers, and small children—came to the gym. It was everyone's victory. As one local put it, "only the cats and dogs stayed home."

In communities like these, sport unifies by reinforcing the division between townspeople and outsiders. A community must have at least two rival teams before its internal divisions can be represented on the playing field. In a place like Bermuda, with multiple sports clubs, competitions among them can dramatize cleavages between local factions while bringing rival supporters together. The clubs, as places to go and drink, also focus daily life for the 59 percent of the adult black male population who are members.

In any case, even if sport divides community members as well as unifying them, it is more than something that alleviates boredom and fills time. Sport promotes communication; it involves people jointly; it provides them with common symbols, a collective identity, and a reason for solidarity.

Sport in the Metropolis

Big cities are full of strangers. The overwhelming size and density of their populations cause inhabitants to develop an aloof, blasé urban attitude, with the consequence that most neighbors are strangers. Population heterogeneity also contributes to the problem of social integration in the metropolis. Typically, immigrant groups of different races, nationalities, ethnicities, and religions accentuate the city's heterogeneity, while internal migrants introduce regional variations on culture. Evolving from distinctions in education, occupation, and status, an elaborate class structure adds another dimension of heterogeneity.

Huge and diverse populations make it difficult for urban-dwellers to sense they belong to an integrated society. Large-scale urban phenomena are difficult to study, yet we need to understand what means are used to confirm the unity of the metropolis and its collective spirit. Sport is one institution that holds together the people of a metropolis and heightens their attachment to the locale. The pomp and pageantry of sport spectacles create excitement and arouse fervor, doing for the people of the metropolis what religious ceremonies do for people in communal societies.

In one of the classic works in sociology, Emile Durkheim suggests that religion is less important as a specific set of beliefs and deities than as an opportunity for public reaffirmation of community. Durkheim argues that the quest for moral solidarity is present even among those who practice the most primitive religion, totemism, which has nothing to do with gods or souls. People of a locality believe they are related to totems (typically animals, but sometimes other natural objects), which are symbolized by emblems that everyone bears. In spite of their lack of blood ties, tribesmen feel related to each other because they share a totem. Team worship, like animal worship, makes all participants intensely aware of their own group membership. By accepting that a particular team represents them symbolically, people enjoy ritual kinship based on that common bond. Their emblem, be it an insignia on a lapel pin or a scarf with team colors, distinguishes fellow fans from both strangers and enemies.

The simile "sport is like religion" refers, simplistically, to people's blind faith in and devotion to their teams. The stadium acts as a cathedral where the followers come together to worship their heroes (a few of whom hold the status of demigods); some literally pray for their success. Durkheim admitted that secular events could be equally successful in reaffirming the common sentiments of a collectivity by creating sacred things out of ordinary ones. Sport spectacles belong to the world of the sacred rather than the profane; fans who say sport provides an escape from "real life" in effect sustain this religious distinction. They are acknowledging that the sporting drama stands apart from mundane reality and allows them to transcend their concrete individual existence. Unlike the isolated entertainment of "escapist" movies and much more like the effect of a religious celebration, sport fosters a sense of identification with the others who shared the experience.

At least since the intercity rivalry of the ancient Greek Olympic Games, glory has been shared by the townspeople of the victorious athletes. Across time and place, sport promoters, whether governments or team management, have told fans they *can* properly assume the team victory as their own. Even if all the athletes are mercenaries and not native sons, once they put on the uniforms that bear the group emblem they become that group's proud representatives. The rooting phenomenon works, says Roberts, precisely because people are willing to believe that "empty uniforms comprise a spiritual container whose meaning is constant, although the flesh filling the uniforms changes ceaselessly." A hero who is traded will be sorely missed and may serve to establish some rooting interest for his new team, but the former archenemy who has come to replace him soon wins the hearts of the fans when he is instrumental in bringing victory to the home team.

Examining Durkheim's theory of ritual solidarity, Collins saw that the greater the number of people present and the more narrowly focused their attention, the more exuberant the mass mood. Major sporting events draw together more people more often than anything else in modern life. Where else do we meet with 50,000 others? With the exception of papal masses, religious events draw no more than a few thousand at most. Rock concerts in the post-Woodstock era could draw as many as 100,000 people for their multiband shows, but now even bands with hit albums are having trouble selling 20,000 tickets; most bands now prefer to play several nights in a smaller auditorium rather than take the risks of promoting one big show. In the auditorium people's attention is drawn to the front, toward the staged action; the spectator looks past thousands of backs of heads to see the principal actors. Sport is staged in the round, in the center of a stadium, so the spectator confronts the emotion apparent on the faces of other spectators and is made even more aware of the mass of humanity sharing the event. Both rock concerts and sport contests, while eliciting chants and cheers, narrowly focus people's attention to arouse their emotions and common sentiments. And devotees of a team or a rock superstar both feel a special bond when they meet others who share their passion.

In a time of increasing sophistication and skepticism, people seem reluctant to leave their private shells to enter the mass mood. Things that were once sacred now seem "hokey." And sporting events seem to be the last bastion of hokey. Fans will abandon so much reserve that they can scream "CHARGE" and join in songs like "Take Me out to the Ball Game" (in the United States) and "We'll Support You Ever More" (in England). A writer describing the Pittsburgh fans during a World Series baseball game against Baltimore said cries of "C'mon family" were heard throughout the game, and signs said "We're all in this together." "While it may be hokey . . . it's undeniably affecting". . . .

Sport in the Nation

National integration has been a problem since the concept of nationalism developed more than three hundred years ago. When we think of a nation, we think of boundaries that include people of common descent, language, customs, and religion, yet the presumption of a homogeneous society is rarely confirmed in reality. For instance, self-determination dissolved the Austro-Hungarian empire, but no boundaries could be devised that would have put all members of a group into their own tidy boundaries. Problems of minorities emerged as unavoidable. Southeast Asia and Africa illustrate how nations were formed by the chance pattern of imperial conquest rather than according to the homogeneity of the people. Many nations include groups divided by the most basic prerequisite for communication—language. The Russian Empire included Turkish-speaking people; Canada is bilingual; Switzerland contains three languages. The Congo Republic contained an estimated 250 tribal-linguistic groups.

National integration is especially problematic for the developing nations. Poor transportation and communication keep regional differences strong. Foreign investments exacerbate divisions within regions by bringing modernity to the major cities of the Third World while leaving the hinterland a hundred years behind. National consciousness in these nations has been retarded by foreign domination of their political, economic, and cultural institutions. These problems are not easily overcome. Just as economic development is essential for a people's independence, so is cultural nationalism. National pride and self-consciousness can be a key instrument for change. Distinctive art, literature, folklore, and music provide a national self-image that helps integrate diverse peoples. Sport has played a crucial role in the development of cultural nationalism in many countries. Sporting victories grant the international recognition that helps developing nations shed their inferiority complexes.

Sport contributes to national integration by giving people of different social classes, ethnicities, races, and religions something to share and use as a basis for their ritual solidarity. Individuals sense numerous loyalties, some of which cut across one another; overarching goals can temporarily unite people in diverse groups and places. State championships unite the provinces with the central city; national contests unite towns, cities, and regions; international competitions focus everyone's identity as national citizens. Everyone who resides within the national borders—the countryside as well as the cities—shares the event.

Sport's remarkable ability to bring diverse people of a nation together is perhaps best illustrated by the controversy over Argentina's hosting the 1978 World Cup championship. In 1973 the leftist Peronists decided to stage the World Cup in order to court popularity. When the right-wing military junta took over in 1976, they declared they would hold the Cup as planned—a decision also calculated to attract popular support. European journalists and others protested Argentina's political turmoil and distrusted its security safeguards. Protests mounted after the military head of the national organizing committee for the 1978 Cup was assassinated on his way to the first press conference. The protests were quieted when Argentina's infamous urban guerrillas, the Montoneros, issued a statement saying they would not disrupt the World Cup since they, too, were *hombres y mujeres del pueblo* (men and women of the people). Left-wing socialists, right-wing militarists, even urban guerrillas can call a truce in the name of sport.

The World

Just as national championships reinforce the fan's identification with his hometown while reminding him of his membership in the society as a whole, international competitions reinforce nationalism while simultaneously uniting people into a global folk culture of idols and teams. Sport figures are more widely recognized than political or intellectual leaders or even performing artists. Brazilians who travel report that they are asked about Pelé by people who would not know where to find Brazil on a map.

Technological advances have helped realize the dream of universal communication. Most important, satellites permit live transmission of televised events that unite audiences around the world. Concrete special events extend the realm of our common experience; what we see together makes us alike. And what we see can convey the pleasures and not just the sorrows of life. At the same moments in time, people virtually everywhere paused to experience the tragedy of John F. Kennedy's funeral, to observe the triumphant first step on the moon, and to share the joy of Prince Charles's wedding. The most recent example demonstrates how technology has expanded the integrative potential of certain events from national to global proportions. The worldwide audience for Prince Charles's marriage to Lady Diana Spencer was estimated at 750 million people in seventy-seven countries. It was a perfect video event for satellite transmission: it was planned far in advance and starred a central figure from the world's most famous royal family.

This event can be compared with Queen Elizabeth's coronation in 1953, when viewers in Italy, Germany, Holland, and France got live reception, along with 53 percent of the population of the British Isles, while the rest of the world had to await film replays. Two sociologists who analyzed that coronation called it "a great act of national communion." Now the pomp and storybook aura of a royal wedding can provide a common vital object of attention for a momentary global communion.

No one really knows who is the most famous person in the world; contenders include Pelé, Muhammed Ali, John Lennon, and Prince Charles. But comparative data do exist for audiences of satellite-televised events, and the major international sporting contests draw together more spectators than anything else. The final game of the 1978 World Cup holds the record to date: more than 2 billion fans watched, including for the first time those in China and South Africa. In other words, *nearly half the world's people shared a single event*. Estimates of the viewing audience for the whole tournament go as high as 20 billion. . . .

Sport is different because it is reciprocal. People in countries that share a love for the same sport also share respect for that sport's best athletes and for distinctive national styles of play. World sporting federations stage truly international events. Where Esperanto failed as the universal language, soccer as the premier world sport has laid a basis for global community by promoting common knowledge, shared symbols, and communication between people of different nations.

2. *For the True Believer*

RICHARD E. LAPCHICK

There is little doubt that sport has become the broadest common cultural denominator in almost all societies. Men and women, blacks and whites, reactionaries and revolutionaries, Soviets and Americans, barefoot village people from the mountains of Kenya and sophisticated urbanites from New Delhi seem to "think sports." The proportion of newsprint devoted to sports is usually as large or larger than that devoted to international events, domestic politics, the economy, the arts, education, or religion. American television, especially on weekends, is saturated with sports events; there are several cable channels devoted to showing sports twenty-four hours a day.

Rabbis, priests, ministers, and politicians use sports metaphors to make their moral or political points. Values taught in sport will make their flocks better Jews, Catholics, Protestants, Muslims, or Americans. Therefore, clergymen don't mind that Sundays are essentially the property of the NFL or the NBA. Religious services have become warm-ups for the bigger game to follow at the stadium. Religion and sport are on a continuum, teaching moral virtue to all who participate.

With so many Americans either playing themselves or watching others play, an enormous subculture has arisen. Many people in the subculture have come to accept a series of age-old verities about sport. I call such people "true believers." Here is their credo: sport can influence everything, for the better. Sport contacts with other nations build friendships, peace, and understanding. Sport has been a major social equalizer in America, leading blacks out of the ghetto through increased educational opportunity, changing attitudes of white teammates and opponents, and increasing employment opportunities at the end of their sports careers. Women can assert themselves on athletic fields in ways that will break down "feminine" stereotypes and, therefore, prepare them to enter executive positions.

But sport goes beyond this; it is an inspiration to everyone. It builds character, motivates individuals, generates teamwork, and teaches discipline through structured and contained competition. Sport is an acceptable outlet for aggressive behavior. Values learned in sport are assets in schools, business—in all phases of life. Good athletes become good citizens and succeed as a consequence of their own dedication and hard work. Those athletes who make the

SOURCE: Richard E. Lapchick, *Broken Promises: Racism in American Sports* (New York: St. Martin's Press, 1984), pp. 159–173.

17

pros have unlimited opportunities when their playing careers end. But, pro or not, everyone benefits from competition; schools, communities, and the nation come together to root for their team.

It is undeniable that there are exceptions to such generalizations but those who have joined the sports subculture see them as only that—as aberrations from the norm. This is because they tend to view society itself as healthy and on the right path. But the draw of sport is so powerful that even many of those who are strong critics of society view sport in the same positive light. The assumptions have been well packaged. Sport is . . . sport does . . . sport will.

Yet obviously, ours is a far from perfect society. And if sport is so good, what went wrong? How have all of us, trained in the value system of athletics, forgotten those values so soon? Could it be that the true believer was misinformed, that sports does not by itself break down barriers? Is it possible that, in fact, we can see a microcosm of the whole society—with all its strengths and weaknesses—in the sports world?

On the international level, sport seems to be as much a source of national friction as it is a source of friendship, peace, and understanding. It is usually benign when we compete with "friendly nations" such as Britain, France, and West Germany. However, since American dominance has shifted in favor of the Soviet Union, Cuba, and the German Democratic Republic, our viewpoint toward them is different. In the late 1960s Americans started to become increasingly critical of the Olympics. We claimed that the Soviets and their Third World clients had politicized the Games that we were trying to protect. The sports media was willing to confirm for us that America doesn't play sports politics, that sports is above politics. How fast they changed when President Carter called for a boycott of the Moscow Olympics in 1980 to punish the Russians for invading Afghanistan. The Carter administration bludgeoned athletes into going along with the boycott, cajoled allies into joining the boycott, and offered incentives to developing nations, especially in Africa, if they would shun the Games. The press, for the most part, tended to ignore the methods being used. Finally, its reporting of the Games tried to paint them as a failure. Yet it is arguable that the Games were a success. Thirty-six new world and seventy-four new Olympic records were set—more records than at any previous Olympics. Eighty-one countries attended. More than 60,000 foreign tourists came to Moscow and an estimated 1.5 billion watched the Games on TV. And the Soviet Union was still in Afghanistan.

Let's examine those instances where America has become openly involved in sports politics. In 1936, we refused to boycott the Nazi Olympics in spite of a massive grass-roots protest against the Berlin Olympics in the United States from 1933 to 1936. In fact, an international boycott collapsed when America agreed to go to Berlin. In the late 1950s President Eisenhower directly intervened when the International Olympic Committee admitted the People's Republic of China (PRC) and excluded Taiwan. The pressure led to another sixteen-year delay in admitting the PRC into the modern Olympics. Throughout the 1960s and into the 1970s, the U.S. government refused visas to athletes from Cuba and the German Democratic Republic. In 1976, President Ford threatened to pull out of the Montreal Games unless Taiwan was admitted. Even so, he refused to go along with the 1976 African boycott that evolved over the racial situation in South Africa. America has never backed any request to boycott South Africa in spite of the fact that the vast majority of nations agreed to end competition with that country as long as apartheid dominates its policy.

What does it tell us when we boycott games to protest communism and do nothing in the face of racism and fascism? A great deal if we look closely.

Women's sports are growing in popularity, and, unlike men's sports, most of them are white dominated. The exceptions are, of course, track and field and, increasingly, basketball. This whiteness helps market sports for television, commercials, and dollars. Most professional women athletes are white and middle to upper-middle class. . . .

Certainly there have been gains for women in sports. Between 1970 and 1980, the number of women who competed in high school sports increased by more than 500 percent. So many more women are competing in colleges that by 1980 the Association for Intercollegiate Athletics for Women (AIAW) had more than 800 member schools, when it did not even exist in 1970. Gains have been so impressive that the NCAA, which did not have women's sports in 1970, has now successfully fought for control of them and has crushed the AIAW. This is the same NCAA that not only didn't support Title IX, which called for more equalization between men's and women's sports, but actively opposed it; the same NCAA that still opposes equal spending for men and women in revenue-producing sports. However, it is difficult to believe there will be much difference between whether women's sports are ultimately controlled by the AIAW or the NCAA. The bottom line is that while women pay more than 50 percent of all tuition and fees, they receive less than 20 percent of the school's athletic budget. Once again, this is still a white middle-class problem. The high-school drop-out rate for Spanish-speaking American women is nearly 75 percent and is only slightly less for black women. They won't have to worry about proper implementation of Title IX.

Everyone knows that professional sport is a business like any other, although most sports values are expected to apply. But in colleges, high schools, and little leagues, sport is thought to be pure. We expect dedication and loyalty to the team, hard work, honesty, discipline, character building, and a commitment to winning through excellence and not through destruction of the opposition. Our coaches are to be philosophers and teachers of these virtues and nurturers of their athletes, both on and off the court.

The truth is very different. "Winning isn't everything, it's the only thing," is a reality. Winning at all costs is the philosophy most coaches believe in, no matter what pieties they may utter. Alumni and boosters pay coaches, players, and families of players. Athletes disregard academics and dream of incomes far beyond their ability. Faculties shrug their shoulders while college presidents say they can't expect athletes to take academics as seriously as other students. Sanctions for violations are rare and selective. Ultimately, it pays to cheat. It is a system gone mad. Win at all costs, at any cost. Why is it happening? The answer, of course, is money.

Athletic budgets are soaring to finance dominant teams that will fill arenas and obtain lucrative TV contracts. Major league baseball's 1983 $1 billion TV contract and the NFL's 1982 TV contract, worth more than $2 billion, are benchmarks for college contracts. A top college team today can earn more from one TV game than it cost to run an entire athletic program in 1975. There are now $10 million-plus athletic budgets all over the country and these figures exclude lucrative booster donations.

The abuses of athletes that were revealed in 1980 seemed to shock many people. The extent of the academic/athletic scandal made claims of such abuses by sports critics like Jack Scott and Harry Edwards in the late 1960s seem insignificant.

History should have told us something. The NCAA lists seven football conferences with sixty schools as the most prominent football conferences in the country. *Before* 1980's scandal broke, forty-two of the sixty had received public disciplinary action. That's 72 percent.

Basketball was even worse. Between 1952 and 1980, there were only two schools (Chicago Loyola in 1963 and Marquette in 1967) that won NCAA championships that were not subject to some form of public disciplinary action at one time or anther because of their basketball programs. . . .

More often than not, the black athlete is the ultimate victim of all these abuses and ends up without an education. However, white athletes are also seriously shortchanged in the process. Both are sucked into the cheating that is so common it seems right. If coaches and athletic administrators are supposed to be their models, then who can fully blame the athlete for taking what must simply appear to be his piece of the pie?

Are players on scholarship "student athletes"? That is what the NCAA calls them. However, evidence shows that high-level players are really athletes first and students second.

William E. (Bud) Davis, president of the University of New Mexico, told *Newsweek*'s Pete Axthelm, "Our recruits were recruited to be athletes, not students. There was never an expectation that they'd get their ass out of bed at eight o'clock to go to class and turn in their assignments."

A report signed by University of Southern California President James H. Zumberge said that between 1970 and 1980, 330 athletes were admitted who did not meet the school's minimum requirements. He said decisions were "based chiefly on athletic prowess as judged by the athletic department, and without normal admissions office review." USC Athletic Director Richard Perry, replying to the charge that only slightly more than half of the athletic team members graduated from USC between 1964–77, noted, "I didn't know of anything that says the purpose of higher education is to procure degrees."

Bill Wall, who was the president of the National Association of Basketball Coaches, said, "I know some coaches who couldn't stop cheating if they wanted to because their alumni and boosters wouldn't let them". . . .

The chain of corruption, commercialization, professionalism, and dehumanization starts early. Parents push their children in the Little League and Pop Warner League. The pressure starts there; the position specialization starts there. The dehumanization starts there. The end of most athletic careers starts there. Parents don't want each child to play in each game. They want *their* child to play the whole game. When the Little League and Pop Warner football instituted a rule that every child had to play, 1,800 teams withdrew from the league. Families move near schools with better athletic programs. Parents in Georgia and Texas are now arranging for their children to repeat the eighth grade to increase their chances for college scholarships five years later by giving them one more year to mature.

Dr. Thomas Tutko, a leading psychologist dealing with children in sports recently told Emily Greenspan, writing in *The New York Times Magazine,* "I'm concerned with how many good athletes have been scarred by injury or burned out psychologically by the time they were fifteen because they were unable to meet the insatiable demands of their parents, their coaches, or their own personal obsession."

The pressures get worse in high school. Many teenagers already have gone through a recruiting process to get there. Coaches even help their families relocate nearer to the school. In December 1980 a father allegedly went to a Michigan coach's home and assaulted him because his son wasn't playing enough. High school teachers regularly "pass on" illiterate players to keep them eligible and the seemingly easy ride to the top has begun. In November 1980, the principal of an Idaho high school punched a referee in the stomach and knocked him down after he thought the ref missed a couple of calls.

For those whose eighth-grade dreams are still alive in the twelfth grade, the good life continues unabated. College coaches offer players a variety of inducements to come to their school. Payoffs have included jobs, housing, cars, clothing, meals, transportation, and direct cash handouts. Frank Lollino, the high school coach of star basketball player Mark Aguirre, told reporters that Aguirre was offered cash, cars, and trips while Lollino was offered cash, trips to Hawaii, and better coaching jobs if he could help get Aguirre. He claimed he was offered $10,000 in cash and $15,000 later if he could deliver Eddie Johnson, Aguirre's teammate, to the recruiter's school. Lollino calls recruiters "bagmen."

Between the athletes and the coaches are the boosters and alumni. Together, they now contribute a significant portion of the athletic budget and almost all of the bagman's money; they have a great deal of control. Through

1980, over half of the actions taken by the NCAA Committee on Infractions have been against booster-related offenses.

Many administrators appear to condone departures from the rules. Some encourage them. After all, a winning team enhances the school's prestige even if it is at the educational expense of the same student-athletes responsible for that prestige. A winner brings in TV money and exposure, gate receipts, and at private institutions, it can mean a drawing card for new students, thus more revenues.

Then, of course, there is the faculty. Many have suggested, even expected, that they obtain more critical academic control as kind of super ombudsmen of athletic practices. However, the reality is they tend to be either fans themselves or feel themselves above sports, thereby absolving themselves of any academic responsibility for athletes.

So who or what is left to make things right? It appears to be the National Collegiate Athletic Association (NCAA), led by Executive Director Walter Byers. The NCAA tells us it is organized solely for the benefit of the amateur student-athlete who participates in sport "for the educational, physical, mental, and social benefits he derives therefrom and to whom athletics is an avocation."

Yet, George Sage, the highly respected sports scholar, writes that the NCAA is a "business organization that is part of the entertainment industry whose product is competitive intercollegiate sports events." He argues that it is a cartel that has a monopoly on the production and sale of the commodity and controls the wages of the labor force. Universities are member firms with no choice but to join if they have big-time programs, for the NCAA runs all national championships and controls all TV rights.

The NCAA regulates everything regarding athletes, who make up the largest single group of employees. It maintains an artificial low wage for them. The "transfer rule" of one-year mandatory ineligibility restricts mobility if a player changes schools; the "five-year rule" allows colleges to red-shirt players; that is, to allow them to sit out a year and defer eligibility, and the "freshmen eligibility rule," which allows freshmen to play varsity sports right away, reduces costs for member firms. All these rules maximize the profits of the schools and dovetail nicely with professional rules by delivering mature athletes to the pros.

Finally, the NCAA is its own police force and penalizes those who violate NCAA rules and regulations. With more than 725 members, the NCAA controls major sport.

With all its power and profit, the NCAA, if it wished, could really come down on corrupt athletic departments, finance a substantial investigation unit, and clean up college sports in a hurry.

However, with its power comes self-interest and self-preservation. If the NCAA went after as many of the major colleges as are suspected violators, there would be few teams eligible to compete for the national championship.

They tread gingerly. Newspapers and the FBI have been uncovering more dirt than the NCAA Investigation Unit.

But where does that leave us? Time-Life ran a major series as President Reagan came into office called "American Renewal." Articles on this theme were included in Time-Life publications such as *Fortune, Money, Time, Life, Discover, People,* and, of course, *Sports Illustrated.* The *SI* piece examined the "elusive topic of the country's moral fiber," looking "at competition in America and its importance not only in sports but in all areas of life." It accepted as fact many of the problem areas that have developed in sport. But like the conservative politicians, its prescriptions for change to decades-old, complex problems were almost unbelievably simplistic.

The formula was that colleges should stop "toadying to the pros," stop carrying athletes who are poorly prepared academically just to win and make money. When that's done, high schools, in "an interesting side effect," will have to prepare athletes academically. If they can do it, "a whole generation of better prepared players-for-life, not just sports, will emerge."

As for coaching corruption, we should severely limit recruiting and give coaches job security. Coaches could then be teachers again and stress team play, require self-sacrifice, insist on striving for excellence in performance and not just victory. If these prescriptions could be implemented, then many of the problems discussed could be solved. However, the simplicity of the prescriptions doesn't account for the deep-rooted nature of the problems. Answers that address the surface can't penetrate to the core.

3. *Sport in Society: An Inspiration or an Opiate?*

JAY J. COAKLEY

People in American society generally see sport in a very positive way. Not only is sport assumed to provide a training ground for the development of desirable character traits and good citizens, but it is also believed to reaffirm a commitment to societal values emphasizing competition, success, and playing by the rules.

Does sport really do all these things? Is it as beneficial and healthy as people believe? These questions have generated considerable disagreement among sport sociologists. It seems that most of us in the sociology of sport are quick to agree that sport is a microcosm of society—that it mirrors the values, structure, and dynamics of the society in which it exists (Eitzen and Sage, 1978). However, we often disagree when it comes to explaining the consequences or the functions of sport in society. This disagreement grows out of the fact that sport sociologists have different theoretical conceptions of how society works. Therefore, they differ on their ideas about how sport functions within society. A description of the two major theoretical approaches used in the sociology of sport will illustrate what I mean.

THE FUNCTIONALIST APPROACH

Sport Is an Inspiration

The majority of sport sociologists assume that society is most accurately conceptualized in terms of a *systems model*. They see society as an organized system of interrelated parts. The system is held together and operates because (1) its individual members generally endorse the same basic values and (2) the major parts in the system (such as the family, education, the economy, government, religion, and sport) all fit together in mutually supportive and constructive ways. In sociology, this theoretical approach is called *functionalism*.

When the functionalists describe and analyze how a society, community, school, or any other system works, they are primarily concerned with how the

SOURCE: Jay J. Coakley, *Sport in Society: Issues and Controversies*, second edition (St. Louis: C. V. Mosby, 1982), pp. 16–30.

parts of that system are related to the operation of the system as a whole. For example, if American society is the system being studied, a person using a functionalist approach would be concerned with how the American family, the economy, government, education, religion, and sport are all related to the smooth operation of the society as a whole. The analysis would focus on the ways in which each of these subparts of society help to keep the larger system going.

The functionalists also assume that a social system will continue to operate smoothly only if the four following things happen:

1. The members of the system must learn the values and the norms (i.e., the general rules or guidelines for behavior) that will lead them to want to do what has to be done to keep the system in operation. This process of shaping the feelings, thoughts, and actions of individuals usually creates some frustration and tension. Therefore, there must also be some channels through which people can let off steam in harmless ways.
2. The system must contain a variety of social mechanisms that bring people together and serve as catalysts for building the social relationships needed for coordinated action. Without a certain degree of cohesion, solidarity, and social integration, coordinated action would be impossible and the social system would stop functioning smoothly.
3. The members of the system must have the opportunity to learn what their goals should be within the system and the socially approved ways of achieving those goals.
4. The social system must be able to adjust to the demands and challenges of the external environment. It must have ways of handling and coping with changes in the social and physical environments so that it can continue to operate with a minimal amount of interference and disruption.

According to those using a functionalist approach, these four "system needs" are the basic minimum requirements for the smooth operation of any social system whether it be a society, community, club, large corporation, or neighborhood convenience store (Parsons and Smelser, 1965). These four basic system requirements are referred to as:

1. The need for pattern maintenance and tension management.
2. The need for integration.
3. The need for goal attainment.
4. The need for adaptation.

When you start with a functionalist conception of how society works, the answer to the question of what sport does for a society or community is likely to emphasize the ways in which sport satisfies the four basic needs of the social system. A brief review of how sport is related to each of these needs is a good way to summarize this approach.

PATTERN MAINTENANCE AND TENSION MANAGEMENT

The functionalists generally conclude that sport provides learning experiences that reinforce and extend the learning occurring in other settings. In other words, sport serves as a backup or a secondary institution for primary social institutions such as the family, school, and church. Through sport people learn the general ways of thinking, feeling, and acting that make them contributing members of society. They become socialized so that they fit into the mainstream of American life and therefore reaffirm the stability and continued operation of our society (Schafer, 1976).[1]

The pattern maintenance function of sport applies to spectators as well as those who are active participants. Sport is structured so that those who watch or play learn the importance of rules, hard work, efficient organization, and a well-defined authority structure. For example, sociologist Gunther Luschen (1967) shows how sport helps to generate the high levels of achievement motivation necessary to sustain the commitment to work required in industrialized countries. Along similar lines, Kleiber and Kelly (1980) have reviewed a number of studies concluding that participation in competitive games helps children learn how to handle adult roles in general and competitive relationships in particular. In fact, some recent discussions of sex roles have suggested that women may be at a disadvantage in business settings partly because they have not been involved in competitive sports to the same degree as their male counterparts (Hennig and Jardim, 1977; Harragan, 1977; Lever, 1978).

Sport has also been thought to serve tension management functions in society by providing both spectators and participants with an outlet for aggressive energy (Vanderzwaag, 1972; Proctor and Eckard, 1976; Marsh, 1978). This idea prompted two widely respected sociologists, Hans Gerth and C. Wright Mills (1954), to suggest the following: "Many mass audience situations, with their 'vicarious' enjoyments, serve psychologically the unintended function of channeling and releasing otherwise unplacable emotions. Thus, great volumes of aggression are 'cathartically' released by crowds of spectators cheering their favorite stars of sport—and jeering the umpire." The idea that sport may serve tension management functions is complex and controversial.

INTEGRATION

A functionalist approach also emphasizes how sport serves to bring people together and provide them with feelings of group unity, a sense of social identification, and a source of personal identity. In short, a functionalist explains how sport creates and reaffirms the linkages between people so that cooperative action is possible. Luschen (1967) outlines how this occurs in the following: "Since sport is also structured along such societal subsystems as different classes, males, urban areas, schools, and communities, it functions for integration. This is obvious also in spectator sport, where the whole country or community identifies with its representatives in a contest. Thus, sport functions as a means of integration, not only for the actual participants, but also for the represented members of such a system."

Sport has been seen to serve integration functions in countries other than the United States also. For example, others have discussed how sport contributes to unity and solidarity in Switzerland (Albonico, 1967), France (Bouet, 1969), Germany (Brockman, 1969), China (Chu and Segrave, 1979), the Soviet Union (Riordan, 1977), and Brazil (Lever, 1981).

Andrzej Wohl (1970), a sport sociologist from Poland, has argued that competitive sport could not exist if it recognized "local, national or racial barriers or differences of world outlook." He points out that sport is so widely used to serve integration functions that it "is no secret for anybody any more."

GOAL ATTAINMENT

Someone using a functionalist approach is likely to see sport as legitimizing and reinforcing the primary goals of the system as well as the means to be used to achieve those goals. In the United States, for example, sport is organized so that successful outcomes are heavily emphasized, and success is generally defined in terms of scores and win-loss records. Just as in the rest of society, the proper way to achieve success in sport is through a combination of competition, hard work, planning, and good organization. Therefore, the sport experience not only serves to legitimize the way things are done in other sectors of society but also it prepares people for participation in those sectors.

In other countries, different aspects of the sport experience are emphasized so that it serves as a supportive model for their goal priorities and the proper means to achieve goals. Capitalist countries are more likely to emphasize output and competition in sport while socialist countries will be more likely to emphasize cooperation and the development of a spirit of collectivism (Morton, 1963). Sport seems to be amazingly flexible in this respect; it has been shaped and defined in a variety of ways to serve goal attainment functions in many different social systems. This point has been developed and explained by Edwards (1973): "Most sports have few, if any, intrinsic and invariably social or political qualities . . . and those qualities which such activities do possess are sufficiently 'liquid' to fit comfortably within many diverse and even conflicting value and cultural traditions."

ADAPTATION

In preindustrial societies it is easy to see how sport serves a system's need for adaptation. Since survival in such societies depends on the development and use of physical skills, participation in games and sport activities is directly related to coping with the surrounding environment (Luschen, 1967). Dunlap (1951) makes this case in her study of the Samoans. Additionally, she found that the "factors of physical strength and endurance which were essential for success in their games were also essential for success in their wars."

In industrial societies, it is more difficult to see how sport satisfies the adaptation needs of the social system. However, in two articles on the functions of sport, Wohl (1970, 1979) has suggested that it is in this area that sport makes its most important contributions. He points out that in any society with technologically advanced transportation and communications systems, sport becomes the only sphere of activities in which physical skills are developed and perfected. Through sport it is possible to measure and extend the range of human motor skills and to adapt them to the environments we have created. Without sport it would be difficult to maintain a population's physical well-being at the levels necessary to keep an industrial society operating efficiently. Sport is so crucial in this regard that Wohl (1979) calls for the use of all the sport sciences to plan and control its development. In this way the contributions of sport to satisfying adaptation needs could be maximized.

In concluding our review of the functionalist approach to sport it should be pointed out that social scientists are not the only ones who use such an approach in explaining the relationship between sport and society. Most people view society and the role of sport in terms very similar to those used by the functionalists. They look for the ways in which sport contributes to the communities in which they live. They see sport providing valuable lessons for their children and opportunities for themselves to release the tensions generated by a job or other life events. Sport gives them something to talk about with strangers as well as friends and it provides occasions for outings and get-togethers. Many people believe that sport can serve as a model of the goals we should strive for and the means we should use in trying to achieve those goals. Finally, sport is viewed as a healthy activity for individuals as well as the entire country; it can extend life and keep us physically prepared to defend our country in case of war.

These beliefs about sport have led to policy decisions on Little League programs, the funding of high school and college athletics, the support of professional teams and the Olympic movement, the development of physical education programs in schools, and the use of sport activities in military academies to prepare young men and women to be "combat ready." The widespread acceptance and the pervasive influence of the functionalist approach make it necessary for us to be aware of its weaknesses.

Limitations of the Functionalist Approach

Using a functionalist approach to answer the question of how sport is related to society can provide us with valuable insights, but it is not without its problems. Such an approach tends to emphasize the positive aspects of sport. This is because those using it often assume that if some part or component of a social system has existed for a long time, it is likely to be contributing to the system in a favorable way; if it were not, it would have been eliminated or gradually faded out of existence on its own. Since sport has been around for some time and is an increasingly significant component of our social system, most functionalists conclude that it *does* make positive contributions to society. This conclusion leads them to ignore or underemphasize the negative aspects of sport. After all, it is also possible that sport could distort values and behavioral guidelines (norms). Sport could destroy motivation, create frustration and tensions, and disrupt social integration. It could impede goal attainment and interfere with methods of coming to terms with the external social and physical environment by diverting a group's attention away from crucial personal and social issues.

Another problem with the functionalist approach is that it is based on the assumption that the needs of the individual parts of a social system overlap with the needs of the system as a whole. The possibility of internal differences or basic conflicts of interests within a social system is inconsistent with the assumption that any system is held together by a combination of common values and an interrelated, mutually supportive set of parts. If the needs of the total system were in serious conflict with the needs of the individual parts, the validity of the functionalist approach would be called into question.

This is one of the major weaknesses of functionalism. Although we may agree that many people in our society hold similar values, can we also argue that the structure of American society serves the needs of everyone equally? It would be naive to assume that it does. In fact, it may even frustrate the needs of certain groups and individuals and generate conflict. To conclude that sport exists because it satisfies the needs of the total system overlooks the possibility that sport may benefit some segments of the population more than others. Furthermore, if the interests of some groups within the system are met at the expense of others, the consequences of sport could be described as positive only if you were viewing them from the perspective of those privileged groups. Unfortunately, a functionalist approach often leads to underemphasizing differences of interests as well as the possibility of exploitation and coercion within the social system. It also leads to ignoring the role of sport in generating conflict and maintaining a structure in which at least some relationships are based on exploitation and coercion.

In sociology the theoretical approach that calls attention to these unpleasant characteristics of social systems and how sport is related to them is called conflict theory.

CONFLICT THEORY

Sport Is an Opiate

Conflict theory is not as popular as functionalism. It does not fit with what most people think about how society is organized and how it operates. Instead of viewing society as a relatively stable system of interrelated parts held together by common values and consensus, conflict theorists view it as an ever-changing set of relationships characterized by inherent differences of interests and held together by force, coercion, and subtle manipulation. They are concerned with the distribution and use of power rather than with common values and integration. Their analysis of society focuses on processes of change rather than on what is required for a social system to continue operating smoothly.

Most beginning students in the sociology of sport are not very receptive to the use of conflict theory in explaining the relationship between sport and society. They say that it is too negativistic and critical of our way of life and the institution of sport. They prefer the functionalist approach because it fits closely with what they have always believed and because it has implications that do not threaten the structure of either society or sport. My response is that although functionalism is useful, it can often lead us to look at the world unrealistically and ignore a dimension of the relationship between sport and society that should be considered. Neither American society nor sport is without problems. Awareness and understanding of these problems require critical thought, and conflict theory is a valuable stimulus for such thought.

Conflict theory is based primarily on an updated revision of the ideas of Karl Marx. Those who use it generally focus their attention on capitalist countries such as the United States but it has also been used to describe and understand any social system in which individuals are perceived as not having significant control over their own lives. According to many conflict theorists this includes capitalist systems along with fascist or military/police regimes and socialist systems controlled by centralized, bureaucratic governments (Brohm, 1978).

In order to understand how conflict theorists view the role of sport in society, we will start with a simplified description of capitalism and how contemporary organized sport fits into its structure. Any capitalist system requires the development of a highly efficient work process through which an increasing number of consumer goods can be mass produced. Industrial bureaucracies have been created to meet this need. This means that in the interest of efficiency and financial profit, workers end up performing highly specialized and alienating jobs. These jobs are generally in the production, marketing and sales, or service departments of large organizations where the workers themselves have little control over what they do and experience little or no excitement or satisfaction in their day-to-day work lives. This situation creates a need for escape and for tension-excitement in their nonwork lives. Within capitalist systems, people are subtly manipulated to seek the satisfaction they need through consumerism and mass entertainment spectacles. Sport in such societies has emerged as a major form of entertainment spectacle as well as a primary context for the consumption of material goods. Additionally, the structure of sport is so much like the structure of work organizations and capitalist society as a whole that it serves to stabilize the system and promote the interests of people who are in positions of power.

Conflict theorists see sport as a distorted form of physical exercise that has been shaped by the needs of a capitalist system of production. A specific example of how sport has developed in this manner has been outlined by Goodman (1979) in an analysis of the history of playground and street life in one of New York City's working class neighborhoods. Goodman shows how the spontaneous, free-flowing play activities of children in New York were literally banned from the streets in order to force participation in organized playground programs. The original goals of the playgrounds are best described through the words of one of the influential playground supervisors early in this century (Chase, 1909): "We want a play factory; we want it to run at top speed on schedule time, with the best machinery and skilled operatives. We want to turn out the maximum product of happiness." Thus the organized activities and sport programs became a means for training the children of immigrants to fit into a world of work founded on time schedules, the stopwatch, and production-conscious supervisors.

For the parents of these children the playground and recreation center programs had a different goal. It was clearly explained in the following section of a 1910 New York City Department of Education report (cited in Goodman, 1979): "The great problem confronting the recreation center principal and teachers is the filling of the leisure time of the working men and women with a combination of recreation and athletic activities which will help make their lives more tolerable." As Goodman points out, the purpose of the centers was to provide controlled leisure activities to take the people's minds off the exploitation and poor working conditions experienced in their jobs. The supervised activities were meant to pacify the workers so that they could tolerate those conditions and continue contributing to the growth of the economy. When they needed to be replaced, the organized playground activities would have prepared their children to take their roles.

Other conflict theorists have not limited their focus to a local community setting. They have talked in more general terms about the relationship between sport and society. Their discussions emphasize four major aspects of the role of sport. These include:

1. How sport generates and intensifies alienation
2. How sport is used by the state and the economically powerful as a tool for coercion and social control
3. How sport promotes commercialism and materialism
4. How sport encourages nationalism, militarism, and sexism

The following sections summarize the discussions of the conflict theorists on each of these four topics.

ALIENATION

According to the conflict theorists sport serves to alienate people from their own bodies. Sport focuses attention on time and output rather than on the individual. Standardized rules and rigid structure destroy the spontaneity, freedom, and inventiveness characteristic in play. Jean-Marie Brohm (1978), a French sport sociologist, explains how sport affects the connection between athletes and their bodies: "[In sport the body is] experienced as an object, an instrument, a technical means to an end, a reified factor of output and productivity, in short, as a machine with the job of producing maximum work and energy." In other words, sport creates a setting in which the body is no longer experienced as a source of self-fulfillment and pleasure in itself. Pleasure and fulfillment depend on *what is done* with the body. Satisfaction is experienced only if the contest is won, if a record is set or a personal goal achieved, and if the body performs the way it has been trained to perform. When this happens sport becomes a "prison of measured time" and alienates athletes from their own bodies (Brohm, 1978).

Mumford (1934) extends the idea of alienation even further. In a classic analysis of contemporary civilization he describes the sport stadium as an "industrial establishment producing running, jumping or football playing machines." Building on this notion conflict theorists argue that commercialized sport (any sport in which profits are sought) reduces athletes to material commodities (Hoch, 1972). Thus the body becomes a tool not only for the setting of records but also for generating financial profits for nonparticipants— from team owners and tournament sponsors to concession operators and parking lot owners. The athletes may also benefit, but their rewards require them to forfeit the control of their bodies and become "gladiators" performing for the benefit of others.

Conflict theorists have pointed to the use of drugs and computer technology in sport as support for their analysis of how sport affects the definition of an athlete's body (Brohm, 1978). When the body is seen as an instrument for setting records and the improvement of times is defined as the measure of human progress, then the use of drugs, even harmful drugs, will be seen as a valuable aid in the quest for achievement. Computer technology used to analyze and improve the body's productive capacity further separates the physical act of sport participation from the subjective experience of the athlete. Just as on the assembly line, efficiency comes to be the major concern in sport and the worker (athlete) loses control over the means of production (the body).

COERCION AND SOCIAL CONTROL

Goodman's (1979) study of the working class neighborhood in New York City led him to conclude that sport in that city was used as a means of making the lives of shop workers more tolerable. Other conflict theorists expand this notion and describe sport as an opiate interfering with an awareness of social problems and subverting collective attempts to solve those problems. According to Hoch (1972), sport perpetuates problems by providing people with either "(1) a temporary high . . . which takes their minds off problem[s] for a while but does nothing to deal with [them]; or (2) a distorted frame of reference or identification which encourages them to look for salvation through patently false channels."

Hoch's description of the personal and social impact of sport is similar to Marx's description of religion in society. To Marx, religion focuses attention on the supernatural, provides people with a psychological lift, and emphasizes improvement through changing the self rather than changing the social order. Religion destroys awareness of material reality and promotes the maintenance of the status quo by giving priority to the goal of spiritual salvation. Marx further concluded that organized religion can be exploited by people in positions of power in society. If the majority of individuals in a society believe that enduring pain, denying pleasure, and accepting their status in this life gains them spiritual salvation, those in power can be reasonably sure that those under their control will be hard working and docile. If those in power go so far as to manifest their own commitment to religion, their hold over the people can be strengthened even further. Such a manifestation would, after all, show that they had something in common with the masses.

Conflict theorists make the case that in an advanced capitalist society where people are not likely to look to the supernatural for answers and explanations, religion may be supplemented by other activities with similar narcotic effects. Hoch points out that these contemporary "opiates" include "sport spectacles, whiskey, and repressively sublimated sex." These combined with other opiates such as nationalism, racism, and sexism distort people's perspectives and encourage self-defeating behavior. Among these, sport stands out as an especially powerful opiate. Unlike the others, sport spectatorship is often accompanied by an extremely intense identification with players, teams, and the values perceived to be the basis for success in athletics. According to Hoch, this identification brings sport further into the lives of the spectators and captures their attention on a long-term basis. When the game ends, fan involvement does not cease, but carries on between games and into the off season. This means that workers think about and discuss the fate of their teams rather than the futility of their own lives. Thus they are less likely to become actively involved in political or revolutionary organizations. Petryszak (1978), in a historical analysis of sport, makes the case that the "ultimate consequence of . . . spectator sports in society is the reduction of the population to a position of complete passivity."

Beyond occupying people's time and distracting their attention and energy, sport helps maintain the position of those in power in other ways. Conflict theorists note that the major contact sports, such as football, hockey, and boxing, promote a justification for the use of "official" violence by those in authority positions. In other words, sport shapes our values in ways that lock us into a social system based on coercion and the exploitive use of power. The more we witness violent sports, the more we are apt to condone the use of official violence in other settings—even when it is directed against us.

Sport also serves the interests of those in power by generating the belief that success can be achieved only through hard work and that hard work always leads to success. Such a belief encourages people to look up to those who are successful as being paragons of virtue and to look down on the failures as being lazy and no good. For example, when teams win consistently their success is attributed to hard work and discipline; when they lose consistently, losing often is blamed on a lack of hustle and poor attitude. Losses lead the fans to call for new players and coaches—not a restructuring of the game or its rules. Hoch (1972) points out that this way of looking at things blinds people to a consideration of the problems inherent in the social and economic structure and engenders the notion that success depends only on attitude and personal effort. It also leads to the belief that failure is to be blamed on the individual alone and is to be accepted as an indication of personal inadequacies and of a need to work harder in the future.

Conflict theorists see sport as a tool for controlling people and maintaining the status quo. It is structured to promote specific political ideas (Helmes, 1978) and to regiment and organize the lives of young people so that they will become productive workers. For adults, the role of spectator reinforces a passive orientation toward life so that they will remain observers rather than the shapers of their own experience (Aronowitz, 1973).

COMMERCIALISM AND MATERIALISM

The conflict theorists emphasize that sport is promoted as a product to be consumed and that it creates a basis for capitalist expansion. For example, increasing numbers of individuals and families are joining athletic clubs where they pay to participate and pay for the lessons teaching them how to participate correctly and efficiently. Creating and satisfying these expanding interests have given rise to an entire new industry. Summer sport resorts, winter sport resorts, and local athletic clubs are all part of this profit-generating industry.

Furthermore, sporting goods manufacturers have found that effective advertising can lead more and more equipment to be defined as absolutely necessary for successful and healthy involvement. Potential consumers have been convinced that if they want to impress other people with their knowledge about the sport experience they have to buy and show off only top-of-the-line equipment. It has come to the point where participants can prove themselves in sport through their ability to consume as well as their ability to master physical skills. Thus sport has been used to lead people to deal with one another in terms of material images rather than in terms of the human quality of experience.

Sport not only creates direct profits but also is used as an advertising medium (Brohm, 1978). Sport spectacles serve as important settings for selling cars, tires, beer, soft drinks, and insurance. The tendency for people to personally identify with athletes is also used to sell other products. The role of athlete, unlike most adult occupational roles, is highly visible, prestigious, and relatively easy to emulate. Therefore, the attachment to sport heroes serves as the basis for the creation of an interest in sport along with a general "need" for consumer goods.

This process affects young people as well as adults. Children are lured into the spectator role and the role of consumer by trading cards, Dallas Cowboy pajamas, Yankee baseball caps, NBA basketball shoes, and a multitude of other products that ultimately create adulthood desires to become season ticket purchasers. Participation in highly specialized sport programs leads children to conclude that the proper equipment is always necessary for a good time and that being a good runner, tennis player, and soccer player depends on owning three different pairs of the best shoes on the market.

NATIONALISM, MILITARISM, AND SEXISM

Conflict theorists point out that sport is used by most countries as the showplace for displaying their national symbols and military strength. In many developing countries, national sport programs are administered by the defense department; in industrialized countries sport is symbolically linked with warfare and strong militaristic orientations. The conflict theorists claim that the collective excitement generated by sport participation and mass spectator events can be converted into unquestioning allegiance to political beliefs and an irrational willingness to defend those beliefs. Nationalistic feelings are fed by an emphasis on demonstrating superiority over other countries and other political systems. Futhermore, sport provides a model of confrontation, which polarizes groups of people and stresses the necessity of being militarily prepared.

Finally, the conflict theorists argue that sport divides the sexes and perpetuates distorted definitions of masculinity and femininity. The organization of contemporary sport not only relegates women to a secondary, supportive role, but also leads people to define masculinity in terms of physical strength and emotional insensitivity. In fact, the model of the successful male is epitomized by the brute strength and the controlled emotions of the athlete. Sport further reinforces sexism by focusing attention on performance differences in selected physical activities. People then use those differences to argue that male superiority is grounded in nature and that the sexes should continue to be separated. This separation obscures the characteristics men and women have in common and locks members of both sexes into restrictive roles.

Conflict theorists see much of contemporary sport as a source of alienation and a tool of exploitation and control serving the needs of economic and political systems rather than the needs of human beings. They generally argue that it is impossible for sport to provide humanizing experiences when the society in which it exists is not humane and creative (Hoch, 1972).

Limitations of the Conflict Theory Approach

Like the functionalist approach, conflict theory has some weaknesses. The conflict theorists make good use of history but they tend to overemphasize the role of capitalism in shaping all aspects of social reality since the Industrial Revolution. Capitalism has been a significant force, but other factors must be taken into account in explaining what has happened during the last two centuries.

The emergence and growth of modern sport is a good case in point. Sport has been strongly influenced by capitalism but the emergence of contemporary sport can be explained in terms of factors that existed prior to the Industrial Revolution. Guttmann (1978) has argued that modern sport is a product of a scientific approach to the world rather than of the needs of capitalist economic systems. This scientific approach to the world grew out of seventeenth century discoveries in mathematics and is characterized by a commitment to quantification, measurement, and experimentation. According to Guttmann this scientific world-view has given rise to contemporary sport. This is the reason why sport is also popular in noncapitalist countries including China, Cuba, Czechoslovakia, and the Soviet Union.

In their analysis of sport, many conflict theorists are too quick to conclude that sport inevitably creates alienation and serves as an "opiate of the masses." They tend to ignore the testimonials of athletes who claim that sport participation, even in a capitalist society, can be a personally creative, expressive, and liberating experience (Slusher, 1967; Spino, 1971; Bannister, 1973; Csikszentmihalyi, 1975; Sadler, 1977). This possibility, of course, is inconsistent with the idea that the athlete's body automatically becomes a tool of production controlled and used for the sake of political and economic goals.

The argument that sport is an opiate also has some weaknesses. It is probably true that athletes and fans are more likely than other people to have attitudes supportive of the status quo. However, it is not known if their involvement in sport caused these attitudes or if the attitudes existed prior to their involvement and caused them to be attracted to sport. It may be that sport attracts people who are already committed to the status quo. If this is the case, it is difficult to argue that sport provides an escape from reality for those who might otherwise be critical of the social order. Research suggests that the most alienated and the most dissatisfied people in society are the least likely to show an interest in sport. In fact, interest and involvement are greatest among those who are the most economically successful (Sillitoe, 1969; Edwards, 1973a; Anderson and Stone, 1979).

Another weakness of conflict theory is that it often overemphasizes the extent to which sport is controlled by those in positions of power in society. The people who control the media, sport facilities, and sport teams do have much to say about the conditions under which top level sport events are experienced and viewed by players and spectators alike. However, it is difficult to argue that all sport involvement is a result of the promotional efforts of capitalists or government bureaucrats. This is especially true when attention is shifted from professional level sport to sport at the local recreational level. Active sport participation generally occurs at levels where the interests of the participants themselves can be used as the basis for creating and developing programs.

Furthermore, certain sports have characteristics making them difficult to control by those who are not participants. Surfing is a good case in point; it does not lend itself to scheduling or television coverage, equipment needs are not extensive, and it does not generate much long-term spectator interest among those who have never been surfers. Therefore, the development of surfing and other similar sports has not been subject to heavy influence from outsiders whose main concerns are generating profits and creating sport spectacles.

SUMMARY AND CONCLUSION: WHO IS RIGHT?

Now that we have looked at the relationship between sport and society (see Table 3-1 for a review) from two different perspectives, which explanation is most correct? Is sport an inspiration or an opiate? I have found that the way people answer this question depends on what they think about the society in which sport exists. For example, those who are generally uncritical of American society will tend to agree with the functionalist approach when they look at sport in the United States. Those who are critical of American society will side with the conflict theorists. However, when the country in question is East Germany or China rather than the United States, some people may shift perspective. Those who do not agree with the way of life in East Germany or China will quickly become conflict theorists in their discussions of sport in these countries; those supportive of socialist systems will tend to become functionalists. It can be confusing to say that sport is an inspiration in one country and an opiate in another.

In order to eliminate some of the confusion on this issue we need detailed research on how the structure of physical activities is related to the subjective experiences of participants (players and spectators). We also need to know how those experiences are related to attitudes and behavior patterns. We can assume that under certain circumstances the consequences of sport will be constructive, and under other circumstances they will be destructive. Our task is to be able to clearly describe the circumstances under which these

TABLE 3-1. Functionalism and Conflict Theory: A Summary of Their Assumptions about the Social Order and Their Explanations of the Relationship between Sport and Society

Functionalist Approach	Conflict Theory
Assumptions about the social order	
Social order based on consensus, common values, and interrelated subsystems	Social order based on coercion, exploitation, and subtle manipulation of individuals
Major concerns in the study of society	
What are the essential parts in structure of social system?	How is power distributed and used in society?
How do social systems continue to operate smoothly?	How do societies change and what can be done to promote change?
Major concerns in the study of sport	
How does sport contribute to basic social system needs such as pattern maintenance and tension management, integration, goal attainment, and adaptation?	How does sport create personal alienation? How is sport used to control thoughts and behavior of people, and maintain economic and political systems serving interests of those in power?
Major conclusions about the sport-society relationship	
Sport is valuable secondary social institution benefiting society as well as individual members of society	Sport is distorted form of physical exercise shaped by needs of autocratic or production-conscious societies
Sport is basically a *source of inspiration* on personal and social level	Sport lacks creative and expressive elements of play; *it is an opiate*
Goals of sport sociology	
To discover ways in which sport's contribution to stability and maintenance of social order can be maximized at all levels	To promote development of humane and creative social order so that sport can be source of expression, creative experiences, and physical well-being
Major weaknesses	
Assumes that existence and popularity of sport prove that it is serving positive functions	Assumes that structures and consequences of sport are totally determined by needs of political and economic order
Ignores possibility of internal differences and basic conflicts of interest within social systems and therefore assumes that sport serves needs of all system parts and individuals equally	Ignores factors other than capitalism in analyzing emergence and development of contemporary sport
	Focuses too much attention on top level spectator sport and overemphasizes extent to which all sport involvement is controlled and structured by power elite

different consequences occur and to explain why they occur the way they do. This means that studies cannot be limited to specific countries or to specific groups of people. We need cross-cultural and comparative research focusing on all dimensions of the phenomenon of sport.

In developing research and exploring these issues we need to be aware of the ideas of both the functionalists and the conflict theorists. Each of their explanations of the relationship between sport and society alerts us to questions that must be asked and hypotheses that must be tested. Unless these and other theoretical perspectives are used our understanding of sport will be needlessly restricted.

Unfortunately, research will never be able to show us what the relationship between sport and society *should* be. It only alerts us to the possibilities and provides us with a starting point for shaping what it will be in the future.

NOTE

1. Although the focus of the examples in this [selection] is the United States, the pattern maintenance function of sport has been described in other countries, including the Soviet Union (Morton, 1963; Riordan, 1977), East Germany (Santomier and Ewees, 1979), China (Johnson, 1973a,b; Chu and Segrave, 1979), Finland (Olin, 1979), Australia (Murray, 1976), and Samoa (Dunlap, 1951).

REFERENCES

Albonico, R. 1967. Modern University Sport as a Contribution to Social Integration. *International Review of Sport Sociology* 2:155–162.

Anderson, D., and G. P. Stone. 1979. A Fifteen-Year Analysis of Socio-Economic Strata Differences in the Meaning Given to Sport by Metropolitans. In M. L. Krotee, ed. *The Dimensions of Sport Sociology*. Leisure Press, New York.

Aronowitz, S. 1973. *False Promises*. McGraw-Hill, New York.

Bannister, F. T. 1980. Search for "White Hopes" threatens Black Athletes. *Ebony* 34(4):130–134.

Brockmann, D. 1969. Sport as an Integrating Factor in the Countryside, *International Review of Sport Sociology* 4:151–170.

Brohm, J-M. 1978. *Sport: A Prison of Measured Time*. Ink Links. London.

Chase, J. H. 1909. How a Director Feels. *Playground* 3(4):13.

Chu, D. B., and J. O. Segrave. 1979. Physical Culture in the People's Republic of China. *Journal of Sport Behavior* 2(3):119–135.

Csikszentmikhalyi, M. 1975. *Beyond Boredom and Anxiety*. Jossey-Bass. San Francisco.

Dunlap, H. L. 1951. Games, Sports, Dancing, and Other Vigorous Recreational Activities and their Function in Samoan Culture. *Research Quarterly* 22(3):298–311.

Edwards, H. 1973. *Sociology of Sport*. Dorsey Press, Homewood, Ill.

Eitzen, D. S., and G. H. Sage. 1978. *Sociology of American Sport*. Wm. C. Brown. Dubuque, Iowa.

Gerth, H., and C. W. Mills. 1953. *Character and Social Structure*. Harcourt Brace Jovanovich, New York.

Goodman, C. 1979. *Choosing Sides*. Schocken, New York.

Guttmann, A. 1978. *From Ritual to Record: The Nature of Modern Sports*. Columbia University Press, New York.

Hennig, M., and A. Jardim. 1977. *The Managerial Woman*. Anchor, New York.

Hoch, P. 1972. *Rip Off the Big Game*. Doubleday, New York.

Johnson, W. O. 1973. Faces on a New China Scroll. *Sports Illustrated* 39(14):42–67.

Kleiber, D. A., and J. R. Kelly. 1980. Leisure, Socialization and the Life Cycle. In S. Iso-Ahola, ed. *Social Psychological Perspectives on Leisure and Recreation*. Charles C. Thomas, Springfield, Ill.

Lever, J. 1978. Sex Differences in the Complexity of Children's Play. *American Sociological Review* 43(4):471–483.

Lever, J. 1980. Multiple Methods of Data Collection: A Note on Divergence. Unpublished manuscript.

Luschen, G. 1967. The Interdependence of Sport and Culture. *International Review of Sport Sociology* 2:127–139.

Marsh, P. 1978. *Aggro: The Illusion of Violence*. J. M. Dent, London.

Morton, H. W. 1963. *Soviet Sport*. Collier, New York.

Mumford, L. 1934. *Technics and Civilization*. Harcourt Brace Jovanovich, New York.

Murray, L. 1979. Some Ideological Qualities of Australian Sport. *Australian Journal of Health, Physical Education and Recreation* 73:7–10.

Olin, K. 1979. Sport, Social Development and Community Decision-Making. *International Review of Sport Sociology* 14(3–4):117–132.

Parsons, T., and N. J. Smelser. 1965. *Economy and Society*. The Free Press, New York.

Petryszak, N. 1978. Spectator Sports as an Aspect of Popular Culture—An Historical View. *Journal of Sport Behavior* 1(1):14–27.

Proctor, R. C., and W. M. Echard. 1976. "Toot-Toot" or Spectator Sports: Psychological and Therapeutic Implications. *American Journal of Sports Medicine* 4(2):78–83.

Riordan, J. 1977. *Sport in Soviet Society*. Cambridge University Press, New York.

Sadler, W. A. 1977. Alienated Youth and Creative Sports Experience. *Journal of the Philosophy of Sport* 4(Fall):83–95.

Santomier, J., and K. Ewees. 1979. Sport, Political Socialization and the German Democratic Republic. In Krotee, M. L. (ed.), *The Dimensions of Sport Sociology*. Leisure Press, West Point, N.Y.

Schafer, W. E. 1976. Sport and Youth Counterculture: Contrasting Socialization Themes. In D. M. Landers, ed. *Social Problems in Athletics*. University of Illinois Press, Urbana, Ill.

Sillitoe, K. 1969. *Planning for Leisure*. University of Keele, London.

Slusher, H. S. 1967. *Man, Sport and Existence*. Lea & Febiger, Philadelphia.

Spino, M. 1971. Running as a Spiritual Experience. In J. Scott, *The Athletic Revolution*. The Free Press, N.Y.

Vanderzwaag, H. J. 1972. *Toward a Philosophy of Sport*. Addison-Wesley, Reading, Mass.

Wohl, A. 1970. Competitive Sport and Its Social Functions. *International Review of Sport Sociology* 5:117–124.

Wohl, A. 1979. Sport and Social Development. *International Review of Sport Sociology* 14(3–4):5–18.

■ FOR FURTHER STUDY

Avedon, Elliot M., and Brian Sutton-Smith. *The Study of Games*. New York: Wiley, 1971.

Caillois, Roger. "The Structure and Classification of Games." *Diogenes* (Winter 1965):62–75.

Edwards, Harry. *Sociology of Sport*. Homewood, Ill.: Dorsey, 1973, pp. 3–61.

Eitzen, D. Stanley, and George H. Sage. *Sociology of North American Sport*. Dubuque, Iowa: Wm. C. Brown, 1986, pp. 1–30.

Figler, Stephen K., *Sport and Play in American Life*. Philadelphia: Saunders, 1981.

Frey, James H., ed. "Contemporary Issues in Sport." *The Annals of the American Academy of Political and Social Science* 445 (September 1979): entire issue.

Gilbert, Bil. "Gleanings from a Troubled Time." *Sports Illustrated* (December 25, 1972):34–46.

Grove, Stephen J., and Richard A. Dodder. "A Study of Functions of Sport." *Journal of Sport Behavior* 2 (May 1979):83–92.

Gruneau, Richard. *Class, Sports, and Social Development*. Amherst, Mass.: University of Massachusetts Press, 1983.

Gruneau, Richard, and John G. Albinson, eds. *Canadian Sport: Sociological Perspectives*. Don Mills, Ontario: Addison-Wesley, 1976.

Guttmann, Allen. *From Record to Ritual: The Nature of Modern Sports*. New York: Columbia University Press, 1978.

Guttmann, Allen. *Sports Spectators*. New York: Columbia University Press, 1986.

Hargreaves, John. *Sport, Power and Culture: A Social and Historical Analysis of Popular Sports in Britain*. New York: St. Martin's Press, 1986.

Huizinga, Johan. *Homo Ludens: A Study of the Play Element in Culture*. Boston: Beacon Press, 1950.

Lapchick, Richard E., ed. *Fractured Focus: Sport as a Reflection of Society*. Lexington, Mass.: D. C. Heath, 1986.

Lowe, Benjamin. "The Sociology of Sports—A Basic Outline." *The Physical Educator* 28 (May 1971):79.

Loy, John W. "The Nature of Sport: A Definitional Effort." *Quest* 10 (May 1968):1–15.

Loy, John W. "A Case for the Sociology of Sport." *Journal of Health, Physical Education and Recreation* 43 (June 1972):50.

Loy, John W. "The Emergence and Development of the Sociology of Sport as an Academic Specialty." *Research Quarterly* 51, no. 1 (1980):91–109.

Loy, John W., Barry D. McPherson, and Gerald Kenyon. *Sport and Social Systems: A Guide to the Analysis, Problems, and Literature*. Reading, Mass.: Addison-Wesley, 1978, pp. 1–64.

Loy, John W., Barry D. McPherson, and Gerald S. Kenyon. *The Sociology of Sport as an Academic Specialty*. CAHPER monograph (no date).

Loy, John W., Gerald S. Kenyon, and Barry D. McPherson, eds. *Sport, Culture and Society*. 2d ed. Philadelphia: Lea and Febiger, 1981.

Luschen, Gunther. "The Sociology of Sport: A Trend Report and Bibliography." *Current Sociology* 15 (1967):5–140.

Luschen, Gunther. "The Development and Scope of a Sociology of Sport." *American Corrective Therapy Journal* 29 (March/April 1975):39–43.

Luschen, Gunther. "Sociology of Sport." *Annual Review of Sociology* 6 (1980):315–347.

Luschen, Gunther, and George H. Sage. "Sport in Sociological Perspective." In *Handbook of Social Science of Sport*, edited by Gunther Luschen and George H. Sage. Champaign, Ill.: Stipes, 1981, pp. 3–21.

McKay, Jim. "Marxism as a Way of Seeing: Beyond the Limits of Current 'Critical' Approaches to Sport." *Sociology of Sport Journal* 3 (September 1986):261–272.

Melnick, Merrill J. "A Critical Look at Sociology of Sport." *Quest* 24 (Summer 1975):34–47.

Melnick, Merrill J. "Toward an Applied Sociology of Sport." *Journal of Sport and Social Issues* 5 (Spring/Summer 1981):1–12.

Michener, James. *Sports in America*. New York: Random House, 1976.

Morford, R. "Is Sport the Struggle or the Triumph?" *Quest* 19 (January 1973):83–87.

Morgan, Willam J. " 'Radical' Social Theory and Sport: A Critique and a Conceptual Emendation." *Sociology of Sport Journal* 2 (March 1985):56–71.

Nixon, Howard L. *Sport and Social Organization*. Indianapolis: Bobbs-Merrill, 1976, pp. 5–8.

Novak, Michael. *The Joy of Sports*. New York: Basic Books, 1976.

Page, Charles H. "The Mounting Interest in Sport." In *Sport and Society*, edited by Charles H. Page and J. T. Talamini. Boston: Little, Brown, 1973, pp. 3–39.

Pankin, Robert M., ed. *Social Approaches to Sport*. London: Associated University Presses, 1982.

Sage, George H. "Sport and the Social Sciences." *The Annals* 445 (September 1979):1–14.

Sage, George H., ed. *Sport and American Society*. 3d ed. Reading, Mass.: Addison-Wesley, 1980.

Schwartz, J. Michael. "Causes and Effects of Spectator Sports." *International Review of Sport Sociology* 8 (1973):25–43.

Scott, Jack. *Athletics for Athletes*. Berkeley, Calif.: Otherways, 1969.

Shaw, David. "The Roots of Rooting," *Psychology Today* 11 (February 1978):48–51.

Shecter, Leonard. *The Jocks*. Indianapolis: Bobbs-Merrill, 1969.

Slusher, Howard. *Man, Sport and Existence: A Critical Analysis*. Philadelphia: Lea and Febiger, 1967.

Snyder, Eldon E., and Elmer Spreitzer. "Sociology of Sport: An Overview." *The Sociological Quarterly* 15 (Fall 1974):467–487.

Vander Zwaag, Harold, and Thomas J. Shechan. *Introduction to Sport Studies: From the Classroom to the Ball Park*. Dubuque, Iowa: Wm. C. Brown, 1978.

Weiss, Paul. *Sport: A Philosophic Inquiry*. Carbondale, Illinois: Southern Illinois Press, 1969.

Whit, William C., ed. "Teaching Sociology of Sport." *Arena Review* 10 (December 1986): entire issue.

Young, T. R., ed. "Critical Perspectives on Sport." *Arena Review* 8 (November 1984): entire issue.

Part Two

Sport as a Microcosm of Society: Cross-Cultural Perspectives

In the following quote, Howard Cosell argues that sport is a reflection of society:

> Once upon a time, the legend had it, there was a world that remained separate and apart from all others, a privileged sanctuary from real life. It was the wonderful world of sport, where every competition was endowed with an inherent purity, every athlete a shining example of noble young manhood, and every owner was motivated by his love of the game and his concern for the public interest. . . . The sports establishment—the commissioners, the owners, the leagues, the National Collegiate Athletic Association—would have us believe the legend. Their unceasing chant is that sport is escapism, pure and simple; that people have enough daily problems to cope with in a complex, divided, and even tormented society; and that the relief provided by sports is essential to the maintenance of an individual mental and emotional equilibrium. There is something to be said for this argument, but this hardly means that the sports establishment should be left untrammeled and that individual injustices should not be exposed. The plain truth is that sport is a reflection of the society, that it is human life in microcosm, that it has within it the maladies of the society, that some athletes drink, that some athletes do take drugs, that there is racism in sport, that the sports establishment is quite capable of defying the public interest, and that in this contemporary civilization sport does invade sociology, economics, law, and politics.[1]

Cosell's argument is also mine—sport *is* a microcosm of society. If we know how sport is organized, the type of games played, the way winners and losers are treated, the type and amount of compensation given the participants, and the way rules are enforced, then we surely also know a great deal about the larger society in which it exists. Conversely, if we know the values of a society, the type of economy, the way minority groups are treated, and the political structure, then we would also have important clues about how sport in that society would likely be organized.

The United States, for example, is a capitalistic society. It is not surprising, then, that in the corporate sport that dominates, American athletes are treated as property. In the professional ranks they are bought and sold. At the college level players once enrolled are unable to switch teams without waiting for a year. Even in youth sports, players are drafted and become the "property" of a given team.

Capitalism is also evident as team owners "carpetbag," i.e., move teams to more lucrative markets. At the same time these owners insist that the cities subsidize the construction of new stadiums, thereby making their franchises more profitable. The players, too, appear to have more loyalty to money than to their teams or fans.

Americans are highly competitive. This is easily seen at work, at school, in dating, and in sport. Persons are evaluated not on their intrinsic worth but on the criterion of achievement. As Sage has written: "Sports have consented to measure the results of sports efforts in terms of performance and product—the terms which prevail in the factory and department store."[2]

Athletes are expected to deny self and sacrifice for the needs of the sponsoring organization. This requires, foremost, an acquiescence to authority. The coach is the ultimate authority, and the players must obey. This is the way bureaucracies operate, and American society is highly bureaucratic whether it be in government, school, church, or business. As Paul Hoch has stated: "In football, like business . . . every pattern of movement on the field is increasingly being brought under the control of a group of non-playing managerial technocrats who sit up in the stands . . . with their headphones and dictate offenses, defenses, special plays, substitutions, and so forth to the players below."[3]

Thus, American sport, like American society, is authoritarian, bureaucratic, and product-oriented. Winning is everything. Athletes use drugs to enhance their performances artificially in order to succeed. Coaches teach their athletes to bend the rules (to feign a foul, to hold without getting caught) in order to win. Even at America's most prestigious universities, coaches offer illegal inducements to athletes to attend their school. And, as long as they win, the administrators at these offending schools usually look the other way. After all, the object is to win, and this "Watergate mentality" permeates sport as it does politics and the business world.

These are but some of the ways that sport mirrors society. In this part we shall examine three illustrations of how sport is a microcosm of society. The first selection, by sociologists Eldon E. Snyder and Elmer A. Spreitzer, shows how baseball has been adapted in Japan to fit the unique social structure of that society.

The second selection, by D. Stanley Eitzen, illustrates what the structure of two major team sports—football and baseball—tells us about Americans and American society.

The concluding selection, by anthropologist Richard Grey Sipes, investigates the relationship between violence-prone societies and violent societies. This is a significant question. If the data show a strong positive correlation between the existence of combative sports and the incidence of war, then we have vivid demonstration of the link between a society's culture and its sports.

NOTES

1. Howard Cosell, "Sports and Good-bye to All That," *The New York Times* (April 5, 1971), p. 33.
2. George H. Sage, "Sports, Culture, and Society," paper presented at the Basic Science of Sport Medicine Conference, Philadelphia (July 14–16, 1974), pp. 10–11.
3. Paul Hoch, *Rip Off the Big Game* (Garden City, New York: Doubleday Anchor, 1972), p. 9.

4. *Baseball in Japan*

ELDON E. SNYDER AND ELMER A. SPREITZER

The case of baseball in Japan represents an interesting example of the way in which cultural differences affect a particular sport. Although the structure of the game is basically the same as in North America, it is clear that the climate and texture of the game are very different in the two cultural settings. An American professor at Tokyo University introduced baseball to his students in 1873. The sport is now immensely popular and draws a crowd at all levels of competition. A national tournament at the high school level lasts ten days and draws about 500,000 spectators in addition to a nationwide television audience (Boersema, 1979, p. 28). At the college level, baseball is televised and draws a following akin to bigtime university rivalries in the United States. The professional baseball leagues attract about 12 million spectators in addition to huge television audiences; several games are broadcast simultaneously on weekend television. Professional baseball in Japan began in 1936 after Babe Ruth and a group of American players toured the country.

Japanese baseball is distinctive in a number of ways that Americans would find quaint. For example, the annual game of musical chairs wherein managers are "replaced" is foreign to Japan. Managers are rarely fired, and when it does take place, a stylized ritual is used to permit the former manager to save face. It is also interesting to note that in Japan baseball games can end in a tie, which is no doubt a reflection of the Japanese emphasis on *process* as well as product. Moreover, the manager and players emphasize the collective goal of winning the pennant even at the expense of individual careers. A manager may call on a star pitcher, therefore, whenever a game is critical. Star pitchers are also used for relief work which commonly results in only two days of rest between starts. Such a heavy use no doubt shortens a career. In a 1958 Japan series, one pitcher worked in six of the seven games, and he once won 42 games in a single season. His career ended at 26 years of age. Nevertheless, a player is unlikely to challenge the system since team loyalty is paramount (Boersema, 1979).

American teams have been playing regularly in Japan since 1951 on an invitational basis. During this period, the teams from America have compiled a record of 163–47–20 (won-lost-tie) against the Japanese teams. The consensus of the visitors is that the Japanese are very competitive in terms of funda-

SOURCE: Eldon E. Snyder and Elmer A. Spreitzer, *Social Aspects of Sport*, second edition (Englewood Cliffs, N.J.: Prentice-Hall, 1983), pp. 53–56.

mentals and basic skills but lack the strength and power of players from America (Boersema, 1979, p. 31). Two foreign players are allowed on each professional team in Japan. Most of the American players are superannuated veterans of the major leagues. The Japanese recruit the Americans with serious attention paid to personal character and personality traits. The objective is to recruit well-mannered and disciplined players who can adapt to the more structured Japanese system and who can bear the rigorous training schedule that begins in January.

It is relevant to note that sumo wrestling ranks as the second most popular sport in Japan, with baseball first. "Both are very ceremonial sports, both require of the competent spectator very minute and careful observation of the quick move made after rather long pauses for ritual and for mental preparation by the athletes" (Cleaver, 1976, p. 120). To the American observer, Japanese baseball seems authoritarian and highly ritualized; however, a brief discussion of traditional Japanese values will suggest that baseball simply mirrors the larger Japanese society. First of all, it might be noted that individualism and egotism are highly stigmatized personality traits in Japan; the following expressions illustrate the value of selflessness in Japanese society:

"Have no self."

"Be wrapped in something long."

"The nail that sticks up will be hammered down."

"If one had no selfish motives but only the supreme values, there would be no self."

"If he serves selflessly, he does not know what service is."

"If he knows what service is, he has a self."

"If you think that you work diligently, it is not true service."

"To think of merits and demerits is egotism."

"Because you do not act as you please, things will, conversely, turn out right for you."

(Minami, 1971, p. 11)

The teamwork that is evident on a Japanese baseball team is paralleled by a remarkable sense of solidarity among industrial workers in Japan (Cleaver, 1976, p. 101). There is a congruity between company policy and worker preferences that precludes alienated labor. Workers consult and advise one another on improved ways of doing a particular piece of work. Although individuals may hold disparate political views off the job, these theoretical differences do not intrude upon team efforts at work. Many leisure activities are organized through the employer as family recreation; this pattern is sometimes referred to as paternalism by Americans. Westerners continually express amazement at the work ethic of industrial workers in Japan. In 1972 an American visitor reported seeing a group of workers assembled one morning outside a factory waiting for the gates to open. While waiting they were singing the company song (Cleaver, 1976, p. 102).

One of the first character traits that Americans note in Japanese is their extreme politeness. The ceremonial and ritual etiquette associated with courtesy in Japan is expressed in a gradation of honorific language which is reflected in vocabulary as well as in grammar. La Barre's (1962) observations concerning Japanese politeness were originally published in 1945 and are therefore probably less applicable to contemporary Japan; nevertheless, his description of the Japanese character is interesting in terms of its contrast with American individualism.

> By contrast, the Japanese pride themselves on their lack of selfish "individualism" and their willingness to pull together in conformity to the "Yamato spirit." Thus it is often extremely difficult in Japanese social relations . . . to get any clear idea on which side of the fence a given person stands, since everyone pretends there is no fence and since all of them seek the protective cloak of apparent conformity to public opinion. There is so much by-play and face-saving, that in the end the Japanese exasperate occidentals as being *emotionally masked* persons with no honesty of expression whatsoever, "inscrutable" and untrustworthy (p. 335).

Haring (1962, p. 389) interprets Japanese politeness as compliance with a code of behavior that specifies correct behavior vis à vis others as a means of maintaining face and one's own self-esteem. The operative question is, "Have I acted correctly?"

The Japanese concepts of self-discipline and self-sacrifice are linked with implicit assumptions concerning skill, competency, and expertness. Self-pity is a foreign concept, as is individual frustration. "In Japan one disciplines oneself to be a good player, and the Japanese attitude is that one undergoes the training with no more consciousness of sacrifice that a man who plays bridge. Of course the training is strict, but that is inherent in the nature of things" (Benedict, 1946, p. 233). Interestingly, competency drives out self-consciousness; thus when one is living on the plane of expertness, Japanese say that he or she is "living as one already dead." Through self-discipline an inherently difficult activity can be made to appear easy. This stress on "competent self-discipline" has some desirable consequences. "They pay much closer attention to behaving competently and they allow themselves fewer alibis than Americans. They do not so often project their dissatisfactions with life upon scapegoats, and they do not so often indulge in self-pity because they have somehow or other not got what Americans call average happiness. They have been trained to pay much closer attention to the 'rust of the body' than is common among Americans" (Benedict, 1946, p. 235).

The highly explicit codes of behavior in Japan account for the structured nature of the individual's response; behavior has the quality of being thoroughly planned. Spontaneous behavior is not admired. The mature individual is assumed to anticipate all emergencies and to be able to meet them calmly. Display of emotion is discouraged (Haring, 1962, p. 389). Similarly, a person who is touchy or easily affronted evidences an insecure ego. In child raising the parents make it clear that claims of the individual ego are to be systematically suppressed. In order to preserve face, "there must therefore be not only a constant checking and correcting of behavior, but also an anxious concern lest any lapse be publicly noted" (LaBarre, 1962, p. 341).

This description of Japanese personality traits and cultural values explains why baseball is so different in the two countries—sport is a value receptacle for society. A respect for authority, devotion to the collectivity, and self-discipline would understandably be conducive to team harmony. In Japanese baseball, doing your own thing is strongly stigmatized—salary disputes, asking for individual exemptions from team policies, temper tantrums, moodiness, complaining, clubhouse lawyers, attacking the umpire, criticizing the manager, mouthing-off to the media, bad-mouthing teammates, violation of training rules, fist fights, and *ad nauseam*. American players in Japan who have behaved in a selfish manner have experienced prompt and strong sanctions (Objski, 1975; Whiting, 1979).

Shenanigans of this type would lead to strong ostracism in a shame culture such as Japan. "Shame is a reaction to other people's criticism. A man is shamed by being openly ridiculed and rejected or by fantasying to himself that he has been ridiculous. In either case it is a potent sanction" (Benedict, 1946, p. 223). In brief, the Japanese place a premium on the quality of the athlete's character; sport performance alone is not sufficient. Thus, the "superbrat" (the columnist Mike Royko's term) is persona non grata in Japanese baseball.

REFERENCES

Benedict, Ruth 1946 *The Chrysanthemum and the Sword: Patterns of Japanese Culture*. Boston: Houghton-Mifflin.
Boersema, James 1979 "Baseball: Oriental Style." *Soldiers* 34 (June):28–31.
Cleaver, Charles G. 1976 *Japanese and Americans: Cultural Parallels and Paradoxes*. Minneapolis: University of Minnesota Press, 1976.
Haring, Douglas G. 1962 "Japanese National Character," in Bernard Silberman (ed.), *Japanese Character and Culture*. Tucson: University of Arizona Press.
La Barre, Weston 1962 "Some Observations on Character Structure in the Orient," in Bernard Silberman (ed.), *Japanese Character and Culture*. Tucson: University of Arizona Press.
Minami, Hiroshi 1971 *Psychology of the Japanese People*. Toronto: University of Toronto Press.
Obojski, Robert 1975 *The Rise of Japanese Baseball Power*. Radnor, Pa.: Chilton.
Whiting, Robert 1979 "You've Gotta Have 'Wa.' " *Sports Illustrated* 51 (September 24):60–71.

5. *The Structure of Sport and Society*

D. STANLEY EITZEN

An important indicator of the essence of a society is the type of sport it glorifies. The examination of the structure of a society's dominant sport provides important clues about that society and its culture. For example, answers to the following questions will greatly inform the observer about that society: Is the sport oriented toward a group (team) or the individual? Does the outcome depend essentially on strength, speed, strategy, deception, or the mastery of intricate moves? Is the activity cerebral or physical? Is the primary goal to win or to enjoy the activity?

Let us begin by looking at what Americans consider the essence of sport—winning—to show how other societies have a different view more consonant with their culture. Sport, as played in America, is an expression of Social Darwinism—a survival-of-the-fittest approach where everyone competes to be alone at the top. Players are cut from teams even in our schools if they are not considered good enough. Tournaments are organized so that only one team or individual is the ultimate winner. Corporations sponsor contests for youngsters such as "Punt, Pass, and Kick," where winners are selected at the local level and proceed through a number of district and regional contests until a winner is declared in each category. In 1974, for instance, there were 1,112,702 entrants in the Punt, Pass, and Kick contest, and only six youngsters ended as winners.[1]

In cooperative, group-centered societies, such sporting activities would seem cruel, even barbaric, because success is achieved only at the cost of the failure of others. These societies, rather, would have sports where the object is something other than winning. For instance:

> The Tangu people of New Guinea play a popular game known as *taketak*, which involves throwing a spinning top into massed lots of stakes driven into the ground. There are two teams. Players of each team try to touch as many stakes with their tops as possible. In the end, however, the participants play not to win but to draw. The game must go on until an exact draw is reached. This requires great skill, since players sometimes must throw their tops into the massed stakes without touching a single one. *Taketak* expresses a prime value in Tangu culture, that is, the concept of moral equivalence, which is reflected in the precise sharing of foodstuffs among the people.[2]

SOURCE: This essay was written for the first edition of this volume and is slightly revised for this edition.

This example demonstrates that a society's sports mirror that society. Co-operative societies have sports that minimize competition, while aggressive societies have highly competitive sports. This raises a question about the nature of the most popular American sports. What do they tell us about ourselves and our society? Let us concentrate on the two most popular team sports—football and baseball—as they are played at the professional level.[3]

THE DIFFERING NATURES OF FOOTBALL AND BASEBALL

Although there are some similarities between football and baseball, for example, cheating is the norm in both,[4] these two sports are basically different. In many ways they are opposites, and these incongruities provide insightful clues about Americans and American society.

Two fundamentally different orientations toward time exist in these two sports. Baseball is not bounded by time while football must adhere to a rigid time schedule. "Baseball is oblivious to time. There is no clock, no two-minute drill. The game flows in a timeless stream with a rhythm of its own."[5] In this way baseball reflects life in rural America as it existed in the not-too-distant past compared to football's emulation of contemporary urban society, where persons have rigid schedules, appointments, and time clocks to punch.

The innings of baseball have no time limit, and if the game is tied at the end of regulation innings, the teams play as many extra innings as it takes to determine a winner. Football, on the other hand, is played for sixty minutes, and if tied at the end, the game goes into "sudden death," that is, the first team to score wins. Thus, even the nomenclature of the two sports—"extra innings" compared to "sudden death"—illustrates a basic difference between them. There are other semantic differences. A baseball player makes an "error," but a football team is "penalized." The object of baseball is to get "home" while the goal of football is to penetrate deep into the opponent's "territory." In baseball there is no home territory to defend; the playing field is shared by both teams. There is no analogue in baseball for the militaristic terms of football, for example, "blitz," "bomb," "trap," "trenches," "field general," "aerial attack," and "ground attack."

Such linguistic differences imply a basic discrepancy between baseball and football. Baseball is essentially a calm and leisurely activity while football is intense, aggressive, and violent. Football is foremost a form of physical combat, whereas baseball is one of technique. A baseball player cannot get to first base because of his strength, aggression, or ability to intimidate. His only way to get there is through skill. In football, however, survival (success) belongs to the most aggressive. Former football player George Sauer has suggested that aggression on the football field leads to success just as it gets one ahead in American society:

How does football justify teaching a man to be aggressive against another man? And how does it justify using that aggression for the ends that it has? I think the values of football as it is now played reflect a segment of thought, a particular kind of thought that is pretty prevalent in our society. The way to do anything in the world, the way to get ahead, is to aggress against somebody, compete against somebody, try to dominate, try to overcome, work your way up the ladder, and in doing so, you have to judge yourself and be judged as what you want to be in relation to somebody else all the time. Given the influence football has on young children, the immense influence it has as a socializing force in society, its impact should be rigorously examined. People learn certain values from watching football, from watching aggression, from watching it performed violently and knowing that these guys are going to get a big chunk of money if they do it well often enough.[6]

The two sports require different mentalities of their athletes. Football players must be aggressive while that is not a necessary ingredient for the baseball player. Also, baseball is a game of repetition and predictable action that is played over a 162-game schedule. The players must stay relaxed and not get too excited because to do so for every game would be too physically and emotionally draining over the six months of the season. Moreover, because the season is so long, players must pace themselves and not let a loss or even a succession of losses get them down. In football, though, losing is intolerable because of the short season (sixteen games). Thus, football players must play each game with extreme intensity. As a result the incidence of taking amphetamines ("uppers") has been much greater among football players than among baseball players. The intensity that characterizes football resembles the tensions and pressures of modern society, contrasted with the more relaxed pace of agrarian life and baseball.

One of the most interesting contrasts between these two sports is the equality of opportunity each offers. Baseball promotes equality while football is essentially unequal. This difference occurs in several ways. First, football originated among college elites and even today requires attending college to play at the professional level. Baseball has never been closely identified with college. Essentially, the way to make it in baseball is to work one's way through the minor leagues rather than by attending college (although that is one route).

A second way that baseball is more egalitarian than football is that it can be played by people of all sizes. There have been small All Star players such as Phil Rizzuto, Bobby Shantz, Pee Wee Reese, Joe Morgan, and Freddie Patek. Football, however, is a big man's game. In football the good, big team defeats the good, small team, whereas in baseball, the good, small team has an equal chance of beating the good, big team.

Baseball is also more equal than football because everyone has the opportunity to be a star. Each position has its stars. Pay is divided about equally by position. Except for designated hitters, all players must play both offense and defense. Thus, each player has the chance to make an outstanding defensive play or to bat in the winning run. Stardom in football is essentially reserved for those who play at certain positions. Only backs, receivers, and kickers score points while others labor in relative obscurity, making it possible for the "glamor boys" to score. This is similar, by the way, to American society, where the richest "players" score all the points, call the plays, and get the glory at the expense of the commoners. There is also a wide variance in pay by position in football.

A final contrast on this equality dimension has to do with the availability of each of the sports to the masses. The average ticket price for major league baseball is approximately one-third that of professional football. The cheaper tickets for baseball allow families to attend and provide live entertainment for members of all social classes. Football, however, excludes families (except for the rich) and members of the lower classes because of the high prices and the necessity of purchasing season tickets.

Another major dimension on which these two sports differ is individualism. Baseball is highly individualistic. Elaborate teamwork is not required except for double plays and defensing sacrifice bunts. Each player struggles to succeed on his own. As Cavanaugh has characterized it:

> Although there are teams in baseball, there is little teamwork. The essence of the game is the individual with or against the ball: pitcher controlling, batter hitting, fielder handling, runner racing the ball. All players are on their own, struggling (like the farmer) to overcome not another human being but nature (the ball). This individualism is demonstrated when the shortstop, cleanly fielding the ball, receives credit for a "chance" even if the first baseman drops the thrown ball. It is demonstrated when a last-place team includes a Cy Young Award-winning pitcher or a league-leading hitter. It is perhaps most clearly manifest in the pitcher-batter duel, the heart of the game, when two men face each other. Baseball is each man doing the best he can for himself and against nature within a loose confederation of fellow individualists he may or may not admire and respect. This reflects a society in which individual effort, drive, and success are esteemed and in which, conversely, failure is deemed the individual's responsibility.[7]

Football, in sharp contrast, is the quintessence of team sports. Every move is planned and practiced in advance. The players in each of the eleven positions have a specific task to perform on every play. Every player is a specialist who must coordinate his actions with the other specialists on the team. So important is each person's play to the whole, that games are filmed and reviewed, with each play then broken down into its components and each player graded. Each player must subordinate his personality for the sake of the team. The coach is typically a stern taskmaster demanding submission of self to the team. The similarity of the football player to the organization man is obvious. So, too, is the parallel between football and the factory or corporation, where intricate and precise movements of all members doing different tasks are required for the attainment of the organization's objective.

CONCLUSION

Sociologist David Riesman in his classic book, *The Lonely Crowd*, noted a shift in American character since World War II.[8] Prior to that war Americans were what Riesman called "inner directed," which fit the demands of an essentially agrarian society. The farmer and the small entrepreneur succeeded on their own merits and efforts. "Rugged individualism" was the necessary ingredient for success. There was the firm belief that everyone was a potential success.

But since the war the United States and Americans have changed. Rural life is replaced by living in cities and suburbs. Individuals now typically are dominated by large bureaucracies, whether they be governments, schools, churches, or factories. In these settings Riesman noted that Americans have become "other directed." Rather than an "automatic pilot" homing the inner-directed person toward an individual goal, the other-directed person has an "antenna" tuned to the values and opinions of others. In short, he or she is a team player and conformist.

Baseball, then, represents what we were—an inner-directed, rural individualistic society. It continues to be popular because of our longing for the peaceful past. Football, on the other hand, is popular now because it symbolizes what we now are—an other-directed, urban-technical corporate-bureaucratic society. Thus these two sports represent cultural contrasts (country vs. city, stability vs. change, harmony vs. conflict, calm vs. intensity, and equality vs. inequality). Each sport contains a fundamental myth that it elaborates for its fans. Baseball represents an island of stability in a confused and confusing world. As such, it provides an antidote for a world of too much action, struggle, pressure, and change. Baseball provides this antidote by being individualistic, unbounded by time, nonviolent, leisurely in pace, and by perpetuating the American myths of equal opportunity, egalitarianism, and potential championship for everyone.

Football represents what we are. Our society is violent. It is highly technical. It is highly bureaucratized, and we are all caught in its impersonal clutches. Football fits contemporary urban-corporate society because it is team-oriented, dominated by the clock, aggressive, characterized by bursts of energy, highly technical, and because it disproportionately rewards individuals at certain positions.

The uniquely American sports of football and baseball, although they represent opposites, provide us with insight about ourselves and our society. What will become of these sports as society changes? Will we continue to find football and baseball so intriguing as society becomes more structured? We know that in the future American society will be short of resources. We know that its citizenry will be older and more educated than at present. We also know that society will become more urban. What will these and other trends mean for society and for sport? One thing is certain—as society changes so, too, will its sports. Does this mean that baseball and football will change? Will another sport emerge that is more attuned with the culture and structure of society? Or will baseball become even more popular as we become more nostalgic for the peaceful, pastoral past?

NOTES

1. D. Stanley Eitzen and George H. Sage, *Sociology of American Sport* (Dubuque, Iowa: Wm. C. Brown, 1978), pp. 68–69.
2. George B. Leonard, "Winning Isn't Everything: It's Nothing," *Intellectual Digest*, 4 (October, 1973), p. 45.
3. Several sources are especially important for the material that follows: Gerald J. Cavanaugh, "Baseball, Football, Images," *New York Times* (October 3, 1976), p. 2S; George Carlin, "Baseball-Football," *An Evening with Wally Londo* (Los Angeles: Little David Records, 1975); Leonard Koppett, "Differing Creeds in Baseball, Football," *Sporting News* (September 6, 1975), pp. 4 and 6; Murray Ross, "Football Red and Baseball Green," *Chicago Review* (January/February 1971), pp. 30–40; Richard Conway, "Baseball: A Discipline that Measures America's Way of Life," *Rocky Mountain News Trend* (October 19, 1975), p. 1; "Behind Baseball's Comeback: It's An Island of Stability," *U.S. News & World Report* (September 19, 1977), pp. 56–57; William Arens, "The Great American Football Ritual," *Natural History*, 84 (October, 1975), pp. 72–80; Susan P. Montague and Robert Morais, "Football Games and Rock Concerts: The Ritual Enactment of American Success Models," *The American Dimension: Cultural Myths and Realities*, William Arens (ed.), (Port Washington, New York: Alfred, 1976), pp. 33–52; and R. C. Crepeau, "Punt or Bunt: A Note in American Culture," *Journal of Sport History*, 3 (Winter 1976), pp. 205–212.
4. Cf., D. Stanley Eitzen, "Sport and Deviance," *Sport in Contemporary Society*, 1st ed. (New York: St. Martin's Press, 1979), pp. 73–87.
5. Crepeau, "Punt or Bunt," p. 211.
6. Quoted in Jack Scott, "The Souring of George Sauer," *Intellectual Digest*, 2 (December 1971), pp. 52–55.
7. Cavanaugh, "Baseball, Football, Images," p. 25S.
8. David Reisman, *The Lonely Crowd* (New Haven: Yale University Press, 1950). The analysis that follows is largely dependent on Crepeau, "Punt or Bunt," pp. 205–212.

6. *Sports as a Control for Aggression*

RICHARD GREY SIPES

From as early as our first recorded thoughts of man, we have been attempting to control what we call aggression. We haven't tried to eliminate it, but rather to have it manifest how, when and where we wish it and to have it absent in all other situations. Most of the time, on a day-to-day basis, we succeed, but we become quite concerned when our control fails and results in muggings, fist fights, child abuse, riots, police brutality or a war not to our benefit.

Can we significantly improve the precision of our control of aggression? I do not think so. My opinion is based on research results[1,2,3] indicating that, with massive effort, we could raise or lower the *general* aggressiveness of a society and its members, but that we cannot control manifestations of aggression much more precisely than we presently do.

Sport has been seen as an activity that can be used to at least influence the manifestation of aggression on the social and individual levels. It is true that sport is theoretically and practically more controllable by social institutions, up to and including the governmental level, than virtually any other widespread activity. How we would use our control of sports, though, depends on which of two opposing models of human behavior we use in our thinking.

TWO MODELS OF BEHAVIOR

According to what I have called the *Drive Discharge Model* of human behavior, there is a certain level of aggression in every individual and in every society. The aggression is like a liquid substance generated by an innate drive or by interaction with the environment. Although its level may vary somewhat from time to time, and from one society to another and one person to another, it generally is higher than desired, and must be discharged along acceptable paths. This is the model with which most psychiatric and psychological writers work, and it is the one most commonly used by the layman. According to this model, we can decrease unwanted manifestations of violence and other aggressive behavior by encouraging its manifestations in innocuous behavior. Sim-

SOURCE: Richard Grey Sipes, "Sports as a Control for Aggression," in *The Humanistic and Mental Health Aspects of Sports, Exercise and Recreation*, Timothy T. Craig (ed.) (Washington, D.C.: American Medical Association, 1976), pp. 46–49.

plistically, we can reduce the frequency of fistfights by increasing the frequency of attendance at boxing matches, and decrease the likelihood of war by increasing combative sports.

The alternative model, which I label the *Culture Pattern Model*, assumes something quite different about human behavior. It stresses the fact that we learn our individual patterns of behavior, and that our culture supplies us with these patterns. It sees individuals and entire societies as fundamentally consistent in most of their behavior patterns, with similar generalized modes manifesting themselves in divergent arenas of action. According to this model, we can decrease unwanted violence and other aggressive behavior by reducing the aggressive component of culture patterns wherever this component is found. Simplistically, we would reduce the frequency of fistfights if we eliminated the sport of boxing, and could reduce the likelihood of war by not engaging in combative sports.

The "treatments" indicated by these two models, then, are mutually exclusive—indeed opposite.

But both models, if we stop here, are only unsubstantiated speculations . . . informed opinions. They must survive rigid, controlled tests if they are to pass to the category of substantiated theories, and they must be in this category before we are justified in acting on them.

TESTING THE MODELS

Both models have been tested through hypotheses logically derived from them. The *Drive Discharge Model* predicts that as the incidence of one form of aggression goes up, the incidence of other forms will go down. We should find a lower incidence of combative sports in societies that are more warlike, and within any given society a lower incidence during periods of increased military activity. So with other forms of aggressive behavior. More warlike societies should have a lower need for—and consequently have a lesser occurrence of—such venting behavior as the practice of malevolent magic, harsh punishment of deviants or body mutilation. More peaceful societies, on the other hand, denied the release of aggression in the form of warfare, should show a higher occurrence of these aggressive outlets. More generally, we could predict that the more any one or more of these aggressive channels are used, the less the remainder are likely to be needed by the society.

The *Culture Pattern Model*, on the other hand, predicts that the above channels, including warfare, are likely to vary directly. That is, a society low in one is most likely going to be low in all and a society high in one probably will be high in all, since the same general orientation or cultural motif will govern these and many other behaviors of, and within, the society.

METHODOLOGY

I subjected these hypotheses to test, using the cross-cultural correlation method. This method has been accepted and employed by anthropologists, sociologists, psychiatrists and psychologists to test numerous hypotheses.[4] It has been brought to a high level of confidence and rigor in recent years.[5]

A cross-cultural correlation study utilizes a representative sample of societies from the universe of human societies. Within this sample it tests for Variable A relative to Variable B. If A and B tend systematically to occur or otherwise vary together (correlation studies are statistical—not mechanical—in orientation and admit of disconformity), it is assumed that there is some functional relationship, direct or indirect, between A and B. A biological parallel is the correlation between the presence (or absence) of certain parasitic protozoans in the bloodstream of humans and the periodic manifestation (or absence) of symptoms we term malaria. The correlation is not unity, but it is strong enough and statistically significant enough to suggest an important functional, perhaps causal, connection between the two phenomena.

THE TEST AND RESULTS

I randomly selected ten warlike and ten peaceful societies throughout the world and ethnographically coded them for the presence or absence of combative type sports.[1] A combative type sport was defined as one involving the acquisition of disputed territory, generally symbolized by the placing of an object in a guarded location (a hockey puck in the cage, a basketball through the ring, or a football at the opponent's end of the field), the subduing of an opponent (as in some—but not all—forms of wrestling), or patently combat situations (fencing, dodging thrown spears, karate). If a society had even one combative sport, it was coded as having combative sports. Of the ten warlike societies, nine had combative sports and one did not. Of the ten peaceful societies, only two had combative sports and eight lacked them. This indicates that warlikeness and combative sports tend to occur together. The *phi* value of this distribution is 0.7035. The Fisher Exact Test shows that the probability of getting this, or a rarer distribution of cases in the same direction, by chance alone is less than 0.0028, or about three in a thousand tries. The test supports the *Culture Pattern Model* and vitiates the *Drive Discharge Model*.

To verify my cross-cultural results, I conducted a temporal-variation study in the United States. The level of military activity was measured by the percent of the adult male population in the United States Armed Forces each year between 1920 and 1970. This spanned three periods of active combat. I used two relatively combative sports: hunting (a participation sport) and attendance at football games (spectator activity). I also used two relatively noncombative sports: race-track betting (participant) and attendance at baseball games (spectator). Yearly measures of activity in these sports were correlated with yearly level of military activity. Technical reasons led me to divide the data into two periods: pre-1946 and post-1946. Of the eight resulting correlation tests, six showed a non-significant—often insignificant—relationship between sports and military activity, or which five were direct. The only significant *inverse* relationship was between military activity and betting in the period following 1946. This was balanced by an equally significant *direct* relationship between military activity and betting in the pre-1946 period. This also is the least sport-like of the four sports used, according to common interpretations. Moreover, if graphed, it becomes evident that the eight-fold increase in betting between 1942 (in the midst of World War II) and 1970 probably was due to increasing affluence, and may have nothing to do with the fact that the percent of males in the military shrank from twenty-five to five in the same period. (During the actual World War II and Korean periods of conflict, there is a strong rise in betting, providing a direct correlation between betting and warfare for that specific time span.)

The *Drive Discharge Model* predicts a negative dischronic relationship between sports and war, whereas the *Cultural Pattern Model* predicts a positive *or no* dischronic relationship over this length of time. The case study test results, therefore, confirm the results of the synchronic cross-cultural study and tend to support the *Cultural Pattern Model* at the expense of the *Drive Discharge Model*.

AN ETHNOSCIENTIFIC STUDY OF SPORTS AND CONFLICT

Professor Kendall Blanchard has conducted a comparative ethnoscientific linguistic analysis and emic conflict-model study of "perceived conflict"—fights, wars, aggressive displays and sports—in the contemporary Choctaw Indian and "Anglo" societies. (This approach studies, in depth, the terms grammar, values and logic used by the members of a culture themselves, to arrive at the *meaning* of behavior in the cultural context.[6]) Through personal correspondence he informs me that his unpublished results[7] support my findings that sports, especially combative team sports, do not serve as functional alternatives to other forms of aggression, such as warfare. Sports and war would appear to be components of a broader cultural pattern.

MALEVOLENT MAGIC, MUTILATION, AND PUNISHMENT

I anticipated the objection that the choice and test of merely two alternative channels of aggression discharge might not give a valid or sufficiently complete picture of the situation. This prompted me to later test three other activities, using the same sample societies and the cross-cultural method.[3] I selected the practice of malevolent magic as a way in which an individual could secretively aggress upon a fellow community member. Cosmetic/status mutilation was chosen because it has been claimed to represent a turning-inward of aggression against one's self (although this claim certainly can be disputed). The punishment of deviants was used because it represents aggression of society against the individual.

Three indicator variables were used to measure malevolent magic: (1) how important such magic looms in the minds of most members of the society (importance), (2) roughly what proportion of misfortunes are attributed to it (scope), (3) the amount of harm it can produce (intensity).

Body mutilation was broken down into tattooing, scarification, piercing, shape molding and amputation. The *measure of mutilation* was the sum of measures of (1) how many different types of mutilation were practiced for cosmetic reasons, by what proportion of the population, and by either male or female or both; and (2) the occasions at which mutilation was used to mark changes in the social status or role (adulthood, marriage, widow(er)-hood) of the individual, male or female or both, and the proportional incidence of such mutilation.

Punishment of deviants was measured as the sum of coding values for the severity of usual punishment for (1) murder, (2) major theft, and (3) forbidden sexual intercourse.

Each of the above three theoretical (indirectly measured) variables, and their indicator (directly measured) variables, was tested against the warlikeness of the societies, and the results of the correlation tests are shown in Table 6-1. (Results of the earlier combative-sports test also are shown for comparison and completeness.) A nonwar summarized aggression value for each society also was computed from all four theoretical variable scores (sports, magic, mutilation and punishment) and tested against warlikeness, with the result of that test also shown. Note that all directly-measured indicator variables show a positive correlation with warlikeness. The more warlike societies are more likely to have higher "aggressiveness" in each of these variables. The results are somewhat more impressive when we look at the theoretical variables—the correlations tend to be more significant. The overall aggressive measure is singularly impressive, with the probability of finding that correlation by chance alone being about five in ten thousand.

These results emphatically support the *Culture Pattern Model* and invalidate the *Drive Discharge Model*. The functional relationship between various aggression-containing activities is one of mutual support, not one of alternative discharge paths.

DISCUSSION

Sports and war (and other "aggressive" forms of behavior) obviously do not, as often claimed, act as alternative channels for the discharge of accumulable aggressive tensions.

TABLE 6-1. Warlikeness Versus Other Traits

	Phi*	CumP**
Malevolent Magic	0.6710	0.0070
Importance	0.4725	0.1002
Scope	0.5164	0.0593
Intensity	0.7135	0.0038
Punishment	0.6250	0.0305
Murder	0.4910	0.0835
Theft	0.5006	0.1186
Sex	0.5774	0.0468
Body Mutilation	0.4000	0.0900
Cosmetic	0.2041	0.3257
Male	0.2182	0.3142
Female	0.2182	0.3142
Status	0.2000	0.3258
Male	0.1005	0.5000
Female	0.1155	0.5000
Sports	0.7035	0.0028
Combined	0.8000	0.0005

*Phi is a statistical measure of strength of association between two dichotomized variables. The higher the value, the stronger the association.
**CumP, computed with Fisher's Exact Probability Test, represents the probability of getting the observed distribution, or one more rare, in the direction predicted by chance alone. The lower the value, the more significant the association.

The *Cultural Pattern Model* seems better able to predict and explain human behavior. It says that each society and its culture (and perhaps each individual?) is characterized by one or more motifs or themes. The consistency typical of any culture leads us to expect to find similar attitudes, orientations and behaviors manifesting themselves in different activities. If indifference to suffering, zero-sum games, bravery, aggressiveness or other generalized characteristics are found strongly present in one activity, they most likely will be found throughout the culture rather than be limited to that one activity.

COMMENT

The hope would seem dim of using sports to influence warfare, or any of the other forms of undesirable aggressive behavior. Aggression by society, or by components thereof, or as manifested in the individuals who make up society, is an integral part of the total cultural configuration. To significantly attenuate one form of aggression would require us to simultaneously attenuate most or all forms; that is, to overhaul our entire culture.

Modification of behavior—individual or social—is difficult at best. If we wish to take on this task, though, my research would indicate that aggressive behavior is best reduced by eliminating combative or conflict-type sports. Attempting to siphon off aggressive tension by promulgating the observation of or participation in aggressive sports is more than a futile effort; to the degree that it had any effect at all, it most likely would raise the level of aggression in other social and individual behavior patterns.

REFERENCES

1. Sipes, R. G.: "War, sports and aggression: an empirical test of two rival theories. *American Anthropology* 75 (1): 64–86, 1973.
2. Sipes, R.G.: War, combative sports and aggression: a preliminary causal model of cultural patterning, in Nettleship M A (ed): *War: Its Causes and Correlates*. The Hague, Mouton Press, 1975.
3. Sipes, R. G., Robertson, B.A.: Malevolent magic, mutilation, punishment, and aggression. Read before the American Anthropological Association, San Francisco, 1975.
4. Naroll, R.: What have we learned from cross-cultural surveys? *Am Anthrop* 72: 1227–1288, 1970.
5. Sipes, R.G.: Rating hologeistic method. *Behav Sci Notes* 7: 157–198, 1972.
6. Tyler, S.A.: *Cognitive Anthropology*. New York, Holt, Rinehart, and Winston, 1969.
7. Blanchard, K.: Team sports and violence: an anthropological perspective. Read before the Association for the Anthropological Study of Play, Detroit, 1975.

■ FOR FURTHER STUDY

Angell, Roger. *The Summer Game*. New York: Viking, 1972.
Angell, Roger, *Five Seasons*, New York: Popular Library, 1978.
Axthelm, Peter. *The City Game*. New York: Harper's Magazine Press, 1970.
Blanchard, Kendall. "Basketball and the Culture-Change Process: The Rimrock Navajo Case," *Council on Anthropology Education Quarterly* 4 (November 1974): 8–13.
Blanchard, Kendall A. "Team Sports and Social Organization among the Mississippi Choctaw." *Tennessee Anthropologist* 1 (1975): 63–70.
Blount, Roy Jr. "Winning: Why We Keep Score." *New York Times Magazine* (September 29, 1985): Part II, pp. 24–27, 46.
Boyle, Robert H. *Sport: Mirror of American Life*, Boston: Little, Brown, 1963.
Brailsford, Dennis. *Sport and Society: Elizabeth to Anne*. Toronto: University of Toronto Press, 1969.
Chu, D. B., and J. O. Segrave. "Physical Culture in the People's Republic of China." *Journal of Sport Behavior* 2, no. 3 (1979): 119–135.

Cozens, Frederick, and Florence Stumpf. *Sports in American Life*. Chicago: University of Chicago Press, 1953.

Crawford, S. A. G. M. "New Zealand Rugby: Vigorous, Violent and Vicious." *Review of Sport & Leisure* 3, no. 1 (1978): 64–84.

Fox, J. R. "Pueblo Baseball: A New Use for Old Witchcraft." *Journal of American Folklore* (January 1961): 9–16.

Gruneau, R. S., and J. G. Albinson. *Canadian Sport: Sociological Perspectives*. Don Mills, Ontario: Addison-Wesley, 1976.

Guttmann, Allen. *From Ritual to Record: The Return of Modern Sports*. New York: Columbia University Press, 1978.

Haerle, Rudolf K., Jr. "Heroes, Success Themes, and Basic Cultural Values in Baseball Autobiographies: 1900–1970." Paper presented at the Third National Meeting of the Popular Culture Association, Indianapolis, 1973.

Hall, Donald. "Baseball Country: A Land of Change and Deja Vu." *New York Times* (October 24, 1976): 2S.

Hoch, Paul. *Rip Off the Big Game: The Exploitation of Sports by the Power Elite*. Garden City, N.Y.: Doubleday Anchor, 1972.

Jenkins, Dan. *Saturday's America*. Boston: Little, Brown, 1971.

Kahn, Roger. *The Boys of Summer*. New York: Harper & Row, 1972.

Kenyon, Gerald S. "Sport and Society: At Odds or in Concert." In *Athletics in America*, edited by Arnold Flath. Corvallis, Oregon: Oregon State University Press, pp. 34–41.

Koppett, Leonard. *The Essence of the Game is Deception*. Boston: Little, Brown, 1973.

Lahr, John. "The Theatre of Sports," *Evergreen Review* 13 (November 1969): 39–76.

Lever, Janet. "Soccer as a Brazilian Way of Life." In *Games, Sports, and Power*, edited by Gregory Stone. New Brunswick, N.J.: Transaction, 1972.

Lewis, George H. "Prole Sport: The Case of Roller Derby." In *Side-Saddle on the Golden Calf: Social Structure and Popular Culture in America*, edited by George H. Lewis. Pacific Palisades, Calif.: Goodyear, 1972, pp. 42–49.

Lipsky, Richard. *How We Play the Game*. Boston: Beacon, 1981.

Lipsyte, Robert. "Varsity Syndrome: The Unkindest Cut." *The Annals* 445 (September 1979): 15–23.

Luschen, Gunther. "The Interdependence of Sport and Culture." *International Review of Sport Sociology* 2 (1967): 27–41.

McIntosh, P. C. *Sport in Society*. London: C. A. Watts, 1963.

McIntyre, Thomas D. "Sport in the German Democratic Republic and the People's Republic of China." *Journal of Physical Education, Recreation, and Dance* 56 (January 1985): 108–111.

McLuhan, Marshall. *Understanding Media: The Extensions of Man*. New York: McGraw-Hill, 1964, pp. 234–245.

Mead, Margaret. "The Pattern of Leisure in Contemporary American Culture." *The Annals of the American Academy of Political and Social Science* (September 1957): 11–15.

Michener, James A. *Sports in America*. New York: Random House, 1976, pp. 420–443.

Morgan, Thomas B. "The American War Game." *Esquire* 64 (October 1965): 68–72, 141–148.

Morton, H. W. *Soviet Sport*. New York: Collier Books, 1963.

Natan, A. *Sport and Society*. London: Bowes and Bowes, 1958.

Nixon, Howard L. *Sport and Social Organization*. Indianapolis: Bobbs-Merrill, 1976, pp. 9–28.

Norflus, David. "Baseball: A Mirror of Japanese Society." *Arena Newsletter* 1 (October 1977): 9–12.

Parrish, Bernie. *They Call It a Game*. New York: Dial, 1971.

Ramsey, Frank, with Frank Deford. "Smart Moves by a Master of Deception." *Sports Illustrated* (December 9, 1963): 57–63.

Riesman, David, and Reuel Denney. "Football in America: A Study of Cultural Diffusion." *American Quarterly* 3 (Winter 1951): 109–319.

Riordan, J. *Sport in Soviet Society*. Cambridge: Cambridge University Press, 1977.

Roberts, J. M., M. J. Arth, and R. R. Bush. "Games in Culture." *American Anthropologist* 61 (August 1959): 597–605.

Roberts, J. M., and Brian Sutton-Smith. "Child Training and Game Involvement." *Ethnology* 1 (April 1962): 166–185.

Sadler, William A., Jr. "Competition Out of Bounds: Sport in American Life." *Quest* 19 (January 1973): 124–132.

Scotch, N. A. "Magic, Sorcery, and Football Among Urban Zulu: A Case of Reinterpretation Under Acculturation." *Journal of Conflict Resolution* (March 1961): 70–74.

Seppanen, Paavo. "The Role of Competitive Sports in Different Societies." Paper delivered at the Seventh World Congress of Sociology, Varna, Bulgaria, September 14–18, 1970.

Sewart, John J. "The Rationalization of Modern Sport: The Case of Professional Football." *Arena Review* 5 (September 1981): 45–53.

Stone, Gregory. "Some Meanings of American Sport." In *60th Proceedings of the College Physical Education Association*. Washington, D.C.: American Association for Health, Physical Education, and Recreation, 1957, pp. 6–29.

Tandy, Ruth E., and Joyce Laflin. "Aggression and Sport: Two Theories." *JOPER* 44 (June 1973): 19–20.

Voigt, David O. "Reflections on Diamonds: Baseball and American Culture." *Journal of Sport History* 1 (Spring 1974): 3–25.

Warshay, Leon H. "Baseball in Its Social Context." In *Social Approaches to Sport*, edited by Robert M. Pankin. London: Associated University Presses, 1982, pp. 225–282.

Wolfe, Tom. "Clean Fun at Riverhead." In *Side-Saddle on the Golden Calf: Social Structure and Popular Culture in America*, edited by George H. Lewis. Pacific Palisades, Calif.: Goodyear, 1972, pp. 37–42.

Zurcher, Louis A., and Arnold Meadow. "On Bullfights and Baseball: An Example of Interaction of Social Institutions." *International Journal of Comparative Sociology* (March 1967): pp. 99–117.

Part Three

Sport and Deviance

Sport and *deviance* would appear on the surface to be antithetical terms. After all, sport contests are bound by rules, school athletes must meet rigid grade and behavior standards in order to compete, and there is a constant monitoring of athletes' behavior because they are public figures and because there are officials and organizations whose primary function is to curb their illegal behaviors. Moreover, sport is assumed by many to promote those character traits deemed desirable by most in society: fair play, sportsmanship, obedience to authority, hard work, and goal orientation.

The selections in this part show, to the contrary, that deviance is not only prevalent in sport but that the structure of sport in American society actually promotes deviance. *Deviance* is defined here as behavior that (1) violates the rules of the game, (2) offends the universal values of sporting behavior and fair play, and (3) illegitimately brings harm to persons or property (violence). The first meaning is self-explanatory. The rules of a sport create deviance by negatively labeling and punishing rule breakers. A fight among players in a soccer game, for example, is easily defined as rule breaking, and the punishment for such conduct is easily dispensed. The other two meanings are normative ones and require further elaboration. These meanings include as deviance those behaviors that violate ideals that are presumed to have universal acceptance. It is assumed that those activities that give an athlete or team an unfair advantage in a sports event are generally abhorred throughout the world of sport. "Unfair" is meant to connote those means that enhance the chances of victory other than through skill, luck, strategy, and ability. In addition to unfairness, the deliberate harming of people and property is generally decried and defined as deviant behavior.

The first selection, by D. Stanley Eitzen, provides an overview of deviance in sport by examining the ethical dilemmas faced by athletes, coaches, administrators, team doctors, fans, and the media. The consequences of immorality in sport and the structural roots of these unethical behaviors are also addressed.

Next we focus on sports violence. As demonstrated by Richard Grey Sipes in Part Two, there is a strain toward consistency in the relationship of sports to society: violent societies have violent sports. There is ample evidence that American society is a violent society (e.g., the history of slavery; the forcible taking of land from native Americans; vigilante law in the west; a foreign policy based on Manifest Destiny; our contemporary violent crime rates, which tend to be about ten times greater than those found in Great Britain, France, Sweden, and Japan; our high rate of imprisonment; and the popularity of violent movies and television). Similarly, violent sports are popular in American society. Athletes often engage in violence outside the rules and spectators at sports events sometimes engage in collective violence. The next two selections describe and explain these phenomena.

Jeffrey H. Goldstein, a professor of psychology, has had a continuing research interest in sports violence. His selection summarizes much of what we know about player and spectator violence. He also raises a number of provocative questions about the relationship of violent sports to society, the effects on players and spectators by type of sport, and the role of competition in precipitating violence.

Jay J. Coakley's selection adds to Goldstein's by providing a systematic model of the multiple causes of violence among sports participants.

The final selection, by Sandy Padwe, focuses on a major problem in sport—drug use by athletes. As recreational drug use in society has increased, so, too, has its use by athletes. Because of the heightened visibility of athletes in society, we have seen the consequences of drug use on some athletes— erratic personal behavior, loss of athletic skill, violence, formal suspension from playing by a team or league, and even death. Athletes also take what might be called "vocational" drugs—that is, drugs taken to enhance sport performance such as steroids and amphetamines. Padwe, senior editor at *Sports Illustrated*, presents a penetrating analysis of drug use by athletes in American society.

7. *Ethical Dilemmas in Sport*

D. STANLEY EITZEN

There is a country tune sung by Kris Kristofferson in which he decries the lack of ethical standards common today. He says, in effect, that it's getting harder to know wrong from right and to separate the winners from the losers. Although the songwriter was referring to alienation in American society in general, the lyrics can be applied to sport. Why are so many big-time sports celebrities often in trouble with the law? Why is the outrageous behavior of coaches not only overlooked but generously rewarded? Why is big-time sport permitted to corrupt our universities? Why is gratuitous violence glorified in sport? Many believe that these problems exist because the world of sports has declined morally—moral values are confused with dollar values, and the win-at-any-price ethic controls the conduct in much of sport (Spander, 1985; Lamme, 1985).

Clearly, it is time for scholars of sport and sports-program administrators to reexamine what sport has become and what it should be, to determine the distorted values that now drive sport, and to consider appropriate alternatives. This essay addresses these issues by considering (1) the need to develop ethical principles to guide sport, (2) the ethical dilemmas that confront sport's various constituencies, (3) the ethical consequences of sport's prevailing and distorted code of ethics, and (4) the structural sources of unethical behavior in sport.

ETHICAL PRINCIPLES

My position is that the following ethical principles must be applied to assess the behavior of coaches, players, spectators, and others involved in sport. The principles represent not only the ideals for which we should strive but also our obligation to sport and its participants.

1. *Athletes must be considered ends and not means.* The outcome for the participants in sport is infinitely more important than the outcome of the contest, the money generated, or other extraneous considerations. Athletes must be treated by coaches and administrators with dignity and respect; they must not be exploited; and they must not be demeaned and

---

SOURCE: This essay was written for the third edition of *Sport in Contemporary Society*.

dehumanized. Further, athletes must respect their opponents and not condone or engage in tactics of intimidation or willful injury. Also, the equipment, procedures, and rules of sport must provide for the relative safety of the participants. As philosopher Paul Weiss has argued, "Sports should begin and be carried out with a concern for the rights of others" (1969: 180).

2. *Competition must be fair.* (a) The administration of leagues and the supervision of contests must be governed by rules impartially applied to all parties. (b) Sport, by definition, is a competition involving physical prowess. Thus, if athletic contests are to be true to the ideals of sport, they must be decided only by differences in physical skill, motivation, strategy, and luck. By doing so we would rule out such activities as cheating or drug use to enhance performance artificially that give an athlete or team an unfair advantage. Efforts made by gamblers and corrupt athletes to fix the outcome of athletic contests violate the spirit of sport.

3. *Participation, leadership, resources, and rewards must be based on achievement rather than on ascribed characteristics.* Sports activities must be characterized by equal access and equal opportunity. Thus, ability and motivation shall decide who participates rather than race, creed, gender, or social position.

4. *The activity must provide for the relative safety of the participants.* The rules of the sport and the required equipment must be designed to protect the athlete. The health and safety of athletes must be considered by coaches and administrators as more important than team performance. Coaches must avoid creating situations that lead to physical ailments such as dehydration and heat prostration. Further, athletes must not purposefully act to injure their opponents except in explicitly pugilistic sports, such as boxing, which themselves may be unethical.

Although these principles are difficult to rebut, there are a few counterarguments that should be mentioned. First, although big-time sport is something that many Americans are proud of, its value is diminished when we consider that winning is the primary objective of most coaches and fans. Sport is an activity that occurs in a society where only the fittest survive. The "win-at-any-cost" ethic means that the end justifies the means. As one football coach stated: "Until three years ago we obeyed every rule and where did it get us? We finished last in the conference. Since that time there isn't a rule we haven't broken. And where are we now? This year we're playing in the Orange Bowl" (quoted in Shea, 1978: 145). Many coaches emulate the legendary football coach Vince Lombardi who argued that hatred of opponents should be used to inspire athletes to a higher level of intensity and increased performance. In Lombardi's words, "To play this game you must have that fire in you, and nothing stokes fire like hate" (quoted in Kramer, 1971). However, such tactics create a disrespect for opponents and a greater likelihood of purposeful injury. Further, by practicing the doctrine of "winning is everything" we diminish or even negate the intrinsic rewards of sports participation (Simon, 1983).

Another counterargument questions the so-called "unethical" nature of sport practices that are so widespread. If everyone is doing it, how can it be wrong? For example, many big-time college sports programs commonly break rules when recruiting; most offensive linemen illegally hold their opponents; many major-league baseball teams have at least one pitcher who illegally applies a foreign substance to the baseball for an unfair advantage; and the majority of world-class weight lifters use illegal anabolic steroids to increase their bulk, strength, and muscle. Therefore, if the majority ignores the rules, are the rules negated? Are these activities truly unethical if "everyone is doing them," and does their common use make them justified? To the contrary, ethics applies to how people *should* behave and not to how they *do* behave (Shea, 1978: 148). If a widespread practice in sport provides an unfair advantage in athletic contests, then it is immoral no mattter how often it is practiced. Rules intended to provide equity for all participants and teams are unconditional (Shea, 1978: 149).

Still another counterargument is that universal principles cannot be successfully applied to sports participation because many of its situations and conditions cannot be ethically categorized. In essence, each ethical principle is a continuum with varying degrees of ethical purity. The question is where to draw the line dividing proper from improper conduct if the distinctions are unclear. For example, we can determine easily that Kermit Washington acted improperly when he gave Rudy Tomjanovich a powerful punch that ended his professional basketball career. But how can we evaluate legal acts of mayhem encouraged by coaches and fans as part of the game? For example, we know that when an athlete takes a bribe to affect the outcome of a contest the action is immoral and illegal. Bowyer has characterized such behavior as ". . . a violation of the cathedral" (1982: 301). But is it a "violation of the sports cathedral" when in basketball a slow home team wets the nets to tighten them and thus decelerate a visiting fast-breaking team by giving the defense artificially gained time to set up their defense? Defenders of such an act would call it "getting a competitive edge," but is the act ethical? The following section examines these questions and others.

ETHICAL DILEMMAS

Several common but questionable practices in sport need to be examined more closely in terms of their ethical meaning and consequences. Such practices include cheating and excessive violence, spectator behavior that violates the ethical principles in varying degrees, and the questionable behavior of coaches, athletes, administrators, sports medicine personnel, and the media. Although space does not permit an exhaustive coverage of all areas of ethical concern in sports, the following discussion highlights many ethical dimensions present in the sports world today.

Cheating and Excessive Violence

The *sine qua non* of sport is competition. The goal is to win. But to be ethical the quest to win must be done in a spirit of fairness. Fairness tends to prevail in certain sports such as tennis and golf, but in other sports the dominant mood is to achieve an unfair advantage over the opponent. Obtaining a competitive edge unfairly is viewed by many participants and others involved as "strategy" rather than cheating (Figler, 1981: 72; Avedon, 1971). In such instances cheating takes two forms—normative and deviant (Eitzen, 1981). *Normative cheating* refers to illegal acts that are, for the most part, accepted as part of the game—coaches encourage or overlook them and rule enforcers such as referees and league commissioners rarely discourage them, impose minimal penalties, or ignore them altogether. *Deviant cheating* refers to illegal acts that are not accepted and that are subject to stern punishment, such as drugging a race horse, accepting a bribe, and tampering with an opponent's equipment.

Our interest here is with normative cheating and how it violates the ethical principles of sport even though it is practiced and deemed acceptable by the majority. Following are some examples of normative cheating—commonly accepted practices for achieving an unfair advantage:

- Basketball players pretend to be fouled in order to receive an undeserved free throw and give the opponent an undeserved foul.
- Basketball players are often coached to bump the lower half of a shooter's body because referees are more likely to be watching the ball and the upper half of the shooter's body.
- Offensive linemen in football are typically coached to use special but illegal techniques to hold or trip the opponent without detection. The Oakland Raiders once were accused of greasing the jerseys of their defensive linemen so that blockers could not hold them so easily—"a clear case of one rulebreaker seizing an edge from another" (Axthelm, 1983).
- Coaches sometimes use loopholes in the rules to take unfair advantage of an opponent. For example, during a 1973 football game between the University of Alabama and the University of California, Alabama had the ball on the California 11 yard line. Alabama sent in their field goal kicker with a tee but a player did not leave the field. California countered by sending in its defensive team against the kick. As the huddle broke, the field goal kicker picked up his tee and dashed off the field, leaving the defense at a distinct disadvantage. Alabama scored on the play and the NCAA Rules Committee later declared such plays illegal because a team cannot simulate a substitution designed to confuse an opponent.

- In baseball it is common for the home team to "doctor" its field to suit its strengths and minimize the strengths of a particular opponent. For example, a fast team can be neutralized or slowed down by digging up or watering the basepaths or by placing sand in the takeoff areas (Ostrow, 1985).
- In baseball the pitcher's application of a foreign substance to the ball in order to disadvantage the hitter is a common but illegal occurrence.
- In baseball a practice called "corking the bat" often occurs in which a bat is hollowed out and the wood replaced with various substances that make it more powerful (Bowyer, 1982: 308–309).
- In ice hockey the blades of the sticks are sometimes curved beyond legal limits to make them more effective.

Many people are fascinated by acts of normative cheating such as these. As sportswriter Pete Axthelm has said, "The next best thing to the home team getting an edge is a game that is on the level. . . . Sports fans love the rules—and the chance that somebody will figure out a way to break them" (1983). There exists a fundamental irony of sport—rule-bounded activities where rule breaking is deemed acceptable. Obviously, a stronger application of ethical principles must be applied if sport is to be rid of this hypocrisy.

Also of ethical concern is normative violence in sport. Many popular sports such as hockey and football encourage player aggression—not only is the very nature of these sports to strike an opponent but they encourage excessive violence with little or no penalty. Hockey is well known for its minimal penalties and its tendency to condone crowd-pleasing violence. Hockey players' fights routinely result in cuts, concussions, and fractures. But why do these athletes participate in violence? Smith (1983) has argued that violence in hockey, as in war, is a socially rewarded behavior. The players believe that aggression (body checking, intimidation, and the like) is vital to winning, and their behavior is approved by fans, coaches, and peers. Young athletes idolize the professionals and attempt to emulate their aggressive behaviors at their level of play, thereby perpetuating violence in the sport.

Normative violence is also an integral part of football (Underwood, 1978; 1984). Players are expected by their peers, coaches, and fans to be "hitters." They are taught to lower their heads to deliver a blow to the opponent and gang tackle—to make the ball carrier "pay the price." By physically punishing their opponents the football team attempts to increase the opponent's likelihood of failure—by causing fumbles, a lack of concentration, exhaustion, or player replacement by less-talented substitutes. These win-at-any-cost tactics are almost universally held among coaches, players, and fans in the United States even though they result in a significantly higher injury rate. How unethical is such within-the-rule but excessive violence? According to John Underwood these practices should be neither tolerated nor condoned: "Brutality is its own fertilizer. From 'get away with what you can' it is a short hop to the deviations that poison sport. . . . But it is not just the acts that border on criminal that are intolerable, it is the permissive atmosphere they spring from. The 'lesser' evils that are given tacit approval as 'techniques' of the game, even within the rules." (1984: 85)

Spectator Behavior

Certain spectator behaviors during sports events can be excessive, such as rioting and throwing objects at players and officials. But do we need also to evaluate other common but unsportspersonlike practices of spectators? For example, the booing of officials or opponents; the cheering of an opponent's injury; and such cheers as "kill Bubba kill" or "blood, blood, blood . . . blood makes the grass grow." Spectators can distract opponents in various ways—by making unusual noises, shouting racial/ethnic slurs, chanting "air ball" when an opponent attempts a free throw, or parading signs that demean visiting athletes (such as those that plagued basketball superstar Patrick Ewing throughout his college career at Georgetown University—"Patrick Ewing Can't Read This Sign," or "Patrick Ewing Is the Missing Link").

The Behavior of Coaches

Coaches commonly engage in a number of ethically questionable acts in their quest for a successful team. Many coaches have been found guilty of offering illegal inducements to prospective athletes, providing illicit payments to athletes, and altering the transcripts of athletes to retain their eligibility. Coaches may deliberately attempt to intimidate officials by inciting a home crowd. They may encourage violence toward opponents, such as in the celebrated case in Iowa where the coach of a high school team playing a team called the "Golden Eagles" spray painted a chicken gold and encouraged his players to stomp it "to death" in the locker room before the contest.

In assessing the ethics of coaches, we might ask the following questions (adapted from Eitzen, 1984c: 199–200):

- Are coaches being ethical when they run practice sessions like a marine boot camp?
- Are coaches being ethical when they physically or verbally assault athletes?
- Are coaches being ethical when they treat adult players like children?
- Are coaches being ethical when they encourage athletes to use drugs to enhance their performances artificially?
- Are coaches being ethical when they encourage athletes to cheat?
- Are high school and college coaches being ethical in their lack of regard for the athletes' educational goals and achievements?

- Are coaches being ethical when they refuse to "blow the whistle" on their coaching peers whom they know to be violating the rules?

The Behavior of Athletic Directors and Other Administrators

The administrators of sport have the overall responsibility of ensuring that their athletic programs abide by the rules and that their coaches behave ethically. They must provide safe conditions for play, properly maintained equipment, and appropriate medical attention. However, are they showing adequate concern for players when, for example, they choose artificial turf over grass, knowing that the rate and severity of injury is higher with artificial turf? There are four other areas where athletic directors and administrators may be involved in questionable ethics:

- Are athletic directors being ethical when they "drag their feet" in providing equal facilities, equipment, and budgets for women's athletic programs?
- Are athletic directors being ethical when they schedule teams that are an obvious mismatch? That is, strong teams are often matched with weak teams to enhance the former team's record and to maintain a high ranking, while the weak teams are encouraged to schedule matches with the strong teams to make more money.
- Are administrators being ethical when they refuse to schedule legitimate opponents? For example, boxing champions often ignore their stiffest competition and fight much easier opponents. In college some powerful teams have refused to play other teams because they did not want to legitimate the latter's status.
- Are administrators being ethical when they make decisions regarding the hiring and firing of coaches strictly on their win-loss record? For the most part school administrators do not fire coaches guilty of shady transgressions *if they win*. As John Underwood has characterized it: "We've told them it doesn't matter how clean they keep their program. It doesn't matter what percentage of their athletes graduate or take a useful place in society. It doesn't even matter how well the coaches teach the sports. All that matters are the flashing scoreboard lights." (1981: 81)

The Behavior of Team Doctors and Trainers

There are essentially two ethical issues facing those involved in sports medicine, especially those in the employ of a school or professional team. Most fundamentally, team doctors and trainers often face a dilemma in terms of their ultimate allegiance; that is, is their responsibility to the employer or to the injured athlete (Eskenazi, 1987)? The employer wants athletes on the field, not in the training room. Thus, the ethical question arises—should pain-killing drugs be administered to an injured player so that he or she can return to action sooner than would be otherwise recommended for the long-term health of the athlete?

The other ethical issue for those in sports medicine is whether they should dispense performance-enhancing drugs to athletes. There may be pressures to do so from coaches and players because "everyone is doing it."

The Behavior of the Media

The media, which devote so much attention to sport, are partly to blame for the unethical behaviors found in sport for several reasons. The media often glorify violence; for example, by showing in slow motion bone-crushing hits accompanied by exclamations of glee and wonder; or by their use of such terms as "assassins" and "enforcers" in referring to violence among players. The media also use violence in the promotions of upcoming telecasts to in-crease the number of viewers. Although less common today than in the past, the media tend not to report the negative side of sport and athletes. For instance, reporter Joe Falls, in discussing the fall of former pitching great Denny McLain who was found guilty of loan sharking, extortion, bookmaking, and possession of cocaine, commented: "As guilty as he [McLain] is, I don't hold him entirely to blame for the way his life turned out. I also blame the people who allowed him to get away with his irresponsible acts. They allowed it because he was Denny McLain, the famous pitcher. Some of these people were in the media. They knew Denny was doing wrong, but they grabbed his coattails and thought they would go for a wild ride." (1985: 18) Sports media persons are faced with an ethical dilemma—that is, what information about athletes should be made public and what is best left alone? Rick Telander of *Sports Illustrated* has written perceptively of this ethical problem facing sports reporters:

> For writers the ethical course is tricky but not impossible. *Milwaukee Journal* sports editor Jim Cohen sums it up thus: "A reporter's job is simply to report accurately and fairly—accurately in the sense that what he writes must be true, and fairly in the sense that what he writes must be relevant and told in the proper perspective. If that's not good enough for the people he's writing about, that's too bad. If it offends the reader, that also is too bad."
>
> The key word here is "fairly." The days when sports writers were "housemen"—bought-off flunkies for the owners—are long gone. But even though independent, writers still must be aware of the effect of their work. They must remember that athletes are real people living in the real world with families, friends, and acquain-tances, and that what goes into print about the athlete affects all these people. A writer can call an athlete a bum or a crybaby or a coward, if he is sure it is warranted, and at times it is. But to be sure of that a writer always has to be thinking, always

examining his motives. He must not take cheap shots for laughs or deal meanness out of vengeance. (1984: 11)

Another area of ethical concern is the media's role in reinforcing negative stereotypes of racial minorities and women. For example, studies have shown that articles in magazines such as *Sports Illustrated* (Corrigan, cited Gerber et al., 1974), *Young Athlete* (Rintala and Birrell, 1984), and others (Hilliard, 1984; Bryant, 1980) underrepresent female athletes, focus their attention on women athletes' physical appearance, and often use sexist language.

Finally, it has been suggested by many that the media legitimate gambling in sports by reporting point spreads (Kaplan, 1983; Straw, 1983; D'Angelo, 1987) and by accepting advertising for betting-sheet touts (Frey and Rose, 1987). But is it unethical to do so? The question is debatable. Because readers seek information about sports and athletes, the media often argue that the First Amendment gives them the freedom to provide that information to the public. On the other hand, in states where gambling is illegal, the media is in effect encouraging an illict activity.

THE ETHICAL CONSEQUENCES OF UNETHICAL PRACTICES IN SPORT

A widely held assumption of parents, educators, and editorial writers is that sport helps youths to understand and accept the moral ideals of society. However, this is not always the case and oftentimes sport, as it is presently conducted in youth leagues, schools, and at the professional level, does not enhance positive character traits. As philosopher Charles Banham has noted, although many do benefit from the sports experience, for others sport "encourages selfishness, envy, conceit, hostility, and bad temper. Far from ventilating the mind, it stifles it. Good sportsmanship may be a product of sport, but so is bad sportsmanship" (Banham, 1965: 62).

The "win-at-any-cost" philosophy guides every level of sport in American society and often leads to cheating by coaches and athletes, to the dehumanization of athletes (Shaw, 1972; Feinstein, 1986), and to their alienation from themselves and their competitors. In view of this, it is not surprising that research has consistently revealed that athletes who participate in sport for long periods of time, who face higher levels of competition, and who are more central to their teams have more negative character traits (Eitzen, 1984b). For instance, Bredemeier (1983; 1984) and Bredemeier and Shields (1986) have shown that reasoning about moral issues in sport is significantly higher for nonathletes than for athletes and for female athletes than for male athletes.

However, we cannot infer with confidence that these studies prove the longer athletes are exposed to sport, the less morally sound they become, in that sport is not only a molding process but also a rigid selection process

(Ogilvie and Tutko, 1971). We can conclude, though, that unethical practices in sport do not lead to positive moral development of the participants. Gresham's law would seem to apply to sport—bad morality tends to defeat good morality; unfairness tends to encourage unfairness (Heinila, 1974: 13). Melvin Tumin's principle of least significant morality also makes this point: "In any social group, the moral behavior of the group as an average will tend to sink to that of the least moral participant, and the least moral participant will, in that sense, control the group unless he is otherwise restrained and/or expelled. . . . Bad money may not always drive out good money, though it almost always does. But 'bad' conduct surely drives out 'good' conduct with predictable vigor and speed." (1964: 127)

THE STRUCTURAL ROOTS OF UNETHICAL BEHAVIOR IN SPORT

How can we begin to understand why cheating, exploitation, and other forms of immoral behavior have become so commonplace in sport? Obviously, there are people who seek unethical options, but they alone cannot account for the present situation. Rather, the sociological approach to rule-breaking and other unethical acts locates them not in the original sin, in the genes, or in the psyches of evil persons, but in the structural conditions of society.

The ethical problems of American sport have their roots in the political economy of society. Critical theorists of the Marxist tradition argue that capitalistic society is dominated by two structural conditions—massification and commodification—that help to explain why people make unethical choices in all areas of social life including sport.

Massification refers to the transformed social relations in society that have been caused by a more specialized division of labor, large-scale commodity production and consumption, widespread use of technology to increase industrial and administrative efficiency, and an increasingly authoritarian state (Hargreaves, 1982: 6). In short, the massification of society is the consequence of the society's increased bureaucratization, rationalization, and routinization. The massification of sport is seen in its increasingly technocratic, specialized, controlled-by-the-elite, and impersonal nature. The apt descriptions of contemporary sport as work, big business, spectacle (Hughes and Coakley, 1984), and power politics suggest how sport mirrors the massification of the larger society.

Two related elements of massification that are manifested in sport increase the likelihood of unethical behavior by its participants. As the tasks in sport become more complex and specialized, the anonymity of the participants increases. This occurs even on a single team, as in football, for example, when the offensive and defensive units practice separately and meet independently with their specialized coaches. Social contact is minimized and the norms of reciprocity that are essential to community are evaded even among teammates (Young and Massey, 1980: 88).

Anonymity among sports participants is also enhanced by short-term and episodic interaction (Young, 1972). Interaction is segmentalized so that participants rarely encounter each other in different roles. As a result, coaches and players, opponents, and other sport participants experience only impersonal relationships, which, in a competitive setting such as in sports, foster a "me-first/goals-regardless-of-the-means" attitude among them. This, in turn, causes unethical acts such as cheating, manipulation, fraud, exploitation, and excessive violence to occur more freely.

Commodification refers to the social, psychological, and cultural uses of social structures for the commercial needs of monopolies (Young, 1984: 7). The commodification process views human beings as objects, or interchangeable parts, that can be manipulated. In the sports realm, team owners and administrators allow profit-maximizing decisions to take precedence over humane considerations. Sports enterprises seek to produce what they can sell, and spectacular sports events attract customers. As a result, sports performances become activities of dis-play. "When sport becomes an activity of *dis*-play, it destroys what is valuable in sport altogether. Sport becomes transformed into a spectacle, played for and shaped into a form which will be 'consumed' by spectators searching for titillating entertainment." (Sewart, 1981: 49)

Violence is encouraged by sport administrators because it attracts spectators. Further, sport's popularity in society makes it a particularly effective vehicle for advertising. Male and female athletes are often portrayed as sex objects to sell products. As Brohm has put it: "They [athletes] are very often advertising 'sandwich-board' men" (1978: 176). Today's top-level athletes, whether so-called amateurs or professionals, are viewed as workers who sell their labor—their ability to draw crowds—to employers. Thus, players and franchises are purchased, bought, and sold for profit. Athletes are treated like machines or instruments that are used to produce victories and income. They are manipulated to produce maximum performance:

Every sport now involves a fantastic *manipulation of human robots* by doctors, psychologists, bio-chemists and trainers. The "manufacturing of champions" is no longer a craft but an industry, calling on specialized laboratories, research institutes, training camps and experimental sport centers. Most top-level athletes are reduced to the status of more or less voluntary guinea pigs. "Hopefuls" are spotted young, the less talented are methodically weeded out and those that remain are then systematically oriented according to their potential. . . . The specialists in this sporting Gulag stop at no human sacrifice in their drive to push back the limits of human capacity and transcend biological barriers. (Brohm, 1978: 18–19)

In short, sport and its participants are like any other commodity—"something to be marketed, packaged, and sold. . . . The consequence of the process of commodification is that the multifarious forms of human activity lose their unique and distinct qualities to the principles of the market" (Sewart, 1981: 47–48).

Under the social conditions resulting from the massification and commodification of sport, coaches, athletes, and spectators are objects to be manipulated and exploited. Winning is the all-consuming goal, and participants are judged exclusively in terms of their ability to meet that goal. The unsuccessful are replaced like the defective parts of a machine. Under these circumstances, opponents *are* enemies. So, too, are teammates, in that they compete for starting positions. "In viewing himself as an object, the worker increasingly relates to other people as objects; he is alienated from the species whereby instead of celebrating his existence through meaningful interaction, he is isolated, asocial and ultimately, like the market within which he exists, amoral." (Sugden, 1981: 59) Under these conditions, where athletes are alienated from one another and exploited by the system, they view one another as means to their ends, reinforcing the "win-at-any-cost" ethic.

CONCLUSION

Sport has the potential to ennoble its participants and society. Athletes strain, strive, and sacrifice to excel. But if sport is to exalt the human spirit, it must be practiced within a context guided by fairness and humane considerations. Most important, the competitors must respect and honor each other—in effect, there should be a bond uniting them and their common sacrifices and shared goals. Those intimately involved in sport—athletes, coaches, administrators, and fans—have critical choices to make. When the goal of winning supersedes other goals, they and sport are diminished, and sport does not achieve its ennobling potential. It is time for those who care about sport to recognize the problems of contemporary sport and to strive for changes.

John Underwood, in writing about the excessive violence in sport, presents an insightful analysis of sport:

> True sportsmanship is not compatible with a win-at-all-cost philosophy. . . . I think it is clear enough that the time is ripe in American sport to realize that a stand for sportsmanship and fair play *without* intimidation or brutality will not tilt the axis on which this planet spins. Competitive sports, in the end, must go beyond sportsmanship. They must reach all the way to "fair play." The essential difference is that fair play involves taking a stand above the legalities of the game. A stand that places winning at a risk but at the same time preserves the dignity and value of sport. It is a moral issue, not a political one. It must be based on the inner conviction that to win by going outside the rules and the spirit of the rules is not really to win at all. (1984: 87)

If we fail to heed Underwood's admonition, then we, as in Kris Kristofferson's lament, will find it hard to "separate the winners from the losers" and "to know what's wrong from right."

REFERENCES

Avedon, E. "The Structural Elements of Games." In *The Study of Games*, edited by E. Evendon and B. Sutton-Smith. New York: John Wiley & Sons, 1971.

Axthelm, P. "Psst, Somebody May be Cheating." *Newsweek* (August 8, 1983): 74.

Banham, C. "Man at Play." *Contemporary Review* 207 (August 1965): 60–65.

Bowyer, J. B. *Cheating: Deception in War & Magic, Games & Sports, Sex & Religion, Politics & Espionage, Art & Science*. New York: St. Martin's, 1982.

Bredemeier, B. J. "Athletic Aggression: A Moral Concern." In *Sports Violence*, edited by J. Goldstein. New York: Springer-Verlag, 1983.

Bredemeier, B. J. "Sport, Gender, and Moral Growth." In *Psychological Foundations of Sport*, edited by J. M. Silva, III, and R. S. Weinberg. Champaign, Ill.: Human Kinetics Publishers, 1984.

Bredemeier, B. J., and David L. Shields. "Athletic Agression: An Issue of Contextual Morality." *Sociology of Sport Journal* 3 (March 1986): 15–28.

Brohm, J. M. *Sport: A Prison of Measured Time*. London: Ink Links, 1978.

Bryant, J. "A Two Year Selective Investigation of the Female in Sport as Reported in the Paper Media." *Arena Review* 4 (May 1980).

D'Angelo, Raymond. "Sports Gambling and the Media." *Arena Review* 11 (May 1987): 1–4.

Eitzen, D. S. "Sport and Deviance." In *Handbook of Social Science of Sport*, edited by G. R. F. Luschen, and G. H. Sage. Champaign, Ill.: Stipes, 1981.

Eitzen, D. S. "Teaching Social Problems: Implications of the Objectivist-Subjectivist Debate." *Society for the Study of Social Problems Newsletter* 16 (Fall 1984a): 10–12.

Eitzen, D. S. "The Dark Side of Coaching and the Building of Character." In *Sport in Contemporary Society*, 2d ed., edited by D. S. Eitzen. New York: St. Martin's, 1984b, pp. 189–192.

Eitzen, D. S. "School Sports and Educational Goals." In *Sport in Contemporary Society*, 2d ed., edited by D. S. Eitzen. New York: St. Martin's, 1984c, pp. 199–202.

Eskenazi, G. "Team Doctors: Operating in a Quandry." *The New York Times* (April 15, 1987): 44.

Falls, J. "Indulgence's Child: McLain's Faults were Worsened by Excuse." *The Sporting News* (March 18, 1985): 18.

Feinstein, John. *A Season on the Brink: A Year with Bob Knight and the Indiana Hoosiers*. New York: Macmillan, 1986.

Figler, S. K. *Sport and Play in American Life*. Philadelphia: Saunders, 1981.

"The Fraud Merchants" [editorial]. *The Sporting News* (March 18, 1983): 8.

Frey, James H., and I. Nelson Rose. "The Role of Sports Information Services in the World of Sports Betting." *Arena Review* 11 (May 1987): 44–51.

Gerber, E. R., J. Felshin, P. Berlin, and W. Wyrick. *The American Woman in Sport*. Reading, Mass.: Addison-Wesley, 1974.

Gilligan, C. *In a Different Voice*. Cambridge, Mass.: Harvard University Press, 1982.

Hargreaves, J. "Theorizing Sport." In *Sport, Culture and Ideology*, edited by J. Hargreaves. London: Routledge and Kegan Paul, 1982, pp. 1–29.

Heinila, K. *Ethics in Sport*. Jyvaskyla, Finland: University of Jyvaskyla, Department of Sociology, 1974.

Hilliard, D. C. Media Images of Male and Female Professional Athletes: An Interpretative Analysis of Magazine Articles. *Sociology of Sport Journal* 1 (no. 3, 1984): 251–262.

Hughes, R., and J. Coakley. "Mass Society and the Commercialization of Sport." *Sociology of Sport Journal* 1 (no. 1, 1984): 57–63.

Kaplan, H. R. "Sports, Gambling and Television: The Emerging Alliance." *Arena Review* 7 (February 1983): 1–11.

Kramer, J., ed. *Lombardi: Winning is the Only Thing*. New York: Pocket Books, 1971.

Lamme, A. J. III. "How Big-Time Athletics Corrupt Universities." *The Christian Science Monitor* (February 25, 1985): 12.

Luschen, G. R. F. "Cheating in Sport." In *Social Problems in Athletics: Essays in the Sociology of Sport*, edited by D. M. Landers. Urbana, Ill.: University of Illinois Press, 1976, pp. 67–77.

Ogilvie, B., and T. Tutko. "Sport: If You Want to Build Character, Try Something Else." *Psychology Today* 5 (October 1971): 61–63.

Ostrow, R. "Tailoring the Ballparks to Fit Needs." *USA Today* (March 21, 1985): C1.

Ramsey, F., and F. Deford. "Smart Moves by a Master of Deception." *Sports Illustrated* (December 9, 1963): 57–63.

Rintala, J., and S. Birrell. "Fair Treatment for the Active Female: A Content Analysis of *Young Athlete* Magazine." *Sociology of Sport Journal* 1 (no. 3, 1984): 231–250.

Sewart, J. J. "The Rationalization of Modern Sport: The Case of Professional Football." *Arena Review* 5 (September 1981): 45–53.

Shaw, G. *Meat on the Hoof: The Hidden World of Texas Football*. New York: St. Martin's, 1972.

Shea, E. J. *Ethical Decisions in Physical Education and Sport*. Springfield, Ill.: Charles C. Thomas, 1978.

Simon, I. "A Humanistic Approach to Sports." *The Humanist* 43 (July/August 1983): 25–26, 32.

Smith, M. D. *Violence and Sport*. Toronto: Butterworth, 1983.

Spander, A. "Blame Civilization for Win-at-All-Costs Code." *The Sporting News* (March 18, 1985): 11.

Straw, P. "Pointspreads and Journalistic Ethics." *Arena Review* 7 (February 1983): 43–45.

Sugden, J. P. "The Sociological Perspective: The Political Economy of Violence in American Sport." *Arena Review* 5 (February 1981): 57–62.

Telander, R. "The Written Word: Player-Press Relationships in American Sports." *Sociology of Sport Journal* 1 (no. 1, 1984): 3–14.

Tumin, M. "Business as a Social System." *Behavioral Science* 9 (no. 2, April 1964): 120–130.

Underwood, J. "An Unfolding Tragedy." *Sports Illustrated* (August 14, 1978): 69–82; (August 21, 1978): 32–56; and (August 28, 1978): 30–41.

Underwood, J. "A Game Plan for America." *Sports Illustrated* (February 23, 1984): 66–80.

Underwood, J. *Spoiled Sport*. Boston: Little, Brown, 1984.

Weiss, P. *Sport: A Philosophic Inquiry*. Carbondale, Ill.: Southern Illinois University Press, 1969.

Young, T. R. *New Sources of Self*. London: Pergamon Press, 1972.

Young, T. R. "The Sociology of Sport: A Critical Overview." *Arena Review* 8 (November 1984): 1–14.

Young, T. R., and G. Massey. "The Dramaturgical Society: A Macro-Analytic Approach to Dramaturgical Analysis." *Qualitative Sociology* 1 (no. 2, 1980): 78–98.

8. *Sports Violence*

JEFFREY H. GOLDSTEIN

Violence surrounds and permeates modern sports to such a degree that it is not unreasonable to suggest that there is a necessary connection between them. Anthropologists have often invoked a Freudian or neo-Freudian theory to explain this relationship. Such a view suggests that engagement in symbolic violence, such as combative sports, is a means of containing human aggression. Aggressive energy building up in the Id requires expression in reality or in fantasy. So, at any rate, said Freud. Violent sports provide just such a vicarious outlet for this energy. Therefore, violent sports—whether engaged in as athlete or witnessed as fan—will syphon off some of this energy, thereby reducing the likelihood of aggressing. In this perspective, violent sports are seen as healthy, indirect channels for the expression and control of aggression.

Interestingly, it was often these same anthropologists who suggested that many sports and games developed precisely for the purpose of training young males in the skills that would later become necessary in warfare. From this perspective, sports are seen as a microcosm, if not of a whole society, then at least of one of its institutions, war.

As research conducted over the last decade or so has shown, the latter position is considerably closer to the present reality than the former. But even here, combative sports serve to teach and stimulate violence not because they are miniature battles waged on the playing field, but because they reflect the values and attitudes of the culture of which they form a part. This conclusion is based on research with athletes and fans conducted by psychologists, sociologists, and anthropologists.

RESEARCH WITH ATHLETES

The prevailing view of athletics is that they are constructive and healthy expressions of energy, including aggressive energy, and that they somehow prepare the athlete for extra-athletic endeavors. They are said to build character, respect for authority, discipline, and perseverance. This is a view fostered by coaches, the sponsors of professional and amateur teams and events, and athletes themselves. It is, in all these instances, self-serving and, for the most part, untrue.

SOURCE: Jeffrey H. Goldstein, "Sports Violence," *National Forum* 62 (Winter 1982), pp. 9–11.

Research with high school and college athletes finds that they are more quick to anger than nonathletes and that those who participate in combative sports, such as hockey and football, respond to frustration with a greater degree of aggression when compared to athletes in noncontact sports and nonathletes. During the course of a single football, hockey, or soccer game, penalties and illegal player violence tend to increase.

Are these effects short-lived? While there is little longitudinal research on the off-season emotionality and behavior of athletes, what little there is suggests that athletes become more, not less, aggressive and hostile as the playing season progresses, and that during the off-season, they are more hostile than noncombative athletes and than nonathletes.[1] Some indirect evidence of the emotional effects of participating in contact sports comes from the fact that football players are twice as likely to suffer from hypertension as the general public and four times as likely to have high blood pressure as track athletes.[2] In short, engaging in aggressive sports does not appear to have any beneficial effects on the expression or control of aggression. It is not a way of "letting off steam," but rather, to use the same crude analogy, a way of allowing steam to build up. If an athlete is engaged in a violent sport, one requiring body-contact with an opponent, he is in a sense practicing aggression, albeit under the rather flexible limits set by rules, officials, and custom. This rehearsal, however, makes it more likely that anger will not dissipate, that instead it will increase, and that the rehearsal will lead to real-life reenactment of aggression some time in the future.

SPORTS FANS

Violence among sports fans during and shortly after a combative game, such as soccer, boxing, and football, is seen as a major social problem in many countries, particularly Great Britain, Brazil, Argentina, and Canada. In recent years, riot police have been called to quell disturbances among fans at the Super Bowl, a college All-Star football game, New York Jets games, and following the Pittsburgh World Series win in 1971, when 100,000 boisterous fans set fires, turned over cars, destroyed public property, and committed more than a dozen rapes. Officials at football and soccer games have been pelted with rocks, bottles, metal darts, and in at least two instances in Latin America, killed by indignant fans.

Do such sports tend to attract the violence-prone spectator, or do they somehow create a propensity toward violence in otherwise nonaggressive spectators? In a study conducted at the 1969 Army-Navy football game, it was found that male spectators were significantly more hostile following the game than prior to it. This was true even for spectators who wanted Army, the winning team, to win, as well as for those who didn't care one way or the other who won the game. No such increase in hostility was found for male spectators at a nonaggressive sport, a college gym meet. In other words, it is not competition per se that leads to an increase in hostility, but apparently the aggressive nature of that competition. Likewise, in an extension and replication of the Army-Navy game study, Arms, Russell, and Sandilands of Canada studied spectators at a professional wrestling match, hockey game, and college swimming meet. At both the wrestling match and the hockey game, aggressiveness increased, while there was no evidence of any increase in aggressiveness at the swim meet.

The evidence is clear that sports fans become increasingly hostile and violent during the course of a single aggressive game. Furthermore, the more aggressive the play on the field, the more aggressive the spectators in the stands become. In an article prepared for the *International Review of Sport Sociology,* M. D. Smith has reported that nearly three-fourths of the incidents of fan violence are preceded by player aggression. It appears that the mere act of witnessing violence is sufficient to increase the tendency toward violence among observers.[3]

The attitudes that spectators bring with them to the arena play an important role in determining the effects of aggressive sports. When fans believe that the athletes intend to injure one another, that hatred exists between them, or when they believe that aggression on the field is intentional, they are more likely to enjoy viewing the game, but also more apt to become hostile or violent themselves. In fact, in an experiment by Berkowitz and Alioto, of the University of Wisconsin, the same aggressive football and boxing scenes were preceded by either a neutral introduction or by one stressing the hatred between the opponents. In the latter case, the students were significantly more aggressive toward someone who later angered them. The effects of witnessing aggressive sports, then, depend to a considerable extent on our interpretation of player aggression.[4]

It is clear from all the evidence at hand, which includes, in addition to scattered studies in the social science literature, lengthy government reports on hockey violence in Canada and soccer hooliganism in Great Britain, that nothing remotely akin to the Freudian notion of aggression catharsis occurs at athletic contests among the vast majority of players or fans in the western world. (Whether such catharsis occurs among viewers of violent films or television programs is somewhat more controversial, but here, too, there is little evidence of any widespread purgation of hostility.)

One explanation for the effects of witnessing violence on observers that has gained favor among psychologists is based on the social learning theory of Albert Bandura of Stanford University. According to this theory, people learn what they observe, and if what they observe goes unpunished, they are likely to repeat it when they find themselves in similar circumstances. Thus, sports fans learn specific aggressive actions by observing aggressive athletes on the playing field engage in unpunished violence. When they later find themselves in similar situations, such as in a competitive event, they are apt to imitate some of those aggressive behaviors.

At what level of abstraction do observers learn what they see? Might they not learn some fairly abstract rules, rather than merely the concrete behaviors of aggressive athletes? Can't they learn that violating rules is often officially condoned? Or that intimidation is a successful strategy in competition? Certainly, when people discuss sports as a microcosm of social life, they are referring to characteristics of sports on just such a level of abstraction.

SPORT AS METAPHOR

Metaphors are often useful devices for leading us to ask questions otherwise overlooked. For example, likening the brain to a computer leads psychologists to avenues of research concerned with information storage and retrieval that hitherto had been ignored. The metaphorical theorist must recognize, however, that the brain is *not* a computer. A metaphor in science is only as good as it is useful, not as a post hoc explanation or justification of events, but as a heuristic device.

When sports are used as a metaphor for society, only selected sports are employed. Football, soccer, boxing, and other contact sports are seen as possessing the necessary points of contact with society to permit the metaphor to stand. Tennis and racquet sports, weight lifting, gymnastics, and track and field are rarely employed as metaphors for society. In other words, sports are *selectively* chosen as analogues of society, implying that there already exist some fairly fixed notions of the nature of society and of sport. We read that high school football is an important part of the school curriculum because it prepares the athlete for "real life," whose goal, we are told, is winning. We read that society involves a contest of survival, that life itself is a competitive contest. We are less apt to read that more than a quarter million youngsters are treated annually in hospital emergency rooms for football injuries. We are also less likely to read that thousands of youngsters are encouraged to repeat a grade in school so that, when they are old enough to play high school football, they will be bigger and more experienced than their teammates. What we are exposed to is the familiar litany of social Darwinism:

I will demand a commitment to excellence and to victory; that is what life is all about.

—Vince Lombardi

Every time you win, you're reborn; when you lose, you die a little.

—George Allen

In this country, when you finish second, no one knows your name.

—Frank McGuire

Winning isn't everything; it's the only thing.

—Vince Lombardi

The metaphor of sport-as-social-microcosm breaks down when it is realized that the primary function of a sport is not victory, though that is one of its essential features. It is incumbent on a player or team to play as well as possible. It is not unlike an implicit rule; without competition, there is no contest. But without cooperation, there is no contest either. Games require a remarkable degree of cooperation among members of a team and between opponents, who must share the same definition of the situation, adopt the same set of rules, and defer to the same impartial officials. Cooperation is the *yin* to competition's *yang*. Sports and games would best be seen, not as metaphors of society, but as integral parts of a society.

Of course, certain societies are more likely to emphasize competitive games and sports than others, depending on their economic structure and on their child rearing strategies. Most of the sports and games that are widespread in Western cultures are games of physical skill, which have been shown by John Roberts and Brian Sutton-Smith to be related to the culture's emphasis on achievement. Rather than serving particular, unique functions in a society, such as providing an indirect outlet for aggression, sports and games may more properly be seen as reflecting the values of the culture. Therefore, it is not surprising in view of the evidence reviewed here that Sipes has reported that those cultures where combative sports are stressed are also those that engage most often in warfare.[5] Of course, the positive relationship between aggressive sports and warfare is not evidence of any causal connection between these events. It is possible, even probable, that both the emphasis on combative sports and the frequency of warfare are themselves both reflections of other, more basic factors.

SPECULATIONS AND SOLUTIONS

What of the many athletes and fans—involved in both contact and noncontact sports—who argue that if it were not for their sport they would probably be more aggressive? Can't athletics be used as an aggression-management technique? One can easily imagine an athlete who feels the need to control his anger, to express it only during appropriate moments in play and in accordance with the rules of the game and the spirit of good sportsmanship. Sports probably *can* be used as vehicles of self-control and self-regulation, but they rarely are.

I believe that nonaggressive sports can serve as anger- (and other forms of emotion-) regulating devices, providing the following conditions are met: (a) an athlete experiences anger prior to play; (b) the game itself is physically and mentally engrossing; and (c) the game does not require physical aggression, such as tackling or blocking, against one's opponent. However, these same conditions may be met in a variety of nonathletic settings. Because humans are the supremely symbolic creatures they are, a remarkable ability exists to transform an emotion, such as a mild personal insult, into a great wrong by rewriting history or reinterpreting the past. For example, a husband who feels slighted by his wife is fully able to reinterpret events of the past, which had hitherto not been interpreted as rejections, as subtle but intentional attempts to undermine his feelings of worth. A slight anger may thus transform into a great one, and it is this greater anger that is apt to be acted upon. If a person is sufficiently distracted from the task of revising history, the slight anger remains minor and, in fact, will dissipate with the passage of time. Sports that require complete attention and concentration may easily serve this distracting function, thereby preventing a negative emotion from becoming more intense, and may even be associated with the reduction of that emotion. This is true not only of sports, but of nearly any physical activity requiring skill and concentration, from chess to pinball machines.

Given the spirit into which most modern-day western sports are entered and witnessed, a series of changes may alleviate the undesirable effects of player and fan violence. Rules prohibiting unnecessary brutality must be written and enforced. It must be made known to players, trainers, managers, owners, and fans that unnecessary violence will not be tolerated, is not desirable, and detracts from the game. Sportscasters and reporters themselves must relearn their conceptions of sports so that they may come to appreciate the role of cooperation, aesthetics, and the various prosocial and positive aspects of noncompetitive athletics.

None of this is to imply that sports, even body-contact sports, *must* have a particular effect on the players' or fans' level of aggression. I do not believe that is so. It is probable that contact sports increase players' and spectators' aggressiveness because of the spirit in which the games are played, viewed, and promoted. If athletes, sportscasters, and fans regained interest in the nonbrutal aspects of competitive sports, if the function of victory in sports were placed in its proper perspective, if sports violence were routinely condemned, then sports would have little or no stimulating effect on subsequent aggression. It is not competition per se that increases aggression, among either players or fans, but the nature and spirit of that competition.

NOTES

1. A. Patterson, Hostility catharsis. *Personality and Social Psychology Bulletin*, 1974, *1*, 195–197. D. Zillmann, R. C. Johnson, & K. D. Day. Provoked and unprovoked aggressiveness in athletes. *Journal of Research in Personality*, 1974, 8, 139–152.

2. R. C. Yeager. *Seasons of shame*. N. Y.: McGraw-Hill, 1979.
3. J. H. Goldstein & R. L. Arms. Effects of observing athletic contests on hostility. *Sociometry*, 1971, *34*, 83–90. R. L. Arms, G. W. Russell, & M. L. Sandilands. Effects on the hostility of spectators of viewing aggressive sports. *Social Psychology Quarterly*, 1979, *42*, 275–279. M. D. Smith. Significant others' influence on the assaultive behaviour of young hockey players. *International Review of Sport Sociology*, 1974, *3/4*, 45–56.
4. L. Berkowitz & J. T. Alioto. The meaning of an observed event as a determinant of its aggressive consequences. *Journal of Personality and Social Psychology*, 1973, *28*, 206–217. D. Zillmann, J. Bryant, & B. S. Sapolsky. The enjoyment of watching sport contest. In J. H. Goldstein (ed.), *Sports, games, and play*. N. Y.: Wiley, 1979.
5. J. M. Roberts & B. Sutton-Smith. Child training and game involvement. *Ethnology*, 1962, *1*, 166–185. R. G. Sipes. War, sports and aggression: An empirical test of two rival theories. *American Anthropologist*, 1973, *75*, 64–86.

9. *The Sociological Perspective: Alternate Causations of Violence in Sport*

JAY J. COAKLEY

INTRODUCTION

Over the past decade, the issue of violence in sport has attracted considerable attention. Journalists have described it (Kennedy, 1975; Lipsyte, 1975; Surface, 1977; Underwood, 1978a,b,c; Yeager, 1979); social scientists have tried to explain it (Smith, 1971, 1974, 1975a,b, 1978, 1979a,b; Berkowitz, 1972; Vaz, 1972, 1974, 1977, 1979; Zillman, and others, 1974; Martens, 1975; Fisher, 1976; Crawford, 1978; Hughes & Coakley, 1978; Gaskell & Pearton, 1979; Pilz, 1979; Poupart, 1979) and athletes have bragged, testified and complained about it (Shaw, 1972; Tatum, 1979).

While violence is not new to sport, much of our recent concern is due to the fact that it has never before affected the safety and well-being of so many athletes and been witnessed by so many spectators. Our concern is also an outgrowth of our increased awareness of the senselessness of violence and the serious consequences it has in the realm of sport. Injury rates in football have reached epidemic proportions; at the professional level, there are as many serious injuries sustained during the season as there are players in the NFL.[1] The assaultive behavior of hockey players has led to criminal charges as well as a long list of serious injuries. Fights and the use of intimidation have directly affected the health and the careers of athletes in other sports such as baseball, basketball and soccer. The consequences of violence have not only been felt on the professional level. Athletes in youth leagues and interscholastic sport programs have also fallen victims to the escalation of violent body contact and the use of aggressive behavior to intimidate opponents.[2]

There is no single cause of violence in sport. Among other things, violence may be influenced by the personality structures of athletes; it may sometimes be the result of frustration or a thoughtless response to other aversive stimuli; or it may simply reflect the cultural norms characteristic in a particular society or population group. In this paper, the goal will be to develop a sociological explanation of violence in sport. Attention will focus on the social processes through which violence has become a part of sport and on the relationship between violence and the socio-structural context in which sport exists.

SOURCE: Jay J. Coakley, "The Sociological Perspective: Alternate Causations of Violence in Sport," *Arena Review* 5 (February 1981), pp. 44–56.

I. VIOLENCE AND THE COMMERCIALIZATION OF SPORT

A number of years ago, Gregory Stone (1955) made the case that sport is comprised of both the elements of "play" and "dis-play." The element of play refers to the participants' personal concern with the dynamics of the activity; the element of dis-play refers to action which symbolically represents the dynamics of the activity for the purpose of making it more amusing to spectators. When sport becomes commercialized, the element of dis-play becomes increasingly important so that spectator interests can be maintained at the levels necessary to profitably stage events.

This does not mean that player skills and finesse cease to be important when sport becomes a form of entertainment. But these dimensions of action in sport become overshadowed by what Furst (1971) has described as heroic values and behavior. When this occurs, athletes tend to emphasize actions displaying courage, daring and endurance. In a society in which violence is either positively valued or mystically imbued, the attributes of courage, daring and endurance may be translated into confrontation, intimidation and aggression.

Spectators may appreciate skillful action but unless they are extremely knowledgeable about the sport being watched, they are likely to key in on heroic displays, including violence. This point was made by Christopher Lasch in his analysis of "The Corruption of Sports": "As spectators become less knowledgeable about the games they watch, they become more sensation-minded and bloodthirsty . . . what corrupts an athletic performance (is) the presence of an unappreciative, ignorant audience and the need to divert it with sensations extrinsic to the performance" (1977:25).

In spite of the fact that violent action jeopardizes the health and safety of athletes and threatens to bring their sport careers to an abrupt, sudden end, they often emphasize heroic values, even in their personal approaches to sport. This is clearly illustrated by Jerry Kramer's description of his pre-game feelings about the opponents he used to face as an offensive lineman on the Green Bay Packers: "I've started day-dreaming about Merlin Olsen. I see myself breaking his leg or knocking him unconscious and then I see myself knocking out a couple of other guys, and then I see us scoring a touchdown and always . . . I see myself the hero" (1968).

The point being made in this section is not simply that violence sells tickets. Violence, *by itself*, may shock and mesmerize people, but it will not fill a football stadium or a hockey arena week after week. In order for violence to take on commercial value, it must be linked to heroic action. People may talk about how they saw Woody Hayes punch an opposing player after a play during the 1978 Gator Bowl. But what they paid to see was young men heroically confronting one another, putting their physical well-being on the line for the sake of achieving a legitimate and valued goal: victory. It is in the quest for victory that violence becomes glorified in the minds of spectators and players.

The marketability of violence is also tied to the fact that it increases the "stakes" associated with the action in sport and it can serve as a confirmation of the commitment and motivation of players. A known "rivalry" between opponents generates interest because it guarantees that the participants are taking the match-up seriously and that they are committed to achieving the goal of victory even if it entails the endurance or infliction of pain and injury. The rhetoric of hate, grudge games and revenge matches by promoters and TV commentators sells events not because of the violence it infers, but because it leads spectators to believe that players are so intent on winning that they will not restrain themselves from doing whatever is needed to achieve their goal.

Instrumental Aggression

Commercialization not only changes the general meaning of sport and the sport experience, but it focuses attention on scores and outcomes. The quest for victory is essential for sport's commercial success. However, unless victories are regularly achieved by a spectator's favorite team, there may be doubts about the commitment of the players. Wins automatically infer motivation and commitment; losses raise doubts about the seriousness of player involvement.

In sports in which intimidation and violence can be affectively used to gain a competitive advantage over opponents and win games and matches, commercialization increases the likelihood that such tactics will be incorporated into the action. One of the things that documents the extent to which this has occurred in many sports is the institutionalization of what some people have called the "enforcer role" on a sport team. An "enforcer" is a member of a team who is formally or informally expected to use aggressive tactics to intimidate, provoke and sometimes, even injure the players from the opposing teams—especially the best players. Dave Schultz, one of the more effective enforcers in professional hockey during the 1970s, explains the simple logic underlying his enforcer role on a team: "It makes sense to try and take out a guy who's more important to his team than I am to mine" (Kennedy, 1975). In most cases, those who play the enforcer role realize that their career in sport depends on being highly aggressive.

A young rookie for the Minnesota North Stars explains that when he was drafted, he knew he was expected to be "a physical player" and that he was not expected to do any scoring. In apologizing for the fact that he did not get involved in very many fights during his first year, he gave the following statement: "There were some situations where I could (have fought), but they were at the end of my shift when I was tired. . . . That's one thing I've got to condition for this summer. I'm going to have to be in better shape for fighting. That's the job." (Dean McGee, *Colorado Springs Gazette-Telegraph*, 5/1/78:6B).

Efforts to control aggression in contact sports will continue to be ineffective as long as many players realize that their paychecks depend upon using aggressive behavior to intimidate other players and attract spectators. When Jack Tatum (1979), the defensive safety for the Oakland Raiders, recklessly crashed into Darryl Stingley after an incomplete pass, breaking Stingley's neck and damaging his spinal cord, a loud cheer came from the stands. After discovering that his action left Stingley almost completely paralyzed for life, Tatum explained, "It was one of those pass plays where I could not possibly have intercepted, so because of what the owners expect of me when they give me my paycheck I automatically reacted to the situation by going for an intimidating hit" (1979:223). It is also interesting to note that this explanation was written in an autobiography that would probably never have been profitably published if Tatum specialized in something other than intimidation on the playing field.

II. VIOLENCE AND THE SOCIAL ORGANIZATION OF SPORT TEAMS

The discussion of violence and the commercialization of sport focused on how the nature of sport and the sport experience are shaped by general social and economic factors. In this section, attention will focus on how violence in sport may also be related to the organization of sport teams themselves. This possibility has been discussed in detail by Hughes and Coakley (1978) and by Coakley (1982); it will only be summarized here.

In heavy contact sports, it is possible that a repressively organized team structure at least partially accounts for the acceptance and the use of violence among players. This is not really a new idea. Research has consistently shown that there is a strong relationship between rigidly organized social structures and the incidence of aggressive behavior among those who are required to cope with such structures (Clemmer, 1958; Sykes, 1958; Milgram, 1963; Zimbardo, 1972; Goldfarb, 1975). Combining this fact with the information indicating that sport teams—especially in the heavy contact sports—are rigidly structured (Friedenberg, 1967; Scott, 1971; Hoch, 1972; Edwards, 1973), leads to the idea that some of the violent behavior of the athletes in these sports is rooted in the repressive control systems of coaches and administrators.

Sykes (1958) has suggested that the high rate of violence in prisons is directly related to the social psychological deprivations experienced by inmates. These deprivations threaten each inmate's (1) feelings of moral worth, (2) adult status, (3) phsyical security, (4) masculinity, and (5) sense of adequacy. In collectively responding to these five threats, inmates develop a social system in which violent behavior comes to be defined as the normative means for establishing status among peers, maintaining self-esteem and protecting one's physical well-being.

In spite of the obvious differences between prisons and sport teams, the athletes on repressively organized teams do experience a set of deprivations similar to those experienced by inmates. Violence is one of the methods that can be used to cope with those deprivations. A brief discussion of how the self-systems of athletes are threatened by repressive controls will illustrate this point.

Threats to Moral Worth

When group membership and personal evaluation come to be defined in moral terms, extreme forms of behavior may not only be encouraged, but they may come to be demanded in the name of loyalty. For athletes, good standing on the team is often defined in moral terms. If an athlete fails to meet performance expectations, the failure is often interpreted as a violation of team trust, and the moral worth of the athlete may be called into question. Violent acts become mechanisms through which the player's moral worth is demonstrated and through which team trust is guaranteed.

Through a combination of formal and informal definitions of what it means to be a team member, a coach can create and sustain a deep-seated fear among players that they may indeed not be worthy of continued membership. Violation of team rules, failure to practice hard, mistakes in a game and above all, quitting the team—each may provide a threat to moral worth. Such a threat becomes a potent force in generating the willingness to disregard the health and welfare of self and others. It is in this way that the capacity to endure pain and inflict it on others takes on a positive moral value—it is for the sake of the team which, in return, provides a reaffirmation of a positive, individual identity. Unfortunately, that reaffirmation is only a temporary one; becoming a permanently trusted team member is rare, if not impossible. One's moral worth must be established day after day, season after season.

Threats to Adult Status

In the literature on team contact sports, there are numerous references to men being treated as boys (Shaw, 1972; Kramer, 1970; Kempton, 1971; Scott 1971). Team decisions are made by coaches in a dictatorial (benevolent and otherwise) fashion. Coaches may even become "father-figures" which further confirms the child status of the athletes. Players are told to obey, not to think (Shaw, 1972); too much thinking may lead a player to be labelled as a "problem athlete" or as "uncoachable" (Scott, 1971). This situation serves to keep the athlete in perpetual doubt about his adult status. Consequently, proving adulthood becomes an important goal, and aggressive and violent behavior becomes an available means to that goal. Even players on the same team will be aggressive toward one another to establish their independence in traditional male terms.

In Rollo May's investigation of the sources of violent behavior, he argues that all human beings need some means of achieving a sense of personal significance. Significance is most likely to be achieved when people have opportunities to make their own decisions and shape their own lives. If these opportunities do not exist, "violence may be the only way individuals or groups can achieve a sense of significance" (May, 1972:44). In a setting or activity in which the restriction of decision-making opportunities is coupled with the demand for physical contact, it would seem that relatively high rates of violent behavior would be quite likely.

Threats to Physical Well-Being

Being able to "take physical punishment and give it back" is crucial to athletes in establishing their status on the team and avoiding physical and verbal harassment from teammates and opponents. John Ferguson, [former] coach of the New York Rangers hockey team, has noted: "If a rookie backs down just once, he'll draw a crowd. Enough guys will want a piece of the kid to run him out of the league" (quoted in *Surface*, 1977). Unfortunately, the acquisition of status and physical security is never final. Periodic "tests" will be made by the opposition if there is even a rumor that someone is "going soft" or is "afraid to hit."

Adding to the threat to one's physical well-being is the manner in which injuries are defined by coaches and athletes. For example, Jerry Kramer candidly reveals that "Vince (Lombardi) took an injury as a personal insult." Another professional football player explains that he has always continued to play when in pain because "I can't dishonor the way I feel about myself as a man" (Looney, 1973).

Similar incidents on high school, college and professional teams indicate that in contact sport, the failure to "hit" or to continue hitting when hurt is defined as irresponsibility by the coach and as a violation to team trust by the players. Through this rather obvious reversal of common sense, abrasions, bruises, torn ligaments and broken bones become potential symbols of personal failure during the game and "badges of courage" in the locker room and the newspaper reports after the game is over.

Threats to Masculinity

British anthropologist Geoffrey Gorer reports that in cultural settings in which sex roles are highly differentiated, expectations for men lead them to demonstrate their uniqueness as males through the display of warrior-like behavior; non-violent societies, on the other hand, tend to have minimal sex role differentiation (1966:47). In all-male settings, the exclusion of the opposite sex not only deprives group members of opportunities for heterosexual expression but also of the sexual complementarity necessary to give meaning to their own sexuality. In light of the popular stereotypes of the sex lives of athletes, it may seem far-fetched to make the case that their masculinity can be threatened even in an all-male environment. However, coaches often respond to the performance failures of players by raising questions about their manhood. Of course, the inference made by the players and coaches is that it is through mastery and domination that manhood is demonstrated and proved. In the all-male setting of contact sport, agressive and violent behavior becomes an avenue of proof of masculinity.

Threats to Personal Feelings of Adequacy

All athletes have to cope with the constant threat of failure and the loss of a sense of adequacy. Within the sport setting, the awareness that continued team membership and the maintenance of specific relationships and lifestyle patterns depend upon effective performances may precipitate aggressive behavior. This is especially true when such behavior is defined as having instrumental value for the team as a whole. When it does, violence becomes the means through which a sense of personal adequacy is achieved and one's status, both inside and outside of the sport setting, is preserved.

Each of these threats calls into question a player's career goals, his self-esteem and his feelings of security as an athlete. In response, violent behavior comes to be collectively justified and even extolled as an integral facet of the contact sport experience. This is one of the ways in which behavior that is defined as illegal and reprehensible in the everyday lives of most people comes to be defined as normal in at least a portion of the lives of many athletes in some of the most popular sports in North America.

III. VIOLENCE AND SOCIALIZATION INTO THE ROLE OF ATHLETE

When the use of intimidation and violence exists at the top levels of competition, it is likely to spill over into sport programs at other levels. Research shows that when young athletes identify with top-level players perceived to be violent, their own sport behavior becomes more violent (Smith, 1974). This is a significant factor, since violent role models are not only very visible but are held in high esteem by many sport fans and are given favorable press coverage and good salaries. When young people see such models rewarded for their behavior and then participate in the same sport under conditions very similar to those in which the model was observed, the level of imitation is likely to be very high (Berkowitz, 1969, 1972a,b).

Young players are also encouraged to use violence by their peers, team-mates and oftentimes, by their parents and coaches. Edmund Vaz (1972) reports that the 13–17-year-old players in Canadian hockey leagues are not only encouraged to be physically aggressive, but are taught techniques of fighting by their coaches. In a study of how players in this age group perceived the attitudes of the significant others in their sport lives, Smith (1975a) found that the players generally anticipated positive sanctions for many of the forms of violent behavior that could be used during a game. The strongest perceived encouragement comes from peers; 65% of the players in the sample thought their peers would approve of starting a fight on the ice. Various other forms of intimidation and violence were perceived by the majority of players to be approved by peers, teammates, coaches and fathers. Mothers were the only significant others perceived to be apprehensive about too much aggressive behavior. However, approximately half of the players perceived their mothers of approving of heavy bodychecking and fighting back after someone else initiated a fight.

Interviews with both players and coaches led Smith (1975a) to conclude that the major factor limiting the players' use of violence and the coaches' approval of such behavior was their fear that it would elicit penalties and therefore jeopardize their teams' chances for success. In other words, their apprehension was based on instrumental concerns rather than any interest in protecting the integrity of the game or the safety of the participants.

The extent to which violence is encouraged and incorporated into the sport experience of young athletes is also influenced by the characteristics of the program in which participation occurs. Programs which restrict participation to the top-level players in various age groups and which emphasize win-loss records, playoffs and tournaments, and personal performance statistics are the ones in which the use of physical intimidation and violence are most prevalent (Tyler & Duthie, 1979; Smith, 1978, 1979a). It is in these programs that players learn to define violence and intimidation as an expected part of their role as athletes. They learn that such behavior not only wins games but is used as an indicator of a player's personal abilities. Therefore, the effective use of violent tactics becomes necessary to an athlete's career success and his access to more immediate forms of external awards.

IV. PLAYER VIOLENCE AND VIOLENCE AMONG SPECTATORS

Sociological research suggests that the aggressive actions of players often serve as catalysts for the violent behavior of those who are watching. The implications of such a possibility are worthy of consideration because there are so many spectators who are attracted to sports in which the use of intimidation and violence is prevalent.

Berkowitz (1972a) has suggested that spectators will usually not define aggression as appropriate for themselves unless they interpret the action in the game or match as being aggressive. He emphasizes that "it's the viewer's interpretation that really matters; the scene isn't really an aggressive stimulus unless he thinks of it as aggression, as the deliberate injury of others" (1972a). When the activities of the players are generally interpreted as non-aggressive, the orientation of the spectators is likely to be quite different. Emotional intensity may be high depending upon the tension-excitement generated by the competitive situation itself, but the aggressive readiness of the spectators is relatively low, and the normal contraints for behavior are not likely to be as loose as they are at an event that is generally interpreted as containing aggressive behavior.

Studies by Goldstein and Arms (1971), Arms, and others (1979) and Lennon and Hatfield (1980) support this explanation. These researchers each compared pre-game and post-game feelings of hostility among spectators at heavy contact sport events (wrestling, football, ice hockey) and non-contact sport events (gymnastics, swimming) and found that only the former produced increases in aggressive tendencies. In other experiments done by Berkowitz, he repeatedly found that subjects who were exposed to a rather brutal boxing match in a seven-minute film segment taken from a movie ("Champion") were more likely than members of a control group to administer shocks to subjects in a learning experiment. In further experiments, he found that when the film of the boxing match or a professional football game was described to subjects as an aggressive confrontation between the opponents, they were more punitive than others who saw the game film, but who were informed that the competing athletes were just doing their jobs, and they were not trying to hurt one another (Berkowitz, 1972a).

A summary of newspaper accounts of actual cases of spectator violence at sport events led Smith (1975b) to conclude that violence breeds violence in real-life settings as well as in the laboratory. He explains:

> In a study of 17 major soccer riots reported in *The New York Times*, over half were preceded by assault (or threats of it) by players, spectators, or police. . . . And some sort of assaultive behavior was said to precede 74 percent of 39 sport crowd outbursts reported in the *Toronto Globe and Mail* during the decade 1963–73. . . . The most frequent type of assault was player attack on opposing players, ranging from individual acts to bench-emptying brawls. In the majority of cases, these were explicitly identified as precipitants of the collective action that followed (1975b:314).

In other cases, Smith found that outbreaks of spectator violence were precipitated by player violence combined with other factors such as unpopular calls by referees. But even if player violence was not the most critical precipitating factor, it was part of a series of events that together created the context in which spectator outbreaks occurred.

In conclusion, it can be stated that the extent to which player violence spills over into the actions of spectators depends upon the spectators' subjective definitions of the players' actions. When the actions of the players are defined as aggressive, the social organization of the crowd is likely to generate a set of orientations and behaviors that can serve as a context conducive to spectator aggression. Actual displays of aggressive behavior, however, depend upon a combination of this context, general social conditions and specific precipitating events between individual spectators. For example, some groups at hockey or football games may define them as physical but non-aggressive; this would provide a basis for a variation in behaviors from one section of a crowd to another and from individual to individual. There may also be specific actions of players in an incidental contact sport, such as baseball or soccer, that some spectators will define as aggressive, and crowd behavior may become more extreme at those times.

SUMMARY

Violence among athletes has many causes. In this paper, attention was directed at those causes grounded in the social processes involved in the sport experience and in the socio-structural context in which sport exists. The commercialization of sport has led to an emphasis on heroic values (including violence) for the purpose of generating and maintaining spectator interest. And violence has come to be used as an effective tactic in winning games and enhancing the commercial reputation and popularity of individual athletes.

Player violence is also rooted in the structure and organization of sport teams themselves. The repressive control systems characteristic of so many heavy contact teams leads players to define violence as not only an expected part of their experience, but as sometimes necessary to maintaining their identities and self-esteem as athletes. Violence becomes a means through which athletes cope with the social psychological deprivations they experience as team members.

The socialization experiences of athletes in many sports includes the learning of violent tactics. The approval of these tactics by significant others in the lives of young athletes serves to intensify the extent to which they incorporate violence into their own sport behavior.

Finally, violence by players sometimes serves as a catalyst for violence among spectators. It not only heightens the emotional intensity of fans, but provides them with attractive models of aggressive behavior.

NOTES

1. A serious injury is defined as one which prevents an athlete from playing in at least one game during the season.
2. Throughout this paper, the terms "violence" and "aggression" are used to refer to behavior which either intends harm or shows a serious disregard for the safety and well-being of self or others.

REFERENCES

Arms, Robert, Gordon W. Russell, and Mark L. Sanderlands. "Effects on the Hostility of Spectators of Viewing Aggressive Sports." *Social Psychology Quarterly*, XLII, No. 3 (1979), 275–279.

Berkowitz, Leonard. Ed. *Roots of Aggression: A Re-examination of the Frustration-Aggression Hypothesis*. New York: Atherton, 1969.

Berkowitz, Leonard. "Sports, Competition, and Aggression." *Proceedings: 4th Canadian Psycho-Motor Learning and Sport Symposium*, Ottawa, Canada, 1972a.

Berkowitz, Leonard. *Social Psychology*. Glenview, Ill.: Scott, Foresman and Company, 1972b.

Clemmer, D. *The Prison Community*. New York: Holt, Rinehart & Winston, Inc., 1958.

Coakley, Jay J. *Sport in Society*. 2d ed. St. Louis: The C. V. Mosby Co., 1982.

Crawford, Scott A. "New Zealand Rugby: Vigorous, Violent & Vicious?" *Review of Sport and Leisure*, III, No. 1 (1978), 64–84.

Edwards, Harry. *Sociology of Sport*. Homewood, Ill.: Dorsey Press, 1973.

Fisher, A. Craig. *Psychology of Sport*. Palo Alto, Calif.: Mayfield Publishing Company, 1976.

Friedenberg, Edgar Z. "Foreword." Slusher, *Man, Sport, and Existence*. Philadelphia: Lea & Febiger, 1967, pp. vii–xiii.

Furst, R. Terry. "Social Change and the Commercialization of Professional Sports." *International Review of Sport Sociology*, VI (1971), 153–170.

Gaskell, George, and Robert Pearton. "Aggression and Sport," Goldstein, Ed. *Sports, Games & Play*. Hillsdale, N.J.: Lawrence Erlbaum Associates, Publishers, 1979, pp. 263–295.

Goldfarb, R. *Jails, The Ultimate Ghetto*. Garden City, N.J.: Anchor Press, 1975.

Goldstein, J., and R. L. Arms. "Effects of Observing Athletic Contests on Hostility." *Sociometry*, XXXIV, No. 1 (1971), 83–90.

Gorer, Geoffrey. "Man Has No 'Killer' Instinct." *The New York Times Magazine*, Section 6, November 27, p. 47.

Hoch, Paul. *Rip Off the Big Game*. New York: Doubleday & Company, Inc., 1972.

Hughes, Robert, and Jay J. Coakley. "Player Violence and the Social Organization of Contact Sport." *Journal of Sport Behavior*, I, No. 4 (1978), 155–168.

Kempton, Murray. "Jock Sniffing." *New York Review of Books*, XVI, No. 2 February 11, 1971, pp. 34–38.

Kennedy, Ray. "Wanted: An End to Mayhem." *Sports Illustrated*, XLIII, No. 20, November 17, 1975, pp. 17–21.

Kramer, Jerry, *Instant Replay*. Ed. Dick Schaap. Cleveland: The World Publishing Company, 1968.

Kramer, Jerry. Ed. *Lombardi: Winning Is the Only Thing*. New York: The World Publishing Company, 1970.

Lasch, Christopher, "The Corruption of Sports." *New York Review of Books*, XXIV, No. 7, April 28, 1977, pp. 24–30.

Lennon, Joseph X., and Frederick C. Hatfield. "The Effects of Crowding and Observation of Athletic Events on Spectator Tendency toward Aggressive Behavior." *Journal of Sport Behavior*, III, No. 2, 61–68.

Lipsyte, Robert. *Sports World*. New York: Quadrangle/The New York Times Book Co., 1975.

Looney, Douglas S. "Play When It Hurts Is More than Just a Job." *The National Observer*, XII, No. 1, January 6, 1973, pp. 1, 12.

Martens, Rainer. *Social Psychology and Physical Activity*. New York: Harper & Row, Publishers, 1975.

May, Rollo. *Power and Innocence: A Search for the Sources of Violence*. New York: W. W. Norton & Co., Inc., 1972.

Pilz, Gunter A. "Attitudes toward Different Forms of Aggressive and Violent Behavior in Competitive Sports: Two Empirical Studies." *Journal of Sport Behavior*, II, No. 1 (1979), 3–26.

Poupart, Jean. "La Violence au Hockey: Une Contingence de Carriere, des Imperatifs Organisationnels." *Deviance et Societe*, III, No. 1 (1979), 47–67.

Scott, Jack. *The Athletic Revolution*. New York: Free Press, 1971.

Shaw, Gary. *Meat on the Hoof*. New York: Dell Publishing Co., Inc., 1972.

Smith, Michael D. "Aggression in Sport: Toward a Role Approach," *Journal of the Canadian Association for Health, Physical Education, & Recreation*, CIIILXXI (1971), 22–25.

Smith, Michael D. "Significant Others' Influence on the Assaultive Behavior of Young Hockey Players." *International Review of Sport Sociology*, IX, Nos. 3–4 (1974), 45–56.

Smith, Michael D. "The Legitimation of Violence: Hockey Players' Perceptions of Their Reference Groups' Sanctions for Assault." *Canadian Review of Sociology and Anthropology*, XII, No. 1 (1975a), 72–80.

Smith, Michael D. "Sport and Collective Violence." Donald W. Ball, and John W. Loy. Eds. *Sport and Social Order: Contributions to the Sociology of Sport*. Reading, Mass.: Addison-Wesley Publishing Company, 1975b.

Smith, Michael D. "Hockey Violence: Interring Some Myths." W. F. Straub. Ed. *Sport Psychology: An Analysis of Athletic Behavior*. Ithaca, N.Y.: Mouvement Publications, 1978.

Smith, Michael D. "Hockey Violence: A Test of the Violent Subculture Hypothesis." *Social Problems*, XXVII, No. 1 (1979), 235–247.

Stone, Gregory. "American Sports—Play and Dis-Play." *Chicago Review*, IX (1955), 83–100.

Surface, Bill. " 'Get the Rook!' " *New York Times Magazine*, Section 6, January 9, 1977, p. 14.

Sykes, Gresham. *The Society of Captives*. Princeton, N.J.: Princeton University Press, 1958.

Tatum, Jack, with Bill Kushner. *They Call Me Assassin*. New York: Everest House, 1979.

Tyler, J. K., and J. H. Duthie. "The Effect of Ice Hockey on Social Development." *Journal of Sport Behavior*, II, No. 1 (February, 1979), 49–59.

Underwood, John. "An Unfolding Tragedy: Brutality." *Sports Illustrated*, XLIX, No. 7, August 14, 1978a, pp. 69–82.

Underwood, John, "Punishment Is a Crime." *Sports Illustrated*, XLIX, No. 8, August 21, 1978b, pp. 32–56.

Underwood, John. "Speed Is All the Rage." *Sports Illustrated*, XLIX, No. 9, August 28, 1978c, pp. 30–34.

Vaz, Edmund. "The Culture of Young Hockey Players: Some Initial Observations." Albert W. Taylor. Ed. *Training—Scientific Basis and Application*. Springfield, Ill.: Charles C. Thomas, 1972, pp. 222–234.

Vaz, Edmund. "What Price Victory? An Analysis of Minor League Players' Attitude Toward Winning." *International Review of Sport Sociology*, IX, No. 2 (1974), 33–55.

Vaz, Edmund. "Institutionalized Rule Violation in Professional Hockey: Perspective and Control Systems." *CAHPER Journal*, XLIII, No. 3 (1977), 6–8, 10–14, 32–34.

Vaz, Edmund. "Institutionalized Rule Violation and Control in Organized Minor League Hockey." *Canadian Journal of Applied Sport Sciences*, IV, No. 1 (1979), 83–90.

Yeager, Robert C. *Seasons of Shame*. New York: McGraw-Hill Book Co., 1979.

Zillman, Dolf, R. C. Johnson, and K. D. Day. "Provoked and Unprovoked Aggressiveness in Athletes." *Journal of Research in Personality*, VIII, No. 2 (1974), 139–152.

Zimbardo, P. "Pathology of Imprisonment." *Transaction*, IX (April 1972), 4–8.

10. *Drugs in Sports: Symptoms of a Deeper Malaise*

SANDY PADWE

For pure hypocrisy, there is little that can match the statement Pete Rozelle, the commissioner of the National Football League, made at a press conference he called July 7 [1986] to announce the details of the N.F.L.'s drug testing program. "Our concern," he said, "is the health and welfare of the players—those taking drugs and those injured by those taking drugs."

When novelist Pat Toomay, a former defensive end for several N.F.L. teams, including the Dallas Cowboys and the Oakland Raiders, heard what Rozelle had said, he laughed. "All of a sudden he's worried," said Toomay, who retired in 1980 after a ten-year career. "Why wasn't he worried twenty years ago? Fifteen years ago? Five? It's been going on forever. What about all those guys running around on amphetamines? Painkillers? Steroids? They just didn't start hurting people last season, you know."

The timing of Rozelle's press conference seemed cynical coming as it did when stories about the death from cocaine intoxication of Len Bias, the Maryland University basketball star, and of Don Rogers, the Cleveland Browns safety, were blanketing the front page, the sports page and the nightly national news telecasts. The league said that the timing was a coincidence and that it had been working on a drug testing program ever since revelations of drug use by six players on the New England Patriots soured the aftermath of Super Bowl XX.

Rozelle is no newcomer to the problem of drugs in the N.F.L. Former St. Louis Cardinals linebacker Dave Meggyesy, now the western director of the N.F.L. Players Association, wrote about it in *Out of Their League* in 1970. *North Dallas Forty,* a novel by Pete Gent, a former receiver for the Cowboys and the New York Giants, remains the quintessential work on the subject of football and drugs.

In 1973, George Burman, a Washington Redskins center, was one of several players who detailed drug abuse, especially amphetamine usage, on the team, only to have his coach, George Allen, say: "I know we don't have a drug problem. I'm not worried about it." (Allen now chairs the President's Council on Physical Fitness.) Later that same year, Representative Harley Staggers and Senator Birch Bayh presided over hearings in Washington on drug abuse

SOURCE: Sandy Padwe, "Drugs in Sports: Symptoms of a Deeper Malaise," *The Nation* (September 27, 1986), pp. 276–279.

in sports. Professional football received plenty of attention, and in 1974 the N.F.L. found its flagship case with the San Diego Chargers. Rozelle fined the team's owners, general manager Harland Svare and eight players a total of $40,000 for violations of league rules on drugs. (Cocaine was not involved.) For years after, whenever someone suggested that the N.F.L. wasn't doing all it could about the problem, league officials would point to the Chargers' fines as proof of how tough they could be. But the fines had little effect on the players, who understood that the league's drug policy was basically cosmetic, aimed at placating public opinion. Drug use hardly changed, according to Toomay and several other players active at the time.

As long as the drugs involved in sports were only amphetamines, steroids, painkillers and a little marijuana here and there, and as long as the books being written about the subject were by dissidents such as Meggyesy and Gent—or, in baseball, Jim Bouton—the commissioners felt no discomfort. The same could be said of the directors of athletics at colleges and universities.

Stories of cocaine abuse moved the drug issue to another level. They outraged the public, made TV advertisers nervous and caught the interest of the sporting press. To a lot of editors, coke was a hotter, trendier drug than amphetamines or anabolic steroids. The use of the latter was limited to enhancing one's performance, and in the anything-goes world of athletic competition no one cares about how players excel, as long as they excel.

For years cocaine had been creeping into the sports world. Warren Jabali, who played for Denver in the old American Basketball Association, told *Newsday* in 1973 that he had heard of cocaine dealers on professional basketball teams. In 1978, Bob Hayes, the former Olympic gold medalist who had earned the title of "the world's fastest human," was arrested for selling cocaine. Hayes had been a wide receiver for "America's team," the Dallas Cowboys, so the shock was even greater when Hayes was imprisoned a year later. After that there seemed to be a new drug scandal on the wires every week, often involving cocaine. Some of the athletes were little-known subs and second-stringers, or solid though obscure starters. But others had plenty of headline value.

By 1985 the question preoccupying the press and the commissioners of professional sports was, Can the integrity of the various games be protected? Rozelle ordered a handful of highly publicized suspensions for cocaine use. But his public relations blitz was nothing compared to the one launched that year by Peter Ueberroth, the commissioner of baseball, who held a series of press conferences on cocaine and granted selective-interviews to journalists from prominent newspapers, magazines and television networks.

Ueberroth's initial strategy was to win public support for a drug testing program, and the public bought it after a parade of big-name players such as Keith Hernandez and Dave Parker testified in a Pittsburgh trial that summer that they had used drugs. When Ueberroth finally announced his testing plan, which basically called for players, general managers, secretaries, mail clerks and minor leaguers to pee into a bottle, there was even more backing for his position. With public opinion favoring testing, a number of minor league players allowed testing clauses to be written into their contracts. That left the Major League Baseball Players Association—which opposes any testing that isn't negotiated under the collective bargaining agreement—to explain why it was trying to protect those players who hadn't signed their civil liberties away in the rush to judgment by the fans and the sporting press, which, by and large, had the rope and noose ready.

Then, one day last spring, Ueberroth simply waved his Olympic torch and proclaimed that baseball was drug-free. Apparently all those clean-cut young men who appeared in the Pittsburgh courtroom had been aberrations.

The deaths of Bias and Rogers were hardly aberrations, though. That's when sports and the streets really met, leaving the fans genuinely shocked at the demise, within such a short period, of two seemingly indestructible athletes. If only the fans had been as concerned through the years about the lives wasted by drug use in cities and on campuses. But athletes are perceived as different, special. In the first wave of news stories about Bias and Rogers, both were portrayed by coaches, family and friends as near-saints, people who would never touch a drug. If Bias and Rogers had died in car accidents, it would have been more understandable—a one- or two-day story. Instead, with the press leading the mourning, the deaths became a rallying point for all those groups who see the issue of drug testing in simplistic yes-or-no terms, the Constitution be damned.

The sports media played a major role in stoking the mob mentality. For the first time athletes had died as a result of cocaine abuse, and that focused the issue for the editors and news directors, who felt the public's anger through mail, polls and telephone calls. If sportswriters and broadcasters and their editors know anything, it's how to get a bet down quickly on a good horse. The Bias/Rogers story was a sure thing.

There was no murkiness now for the sports news managers, no departmental generation gap to bridge. Most of the older editors and writers neither understood nor cared about drugs, while the younger generation had been exposed to drug use since college. But both were happy to ignore the warning signals around them. In fact, some young sportswriters had exchanged good weed and good coke during interviews with athletes. It proved the reporter was one of the guys and could be trusted not to write about sensitive subjects, just as the older guys had proved it for all those years by not writing about boozing and whoring. Why spoil a good thing and cut off a source by getting into the real touchy stuff?

If you want to know what's really happening in sports, the place to find out is not usually on the printed page or on the evening telecasts. It's in the press room before and after games, where, over the free food and booze, the writers talk about who's drugged out and whose groin pull is really the clap. Of course, the gossip is off-the-record stuff, passed on by some coach, general manager or agent, or even a player. Quite often it's leaked as part of a whispering campaign by someone who wants to harm the victim for any of a variety of reasons. The best way to get rid of a malcontent or a hypochondriac or a druggie is to plant some gossip with a writer and have the writer pass it on along the grapevine. Pretty soon your problem vanishes to some other team or right out of the league.

There's a culture within a culture operating in sports. On one side, you have a predominantly white power structure, consisting of management and the press, which is serviced by management's powerful public relations machine. On the other side are the athletes, many of whom come from racial, ethnic and youth cultures with values and peer pressures completely antithetical to those of the people in control. You won't get a clear understanding of the inner workings of this culture from the press because most sports departments have an aversion to sociological issues and the abstractions they spawn. So all those competing forces just fester, bothering the daylights out of the fans, who don't quite comprehend what's going on and don't quite want to know.

From management's point of view, until Bias and Rogers died the real issues had been contained beautifully. The sports press—with a few troublesome exceptions—had been numbed. It sat there nodding off in front of the fire, feet up, full-bellied and belching like some Dickensian character in a country inn. So when the two men died, the press reacted predictably and hypocritically, with horror and wonder, as if it had just discovered that there is a real world out there which wasn't created by the P.R. people. Drugs? Right here in River City? Could it be?

Moral indignation oozed from nearly every VDT and microphone. The public expected indignation, but it didn't want the front page transferred to the sports page. As Wilfrid Sheed wrote in *Harper's* in 1984: "Sports continues its rounds as the Magnificent Evasion, since it also keeps us away from the bad news at home and in one's psyche. Many men, and a spattering of women, talk about sports from morning to night for fear something else might get in." The last thing the public wants to read about on the sports page is drugs, politics, antitrust suits, or questions about racism and sexism and colliding cultures. The more drug stories that appear in the papers or on TV, the angrier the public gets. Fans regard such stories as a personal affront, an invasion of sacred territory, a defilement of the temple. They cling to the concept of the athlete as role model, and there are plenty of politicians, commissioners, sportswriters and broadcasters to tell them that's the way it should be.

Why is the public so outraged when some quarterback or third baseman is picked up on a cocaine charge? When a John Belushi self-destructs, there is no outcry for the drug testing of actors. Outrage, it seems, is reserved for sports. When *Sports Illustrated* polled 2,000 adults about their views on sports last spring, it was no surprise that 73 percent of the respondents favored drug testing. A wonderful follow-up question to anyone who favors testing for athletes is whether that person would accept such examinations as a condition for employment. It also would be interesting to poll the members of the baseball, basketball, football and hockey writers associations to see if their members would submit to random drug testing.

Testing is not the simple answer in sports. There are questions about the testing procedures themselves that have not been answered. The tests are hardly infallible. And, then, do you test just for hard drugs or for the performance-enhancing drugs too? Rozelle's plan does not call for steroid testing, which is laughable given the evidence available about steroid use throughout the league. The N.F.L. says it is still working on the testing methodology. The questions over testing will deeply affect the players' future, not to mention their civil liberties as well as those of every other American. Civil libertarians are finally learning how powerful sport is in the United States and how law-enforcement officials and politicians can take advantage of the emotion of the moment to swing the debate over drug testing in their favor, if not in the Constitution's.

The public must realize that athletes are not heroes. Simply putting on a uniform does not make them better people or give them a greater standard of behavior to uphold. Too many athletes are overpampered individuals who have been told all their life that they are special because they can throw a ball or run swiftly. They are eased through colleges and universities when they should be learning to read and write. Not only do they accept it, they expect it. They are the recipients of money, clothes, cars, women and drugs from all manner of people, while teachers, coaches, administrators and even some parents look the other way. Many athletes fully understand sport's amorality and don't even try to distinguish right from wrong.

If college and pro teams look away while the players pump themselves full of steroids, painkillers and amphetamines so they can play when they are hurt, why should athletes think there is anything wrong with doing coke with friends to relax? To be consistent, the press and the fans should be as concerned about athletes' use of painkillers or performance-enhancing drugs as they are about cocaine. Does the reason they aren't have anything to do with America's love affair with winning? Athletes are revered for scoring touchdowns, runs and baskets by a group of individuals to whom winning—or covering the point spread—has become an end in itself. Players get the message: Use whatever means it takes to get the score in your team's favor. Such an attitude skews values completely and bleeds all the beauty from our games.

For their part, the teams and schools expect the athletes to be paragons of virtue and role models. They make the players live this hypocrisy in order to receive financial benefits. As the system unravels—and it is unraveling faster than Roger Clemens can throw a baseball—the impulse will be to reach for a panacea like drug testing rather than to deal with much deeper, much more complex problems, which go to the very core of sport in America. Instead of calling for testing, the people with the nooses should be checking the foundation. It's about to collapse.

■ FOR FURTHER STUDY

Arms, Robert L., Gordon W. Russell, and Mark L. Sandilands. "Effects on the Hostility of Spectators Viewing Aggressive Sports." *Social Psychology Quarterly* 43, no. 3 (1979): 275–279.

Atyeo, Don. *Blood and Guts: Violence in Sports*. New York: Paddington, 1979.

Berkow, Ira. "The Abundance of Skullduggery in Baseball." *The New York Times* (August 23, 1987): 20.

Brady, Erik. "Craftsmen Ply Tricks of the Trade." *USA Today* (August 5, 1987): Cl.

Bredemeier, Brenda Jo, and David L. Shields. "Values and Violence in Sports Today." *Psychology Today* 19 (October 1985): 23–32.

Bredemeier, Brenda Jo, and David L. Shields. "Athletic Aggression: An Issue of Contextual Morality." *Sociology of Sport Journal* 3 (March 1986): 15–28.

Burt, John J. "Drugs and the Modern Athlete: The Legacy of Lenny Bias and Don Rogers." *Journal of Physical Education, Recreation, and Dance* 58 (May/June 1987): 74–79.

Carroll, R. "Football Hooliganism in England." *International Review of Sport Sociology* 15, no. 2 (1980):77–92.

Case, Robert W., and Robert L. Boucher. "Spectator Violence." *Journal of Sport and Social Issues* 5 (Fall/Winter 1981): 1–14.

Celozzi, Matthew J., Richard Kazelskis, and Kenneth U. Gutsch. "The Relationship Between Viewing Television Violence in Ice Hockey and Subsequent Levels of Personal Aggression." *Journal of Sport Behavior* 4 (December 1981): 157–162.

Chass, Murray. "True Confessions: A Pitcher Tells How to Cheat." *The New York Times* (July 26, 1987): 18.

Chass, Murray, and Michael Goodwin. "Drug Abuse in Baseball." In *Fractured Focus*, edited by Richard E. Lapchick. Lexington, Mass.: D. C. Heath, 1986, pp. 277–309.

Curry, Timothy, and Robert M. Jiobu. *Sports: A Social Perspective*. Englewood Cliffs, N.J.: Prentice-Hall, 1984, pp. 211–255.

Edwards, Harry, and Van Rackages. "The Dynamics of Violence in American Sport." *Journal of Sport and Social Issues* 7 (Summer/Fall 1977): 3–31.

Eitzen, D. Stanley. "Violence in Professional Sports and Public Policy." In *Government and Sport*, edited by Arthur T. Johnson and James H. Frey. Totowa, N.J.: Rowman and Allanheld, 1985, pp. 95–116.

Frey, James H., ed. "Gambling in Sports." *Arena Review* 11 (May 1987): entire issue.

Goldstein, Jeffrey H., and Robert L. Arms. "Effects of Observing Athletic Contests on Hostility." *Sociometry* 34 (March 1971): 83–90.

Hersch, Hank. "It's War Out There!" *Sports Illustrated* (July 20, 1987): 14–17.

Hillsbery, Kief, "Clockwork Orange County." *Outside* (August/September 1982): 55–59, 72–74.

Horrow, Rick, ed. "Violence in Sport." *Arena Review* 5 (February 1981): entire issue.

Hughes, Robert H., and Jay J. Coakley. "Player Violence and the Social Organization of Contact Sport." *Journal of Sport Behavior* 1 (November 1978): 155–168.

Johnson, William Oscar. "Steroids: A Problem of Huge Dimensions." *Sports Illustrated* (May 13, 1985): 38–61.

Lang, Gladys E. "Riotous Outbursts in Sports Events." In *Handbook of Social Science of Sport*, edited by Gunther Luschen and George H. Sage. Champaign, Ill.: Stipes, 1981, 415–536.

Lennon, Joseph X. "The Effects of Crowding and Observation of Athletic Events on Spectator Tendency Toward Aggressive Behavior." *Journal of Sport Behavior* 3 (May 1980): 61–68.

McIntosh, Peter. *Fair Play: Ethics in Sport and Education*. London: Heinemann, 1979.

Pilz, Gunter A. "Attitudes Toward Different Forms of Aggressive Behaviors in Competitive Sports." *Journal of Sport Behavior* 2 (February 1979): 3–26.

Rostaing, Bjarne, and Robert Sullivan. "Triumphs Tainted with Blood." *Sports Illustrated* (January 21, 1985): 12–21.

Royce, Joseph. "Play in Violent and Non-Violent Cultures." *Anthropos* 75 nos. 5–6 (1980): 799–822.

Schneider, John, and D. Stanley Eitzen. "The Structure of Sport and Participant Violence." Paper presented at the meetings of the North American Society for Sociology of Sport, Toronto (November 4–7, 1982).

Smith, Michael D. "Sport and Collective Violence." In *Sport and Social Order*, edited by Donald Ball and John Loy. Reading, Mass.: Addison-Wesley, 1975, pp. 281–300.

Smith, Michael D. "Hockey Violence: Interring Some Myths." In *Sport Psychology: An Analysis of Athletic Behavior*, edited by William F. Straub. Ithaca, New York: Movement Publications, 1978, pp. 141–146.

Smith, Michael D. "Towards an Explanation of Hockey Violence." *Canadian Journal of Sociology* 4, no. 1 (1979): 105–124.

Smith, Michael D. "Hockey Violence: A Test of the Violent Subculture Hypothesis." *Social Problems* 27 (1979):235–247.

Smith, Michael D. *Violence and Sport*. Toronto: Butterworth, 1983.

Sugden, John P. "The Sociological Perspective: The Political Economy of Violence in American Sport." *Arena Review* 5 (February 1981): 57–62.

Taylor, Ian. "Football Mad: A Speculative Sociology of Football Hooliganism," In *Sociology of Sport*, edited by Eric Dunning. London: Cass, 1971, pp. 352–377.

Taylor, William N. "Gigantic Athletes: The Dilemma of Human Growth Hormone." *The Futurist* 19 (August 1985): 8–12.

Thirer, Joel. "The Effect of Observing Filmed Violence on the Aggressive Attitudes of Female Athletes and Non-Athletes." *Journal of Sport Behavior* 1 (February 1978): 28–36.

Underwood, John. "An Unfolding Tragedy." *Sports Illustrated* (August 14, 1978): 69–82; (August 21, 1978): 32–56; and (August 28, 1978): 30–41.

Zimmerman, Paul. "The Agony Must End." *Sports Illustrated* (November 10, 1986): 16–21.

Part Four

Sport and Socialization

Children play in all societies. The ways in which adults structure children's play are often interesting clues about a society. To what extent are children allowed to be spontaneous in their play? What equipment is provided the children? What games are part of the culture and are they aggressive, ritualistic, or imaginative? Do adults minimally supervise or absolutely control the activities?

The involvement of young people in adult-supervised sport is characteristic of contemporary American society. Today, millions of youth are involved in organized baseball, football, hockey, basketball, and soccer leagues. Others are involved in swimming, golf, tennis, and gymnastics at a highly competitive level.

Why do so many parents in so many communities strongly support organized sports programs for youth? Primarily because most people believe that sports participation has positive benefits for those involved. The following quotation from *Time* summarizes this assumption:

> Sport has always been one of the primary means of civilizing the human animal, of inculcating the character traits a society desires. Wellington in his famous aphorism insisted that the Battle of Waterloo had been won on the playing fields of Eton. The lessons learned on the playing field are among the most basic: the setting of goals and joining with others to achieve them; an understanding of and respect for rules; the persistence to hone ability into skill, prowess into perfection. In games, children learn that success is possible and that failure can be overcome. Championships may be won; when lost, wait until next year. In practicing such skills as fielding a grounder and hitting a tennis ball, young athletes develop work patterns and attitudes that carry over into college, the marketplace and all of life.[1]

However parents often ignore the negative side of sports participation, a position that is summarized by Charles Banham:

It [the conventional argument that sport builds character] is not sound because it assumes that everyone will benefit from sport in the complacently prescribed manner. A minority do so benefit. A few have the temperament that responds healthily to all the demands. These are the only ones able to develop an attractively active character. Sport can put fresh air in the mind, if it's the right mind; it can give muscle to the personality, if it's the right personality. But for the rest, it encourages selfishness, envy, conceit, hostility, and bad temper. Far from ventilating the mind, it stifles it. Good sportsmanship may be a product of sport, but so is bad sportsmanship.[2]

The problem is that sports produce positive and negative outcomes. This dualistic quality of sport is summarized by Terry Orlick:

For every positive psychological or social outcome in sports, there are possible negative outcomes. For example, sports can offer a child group membership or group exclusion, acceptance or rejection, positive feedback or negative feedback, a sense of accomplishment or a sense of failure, evidence of self-worth or a lack of evidence of self-worth. Likewise, sports can develop cooperation and a concern for others, but they can also develop intense rivalry and a complete lack of concern for others.[3]

The first selection in this part, by sociologist Jay J. Coakley, describes the organized youth sports of today and compares them with the spontaneous games more characteristic of youth in previous generations. The second selection, by John Underwood, critiques adult-sponsored youth sports and offers suggestions for how they might be changed to benefit the participants. The final selection, by D. Stanley Eitzen, examines the consequences of the coach-athlete relationship on youths. As Eitzen points out, coaches often have a great impact on the socialization of youth. Although the more typical emphasis has been on the positive influences of coaches in character-building, Eitzen argues that many potential negative outcomes exist as well.

NOTES

1. "Comes the Revolution: Joining the Game at Last, Women are Transforming American Athletics," *Time* (June 26, 1978), p. 55.
2. Charles Banham, "Man at Play," *Contemporary Review*, 207 (August 1965), 62.
3. T. D. Orlick, "The Sports Environment: A Capacity to Enhance—A Capacity to Destroy," paper presented at the Canadian Symposium of Psycho-Motor Learning and Sports Psychology (1974), p. 2.

11. *Play Group Versus Organized Competitive Team: A Comparison*

JAY J. COAKLEY

One way to begin to grasp the nature and extent of the impact of participation in sport is to try to understand the sport group as a context for the behavior and the relationships of youngsters. In a 1968 symposium on the sociology of sport, Gunther Luschen from the University of Illinois delivered a paper entitled "Small Group Research and the Group in Sport." While discussing the variety of different group contexts in which sport activities occur, he contrasted the spontaneously formed casual play group with the organized competitive team. He was primarily interested in the social organization and the amount of structural differentiation existing in sport groups in general, but some of his ideas give us a basis for comparing the characteristics of the spontaneous play group and the organized competitive Little League team in terms of their implications for youngsters. In general, any group engaging in competitive physical activity can be described in terms of the extent and complexity of its formal organization. Simply put, we can employ a continuum along which such groups could be located depending on how formally organized they are. Figure 11-1 illustrates this idea.

The spontaneous play group is an example of a context for competitive physical activities in which formal organization is absent. Its polar opposite is the sponsored competitive team in an organized league. It follows that the amount of formal organization has implications for the actions of group members, for their relationships with one another, and for the nature of their experiences. Table 11-1 outlines the characteristics of the two groups that would most closely approximate the polar extremes on the continuum.

Before going any further, I should point out that the two descriptions in Table 11-1 represent "ideal type" groups. In other words, the respective sets of characteristics represent hypothetical concepts that emphasize each group's most identifiable and important elements. Ideal types are necessarily extreme or exaggerated examples of the phenomenon under investigation and as such are to be used for purposes of comparison rather than as depictions of reality. Our concern here is to look at an actual group in which youngsters participate and to compare the actual group with the ideal types in order to make an assessment of what the real group might be like as a context for experience. Of

SOURCE: Jay J. Coakley, *Sport in Society: Issues and Controversies* (St. Louis: C.V. Mosby, 1978), pp. 96–103.

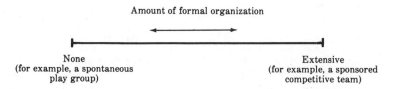

Amount of formal organization

None
(for example, a spontaneous
play group)

Extensive
(for example, a sponsored
competitive team)

FIGURE 11-1   A formal organization continuum for groups in competitive physical activities.

course, the real group will not be an exact replica of either of the ideal types, but will more or less resemble one or the other.

GETTING THE GAME STARTED

The characteristics of each group suggest that the differences between the spontaneous play group and the organized competitive team would be quite apparent as soon as initial contact between the participants occurs. In the spontaneous play group, we might expect that the majority of time would be spent on dealing with organizational problems such as establishing goals, defining means to those goals, and developing expectations of both a general and a specific nature for each of the participants. Being a member of a *completely* spontaneous play group would probably be similar to being involved in the initial organizational meeting of a group of unacquainted college freshmen who are supposed to come up with a class project. Both would involve a combination of some fun, a good deal of confusion, much talking, and little action. For the context of the organized competitive team, we might imagine a supervisor (coach) blowing a whistle that brings a group of preselected youngsters of similar ages and abilities running to fall into a routine formation to await an already known command. This would resemble a "brave new world" of sport where there would be some action, a good deal of listening to instructions, much routinization, and little fun. Fortunately, most group contexts for youngsters' sport participation fall somewhere between these two extremes. The trick is, of course, to find which points on the continuum would have a maximization of both fun and action along with the other characteristics seen as most beneficial to the young participants' development.

From my observations of youngsters in backyards, gyms, parks, and playgrounds, I have concluded that, for the most part, they are quite efficient in organizing their sport activities. The primary organizational details are often partially worked out by physical setting, available equipment, and time of the year, all of which influence the choice of activity and the form the activity will take. To the extent that the participants know one another and have played with each other before, there will be a minimum amount of time devoted to

TABLE 11-1. Comparison of Two Groups*

The Spontaneous Play Group: No Formal Organization	The Sponsored Competitive Team: High Formal Organization
Action is an outgrowth of the interpersonal relationships and of the decision-making processes of participating members.	Action is an outgrowth of a predesignated system of role relationships and of the role-learning abilities of group members.
Rewards are primarily intrinsic and are a function of the experience and the extent of the interpersonal skills of the group members.	Rewards are primarily extrinsic and are a function of the combined technical skills of group members.
Meanings attached to actions and situations are emergent and are subject to changes over time.	Meanings are predominantly predefined and are relatively static from one situation to the next.
Group integration is based on the process of exchange between group members.	Group integration is based on an awareness of and conformity to a formalized set of norms.
Norms governing action are emergent, and interpretation is variable.	Norms are highly formalized and specific, with variability resulting from official judgements.
Social control is internally generated among members and is dependent on commitment.	Social control is administered by an external agent and is dependent on obedience.
Sanctions are informal and are directly related to the maintenance of action in the situation.	Sanctions are formal and are related to the preservation of values as well as order.
Individual freedom is high, with variability a function of the group's status structure.	Individual freedom is limited to the flexibility tolerated within role expectations.
Group is generally characterized by structural instability.	Group is generally characterized by structural stability.

*A study of the game-playing behavior of elementary school children done by Sylvia Polgar (1976) provides empirical support for the comparison made in this table.

the formation of norms—rules from previous games can be used. But despite the ability of most youngsters to get a competitive physical activity going, there seems to be a tendency for adults to become impatient with some of the "childish" disagreements of the young participants. Adults often become impatient because they do not understand the youngsters' "distortions" of the games—games the adults know are supposed to be played another way. Adults who want to teach youngsters to play the game the *right way* and to help young players avoid disagreements and discussions in order to build up more action time seem to be everywhere. These adults see a very clear need for organization, that is, establishing regular practice times, scheduling contests, and giving positive rewards and encouragement to those whose performances are seen as deserving. Although their motives may be commendable, these adults usually fail to consider all of the differences between the informally organized group and the formally organized team.

Most importantly, the game in the park is in the control of the youngsters themselves, whereas the organized competitive team is supervised and controlled by adults (Polgar, 1976). In the play group, getting the game under way depends on the group members being able to communicate well enough to make organizational decisions and to evoke enough cooperation so that a sufficient amount of the group's behavior is conducive to the achievement of the goals of the game, however they have been defined. In this situation, interpersonal skills are crucial, and youngsters will probably be quick to realize that playing the game depends on being able to develop and maintain positive relationships or, at least, learning to cope with interpersonal problems in a way that will permit cooperative action. This constitutes a valuable set of experiences that become less available to participants as the amount of the group's formal organization increases. It is a rare adult coach who allows youngsters to make many decisions on how the game should be organized and played. In fact, most decisions have been made for the coach; the availability of the practice field has been decided, the roles defined, the rules made, the sanctions outlined, the team colors picked, the games scheduled, etc. Occasionally the players are allowed to vote on their team name, but that happens only if the team is new and does not already have one. In all, *the emphasis in the organized setting is on the development of sport skills, not on the development of interpersonal skills.*

PLAY OF THE GAME

Differences between the two groups do not disappear once the game begins. For the spontaneous play group, the game experience is likely to be defined as an end itself, whereas for the organized team, the game is a means to an end. In the play group, the game is unlikely to have implications beyond the setting in which it occurs, and the participants are primarily concerned with managing the situation so that *action* can be preserved for as long as possible. To this end, it is quite common for the participating youngsters to develop sets of norms accompanied by rather complex sets of qualifications and to establish handicaps for certain participants. These tactics serve to compensate for skill differences and to ensure that the game can proceed with scores close enough so that excitement and satisfaction can be maximized for as many of the players as possible. For example, if one of the pitchers in an informal baseball game were bigger or stronger than the rest of the youngsters, he/she would be required to pitch the ball with "an arch on it" to minimize the ball's speed and to allow all the batters a chance to hit it. Exceptionally good batters might be required to bat left-handed (if they were right-handed) to minimize the chances of hitting a home run every time they came to bat. A youngster having a hard time hitting the ball might be given more than three strikes, and the pitcher might make a special effort to "put the ball over the plate" so that the batter would have a good chance of hitting the ball rather than striking out. Since a strikeout is a relatively unexciting event in a game where the primary goal is the involvement of all players, one of the most frequently made comments directed to the pitcher by his/her teammates in the field is "C'mon, let'em hit it!"

Similar examples of norm qualifications and handicap systems can be found in other sport groups characterized by a low degree of formal organization. Sometimes these little adaptations can be very clever, and, of course, some participants have to be warned if they seem to be taking unfair advantage of them. This may occur in cases where a young player tends to call time-outs whenever the opposition has his team at a disadvantage or when someone begins to overuse an interference or a "do-over" call to nullify a mistake or a failure to make a play. Although the system of qualifications and handicaps may serve to allow the participants to have another chance when they make mistakes and to avoid the embarrassment associated with a relative lack of skills, the major function of such systems seems to be to equalize not only the players, but also the teams competing against one another. Through such techniques, scores will remain close enough that neither team will give up and destroy the game by quitting. In a sense, the players make an attempt to control the competition so that the fun of all will be safeguarded. Adults do the same thing when given the chance. None of us enjoys being overwhelmed by an opponent or overcoming an opponent so weak that we never had to make an effort.

For the formally organized competitive team, however, the play of the game may be considerably different. The goal of victory or the promotion of the team's place in the league standings replaces the goal of maximizing individual participant satisfaction. The meanings and rewards attached to the game are largely a function of how the experience is related to a desired outcome—either victory or "a good show." Players may even be told that a good personal performance is almost always nullified by a team defeat and that to feel satisfied with yourself without a team victory is selfish (as they say in the locker room, "There is no 'u' in team" or "Defeat is worse than death because you have to live with defeat").

Since victories are a consequence of the combined skills of the team members, such skills are to be practiced and improved and then utilized in ways that maximize the chances for team success. Granting the other team a handicap is quite rare unless any chance for victory is out of their grasp. If this is the case, the weaker players may be substituted in the lineup of the stronger team *unless,* of course, a one-sided score will serve the purpose of increasing the team's prestige or intimidating future opponents.

Also, if one player's skill level far exceeds that of the other participants, that player will often be used where he can be most effective. In the Little League game, it is frequently the bigger youngster with the strongest arm who is made the pitcher. This may help to ensure a team's chance for victory, but it also serves to nearly eliminate the rest of the team's chances for making fielding plays and for being involved in the defensive play of the game. In a 6-inning game, the fact that a large number of the 18 total outs for the opponents come as strikeouts means that a number of fielders may never have a chance to even touch the ball while they are out in the field. A similar thing happens in football. The youth-league team often puts its biggest and strongest players in the backfield rather than in the line. The game then consists of giving those youngsters the ball on nearly every play. For the smaller players on the defensive team, the primary task may be getting out of the way of the runner to avoid being stepped on. Thus on the organized team, intimidation may become a part of playing strategy. Unfortunately, intimidation increases apprehension and inhibits some of the action in the game as well as the involvement of some of the players. Generally, it seems that on the organized team the tendency to employ the skills of the players to win games takes precedence over devising handicaps to ensure fun and widespread participation.

One way to become aware of some of the differences between the informal play group and the formally organized competitive team is to ask the participants in each group the scores of their games. In the formally organized setting, the scores are often one-sided with members of the winning team even boasting about how they won their last football game 77 to 6, their last baseball game 23 to 1, or their last soccer game 14 to 0. Such scores lead me to question the amount of fun had by the players. In the case of the losers, it would be rare to find players who would be able to maintain an interest in a game when they are so completely beaten. If the winners say they enjoyed themselves, the lesson they may be learning through such an experience should be seriously questioned. It may be that the major lesson is if your opponents happen to be weak, take advantage of that weakness so totally that they will never be able to make a comeback. Such experiences, instead of instilling positive relationships and a sincere interest in sport activities, are apt to encourage distorted assessments of self-worth and to turn youngsters off to activities that, in modified forms, could provide them with years of enjoyment.

In addition to the differences in how the game is organized and how the action is initiated, there are also differences in how action for the two groups is maintained. In the informally organized group, the members are held together through the operation of some elementary processes of exchange that, in a sense, serve as the basis for the participants obtaining what they think they deserve out of the experience (Polgar, 1976). When the range of abilities is great, the older, bigger, more talented participants have to compromise some of their abilities so that the younger, smaller, and less talented will have a chance to gain the rewards necessary to continue playing. The play of the game depends on maintaining a necessary level of commitment among all participants. This commitment then serves as a basis for social control during the action. Although there are some exceptions, those in the group with the highest combined skill and social prestige levels act as leaders and serve as models of normal behavior. For these individuals to deviate from the norms in any consistent manner would most likely earn them the reputation of being cheaters or bad sports. In fact, consistent deviation from the group norms by any of the participants is likely to be defined by the others as disruptive, and the violator will be reminded of his/her infraction through some type of warning or through a threat of future exclusion from group activities. When sanctions are employed in the informal play group, they usually serve an instrumental function—they bring behavior in line so that the game can continue. Sanctions are usually not intended to reinforce status distinctions, to preserve an established social structure, or to safeguard values and principles. Interestingly, self-enforcement of norms in the play group is usually quite effective. Deviation is not totally eliminated, but it is kept within the limits necessary to preserve action in the game. The emphasis is not so much on keeping norms sacred, but on making sure that the norms serve to maintain the goal of action. In fact, norms may change or be reinterpreted for specific individuals or in specific situations so that the level of action in the play activities can be maximized. The importance of maintaining a certain level of action is demonstrated by the informal sanctions directed at a participant who might always be insisting on too rigid an enforcement of norms. This is the person who continually cries "foul" or who always spots a penalty. To be persistent in such a hard-nosed approach to norm enforcement will probably earn the player the nonendearing reputation of being a baby, a crier, or a complainer.

In the informally organized play group, the most disruptive kind of deviant is the one who does not care about the game. It is interesting that the group will usually tolerate any number of different performance styles, forms, and individual innovations as long as they do not destroy action. Batting left-handed when one is right-handed is okay if the batter is at least likely to hit the ball, thus keeping the action going. Throwing behind-the-back passes and trying a crazy shot in basketball or running an unplanned pass pattern in football are all considered part of the game in the play group *if action is not destroyed*. Joking around will frequently be tolerated and sometimes even encouraged *if action can continue*. But if such behavior moves beyond the level of seriousness required to maintain satisfying action for all the participants, commitment decreases, and the group is likely to dissolve. In line with this, usually those participants with the highest amount of skill are allowed the greatest amount of freedom to play "as the spirit moves them." Although such behavior may seem to indicate a lack of seriousness to the outsider, the skill of the player is developed enough to avoid a "disruptive" amount of mistakes. At the same time, such freedom gives high-ability participants a means through which their interest level can be maintained. Similar free-wheeling behavior by a low-ability participant would be viewed with disfavor, since the behavior would frequently bring the action level below what would be defined as acceptable by the rest of the group.

In contrast to the play group, the maintenance of action on the formally organized team depends on an initial commitment to playing as a part of the team. This commitment then serves as a basis for learning and conforming to a preestablished set of norms.[1] The norms apply equally to everyone, and control is administered through the coach-supervisor. Regardless of how priorities are set with respect to goals, goal achievement rests primarily on obedience to the coach's directives rather than on the generation of personal interests based on mutually satisfying social exchange processes. Within the structure of the organized competitive team, deviation from the norms is defined as serious not only when it disrupts action, but also when it *could* have been disruptive or when it somehow challenges the organized structure through which action occurs. Thus sanctions take on a value-supportive function as well as an instrumental function. This is demonstrated by the coaches who constantly worry about their own authority, that is, whether they command the respect of their players.

In the interest of developing technical skills, the norms for the formally organized competitive team restrict not only the range of a player's action, but also the form of such actions. Unique batting, throwing, running, shooting, or kicking styles must be abandoned in the face of what the coach considers to be correct form. Joking around on the part of any team member is usually not tolerated regardless of the player's abilities, and the demonstration of skills is usually limited to the fundamentals of the game.

If commitment cannot be maintained under these circumstances, players are often not allowed to quit. They may be told by the coach that "We all have to take our bumps to be part of a team" or "Quitters never win and winners never quit." Parents may also point out that "Once you join a team, it is your duty to stick it out for the whole season" or "We paid our money for you to play the whole season; don't waste what we've given you." With this kind of feedback, even a total absence of personal commitment to the sport activity may not lead to withdrawal from participation. What keeps youngsters going is a commitment to personal honor and integrity or obedience to a few significant people in their lives.

WHEN THE GAME IS OVER: MEANING AND CONSEQUENCES

The implications of the game after completion are different for the members of the informal play group than they are for the members of the formally organized competitive team. For the latter, the game goes on record as a win or a loss. If the score was close, both winners and losers may initially qualify the outcome in terms of that closeness.[2] But, as other games are played, all losses and wins are grouped respectively regardless of the closeness of scores. In the informal play group, the score of a game may be discussed while walking home; however, it is usually forgotten quickly and considered insignificant in light of the actions of individual players. Any feelings of elation that accompany victory or of let-down that accompany defeat are shortlived in the play group—you always begin again on the next day, in the next game, or with the next activity. For the organized competitive team, such feelings are less transitory and are often renewed at some future date when there is a chance to avenge a previous loss or to show that a past victory was not just a fluke. Related to this is the fact that the organized team is usually geared to winning, with the coaches and players always reminding themselves, in the Norman Vincent Peale tradition, that "We can win . . . if we only play like we can." This may lead to defining victories as the expected outcomes of games and losses as those outcomes that occur when you do not perform as you are able. When this happens, the elation and satisfaction associated with winning can be buried by the determination to win the next one, the next one, and so on. Losses, however, are not so quickly put away. They tend to follow you as a reminder of past failures to accomplish what you could have if you had executed your collective skills properly. The element of fun in such a setting is of only minor importance and may be eliminated by the seriousness and determination associated with the activity.

The final difference between the two groups is related to the stability of each. The informal play group is characteristically unstable, whereas the opposite is true of the organized team. If minimal levels of commitment cannot be maintained among some members of the play group, the group may simply dissolve. Dissolution may also result from outside forces. For example, since parents are not involved in the organization of the play group, they may not go out of their way to plan for their youngster's participation by delaying or arranging family activities around the time of the group's existence. When a parent calls a youngster home, the entire group may be in serious jeopardy. Other problems that contribute to instability are being told that you cannot play in the street, that someone's yard is off limits, that park space is inaccessible, or that necessary equipment is broken or unavailable. These problems usually do not exist for the organized team. Consent by parents almost guarantees the presence of a player at a scheduled practice or game, space and equipment are reserved in advance, and substitute players are available when something happens to a regular team member. Because the team is built around a structure of roles rather than a series of interacting persons, players can be replaced without serious disruption, and the action can continue.

NOTES

1. In some cases, "commitment" may not be totally voluntary on the part of the player. Parents may sign up a son or daughter without the youngster's full consent or may along with peers, subtly coerce the youngster to play.
2. Such qualifications are, of course, used for different effects. Winners use them to show that their challengers were able or that victory came under pressure. Losers use them to show how close they came to victory.

12. *What's Wrong with Organized Youth Sports and What We Should Do about It*

JOHN UNDERWOOD

I am against little league sport. Not *some* little league sport. *All* little league sport. In principle, in fact, in perpetuity.

I will go to my grave believing little league sport is bad for the youth of America, because I don't see the swamp being cleared in my lifetime. Just the opposite. The swamp gets bigger every day.

I have in front of me a picture that depicts little league sport in all its glory. The picture got wide currency. As a brute-face example of human behavior, it probably could have been worse, but it involved women and that made it *seem* worse.

In the picture, one woman, identified as a mother from Burlington, Ontario, is wearing brief shorts and a tank top and high-heeled wedgies. She is shown lashing out with her wedged foot at another mother from East Brunswick, New Jersey. Mother number two is in a stance reminiscent of the basic feminine approach to schoolyard aggression: she has her hands up tentatively and her mouth thrust forward. Her tongue appears to be out. A third woman, looking harried and small, is in the middle, arms spread like a referee's, trying . . . to keep the combatants apart.

The altercation occurred not outside a bowling alley or a PTA meeting or some other likely arena, but on a children's soccer field after a game between two teams of ten-year-olds. According to accounts in the Toronto *Globe and Mail*, the game had been marred by unsightly incidents. Players on both sides were flagged for rough play; their fathers argued on the sidelines.

As the sportsmanship and language on and off the field deteriorated, at least one adult male was seen making vulgar gestures. The two mothers happened onto the field and into the fray immediately after the game. They were suddenly the center of it. East Brunswick Mom said she was kicked and scratched, and had her watch knocked off. Burlington Mom said she had only retaliated because her son had been "whacked on the face" by representatives of the other side. She said her kick missed the target, and she was sorry it had.

According to the *New York Times*, which hopped on the picture for its social implications, the embroglio served as still another reminder of "what can happen when adults become involved in the play of their children." The *Times*, quite accurately, saw it as an indication that the recent growth of kids'

SOURCE: John Underwood, *Spoiled Sport* (Boston: Little Brown, 1984), pp. 154–173.

soccer had finally brought the game down to par with other organized kids sports (Pop Warner and various brands of football, Little League baseball, etc.) in their ability to distort youthful competition.

The scenario contained all the familiar elements.

Involved soccer parents building fields, making schedules, holding player drafts, conducting car pools, all-star games and tournaments, peddling Cokes and candy bars, and generally butting in on every phase of the operation.

Soccer moms and pops crowding the sidelines of every game to encourage their pint-size warriors, their teeth clenched and the veins standing out on their necks.

Full-grown officials towering over the action like Gulliver over the Lilliputians, their whistles blaring authoritatively.

Coaches yelling and screaming at the players, and sometimes at the officials. And vice-versa.

Right on their heels were the sports psychologists, professional and otherwise, always out in force nowadays to measure the fallout from such activities. They got it from every corner. Parents complained about unfit coaches (pictured as frustrated ex-jocks and fantasizers, pressuring children into the hard lessons of "win-at-any-cost" sports ethics). Kids complained about both, albeit with less volume. (What, after all, did they know? Participants in youth sports are not obliged a say in when they play, or how much they play, or what position they play. Just be on time, Sonny, and make sure your jersey is laundered.)

In other words, soccer had arrived. Business as usual in the little leagues. And except for the photographic evidence (Burlington Mom versus East Brunswick Mom), even the violence was not new. Stark examples of how really obsessed adults can get over the games of their children have, in fact, been frequent newsmakers.

Cheating in every form, intimidations, threats, fistfights, riots, bribes, lawsuits—youth sport has been treated to all of it. A few years ago in a small Florida town named Kissimmee (imagine that) a mob of adults acknowledged the efforts of the four coaches of a winning team of twelve-year-old football players by attacking them with clubs and pipes. One coach wound up in the hospital. A cry from the crowd ("He's dead!") apparently sated the mob and it withdrew just before the constables arrived.

The more organized they are and the broader their physical and fiscal demands on the community, the closer youth sports come to being one long, jangling repository of criticism.

From the watchdogs of our collective psyches, they now draw an almost unanimous condemnation.

"Abolish the little leagues," says philosopher Paul Weiss.

"They're destructive; they delude us with their chummy qualities and we fail to see the disabling psychological effects," says Dr. Rollo May, the psychoanalyst.

"Forbid'em," says Harvard's David Riesman (*The Lonely Crowd*). Riesman says the cradle is robbed for girls by preteen pregnancies, and for boys by "this kind of athletic flirtation."

Whom to blame? More appropriately, whom to blame first?

Although it would not be inaccurate to say Mom and Pop and all those facsimile Knute Rocknes who clutter the sidelines of play every weekend, it would be better to examine first what atmospheric change occurred to create such boors. The first, the most prominent one, is the indirect influence: the unfortunate emergence (thanks to television) of an imperfect role model. The professionals.

The change from the adulation of the fictional athletic hero who played for fun (or whatever Frank Merriwell and Chip Hilton played for) to the real ones who play for pay has had a grotesque ripple effect throughout sport, even to levels where fame and fortune are only the stuff of adolescent dreams and wishes. Even for those who want nothing more than the healthy diversion sport should provide.

The model is irresistible, because it is brightly packaged and ubiquitous. A pervasive influence. "Big league" is easily perceived as "the only way to do" sport. If you can't *be* big league, you can *act* big league and *look* big league, and never mind that you are only nine years old. Those responsible for the conduct of kids' sports, themselves willing foils, pass this on, even to those who have absolutely no idea of the fallout—the parents.

To visit on such small heads the pressure to win, the pressure to be "just like Reggie J or Dr. J," is indecent. To dress them up to look like professionals, in costumes ten times more costly than they need for play at such experimental levels, is ridiculous. With such overkill, we take away the very qualities that competitive sports are designed to give the growing-up process.

I discussed this by long distance one afternoon with Dr. Benjamin Spock, the baby doctor-activist. Not surprisingly, he agreed. As an ex-Olympian who appreciated the need to start early in sport, Spock was nevertheless appalled while living in Cleveland to find parents bringing bleary-eyed pre-teenage figure skaters to the ice rink at five A.M. to practice. "That's not fun," he said, "that's a family conspiracy."

The one clearcut incentive for sport, at least at these formative stages, is to have fun. Period. When you take the fun out, it is not sport but exploitation. One could argue correctly that there is no hope for this at the professional level, where the stakes are so high and the ideals so confused, but at least those athletes are rewarded for their toil.

The ultimate exploitation is the little leagues. There, adult domination deprives children of the chance to grow naturally in sport, the chance to learn about competition's ups and downs without parental approval (or worse, disapproval), and without the weight of "big league" settings and imitations. To learn, through trial and error, entrepreneurial gifts as well as athletic skills. Organizing games. Playing them. Being their own umpires.

A game should never be more important than the child who plays it. The outcome of an athletic contest should never be as significant as the pleasure and education the participant might derive.

Such an activity totally loses its meaning when sport is transformed into a plaything for a segment of society *other* than the kids. A segment that very well might be making sport a refuge for its own hangups—a place to go not to appreciate the intrinsic values of pure sport (the joy of competing just for the hell of it), but to get away from the inflation, the bomb, the refugee influx or the impending visit of the divorce lawyer.

Too many parents confer on sport their worst anxieties, bequeathing to children the same dogged intensities that make them the cocktail party bores they are. Or, for that matter, the deadbeats they are. There have been many sick-sad examples. Recently a Dallas father who had coached his four children in little league football, baseball, and basketball, was found to have "borrowed" $10,000 from a kids' league treasury. He said he needed it to cover his losses in the automobile business.

For many parents, involvement is a form of "buying in," much the same way they buy in to a pro team—wearing silly T-shirts, unfurling banners, screaming obscenities. Some psychologists say it is a sign of their own failures to achieve, of trying to identify with the success of their progeny. In this setting success is measured totally by win or lose, and when their children lose, it is as if they have lost themselves. And that they *really* can't take.

Sports psychologist Bruce Ogilvie told me he once took a tape recorder to a little league football game and set it up near the stands. "You've never heard such vile, vicious language," he said. "With clenched fists and livid faces those parents goaded their children with nasty needling [and] yelled at the referee as if he were a criminal."

And what happens to the children through all this? To begin with, says Ogilvie, "they are mostly lost in the maze of extrinsic things going on around them. The activity no longer has any sustenance for them. They are merely the vehicles from which the adults derive their kicks." Watch for yourself, he says, when a team of eight-year-olds is on the field—staring at the sky, twirling their gloves (or helmets) in the air, turning to watch the planes go over. Detached, uncommitted, turned off.

I filled in one afternoon—with more than some reservations—as the substitute coach of my son's team of eight- and nine-year-olds. The regular coach, an Earl Weaver impersonator, had to get a tooth extracted and told me "somebody had to be there for this crucial game." Crucial or not, I made up my mind I would not interfere. I screwed myself to the bench and, except for helping the boys make out the lineup card and yelling out an occasional "thattababy," clammed up.

From there I watched as (1) the other team's coach baited the teenage umpire into an ugly argument, (2) a third team's coach "scouted" both teams with elaborate charts and colored pencils, (3) a gung-ho mother of one of our star players gently prodded me for "not caring," and (4) our team won or lost the crucial game. I'm not sure which.

As we were driving home, I asked my son if he liked baseball. He seemed to think the question called for honesty, and although he knew I loved the game and welcomed any opportunity for a little catch, must have sensed my impartiality. "Not really," he said. I was disappointed but not surprised.

Being turned off is the one extreme. At the other is the totally addicted child who finds in sport (or has been made to find) an opportunity for status and expression, maybe even with an eye out for the money when time and his own well-charted development take him to the stars.

Parents of such children literally get inside their progeny's bloodstream. They become obsessed with the heady notion that they have sired the next Tracy Austin, the next Kurt Thomas, the next Steve Carlton. Forcing (or at least encouraging) their children to give up social lives, and other sports, and maybe even academics, to gain—what?

More often than not, to wake up on the far side of the experience to discover that there were thousands of other eight-year-olds doing exactly the same thing. Believing implicitly that dogged determination and countless repetitions would get them to the top—or to whatever they perceive the top to be. Only to find it doesn't happen that way at all, except for a select handful.

Parents who fall into this trap, says New Yorker Emily Greenspan, a former "obsessed ice skater," see the "spark of athletic precocity in their children and [being eager] to produce a winner, change fun to fear." For parents who become immersed in their child's athletic career, says Ms. Greenspan, it soon becomes *their* career, and the confusion does not reveal itself as "bad" until it is too late.

The John McEnroes and Dorothy Hamills who succeed would tell us it was "worth it."

But would we get the same response from the thousands who are shoved into this time warp and do *not* make it? Even to a local championship? These veterans of domestic sports wars who were never told by a caring, qualified person that they were just not good enough to aspire so high? Who woke up at thirty without medals or, worse, without the sport that had kept them sociologically afloat all those years? Who found too late that the odds were frightfully against them from the start?

The return to earth can be traumatic. Psychologist Terry Orlick of Ottawa, himself an ex-jock, handled the case of a girl who, due to injury, had to give up competitive swimming. Her life had been rigidly programmed in what Orlick calls this "industrialized" kind of specialization, where the high expectation of the individual in one field makes it difficult for him to enter others, and, not wanting to risk failure, he avoids or withdraws from anything else.

The girl reentered society with some shocking realities. She had "terrible identity problems. She was totally withdrawn. It was a painful process. She did not even know how to buy a regular brassiere for herself."

And what of the coaches? Not just the coaches of these special kids—for most of them are, at least, qualified—but the vast number who stumble and bumble into youth sports. Well-intentioned fathers who offer their time, but also their twisted notions of what coaching children in competition is all about (what it is *not* all about is their trying to imitate Earl Weaver). Turning kids off or burning them out with their own bizarre applications of win-at-any-cost.

Larry Csonka, the former all-NFL fullback, followed the progress of a kids' football team near his home in Fort Lauderdale. Csonka is not a man who recoils from spilled blood—his or anybody else's. But he was horrified by little league football. "The coaches didn't know much about what they were doing," he said. "They just yelled a lot. They acted like they imagined Lombardi or Shula would act. Why, they had those eight-year-olds running *gassers* [postpractice wind sprints], for crying out loud." Csonka would not let his kids play little league football.

Influenced by the wrong examples, plagued with slogans about the "need" to win and the "fanatical drive" to win, such men make the score its own biggest reward, and dilute for their own children the pleasure of the competitive experience. The worst thing to be said about them, however, is that they are not qualified. An unqualified coach is a dangerous person.

Thousands of youngsters are injured every year because they have been taught improper techniques for their size and skill level. Damaged elbows are common among young baseball pitchers (so common that "Little League elbow" is a recognized name for a specific ailment); freestyle swimmers suffer a specific kind of shoulder injury; football players get hurt in many ways, even at a level where the danger of injury is minimized because they just don't deliver that many foot-pounds at impact.

Whether the potential for damage is physical or psychological, the threat is always there, and even coaches at the more advanced levels do some astonishingly stupid things when the well-being of their athletes interferes with their drive to win. A high-school football coach in the Midwest lost a star player to appendicitis before a key game. The game was lost. The next day the coach had the team physician check those players whose appendixes were intact, and tried to get him to have the appendixes removed. The doctor refused. He said the coach had no right to make such a demand.

But youth league coaches *do* have the right to say who gets to play and how much they play, and it is here that organized youth sports do their dirtiest work. Bruce Ogilvie laments the "sickening arrogance" of little league coaches forcing eight-, ten-, and twelve-year-olds to sit on the bench while others participate, learning nothing beyond the elitism of sport. To practice and not to play, or to play "a little," is a downer for a youngster who is getting his feet wet in sport. There is nothing right or good to say about it. Token appearances—an inning or two, a couple of minutes in the fourth quarter—are no less demoralizing. They may, in fact, do the greater harm.

There is a growing concern among the custodians of youth sports that many kids who are so stigmatized (you can bet *they* know what sitting on a bench means) are not coming back for more. The dropout rate is epidemic, especially in football. Instead of being a place where the love for competition is inspired, the games become a place where interest dies, especially among white middle-class kids who have so many alternatives to flee to.

My own son never returned to baseball. I was saddened—not for myself, because I had no illusions about what it could lead to—but for him. He was turned off to a great game.

A couple of years ago, the Concord, New Hampshire, Pop Warner team won the state championship with a 9–1 record that included seven shutouts. The next year, when the coach called his first practice, instead of a hundred or so, only twenty-two players reported—and two of them were over the weight limit. The coach said he "couldn't understand it." Alarmingly, the discouragement apparently filters *up*ward. High schools across the country are suffering drastic turnout and attendance declines in football, and many schools have dropped the sport.

The negatives in the experience are compounded when the child not only suffers the premature rejection that bench-riding imposes, but is channeled into positions in team sports that deprive him of the joys that make the game fun in the first place. Eventually, physical development and skill limitations will make those positions acceptable as the best way to stay in.

But you do not protect a youthful baseball player from his inadequacies in the field by making him a "designated hitter." And a right guard on a little league football team, tasting football for the first time, will *never* know the pleasure of running the ball, passing it or catching it. The fun things of football. Worse, he will probably get bored right out of the game. Maybe all games. When you take the fun out, you risk turning a kid away from competitive sports, never to return. Afraid. Turned off. Tuned out.

All in all, the process adds up to what one former high-school and grade-school coach calls "no more than a sophisticated form of child abuse." Brother R. E. Piqott, C.F.C., says that many kids who play at eight or ten stop playing in high school because they get fed up with "the excessive competition, the screaming adults and the absence of fun."

Adults calling ten-year-old basketball players "chokers" and berating little guys who are afraid to take a bat off their shoulder as having "no guts," is pressure of the worst kind. To think that kids learn in this crucible of scrutiny is not rational. It not only takes the fun out, it could very well kill their chances to progress. A double whammy.

What, then, do we do about it?

It would be simple enough to say that the first thing to do is dissolve the partnership. Turn in the fancy uniforms and tear up the schedules. Sweep the sidelines clean of screaming parents and ersatz coaches. Go back to the sandlots. Certainly no other country organizes children for play the way we do, and there is evidence enough that when he or she is *too* organized, *too* structured, the young athlete winds up dispirited.

An ironic object lesson in this kind of bungling was provided in *Sports Illustrated*. A Canadian coach lamented that the Soviet Union's hockey program had benefited from an *un*regimented approach to the sport, an ideological contradiction he could not believe. The Russians had routed coach Scotty Bowman's Team Canada in the Canada Cup tournament, and Bowman said he thought he knew why.

On a visit to Moscow he had been struck by the contrast between the approach to the game there and in U.S. and Canadian cities. In Russia, he said, the neighborhoods were alive with kids skating on their own; "they did not even start organizing until age twelve or so." Bowman said it would be better to let youngsters learn skating skills that way, and was joined in his belief by the National Hockey League's Bobby Orr: "Parents," said all-timer Orr, "are ruining hockey by organizing kids too early."

As a child growing up in South Florida, I divided many of my summers between Miami and Key West, playing the days away at the nearby parks and playgrounds. Without coaxing, without instruction, we moved from game to game and sport to sport with effortless enthusiasm. We made contests of little "practice games," not just to improve techniques but to get more out of the fun parts of the game—hitting "pepper" in baseball, playing one-on-one basketball. We concocted new methods to score so that we could play no matter how many we were or how limited the field. Stickball, of course, was a must.

Ed Kranepool, who played for the New York Mets from age seventeen to his retirement at thirty-four, fondly recalls growing up in the baseball sandlots of the Bronx, choosing up sides, setting the rules, playing two or three freeform games a day. "Adults had nothing to do with our games," he says. "We weren't an organized entity. The games were, in fact, disorganized fun. That's what sports for little kids should be. My initial frustration in sports began when I joined the local little league as a ten-year-old."

But nostalgia is one thing, hard realities are another. It is too late to go back. Times *have* changed. Youth sport would be better served if we thought more in terms of accommodating the need for fun with the facts of community life as they now exist. By its very definition competitive amateur sport implies "love" (from the Latin *amator*, "lover"); an amateur competes out of love.

But the vacant lot other generations played on as kids, for the love of it, is not likely to be there now. . . .

And the fields our tax monies have provided for "organized" play are. . . .

And adjusting to the change might be imperative because, alas, kids no longer just naturally gravitate to the athletic fields on Saturday morning. Affluence has had an anesthetizing effect. Kids sleep in on Saturday. Kids watch cartoons and play electronic games, and complain about the heat if they are asked to leave their air-conditioned caves.

In this respect, the little league Moms and Pops are doing their children a great service by getting them involved. Waking them up, getting them out.

It is also true that the world these kids now face *is* more structured. Being more crowded, it needs to be. The trick, then, is to modify the programs so that the children will be the first, not the last, to benefit. In a sense, therefore, part of the problem—organization—is also part of the solution.

By all means organize, or help the kids do it. Schedule games and fill the fields with players. Outfit them (reasonably, inexpensively), car-pool them, encourage them. Get them to the field on time.

But then step back and let them play.

Let *all* of them play.

Step *way* back so that even if you are seen you will not be heard. Resist the urge to monitor and regulate, and to choose their teams for them.

And, most of all, resist the urge to coach them.

The need for coaching is understood in sport. Being a coach for youth is a high calling, but it would be far better for children if we separated the coaches of little leagues from those who would be coach but have no business at it.

The time has come to understand the need for a basic separation of interest and support: that it is one thing to encourage your child, and play catch with him, and hit balls to him, but it is quite another to take on the mantle of coach for him and his peers.

Qualified coaching is essential to the learning process, but kids at that formative stage should not be overcoached, and not be coached at all by well-intentioned part-timers. Kids just starting in sport need an adjustment period, a time to "fail" in private. They need *ample* time to experiment, to try things, to test the limits of their own bodies without close scrutiny.

When the time is ripe, one professional coach for two or three or even four teams at the park should be adequate. One qualified person to provide the needed guidance and instruction.

The money parents spend "getting involved" could well go toward paying the salary of such a coach, and supplying *his* needs, since they will directly benefit the children. To such a coach (a physical education major, preferably; one who has participated in the games at a skilled level) the youngsters can come to learn techniques, or to satisfy a rule question, or to referee an argument.

A coach who would be there but only to instruct, not to involve himself in the winning and losing of what, after all, are inconsequential contests.

A coach, in short, who would stand above "win-at-any-cost."

Child's play is not trivial. It is important stuff. But first it must be fun. Win-at-any-cost *dulls* sport. The games themselves are robbed of the qualities that make them exciting for us (a reason we invent them in the first place) when a coach's frantic need to win translates into dogged efforts *not to lose*. Play, then, instead of freewheeling and uplifting, becomes conservative, cautious and calculated—the opposite of uplifting. The skills of players are "sat upon" while the coach protects his lead.

Such distortions of sport happen all the time at the professional and major college levels. They should *never* happen at the little league level. But, of course, they do.

The influence of the role model filters down rapidly and helps create men and boys so paralyzed by exaggerated importance of "the score" that they think it's okay to make bench-riders out of ten-year-olds. That it's okay to shut lesser players off from the learning process while their more adept peers get the job done. The job being to win.

What makes this profoundly sad in little league play is that it is sanctioned by the very people who should be most opposed to it—the parents. Eventually they even become accomplices in the crime.

There is nothing wrong with Mom helping arrange for bats and balls and caps, and maybe solving a transportation problem or two. And there is nothing wrong with Dad hitting fungoes to the guys or filling in when an adult is needed for counsel. But it *is* wrong for them to contribute in any way to a distortion of the purpose of playing games. And it *is* wrong for someone who only *thinks* he knows the game to coach young people in the development of their skills.

A little leaguer is in far greater danger of being overcoached than he is being poorly coached. Of being numbed by drills and practices rather than discouraged by his own lack of skills. Every study I have seen on youth sport has come up with the same conclusion: kids would rather play than practice. They are not interested in "refinements" and "techniques" when they are just starting out; they are only interested in playing.

Terry Orlick surveyed the motivational instincts of one thousand children involved in youth sport; of those, ninety-five percent chose "fun" as their reason for playing sports. *Ninety* percent said they'd rather play for a "loser" than sit on a "winner's" bench.

Because most parents instinctively sense this, much deceit is practiced by little league administrators to keep parents from revolting. Many leagues brag of rules that say "everybody plays." More often than not what that means is a token involvement for the lesser kids, while the best play every down or every inning.

The ill effects of such deceit should be obvious enough. If all an unskilled youngster does is make brief appearances (at positions where he can do the least harm), he will not improve. And he will in all likelihood have his confidence shaken as well. He may, in fact, wind up knowing sport only as what writer Robert Lipsyte calls the "chain-gang joylessness of drills and practices." *Not* fun, but a dead end of pseudo-participation.

The solution here is so simple. But to reach it we must accept all around that *to play* is the object. The only reason to have a league.

And in youth sport, *every*body plays.

Every game.

The whole game.

If the league is so loaded with players that the benches are crowded on Saturday afternoon, divide the teams again. Create more teams. Let them play on another field, or at another time. But let them play without concern for "starting lineups" and star-status.

Those discriminations will come naturally later, in high school, say, when skills are clearly defined and a level of team excellence is worth striving for. Eight-year-old kids don't have to know how good or bad they are; they don't need to be reminded by adults, or discouraged from the outset by elitism. They will gravitate naturally to the players whose skills they are more comfortable with—school friends, neighborhood buddies.

In this light, it would be infinitely better to let them choose their own teams. Player drafts of pre-adolescents are the height of absurdity. Let the coach at the park set the game times and structure the leagues, but let the kids pick their own teams, away from the pressure (and needs) of their parents.

And then let them forgo ninety percent of the practicing they do to play. Play *instead* of practice. Kids are great imitators. Most of the things coaches and quasi-coaches try to teach at that level they will pick up themselves anyway. They will learn faster by playing. A baseball or basketball game a day if they want. Maybe two if there is time.

Kids ten to twelve years old could play a football game every day. Not eleven-man-to-a-side, blood-and-guts football, but six- or eight-man football, where they can all get a chance to pass and catch and run with the ball, and to sharpen their skills without drudgery, and to quit if they get tired. Or if they get bored.

Let the kids decide because they know more than you how much they want to play, and at what position, and how much the game means to them. Take those decisions away from the coach and that legion of parent-coaches who get in the way.

(Make no mistake. The kids expect more maturity and good sense from their coaches than they are getting. A questionnaire was sent to parents and players in a Southwest youth football league a few years ago. Forty-one percent of the kids complained that the coaches yelled too much; thirty-six percent said the coaches were poor losers and poor examples.)

Furthermore, youth sport should throw off the trappings of the "big time"—the expensive costumes, the extravagant awards and trophies, the banquets, the all-star games.

"Look at some of the trophies kids are awarded," says Kranepool. "Where's the incentive to carry on after getting that kind of hardware?" Kids, he argues correctly, will develop in sport without bribery. "Don't worry, the good players will stay with the game, and plenty of kids written off as failures will blossom into fine players. I've seen a lot of premature stars in the little league. I played against them. They aren't playing now."

As for the conduct of the games themselves, two changes should be made across the board. The parameters of play should always reflect the size and abilities of the players (e.g., the fields they play on should be tailored—cut to fit). Kids do that naturally in the sandlots. And then, most importantly, let them learn the rules and be made to go by them without having policemen blowing whistles in their faces. Let them take on for themselves the burden of sportsmanship by umpiring their own games.

Children should learn for themselves that rules are made for a reason, and the reason translates into the betterment of the sport. To deprive them of the chance to develop a respect for playing *within* the rules is wrong. When they learn this sensitivity, sport will be made more meaningful because they will know that it is not only unfair to win by cheating, it is not sporting. That to win outside the rules, or by bending the rules, is not to win at all.

Ideals are set in childhood and tend to erode and be corrupted with age. But we should at least *start* with high ideals. A principle of sport (beyond fun) is that it teaches us to sublimate aggression and violence and cheating, not encourage those things. When this is not done, it is appallingly clear that sport suffers. When you push a kid away from the good lessons of sport, toward "anything it takes to win," he suffers.

We have a lot to work on—and to work against. Youth sport is serious stuff because it may well be the youngster's most powerful influence. Its course *can* be redirected. Throwing out the little league babies with the dirty little league bath water is not necessary. The mechanics of youth sport are not unalterably bad. Life at the park is possible without the bloodcurdling yells and bloodthirsty parents, and without fanatical coaches living out their fantasies. We have gone out of control, but we can get back *in* control.

Beyond the above, what it will take is not more criticism, but more caring. Dad has to know that he may have "gone too far" by professionalizing Tommy at eight or ten; that organization is not all bad, that some specializing is necessary at times to refine the skills of a gifted youngster, but we have "gone too far" when we make his specialty a tyranny instead of a simple quest for excellence. That we have gone "out of control."

Dad has to know that a *laissez-faire* attitude will not close the playgrounds or stunt his child's development in sport; that pressuring the child, and burdening him with winning, is counterproductive. And Mom has to be made to know that her screeching when Tommy drops the ball *is* bad—bad for her, and bad for Tommy. Most Moms want Tommy to have a good experience; they just don't understand how counterproductive their conduct is. They have to be made aware that they are "out of control."

Almost any great athlete who has reached star status will tell you how excellence in sports has had a lifelong benefit, knocking down personal and social barriers, learning how to interact with people, overcoming prejudice. Ronald Reagan once described in glowing terms the "inner confidence" he learned from playing sports. *How* he learned is every bit as important as the fact that he learned. That is where the reform in youth sport is needed. Says Jeanne Austin, mother of Tracy and four other tennis-playing Austins: "The child has to want it, not you. Don't emphasize trophies or being first. *Do* talk about the fun, and the friends you can make, and the benefits of exercise."

Be assured. The most important thing about playing sports is to *play*. To take part, with all the good that implies. It is okay to try to win, and there is an undeniable joy in winning. But it is enough to take part. Because from *that* pleasure springs all the benefits that sport can provide. To insist on it for our children is the least we can do.

13. *The Dark Side of Coaching and the Building of Character*

D. STANLEY EITZEN

A widespread belief in our society is that coaches are significant role models for their charges. Communities and school administrators commonly expect their coaches to instill in athletes the important values of competitiveness, aggressiveness, hard work to obtain goals, acceptance of discipline, subordination of self to the success of the team, and striving for excellence. Snyder has shown in a study of slogans placed in locker rooms by coaches that coaches explicitly press these values on their athletes.[1]

Snyder has suggested in another article several aspects of the context within which competition takes place that affect the receptivity of participants to the values of the coach:[2]

1. The more the involvement in the activity, the greater the probability that the individual will acquire the skills and attitudes the coach desires. Since team captains are the most centrally involved, they will be most susceptible to the socialization of the coach, followed in order by starting players, then substitutes.
2. The more voluntary the individual's participation in the activity, the greater the coach's influence on the participant. By contrast, players pressured by external constraints to participate will be relatively unaffected by the coach's influence.
3. The more expressive the relationship between the socializer (coach) and the "socializee" (player), the greater the probability of value transmission. (An expressive relationship is one where the coach cares about the physical and emotional well-being of the athlete.)
4. The greater the prestige and power of the socializer, the greater his or her influence on athletes. The more the coach is admired and held in awe (based directly, in most cases, on winning percentage), the more his or her wishes will be adopted. According to the statements of his former players, Vince Lombardi was just such a coach.[3]
5. The more that sport participation is believed by the participant to be a means of achieving upward social mobility, the greater the possibility of acquiring the values of the coach.

This essay was written for the second edition of this text.

These conditions of optimal influence by coaches have several implications. Most significant, they suggest strongly that coaches will have a profound influence on athletes. Many young people, especially boys in our society and increasingly girls, want desperately to be athletes. They admire older athletes and coaches. They are willing to sacrifice and obey coaches because they believe they can be successful in sport.

A second implication is that the younger the athlete, the more likely the values of coaches will be transmitted. Playing in youth sports, junior high school, and high school is likely to be voluntary and fun compared with college and professional sports. Also the relationship between coach and athlete is more likely to be an expressive one.

The third implication, and the focus of this essay, is if coaches are successful as role models, exactly what are they transmitting to their athletes? Clearly, some coaches are important and positive influences on their athletes, often serving as parental substitutes, and providing a high sense of morality, a model of fairness, humane concerns for their athletes, and personal maturity. But some coaches do not always offer such positive character traits and behaviors. Some coaches fit George Halas's characterization of George Allen as he testified in court, concerning Allen's breach of contract: "This man lies. He is an opportunist. He is a schemer. He will cheat. He will do anything to insure victory. . . . He has no character whatsoever. . . . He is a man thoroughly without principle."[4]

Many coaches cheat. They may hold practices in violation of the rules. They may "doctor" the playing field or playing equipment to give their team an unfair advantage. At the college level, many coaches have violated the rules by giving athletes illegal payments, altering the transcripts of athletes, hiring surrogate test takers for their marginal student-athletes, and enrolling them in "phantom courses." What values are being transmitted to athletes by these kind of coaches?

Many coaches explicitly teach their athletes to cheat. In Fort Collins, Colorado, a coach of fifth graders taught his basketball players to step on the feet of the opposing players during free throws to give them the advantage on rebounds. In baseball a pitcher may be taught how to rough up the ball or place a foreign substance on it to obtain an unfair advantage over the batter. In football a lineman may be taught how to hold without getting caught. Athletes may be encouraged by their coaches to put opponents off-balance psychologically through heckling, name-calling, and other forms of "gamesmanship." Basketball players may be taught how to pretend that they were fouled so that officials will award them undeserved free throws. Would a coach voluntarily disallow a score if it had been gained by undetected illegal means? Perhaps in golf, where the norms promote honesty, but rarely in sports such as football, basketball, or baseball. What, then, is being taught? Sportsmanship? Positive character traits?

Some coaches, in their zeal to be successful, also are guilty of behaviors that brutalize and demean their athletes—actions that in other contexts would not be tolerated. Character building and dehumanizing practices are not compatible. How is character shaped when one is humiliated and demeaned? How is it affected when the individual is treated like an interchangeable part in a machine?[5] This occurs, for example, when an athlete is given pain killers for an injury in order to play, even though there may be long-range negative health consequences.

The athlete also is dehumanized by being treated as a perpetual adolescent, as someone who cannot be trusted. What is the effect on the character of athletes who are told how to dress, when and how to cut their hair, when they should be in bed, and the like? Does such autocratic behavior by coaches build autonomous, self-reliant, self-disciplined individuals? We delude ourselves if we believe that authoritarianism begets good character unless good character is meant to denote submission, compliance, dependence, and conformity.

There is a body of evidence which suggests that the longer one participates, the higher the level of competition, and the more central an athlete is to the team, the more negative character traits that prevail. Some examples include:

- A study of athletes found those at state universities were more likely to cheat than those at state colleges. Also, football players were more likely to cheat than athletes in other sports.[6]
- A study of college athletes revealed an inverse relationship between sportsmanship and involvement in the sports system. In order of sportsmanship: (1) athletes without a scholarship; (2) nonletter winners; (3) letter winers; and (4) full-ride scholarship holders.[7]
- A study comparing athletes and nonathletes in the ninth grade, twelfth grade, and college upperclassmen found that the high school athletes possessed desirable personal-social psychological characteristics to a greater extent than nonparticipants. But, the reverse was true at the college level.[8]
- A number of studies have noted that high school athletes are more likely to have higher grade point averages and higher educational aspirations than nonathletes.[9] Again, there seems to be a reversal when athletes are compared with nonathletes at the college level. A study comparing athletes with nonathletes over a 10-year period at one major university found that athletes in the major revenue sports of football and basketball were the least likely to graduate and had the lowest grade point averages, compared with other athletes and nonathletes. Similarly (and related, most likely, to their relationship to the revenue sports), the greater the scholarship aid to the athlete, the poorer the performance in school.[10]

We cannot determine from these studies whether the length of exposure to the influence of coaches promotes these negative character traits. This is because, as Ogilvie and Tutko have noted from their studies of over 15,000 athletes, sport is not so much a molding process but a selection process.[11] Although we cannot generalize with certainty about the socialization impact of coaches, two conclusions seem appropriate: (1) coaches do try to instill values in their athletes that are congruent with American values; and (2) the behaviors of many coaches may negate the positive traits they hope to promote and even have the opposite effect on the athletes they seek to shape.

NOTES

1. Eldon E. Snyder, "Athletic Dressing Room Slogans as Folklore: A Means of Socialization," *International Review of Sport Sociology* 7 (1972), 89–102.
2. Eldon E. Snyder, "Aspects of Socialization in Sports and Physical Education," *Quest* 14 (June 1970), 1–7.
3. Jerry Kramer (ed.), *Lombardi: Winning Is the Only Thing* (New York: Pocket Books, 1971).
4. Quoted in Wells Twombly, "Football is Allen's Entire World," *The Sporting News* (January 6, 1973), 8.
5. See Howard L. Nixon, "Sport, Socialization, and Youth," *Review of Sport and Leisure* 1 (Fall 1976), 21.
6. William L. Lakie, "Expressed Attitudes of Various Groups of Athletes Toward Athletic Competition," *The Research Quarterly* 35 (December 1964), 497–503.
7. Deane E. Richardson, "Ethical Conduct in Sport Situations," Sixty-sixth Annual Proceedings of the National College Physical Education Association (1962), pp. 98–104.
8. Jack Schendel, "Psychological Differences Between Athletes and Nonparticipants in Athletics at Three Educational Levels," *The Research Quarterly* 36 (March 1965), 52–67.
9. For a summary of the research findings see Eldon E. Snyder and Elmer Spreitzer, *Social Aspects of Sport,* second edition (Englewood Cliffs, New Jersey: Prentice-Hall, 1983), pp. 123–137.
10. Dean Purdy, D. Stanley Eitzen, and Rick Hufnagel, "Are Athletes Students? The Educational Attainment of College Athletes," *Social Problems* 29 (April 1982), 439–448. For a similar conclusion using data on Notre Dame see Allen Sack and Robert Thiel, "College Football and Social Mobility," *Sociology of Education* 52 (January 1979), 60–66.
11. Bruce Ogilvie and Thomas Tutko, "Sport: If You Want to Build Character, Try Something Else," *Psychology Today* 5 (October 1971), 61–63.

■ FOR FURTHER STUDY

Ball, Donald W. "Failure in Sport." *American Sociological Review* 41 (August 1976): 726–739.

Berlage, Gai Ingham. "Are Children's Competitive Team Sports Teaching Corporate Values?" *Arena Review* 6 (May 1982): 15–21.

Berryman, John. "From the Cradle to the Playing Field: America's Emphasis on Highly Organized Competitive Sports for Preadolescent Boys." *Journal of Sport History* 21 (1975): 112–131.

Brower, Jonathan G., ed. "Children in Sport." *Arena Review* 1 (Winter 1978): entire issue.

Brower, Jonathan J. "The Professionalization of Youth Sports." *The Annals* 445 (September 1979): 39–46.

Brower, Jonathan J. "Little League Baseballism: Adult Dominance in a 'Child's

Game.' " Paper presented at the Pacific Sociological Association meetings (Victoria, B.C.: April 1975).

Coakley, Jay J. "Play, Games, and Sport: Developmental Implications for Young People." *Journal of Sport Behavior* 3 (August 1980): 99–118.

Devereux, Edward C. "Backyard Versus Little League Baseball: The Impoverishment of Children's Games." In *Social Problems in Athletics*, edited by Daniel M. Landers. Urbana: University of Illinois Press, 1976, pp. 37–56.

Dubois, Paul E. "The Youth Sport Coach as an Agent of Socialization." *Journal of Sport Behavior* 4 (June 1981): 95–107.

Dubois, Paul E. "The Effect of Participation in Sport on the Value Orientations of Young Athletes." *Sociology of Sport Journal* 3 (March 1986): 29–42.

Fine, Gary Alan. "Team Sports, Seasonal Histories, Significant Events: Little League Baseball and the Creation of Collective Meaning." *Sociology of Sport Journal* 2 (December 1985): 299–313.

Fine, Gary Alan. *With the Boys: Little League Baseball and Preadolescent Culture*. Chicago: University of Chicago Press, 1987.

Geoffrey, G. W. "Reward System in Children's Games: The Attraction of Game Interaction in Little League Baseball." *Review of Sport and Leisure* 1 (Fall 1976): 93–121.

Godshall, R. W. "Junior League Football." *Journal of Sports Medicine* 3 (1975): 139–144.

Gould, Daniel, et al. "Reasons for Attrition in Competitive Youth Swimming." *Journal of Sport Behavior* 5 (September 1982): 155–165.

Hale, Creighton. "Athletics for Pre-High School Age Children," *JOPER* 30 (December 1959): 19–21, 43.

Harris, Donald S., and D. Stanley Eitzen. "The Consequences of Failure in Sport." *Urbal Life* 7 (July 1978).

Havemann, Ernest. "Down Will Come Baby, Cycle and All." *Sports Illustrated* 39 (August 13, 1973): 42–49.

Herron, R., and Brian Sutton-Smith. *Child's Play*. New York: John Wiley, 1971.

Horn, Jack. "Parent Egos Take the Fun Out of Little League." *Psychology Today* (September 1977): 18, 22.

Kaufman, Michael Jay, and Joseph Popper. "Pee Wee Pill Poppers." *Sport* 63 (December 1976): 16–25.

Kay, R. S., D. W. Felker, and R. O. Varoz. "Sports Interests and Abilities as Contributors to Self-Concept in Junior High School Boys." *Research Quarterly* 43 (1972): 209–215.

Kirshenbaum, Terry. "They're Pooling Their Talent." *Sports Illustrated* (July 10, 1978): 32–43.

Kohn, Alfie. "Why Competition?" *The Humanist* 40 (January/February 1980): 14–15, 49.

Krotee, March L. "The Effects of Various Physical Activity Situational Settings on the Anxiety Level of Children." *Journal of Sport Behavior* 3 (November 1980): 158–164.

Lever, Janet. "Sex Differences in the Games Children Play." *Social Problems* 23 (1976): 479–487.

Lever, Janet. "Sex Differences in the Complexity of Children's Play and Games." *American Sociological Review* 43 (August 1978): 471–483.

Lidz, Franz. "BMXing It Up with the Rad Crowd." *Sports Illustrated* (December 8, 1986): 28–36.

Lowe, Benjamin, and Mark H. Payne. "To Be a Red-Blooded American Boy." *Journal of Popular Culture* 8 (Fall 1974): 383–391.

Loy, John W., and Alan Ingham. "Play, Games, and Sport in the Psychosociological

Development of Children and Youth." In *Physical Activity: Human Growth and Development,* edited by G. L. Rarick. New York: Academic Press, 1973, pp. 257–302.

Maggard, Bob. "Avoiding the Negative: Blue Jeans Baseball." *JOPER* 49 (March 1978): 47.

Magill, R., et al. *Children and Youth in Sport: A Contemporary Anthology.* Urbana, Illinois: Human Kinetics, 1978.

Martens, Rainer, ed. *Joy and Sadness in Children's Sports.* Champaign, Ill.: Human Kinetics Publishers, 1978.

Martens, Rainer, and Vern Seefeldt, eds. *Guidelines in Children's Sports.* Washington, D.C.: American Alliance for Health, Physical Education, and Recreation, 1978.

McDermott, Barry. "The Glitter Has Gone." *Sports Illustrated* (November 8, 1982): 82–96.

McPherson, Barry, et al. "The Social System of Age Group Swimming." *Canadian Journal of Applied Sport Science* 5, no. 3 (1980): 142–145.

Mehl, Jack, and William W. Davis. "Youth Sports for Fun—and Whose Benefit?" *JOPER* 49 (March 1978): 48–49.

Orlick, Terry, and Cal Botterill. *Every Kid Can Win.* Chicago: Nelson-Hall, 1975.

Phillips, John C., and Walter E. Schafer, "Consequences of Participation in Interscholastic Sports: A Review and Prospectus." *Pacific Sociological Review* 14 (July 1971): 328–338.

Purdy, Dean A., Steven E. Haufler, and D. Stanley Eitzen. "Stress Among Child Athletes: Perceptions by Parents, Coaches, and Athletes." *Journal of Sport Behavior* 4 (February 1981): 33–46.

Purdy, Dean A., D. Stanley Eitzen, and Steven E. Haufler. "Age-Group Swimming: Contributing Factors and Consequences." *Journal of Sport Behavior* 5 (March 1982): 28–43.

Reese, Don, and John Underwood. "I'm Not Worth a Damn." *Sports Illustrated* (June 14, 1982): 66–82.

Rehberg, R. A. "Behavioral and Attitudinal Consequences of High School Interscholastic Sports: A Speculative Consideration." *Adolescence* 4 (Spring 1969): 69–88.

Richardson, D. "Ethical Conduct in Sport Situations." *66th Proceedings of* the National College Physical Education Association for Men (Washington, D.C.: National College Physical Education Association for Men, 1962).

Sage, George H. "Parental Influence and Socialization into Sport for Male and Female Intercollegiate Athletes." *Journal of Sport and Social Issues* 4 (Fall/Winter 1980): 1–13.

Scanlan, T. K. "The Effects of Success-Failure on the Perception of Threat in a Competitive Situation." *Research Quarterly* 48 (1977): 144–153.

Schafer, Walter E. "Participation in Interscholastic Athletics and Delinquency: A Preliminary Study." *Social Problems* 17 (Summer 1969): 40–47.

Schendel, Jack. "Psychological Differences Between Athletes and Nonparticipants at Three Educational Levels." *Research Quarterly* 36 (March 1965): 52–67.

Seefeldt, Vern. *Joint Legislative Study on Youth Sports Programs.* East Lansing, Michigan: Michigan State University, Department of Physical Education (1978), Parts I, II, and III.

Seefeldt, Vern, and John Haubenstricker, "Competitive Athletics for Children—The Michigan Study." *JOPER* 49 (March 1978): 38–41.

Simon, Julie A. "America's Attitudes Toward Youth Sports." *The Physical Educator* 36 (December 1979): 186–190.

Simon, Julie A., and Rainer Martens, "Children's Anxiety in Sport and Nonsport Evaluation Activities." *Journal of Sport Psychology* 1, no. 2 (1979): 160–169.

Smith, Ronald, et al. "Psychology and the Bad News Bears." In *Psychology of Motor Learning and Sport,* edited by Glyn C. Roberts and Karl M. Newell. Champaign, Ill: Human Kinetics, 1979, pp. 109–130.

Smoll, F., and R. Smith, eds. *Psychological Perspectives in Youth Sport.* Washington, D.C.: Hemisphere, 1978.

Smoll, Frank L., Ronald E. Smith, and Bill Curtis. "Behavioral Guidelines for Youth Sport Coaches." *JOPER* 49 (March 1978): 44–47.

Snyder, Eldon. "Aspects of Socialization in Sports and Physical Education." *Quest* 14 (June 1970): 1–7.

Snyder, Eldon E. "Athletic Dressing Room Slogans as Folklore: A Means of Socialization." *International Review of Sport Sociology* 7 (1972): 89–102.

Snyder, Eldon E., and Elmer Spreitzer. "Basic Assumptions in the World of Sports." *Quest* 24 (Summer 1975): 3–9.

Snyder, Eldon E., and Elmer Spreitzer. "Orientations Toward Sport: Intrinsic, Normative, and Extrinsic." *Journal of Sport Psychology* 1, no. 2 (1979): 170–175.

Stevenson, Christopher. "Socialization Effects of Participation in Sport: A Critical Review of the Research." *Research Quarterly* 46 (October 1975): 287–301.

Stevenson, Christopher L. "College Athletics and 'Character': The Decline and Fall of Socialization Research." In *Sport and Higher Education,* edited by Donald Chu, Jeffrey O. Segrave, and Beverly J. Becker. Champaign, Ill.: Human Kinetics, 1985, pp. 249–266.

Stone, Gregory P. "The Play of Little Children." *Quest* 4 (Spring 1965): 23–31.

Telander, Rick. "The Descent of a Man." *Sports Illustrated* (March 8, 1982): 62–70.

Voigt, David. *A Little League Journal.* Bowling Green, Ohio: Bowling Green University Popular Press, 1974.

Waid, R. "Child Abuse: Reader's Forum." *Runner's World* (September 1979): 16.

Watson, G. G. "Family Organization and Little League Baseball." *International Review of Sports Sociology* 9 (1974): 5–31.

Watson, G. G. "Games, Socialization and Parental Values: Social Class Differences in Parental Evaluation of Little League Baseball." *International Review of Sport Sociology* 12 (1977): 17–47.

Weiss, Maureen R., and Daniel Gould, eds. *Sport for Children and Youths.* Champaign, Ill.: Human Kinetics Publishers, 1986.

Weiss, Maureen R., and Becky L. Sisley. "Where Have All the Coaches Gone?" *Sociology of Sport Journal* 1 (December 1984): 332–347.

Yablonsky, Lewis, and Jonathan J. Brower. *The Little League Game.* New York: Times Books, 1979.

Part Five

Big-Time College Sport

Interschool sports are found in almost all American schools and at all levels. There are many reasons for this universality. Sports unite all segments of a school and the community or neighborhood they represent. School sports remind constituents of the school, which may lead to monetary and other forms of support. School administrators can use sport as a useful tool for social control. But the most important reason for the universality of school sports is the widespread belief that educational goals are accomplished through sport. There is much merit to this view; sports do contribute to physical fitness, to learning the value of hard work and perseverence, and to being goal-oriented. There is some evidence that sports participation leads to better grades, higher academic aspirations, and positive self-concept.

However, there also is a negative side to school sports. They are elitist, since only the gifted participate. Sports often overshadow academic endeavors (e.g., athletes are disproportionately rewarded and schools devote too much time and money to athletics that could be diverted to academic activities). Where winning is paramount—and where is this not the case?—the pressure becomes intense. This pressure has several negative consequences, the most important of which is that participants are prevented from fully enjoying sport. The pressure is too great for many youngsters. The game is work. It is a business.

The pressure to win also contributes to abuse by coaches, poor sportsmanship, dislike of opponents, intolerance of losers, and cheating. Most significant, although not usually considered so, is that while sport is a success-oriented activity, it is fraught with failure (losing teams, bench warmers, would-be participants cut from teams, the humiliation of letting down your teammates and school, and so on). For every ego enhanced by sport, how many have been bruised?

While this description fits all types of schools, big-time college sports deserve special attention for they have unique problems. Athletes in these settings are athletes first and students second; thus they are robbed of a first-class education. They are robbed by the tremendous demands on their time and energy. This problem is further enhanced by athletes being segregated from the student body (in special classes, housed in athletic dorms); thus they are deprived of a variety of influences that college normally facilitates.

Another problem of college sports is that they tend to be ultraelitist. The money and facilities go disproportionately to the *male* athletes in the revenue-producing sports rather than to intramurals, minor sports, and club sports.

The greatest scandal involving college sports is the illegal and immoral behavior of overzealous coaches, school authorities, and alumni in recruiting athletes. In the quest to bring the best athletes to a school, players have been given monetary inducements, sexual favors, forged transcripts, and surrogates to take their entrance exams. In addition to the illegality of these acts, two fundamental problems exist with these recruiting violations: (1) such behaviors have no place in an educational setting, yet they are done by some educators and condoned by others, and (2) these illicit practices by so-called respected authorities transmit two major lessons—that greed is the ultimate value and that the act of winning supersedes how one wins.

Finally, the win-at-any-cost ethic that prevails in many of America's institutions of higher learning puts undue pressure on coaches. They must win to keep their jobs. Hence, some drive their athletes too hard or too brutally. Some demand total control over their players on and off the playing field. Some use illegal tactics to gain advantage (not only in recruiting but also in breaking the rules regarding the allowed number of practices, ineligible players, and unfair techniques). But coaches are not the problem. They represent a symptom of the process by which school sports are big business and where winning is the only avenue to achieve success.

The articles in Part Five reflect on these problems and offer some solutions. The first article, by sociologists Peter and Patricia Adler, reports their first-hand observations of college athletes' involvement in academics. The second selection, by sociologist Harry Edwards, focuses on black student-athletes. His conclusion is profound—" 'dumb jocks' are not born; they are being systematically created." The next selection, by physical educator George H. Sage, examines the efforts made by the regulatory body of college sports—the NCAA—to solve the problems of big-time sports. As Sage points out, the NCAA typically focuses its attention on the problem athletes ("blaming the victim") rather than addressing the structural sources of the problems. The final selection by law professor John C. Weistart, presents concrete suggestions for reforming big-time college sports.

14. *From Idealism to Pragmatic Detachment: The Academic Performance of College Athletes*

PETER ADLER AND PATRICIA A. ADLER

In recent years, the relationship between the athletic participation and academic performance of college athletes has become a topic of scholarly concern. The sociological literature in this area, however, has been inconsistent in its findings. Some studies have cited a weak positive relationship, claiming that although most college athletes had poor academic records in high school, they have higher GPAs, lower attrition rates, and a greater likelihood of graduating than nonathletes because they receive extra tutoring, more attention, and special "breaks" (Hanks and Eckland, 1976; Henschen and Fry, 1984; Michener, 1976; Shapiro, 1984). But most studies of college athletes have found a negative relationship between athletic participation and academic performance. These studies conclude that athletes are unprepared for and uninterested in academics, that they come to college to advance their athletic careers rather than their academic careers; therefore, they have lower GPAs, higher attrition rates, and lower chances of graduating than other students (Cross, 1973; Edwards, 1984; Harrison, 1976; Nyquist, 1979; Purdy, Eitzen, and Hufnagel, 1982; Sack and Thiel, 1979; Spivey and Jones, 1975; Webb, 1968).

Our research, which also finds a negative relationship, extends previous studies in several ways. First, we show that although most college athletes ultimately become disillusioned with and detached from academics, many begin their college careers idealistically, caring about academics and intending to graduate. Second, we show that the structure of college athletics fosters the academic deindividuation of athletes. We trace the stages through which athletes progress as they become socialized to their position in the university environment and learn its structural characteristics. We describe how their academic goals and behavior become increasingly influenced by their athletic involvement. The initial academic aspirations of freshman athletes are considerably varied, but these various individual ideals gradually give way under the force of the structural conditions athletes encounter. Thus, by the time athletes complete their eligibility requirements, their academic attitudes and

SOURCE: Peter Adler and Patricia A. Adler, "From Idealism to Pragmatic Detachment: The Academic Performance of College Athletes," *Sociology of Education* 58 (October 1985), pp. 241–250.

goals closely resemble each other's. This process, which reduces individual differences between athletes, is accompanied by collective academic detachment and diminished academic performance. Third, using a longitudinal analysis of process and change, made possible by our method of data collection, we show the influence of interconnecting factors on athletes' progression through college. This is the first systematic participant-observation study of college athletics. Such an in-depth, ethnographic investigation of this area (suggested by Coakley, 1982; Fine, 1979; Loy, McPherson, and Kenyon, 1978; Purdy et al., 1982) is useful for two reasons: (1) it enables us to determine whether athletic participation hinders or enhances academic performance, and (2) it reveals the factors and processes that produce this relationship.

We begin by discussing the setting in which this study was conducted and our involvement with members of the scene. We then examine the athletes' academic attitudes, goals, and involvement in their first months on campus. Next, we analyze their involvement in three spheres of university life— athletic, social, and classroom—and the impact of this involvement on their academic attitudes and performance. Last, we discuss the series of pragmatic adjustments they forge, which reflect the gradual erosion of their earlier academic goals and idealism. We conclude by offering a structural analysis of athletes' experiences within the university, which shows how and why they become progressively alienated and detached from academics. We suggest several educational and athletic policies that might help to ameliorate this situation.

METHODS AND SETTING

The Research

Over a four-year period (1980–1984), we conducted a participant-observation study of a major college basketball team. We used team field research strategies (Douglas, 1976) and differentiated, multiperspectival roles to enhance our data gathering and analysis. I (first author) was initially granted access to the team because the coaches became interested in our earlier works on the sociology of sport (Adler and Adler, 1978; Adler, 1981). After reading these and talking with me, they perceived me as an expert who could provide valuable counsel on interpersonal, organizational, and academic matters. Although college and professional sports settings are generally characterized by secrecy and an extreme sensitivity to the insider-outsider distinction (see Jonassohn, Turowetz, and Gruneau, 1981), I gradually gained the trust of significant gatekeepers, particularly the head coach, and was granted the status and privileges of an assistant coach. As the "team sociologist," my primary duty was to informally counsel players on social, academic, and personal matters and help them make the adjustment to college life and athletics.

This role allowed me to become especially close to the athletes, who came to me with their problems, worries, or disgruntlements. Becoming an active member (Adler and Adler, 1987) and interacting with other members on a daily basis was also the only way I could penetrate the inner sanctum and achieve the type of rapport and trust necessary for the study.[1]

The second author assumed the outsider role, "debriefing" me when I returned from the setting, looking for sociological patterns in the data, and ensuring that I retained a sociological perspective on my involvement. She helped me conduct a series of intensive, taped interviews with 7 of the coaches and with the 38 basketball players who passed through the program during the four years.[2] She also helped construct the final analysis and written reports.

The Setting

The research was conducted at a medium-size (6,000 students) private university (hereafter referred to as "the University") in the mid-south-central portion of the United States. Most of the students were white, suburban, and middle class. The University, which was striving to become one of the finer private universities in the region, had fairly rigorous academic standards. The athletic department, as a whole, had a very successful recent history: The women's golf team was ranked in the top three nationally, the football team had won their conference in each of the previous four seasons, and the basketball team was ranked in the top forty of Division I NCAA schools and in the top twenty for most of two seasons. They had played in postseason tournaments every year, and in four complete seasons they had won approximately four times as many games as they had lost. Players were generally recruited from the surrounding region. Most of them came from the lower and middle classes, and 70 percent of them were black. In general, the basketball program represented what Coakley (1982) and Frey (1982) have termed big-time college athletics. Although it could not compare to the upper echelon of established basketball dynasties or to the really large athletic programs that wield enormous recruiting and operating budgets, its recent success has compensated for its small size and lack of historical tradition. The University's basketball program could best be described as up-and-coming. Because the basketball team (along with other teams in the athletic department) was ranked nationally and sent graduating members into the professional leagues, the entire athletic milieu was imbued with a sense of seriousness and purpose.

---

[1] For a more detailed discussion of the methodological issues involved in this research, see Adler (1984).

[2] Some individuals were interviewed several times, at various stages of their socialization process.

ACADEMIC EXPECTATIONS

Contrary to the recent negative thought, noted earlier, most of the athletes we observed entered the University feeling idealistic about their impending academic experience and optimistic about their likelihood of graduating. Their idealistic orientation and aspirations derived from several sources. First, they had received numerous cultural messages that a college education would enhance their ability to be successful in our society (cf. Semyonov and Yuchtman-Yaar, 1981). These messages were reinforced by their families, their most outspoken significant others. One sophomore described his family's involvement in his academic career: "When my mom calls she always asks me, first, 'How you feelin','' second, 'How you doin' in school?' She won't even let me talk 'bout basketball 'til she hear I'm doin' okay in school. She always be thinkin' 'bout my future and wantin' me to get that degree." College coaches also reinforced these messages. During recruitment, the coaches stressed the positive aspects of a college education and the importance of graduating (cf. Cross, 1973). The athletes accepted the rhetoric of these sports personnel (what Tannenbaum and Noah [1959] called "sportuguese"), but they never really considered what a higher education entailed. Thus, a third factor fostering their optimism about academics was their naïve assumption that after attending college for four years they would automatically get a degree. They never anticipated the amount or kind of academic work they would have to do to earn that degree. Many of them had not taken a sequence of college preparatory courses in high school.[3] Thus, their optimism was based largely on their "successful" academic careers in high school ("I graduated high school, didn't I?") and on their belief that as college athletes they would be academically pampered ("I heard you can get breaks on grades because you're an athlete"). Arriving freshmen commonly held the following set of prior expectations about their future academic performance: (1) they would go to classes and do the work (more broadly conceived as "putting the time in"); (2) they would graduate and get a degree; and (3) there would be no problem.

Of the entering athletes we observed, 47 percent ($n = 18$) requested placement in preprofessional majors in the colleges of business, engineering, or arts and sciences, indicating their initially high academic aspirations and expectations. One sophomore gave the rationale behind his choice of a major: "You come in, you want to make money. How do you make money? You go into business. How do you go into business? You major in business, and you end up having to take these business courses, and you really don't think about it. It sounds okay." Despite warnings from coaches and older teammates that

---

[3] Several sociological studies have noted that the admission standards for athletes are lower than those for the general student body, leading to the admission of academically marginal, ill-prepared students (Edwards, 1984; Purdy et al., 1982; Sack, 1977; Shapiro, 1984; Spady, 1970).

it would be difficult to complete this coursework and play ball, they felt they could easily handle the demands.

Another group of freshmen, who had no specific career aspirations beyond playing professional basketball (45 percent, $n = 17$), were enrolled by their coaches in more "manageable," athletic-related majors such as physical education or recreation.[4] However, most of these individuals believed that they too would get a degree. Though they had no clear academic goals, they figured that they would somehow make it through satisfactorily. Only a small number of individuals in our sample (8 percent, $n = 3$) entered college with no aspirations of getting a degree. Either these individuals were such highly touted high school players that they entered college expecting to turn professional before their athletic eligibility expired, or they were uninterested in academics but had no other plans. Their main concern, then, was to remain eligible to play ball. But they never seriously considered the possibility that they would be barred from competition because of low grades.

In their first few months on campus, athletes' early idealism was strengthened. During these summer months, the coaches repeatedly stressed the importance of "getting that piece of paper." Once the school year began, freshman athletes attended required study halls nightly, were told how to get tutors, and were constantly reminded by the coach to go to class. One freshman, interviewed during the preseason, indicated his acceptance of the coaches' rhetoric: "If I can use my basketball ability to open up the door to get an education, hopefully I can use my degree to open up the door to get a good job. . . . I think that's really important to Coach, too, 'cause in practice he always be mentioning how important the degree is an' everything."

Although these athletes unquestionably cared more about their athletic and social lives than their academic performance, getting through school, at least in the abstract, was still important to them. For most, this period of early idealism lasted until the end of their freshman year. After this time, their naïve, early idealism gradually became replaced by disappointment and growing cynicism as they realized how difficult it was to keep up with their schoolwork. They encountered unexpected problems in the articulation of the athletic, social, and academic spheres of the University.

ATHLETIC EXPERIENCES

A major difference athletes encountered in moving from high school to college lay in the size of the athletic sphere. In high school, athletics was primary to their self-identities; but in college, it played an even more central role in their

---

[4] This figure includes a small number of athletes who decided, usually during their sophomore or junior years, not to play professionally but to go into an athletically related occupation such as coaching.

lives. It dominated all facets of their existence, including their academic involvement and performance.

A primary change in their athletic involvement was rooted in the *professionalization* of the sport. Upon entering college, freshman athletes immediately noticed its commercialization (cf. Coakley, 1982; Eitzen, 1979; Hoch, 1972; Sack, 1977; Underwood, 1980). They were no longer playing for enjoyment. This was big business ("there's a lotta money ridin' on us"). As a result, basketball changed from a recreation to an occupation (cf. Ingham, 1975). The occupational dimensions of the sport and their desire to perform well intensified the pressure to win (cf. Odenkirk, 1981; Underwood, 1980). A senior described this emphasis on winning: "In college the coaches be a lot more concerned on winning and the money comin' in. If they don't win, they may get the boot, and so they pass that pressure on to us athletes. I go to bed every night and I be thinkin' 'bout basketball. That's what college athletics do to you. It take over you mind."

Professionalization also brought with it the fame and glamour of media attention. During the season, athletes were regularly in the newspaper and on television and were greeted as celebrities whenever they ventured off campus. Overall, then, the professionalization of college athletics drew athletes' focus to this arena and riveted it there.

Playing on the basketball team also demanded a larger share of athletes' *time* in college than it had in high school. In addition to the three hours of practice daily ("two-a-days" on weekends during the preseason), players were expected to watch films of other teams, to be available for team meetings, to return to their dorm rooms by curfew, and to leave the campus for two to five days at a time for road trips.[5] They also had to spend a certain amount of their time with athletically related others: the media, fans, and boosters (rich businesspersons who contributed money and wanted to feel close to the program). This involvement often conflicted with potential academic time: Afternoon practice conflicted with the required courses or labs in certain majors, games and road trips conflicted with the time athletes needed for exams and term papers, and booster functions cut into their discretionary time. By the end of their first year, most athletes acknowledged that their athletic-related activities affected their academic performance. As one senior explained: "We got to go two-a-days, get up as early as the average student, go to school, then go to practice for three hours like nothing you have ever strained. . . . It's brutal 'cause you be so tired. Fatigue is what makes a lot of those guys say 'Chuck it, I'm goin' to sleep.' You don't feel like sittin' there an' readin' a book, an' you not goin' comprehend that much anyway 'cause you so tired." Fatigue (cf. Edwards, 1984) and restricted time for studying caused many athletes to give

---

[5] Edwards (1984:7) has estimated that during the season, basketball players spend fifty hours a week preparing for, participating in, recovering from, and traveling to games.

up and cease caring about their academic work. Thus, rather than use the little free time they had to catch up on their studies, they usually chose to spend it socializing or just sleeping.

Athletes' academic performance was also affected by *coaches' intervention* in their academic lives. Assistant coaches handled academic matters for the athletes, declaring their majors, registering them for courses, adjusting their schedules, and periodically contacting their professors (to monitor their progress). Athletes, therefore, were largely uninvolved in academic decision-making and did not interact directly with professors, academic counselors, or academic administrators. As a result, they failed to develop the knowledge, initiative, or, in many cases, the interest to handle these academic matters themselves. As one sophomore stated, "The day before class you go up to the office and they hand you a card that got your schedule all filled out on it. You don't say nothin' or think nothin' 'bout it, you just go. And it kinda make you feel like you not involved in it, 'cause you don't have nothin' to do with it. Like it's they's job, not yours."

Because the coaches managed these administrative matters, the athletes developed a false sense of security, a feeling that someone was looking out for them academically and would make sure that they were given another chance, a feeling that they could foul up and not have to pay the consequences. They believed that their coaches dominated their professors and the administrators, that they would be "taken care of" academically, and that they need not involve themselves in this arena. This also led them to distance themselves from their academics and to diminish their effort.

Having formed this belief, many athletes were surprised to discover, usually sometime during their sophomore or junior year, that this overseeing and management extended to administrative areas only. Coaches placed them in their courses, but they could not guarantee them special breaks. Athletes then realized, often too late, that they were responsible for attending classes and completing their assignments on their own and that they had to do the same work that other students did to pass their courses. Many athletes were shepherded through high school; therefore, they were ill-equipped to assume responsibilities in college and often failed to fulfill them.

Finally, the athletes received greater *reinforcement* for athletic performance than for academic performance. No one closely monitored their academic behavior, but they were carefully watched at games, practices, booster functions, and on road trips. The celebrity and social status they derived from the media, boosters, and fans brought them immediate gratification, which the academic realm, with its emphasis on future rewards, could not offer.

With a few exceptions, athletes' experiences within the academic realm brought neither close contact nor positive reinforcement. Like many other college students, athletes generally found their professors aloof and uninterested. One freshman gave his impressions of college professors:

At my high school back home, the teachers would make sure everyone done the reading before we went on to the next subject. The teachers really cared if the students got behind, so sometimes they would teach individually. But here, by the next time the class meets, they ask if anyone has any questions, and if no one says anything, then most of them would give a pop quiz. I cannot really say the teachers care here, because if you get behind it's your problem, not theirs.

Given the paucity of contact with the faculty, the lack of reinforcement within the academic realm, and the omnipresence of the coaches, media, fans, and boosters, who provided both positive and negative feedback on daily athletic performance, it became easier for athletes to turn away from academics and concentrate their efforts on sport.

SOCIAL EXPERIENCES

The athletes' social experiences also affected their academic performance. Their social lives at the University were dominated by their relationships with other athletes. They had initially expected to derive both friendship and status recognition from a wide variety of students, both athletes and nonathletes, as they had in high school (cf. Coleman, 1961; Cusick, 1973; Eitzen, 1975; Rehberg and Schafer, 1968; Spady, 1970). But instead of being socially integrated, they found themselves isolated (cf. Antonelli, 1970). They were isolated geographically because they were housed in the athletes' dorm in a remote part of campus. They were cut off temporally by the demands of their practices, games, study halls, and booster functions. They were isolated culturally by their racial and socioeconomic differences from the rest of the student body. They were isolated physically by their size and build, which many students, especially women, found intimidating. A freshman described his feelings of social alienation:

This school is nothing like I thought it would be when I left home. The social life is very different and I have to adjust to it. A main problem for me are the white people. Where I grew up, all my friends were black, so I really don't know how to act toward whites. Here, when I speak to some of them, they just give me a fake smile. I really can't understand the people here because this is college and everyone should have a good time socially.

Since they had few opportunities to interact with nonathletes, they formed extremely strong social bonds among themselves. Housed together in a dorm reserved almost exclusively for male athletes (primarily football and basketball players), they were bonded together into a reference group and peer subculture. Relations within this group were especially cohesive because they lived, played, and travelled together.

Within the dorm, athletes exchanged information about various individuals and how to handle certain situations. This helped them form common attitudes and beliefs about their athletic, social, and academic experiences. The peer subculture thus provided them with a set of norms and values that guided their interpretations and behavior within these three realms.

One of the most predominant influences of the peer subculture was its anti-intellectual and anti-academic character (cf. Coleman, 1960; Sack, 1977). Typically, dorm conversation centered on the athletic or social dimensions of the athletes' lives; little reference was made to academic, cultural, or intellectual pursuits (cf. Meggysey, 1971; Shaw, 1972). As one junior remarked, "If a athlete was living in the dorm with just ordinary people, what do you think they'll be talkin' about? Ordinary things. But you got all athletes here. What are they goin' be talkin' about? It won't be Reaganomics, believe me. It'll definitely be *Sports Illustrated*." Separating athletes from other students thus made their athletic reality dominant and distanced them from any academic inclinations they may have had. The same athlete continued:

> The two images are set apart because one side of us is, "My momma send me to school to be an engineer, and in order to be an engineer I gots to go to class every day and study hard," and the other side is "I come to school to play basketball. I didn't come to school to study that hard." So to keep those two images apart, to keep you thinking basketball night and day, they puts you in with all these other jocks dreamin' in they dream worlds.

The athletes' peer subculture also subverted academic orientations by discouraging them from exerting effort in academics. In fact, individuals who displayed too much interest, effort, or success in academics were often ridiculed, as one player described: "When most of the other guys are making D's and F's, if I work hard and get a B on a test, if I go back to the dorm and they all see I got a B, then they goin' snap on [make fun of] me. So most of the guys, they don't try. They all act like it's a big joke." Like the Chicano subculture Horowitz (1983) observed, the athletes' peer subculture valued education in the abstract, yet the commitments valued by the athletes' subculture conflicted with the commitments necessary to make that value carry over into practical reality. Their peers thus provided them with excuses and justifications that legitimated their poor academic performance and neutralized the importance of this realm in their self-identities.

CLASSROOM EXPERIENCES

Athletes' attitudes toward academics and their effort and performance were also affected by the difficulties and disillusionments they encountered in the classroom. Athletes believed that many professors labeled them as jocks be-

cause they looked different from most of the other students, they were sur-
rounded in their classes by other athletes, and they were identified by coaches
early in the semester to the professors as athletes. They perceived, then, that
professors treated them differently from the general student body. On the one
hand, because of the widely held subcultural lore that as college athletes they
would have special privileges and because of the important and visible role
they played at the University, they commonly thought that professors would
accord them greater tolerance—i.e., extra tutoring sessions, relaxed dead-
lines, relaxed academic standards (cf. Raney, Knapp, and Small, 1983). This
perception was fostered by their placement, especially in their freshman year,
in courses taught by sympathetic faculty members who tried to give them
extra attention or assistance. Because of these placements, athletes often began college thinking that academics would not be a major concern. On the
other hand, athletes also encountered a number of less sympathetic professors
who they thought stereotyped them as dumb jocks or cocky athletes. In these
cases they "rejected the rejectors" (Sykes and Matza, 1957), using persecution
as a rationale for disengaging from academics. One player discussed his experiences with professors:

> Some are goin' help you, if they can, and you can always tell who they are 'cause
> you got a bunch o' athletes in your class. Some try to make it harder on you.
> They're out to get you 'cause they feel like you living like a king and it shouldn't be
> that way. With those jerks, it don't matter how hard you try. They gonna flunk you
> just 'cause you a athlete.

This differential treatment served to reinforce their perceptions that they
were athletes more than students. Therefore, when they returned to their
dorm rooms at night, exhausted and sore from practicing, it became easier for
them to rationalize, procrastinate, and "fritter" (Bernstein, 1978) their time
away instead of studying.

Athletes also became uninterested in academics because of the *content* of
their classes. Many individuals placed in physical education or recreation
courses, even those who were fairly uninterested in academics from the beginning, felt that their courses lacked academic or practical merit and were either
comical, demeaning, or both. One sophomore articulated the commonly held
view: "How could I get into this stuff? They got me takin' nutrition, mental
retardation, square dancing, and camp counseling. I thought I was goin' learn
something here. It's a bunch o' b.s."

When athletes enrolled in more advanced or demanding courses to fulfill
their requirements, they often found themselves unequipped for the type of
work expected. Because of their inadequate academic backgrounds, poor
study habits, tight schedules, peer distractions, and waning motivation, the
athletes often became frustrated and bored. Their anticipated positive feedback from academics was replaced by a series of disappointments from low

grades and failed classes. One player described how his failures made him feel inadequate and uncertain: "When I first came here I thought I'd be goin' to class all the time and I'd study and that be it. But I sure didn't think it meant studyin' all the time. Back in high school you just be memorizin' things, but that's not what they want here. Back in high school I thought I be a pretty good student, but now I don't know."

Athletes' experiences in the classroom were thus very different from their preconceptions. The work was harder and they were not taken care of to the extent they had imagined. Because of the intense competition in the athletic arena, they became obsessed with success (Harris and Eitzen, 1978). Their frequent academic failures (or, at best, mediocre grades) led to their embarrassment and despair, which caused them to engage in role-distancing (Ball, 1976) and to abandon some of the self-investment they had made in their academic performance. To be safe, it was better not to try than to try and not succeed. As we noted earlier, this posture was reinforced by their peer subculture.

ACADEMIC ADJUSTMENTS

As college athletes progressed through school, they changed their perspectives and priorities, re-evaluating the feasibility of their original optimistic, albeit casually formed, academic goals. This caused them to effect a series of *pragmatic adjustments* in their academic attitudes, efforts, and goals.

First, whenever possible, athletes externalized the blame for their academic failures. Failures, for instance, were not caused by their own inadequacies or lack of effort but by boring professors, stupid courses, exhaustion, the coaches' demands, or injury. This allowed them to accept the frequent signs of failure more easily and served as an important neutralizing mechanism for their competitiveness.

More importantly, athletes re-examined their academic goals. Because of their initially optimistic expectations, some athletes had declared majors based on career choices that sounded good to them or their parents (e.g., doctor, teacher, engineer, or businessman). About one fourth of the individuals who began in preprofessional majors stayed in these majors all the way through college and graduated.[6] Nevertheless, these individuals generally expended less effort and had less success than they had initially anticipated. Though they graduated in their original major, their academic performance was largely characterized by an attitude of getting by; in most cases, they achieved only the minimum GPA and took the minimum number of hours required for eligibility. One junior described how his attitude toward academ-

---

[6] These figures represent rough estimates based on the number of individuals who graduated, the number of individuals who used up their eligibility, and projections for individuals still in the program. They are intended to be suggestive rather than exact.

ics had changed during his years at college: "If I was a student like most other students I could do well, but when you play the calibre of ball we do, you just can't be an above-average student. What I strive for now is just to be an average student. My best GPA was 2.75. You just don't find the time to do all the reading."

More commonly, athletes in preprofessional majors found that a more concrete adjustment was necessary. The remaining three quarters of this group dropped out of preprofessional programs and enrolled in more manageable majors. This shift indicated that they had abandoned both their academic idealism and their earlier career goals. Nevertheless, they still maintained the goal of graduating, regardless of the major. As one player commented, "Look at George [a former player]. He was a rec major, but now he's got a great job in sales, working for some booster. It don't matter what you major in as long as you keep your nose clean and get that piece of paper."

Athletes who began their college careers with lower academic aspirations, majoring in physical education or recreation, made corresponding adjustments. Approximately one fifth of these athletes held onto their initial goal and graduated in one of these fields. But like the preprofessional majors, they did not perform as well as they had planned. The other four fifths realized, usually relatively late, that their chances of graduating from college were slight. This genuinely distressed them, because getting a degree had become both a hope and an expectation. They shifted their orientation, then, toward maintaining their athletic eligibility. A junior's remarks illustrate how this shift affected his attitude toward academics:

> I used to done thought I was goin' to school, but now I know it's not for real. . . . I don't have no academic goals no more. A player a coach is counting on, that's all he think about is ball. That's what he signed to do. So what you gotta do is show up, show your smilin' face, try as hard as you can. Don't just lay over in the room. That's all the coach can ask. Or else you may not find yourself playing next year.

By their senior year, when they had completed their final eligibility requirements, many members of this last group entirely abandoned their concern with their academic performance.[7] As one senior put it, "I just be waitin', man. I be waitin' for my shot at the NBA. I be thinking about that all the time. Once the season is over, I be splittin'. I don't see no reason to go to classes no more."

As a result of their experiences at the University, athletes grew increasingly cynical about and uninterested in academics. They accepted their marginal status and lowered their academic interest, effort, and goals. They progressively detached themselves from caring about or identifying themselves with this sphere.

---

[7] Ironically, however, even the marginal players never abandoned their dreams of making it in the NBA.

DISCUSSION

We have just described how college athletes progress from an early phase of idealism about their impending academic experiences to an eventual state of pragmatic detachment. The initial differences among the athletes in academic aptitudes, skills, and expectations eventually erode, causing even motivated freshmen to slip into a pattern of diminished interest and effort. The universality of this transformation (albeit with variations) suggests that there is something endemic to universities with big-time athletic programs that significantly affects athletes' orientations and behavior. An overview of the structural characteristics and embedded processes athletes encounter can help explain how and why their behavior changes.

First, athletes are overwhelmed by the demands and intensity of the athletic realm, which absorbs their concentration and commitment. They react by willingly entering the vortex of media celebrity and fantasies about future professional athletic careers. Second, athletes find themselves socially isolated from other students because of their geographic and temporal separation and their physical and cultural differences. In this way, athletes resemble Simmel's strangers—i.e., individuals who are full-fledged members of the group yet at the same time are outside of the group (cited in Wolff, 1950:402–408). By being part of, but not like, the larger student body, athletes experience the tension between nearness and distance. This heightens their sensitivity to their strangeness and focuses their attention on those elements they do not share with other students. As a result, the internal cohesion of their peer subculture becomes strengthened and their self-identities become more firmly anchored within it. Finally, for many athletes, the gap between their academic abilities and the university's expectations brings failure, frustration, and alienation. The peer subculture exacerbates the situation by devaluing academic involvement and neutralizing academic failure. Athletes respond by gradually withdrawing from their commitment to academics.

These structural factors are ultimately much stronger predictors of athletes' academic success than any of their initial individual characteristics. Their early academic involvement varies according to their goals, intelligence, talents, parents' attitudes, and other individual attributes, but the common structure of their experiences erodes many of these distinctions. Some athletes excel in all areas of college, and their success is well-publicized (cf. Looney, 1984). But most college athletes become disillusioned with academics by the time their athletic eligibility expires. This combination of structural factors influencing athletes' behavior, admittedly an extreme example, could also explain the academic careers of other students. Students who are distracted by an outside interest (i.e., a job or an avocation), who belong to a peer group that de-emphasizes the value of academics (i.e., a fraternity), and who become frustrated in the academic realm are likely to be academically unsuccessful in college.

The transformation athletes undergo corresponds to Goffman's (1959) conception of occupational role progression, in which the attitudes of persons socialized to a new social status (here, college athlete) evolve from belief to disbelief. This process begins with the learning and internalization of charter values. For college athletes, this occurs during the final year of high school and the freshman year of college, when they form moderately high aspirations and expectations about their academic futures. A period of desocialization then ensues, in which athletes progressively realize the structural constraints framing their situation. They become unable to accommodate the myriad, often conflicting, expectations and demands confronting them. As a result, they make choices and establish priorities that compromise their early idealism. Expediency thus supplants a concern for academics (Ingham and Smith, 1974), leading them to engage in role-distancing and to forge pragmatic adaptations that undermine their academic performance.

This in-depth investigation confirms the findings and interpretations of those studies positing a negative relationship between athletic participation and academic performance at universities with big-time athletic programs. We extend these analyses by showing that college athletes' academic performance is multifaceted and is determined less by demographic characteristics and high school experiences than by the structure of their college experiences. Athletes progress through a pattern of experiences, which first raises their hopes and then diminishes their opportunities for attaining the professed goals of the educational system.

Given the revenue that athletic programs generate, it may be unrealistic to expect this structure to change dramatically. However, there are several policy implications that can be derived from this research. First, athletes should be sheltered, as much as possible, from the enticing whirlwind of celebrity. This can best be accomplished by reinstituting the ban on freshman eligibility. Second, athletic dorms should be abolished and athletes should be better integrated into the larger university culture. In these ways we can begin to transform college athletes from strangers into neighbors. Third, athletes should be provided with more academic role models and advisors. The current arrangement, in which athletic personnel masquerade as academic advisors, functions counterproductively to the academic goals of the university. Only after these changes are made can college athletes begin to meet the goals of the educational system.

REFERENCES

Adler, P., *Momentum: A Theory of Social Action*. Beverly Hills, CA: Sage, 1981.
Adler, P., "The sociologist as celebrity: The role of the media in field research." *Qualitative Sociology* (1984) 7:310–26.

Adler, P., and P. A. Adler, "The role of momentum in sport." *Urban Life* (1978) 7:153–76.

Adler, P. A. and P. Adler, *Joining the Crowd: Membership Roles in Field Research*. Beverly Hills, CA: Sage.

Antonelli, F., "Psychological problems of top-level athletes." *International Journal of Sport Psychology* (1970) 1:34–39.

Ball, D., "Failure in sport." *American Sociological Review* (1976) 41:726–39.

Bernstein, S., "Getting it done: Notes on student fritters." Pp. 17–23 in J. Lofland (ed.), *Interaction in Everyday Life*. Beverly Hills, CA: Sage, 1978.

Coakley, J. J., *Sport in Society*. 2nd ed. St. Louis: Mosby, 1982.

Coleman, J. S., "Adolescent subculture and academic achievement." *American Journal of Sociology* (1960) 65:337–47.

Coleman, J. S., *The Adolescent Society*. New York: Free Press, 1961.

Cross, H. M., "The college athlete and the institution." *Law and Contemporary Problems* (1973) 38:151–71.

Cusick, P. A., *Inside High School*. New York: Holt, Rinehart and Winston, 1973.

Douglas, J. D., *Investigative Social Research*. Beverly Hills, CA: Sage, 1976.

Edwards, H., "The collegiate arms race: Origins and implications of the 'Rule 48' controversy." *Journal of Sport and Social Issues* (1984) 8:4–22.

Eitzen, D. S., "Athletics in the status system of male adolescents: A replication of Coleman's 'The Adolescent Society'." *Adolescence* (1975) 10:268–76.

Eitzen, D. S., "Sport and deviance." Pp. 73–89 in D. S. Eitzen (ed.), *Sport in Contemporary Society*. New York: St. Martin's, 1979.

Fine, G. A., "Preadolescent socialization through organized athletics: The construction of moral meanings in little league baseball." Pp. 79–105 in M. Krotee (ed.), *Dimensions of Sport Sociology*. Corning, NY: Leisure Press, 1979.

Frey, J. H., "Boosterism, scarce resources and institutional control: The future of American intercollegiate athletics." *International Review of Sport Sociology* (1982) 17:53–70.

Goffman, E., *The Presentation of Self in Everyday Life*. Garden City, NY: Anchor Doubleday, 1959.

Hanks, M. P. and B. K. Eckland, "Athletics and social participation in the educational attainment process." *Sociology of Education* (1976) 49:271–94.

Harris, D. S. and D. S. Eitzen, "The consequences of failure in sport." *Urban Life* (1978) 7:177–188.

Harrison, J. H., "Intercollegiate football participation and academic achievement." Paper presented at the Annual Meeting of the Southwestern Sociological Association, Dallas, 1976.

Henschen, K. P. and D. Fry, "An archival study of the relationship of intercollegiate athletic participation and graduation." *Sociology of Sport Journal* (1984) 1:52–56.

Hoch, P., *Rip Off the Big Game*. New York: Doubleday, 1972.

Horowitz, R., *Honor and the American Dream*. New Brunswick, NJ: Rutgers University Press, 1983.

Ingham, A. G., "Occupational subcultures in the work world of sport." Pp. 337–89 in D. W. Ball and J. W. Loy (eds.), *Sport and Social Order: Contributions to the Sociology of Sport*. Reading, MA: Addison-Wesley, 1975.

Ingham, A. G. and M. D. Smith, "The social implications of the interaction between spectators and athletes." Pp. 189–224 in J. Wilmore (ed.), *Exercise and Sport Science Reviews*. Vol. 2. New York: Academic Press, 1974.

Jonassohn, K., A. Turowetz, and R. Gruneau, "Research methods in the sociology of sport." *Qualitative Sociology* (1981) 4:179–97.

Looney, D. S., "He came out picture perfect." *Sports Illustrated* (1984) 60, 22:44–50.

Loy, J W., B. D. McPherson, and G. Kenyon, *Sport and Social Systems*. Reading, MA: Addison-Wesley, 1978.
Meggysey, D., *Out of Their League*. Berkeley, CA: Ramparts, 1971.
Michener, J. A., *Sports in America*. New York: Random House, 1976.
Nyquist, E. B., "Wine, women, and money: College athletics today and tomorrow." *Educational Review* (1979) 60:376–93.
Odenkirk, J. E., "Intercollegiate athletics: Big business or sport?" *Academe* (1981) 67:62–66.
Purdy, D. A., D. S. Eitzen, and R. Hufnagel, "Are athletes also students? The educational attainment of college athletes." *Social Problems* (1982) 29:439–48.
Raney, J., T. Knapp, and M. Small, "Pass one for the gipper: Student athletes and university coursework." *Arena Review* (1983) 7:53–59.
Rehberg, R. A. and W. E. Schafer, "Participation in interscholastic athletics and college expectations." *American Journal of Sociology* (1968) 73:732–40.
Sack, A. L., "Big time college football. Whose free ride?" *Quest* (1977) 27:87–97.
Sack, A. L. and R. Thiel, "College football and social mobility: A case study of Notre Dame football players." *Sociology of Education* (1979) 52:60–66.
Semyonov, M. and E. Yuchtman-Yaar, "Professional sports as an alternative channel of social mobility." *Sociological Inquiry* (1981) 1:47–53.
Shapiro, B., "Intercollegiate athletic participation and academic achievement: A case study of Michigan State University student-athletes." *Sociology of Sport Journal* (1984) 1:46–51.
Shaw, G., *Meat on the Hoof*. New York: St. Martin's, 1972.
Spady, W. G., "Lament for the letterman: Effects of peer status and extra-curricular activities on goals and achievements." *American Journal of Sociology* (1970) 75:680–702.
Spivey, D. and T. A. Jones, "Intercollegiate athletic servitude: A case study of the black Illinois student-athletes, 1931–1967." *Social Science Quarterly* (1975) 55:939–47.
Sykes, G. M. and D. Matza, "Techniques of neutralization." *American Sociological Review* (1957) 22:664–70.
Tannenbaum, P. M. and J. E. Noah, "Sportuguese: A study of sports page communication." *Journalism Quarterly* (1959) 36:163–70.
Underwood, J., "The writing is on the wall." *Sports Illustrated* (1980) 52, 21:36–71.
Webb, H., "Social backgrounds of college athletes." Paper presented at the Annual Meeting of the American Alliance for Health, Physical Education, and Recreation, St. Louis, 1968.
Wolff, K. H. (ed. and trans.), *The Sociology of Georg Simmel*. New York: Free Press, 1950.

15. *The Black "Dumb Jock": An American Sports Tragedy*

HARRY EDWARDS

Historically, widely experienced socioeconomic hardships in this country have always had an impact on blacks *first* and almost always *worst*. The circumstances of the black student athlete in the 1980s affirm the validity of this contention.

For as long as organized sports participation has been associated with American education, the traditionally somewhat comic, not altogether unappealing "dumb jock" image of the student athlete has endured. Though over the years there have been some notable efforts by journalists, academicians, and sports activists to expose the desperately serious realities masked by this caricature, only recently has American society been jolted into recognizing the extensive and tragic implications of widespread educational mediocrity and failure among student athletes, and—no less importantly—that "dumb jocks" are not born; they are being systematically created.

The fact of negative academic outcomes, then, does not in and of itself significantly distinguish the careers of black student athletes from those of their non-black peers in sports to which blacks have access in numbers—most particularly in basketball and football. Rather, it is the disparate character of black student athletes' educational experiences that has spawned special concern.

Black student athletes from the outset have the proverbial "three strikes" against them. They must contend, of course, with the connotations and social reverberations of the traditional "dumb jock" caricature.

But black student athletes are burdened also with the insidiously racist implications of the myth of "innate black athletic superiority," and the more blatantly racist sterotype of the "dumb Negro" condemned by racial heritage to intellectual inferiority. Under circumstances where there exists a pervasive belief in the mutual exclusivity of physical and intellectual capability, and where, furthermore, popular sentiment and even some claimed "scientific evidence" buttress notions of race-linked black proclivities for both athletic prowess and intellectual deficiency, it should come as no surprise that the shameful situation of the black student athlete has been for so long not only widely tolerated but expected and institutionally accommodated.

But the exploitation of black student athletes is not occasioned and perpet-

---

SOURCE: Harry Edwards, "The Black 'Dumb Jock': An American Sports Tragedy," *The College Board Review* 131 (Spring 1984), pp. 8–13.

uated merely through the unwitting interplay of sportslore and racist stereo-types. The sociological etiology of their circumstances is far more complex. Many of the social forces determining black student athletes' extraordinary vulnerability to athletic exploitation have been affecting black society gener-ally and the black family in particular for decades.

Sports, over the last 40 years, have accrued a reputation in black society for providing extraordinary, if not exemplary, socioeconomic advancement opportunities. This perspective has its origins in black identification with the athletic exploits and fortunes of Jesse Owens, Joe Louis, Jackie Robinson, and other pre- and early post-World War II black sports heroes. In the contempo-rary context, blacks also find ample, if only ostensible, vindication of their overwhelmingly positive perspectives on sports. For instance, though blacks constitute only 12 percent of the U.S. population, in 1983 just over 55 percent of the players in the National Football League were black, while 25 of the 28 first round National Football League (NFL) draft choices in 1981 were black. As for the other two major professional team sports, 74 percent of the players making National Basketball Association rosters and 81 percent of the starters during the 1981–82 season were black, while blacks constituted 19 percent of America's major league baseball players at the beginning of the 1983 season.

Black representation on sports honor rolls has been even more dispropor-tionate. For example, the last 10 Heisman Trophy awards have gone to black collegiate football players. In the final rushing statistics for the 1982 NFL season, 36 of the top 40 running backs were black. In 1982, not a single white athlete was named to the first team of a major Division I all-American basket-ball roster. Similarly, 21 of the 24 athletes selected for the 1982 National Basketball Association (NBA) All-Star game were black. And since 1958, whites have won the NBA's Most Valuable Player title only three times as opposed to 20 times for blacks. And, of course, boxing championships in the heavier weight divisions and "most valuable player" designations in both colle-giate and professional basketball have been dominated by black athletes since the 1960s.

Black society's already inordinately positive disposition toward sport has been further reinforced through black athletes' disproportionately high visibil-ity in the mass media, compared to other high prestige occupational role models (e.g., doctors, lawyers, engineers, and college professors).

Black families' attitudes and expectations concerning sports, then, are deeply influenced by the media and by perspectives on sports held more generally in black society. Research carried out by Melvin Oliver of UCLA discloses, for example, that black families are four times more likely than white families to view their children's involvement in community sports as a "start in athletic activity that may lead to a career in professional sports."

The already heightened black emphasis upon sports achievement that is fostered through myths, stereotypes, family and community attitudes, and the media is further intensified by black youths' early educational and athletic experiences. For example, as soon as someone finds that a particular black youngster can run a little faster, throw a little harder, or jump a little higher than all of his grammar school peers, that kid becomes—as sportscaster Frank Gifford would say—something "really special." What this usually means is that, beyond sports excellence, from that point on little else is expected of him. By the time many black student athletes finish their junior high school sports eligibility and move on to high school, so little has been demanded of them academically that no one any longer even expects anything of them intellectually.

As a result of a lack of creditable academic expectations and standards, and the disproportionate emphasis placed upon developing their athletic talents from early childhood, an estimated 25–35 percent of high school black athletes qualifying for scholarships on athletic grounds cannot accept those scholarships because of accumulated high school academic deficiencies. Many of these young men eventually end up in what is called, appropriately enough, the "slave trade"—a nationwide phenomenon involving independent scouts (some would call them "flesh peddlers") who, for a fee (usually paid by a four-year college) searches out talented but academically "high risk" black athletes and places them in an accommodating junior college where their athletic skills are further honed through participation in sports for the junior college while they accumulate grades sufficient to permit them to transfer to the sponsoring four-year school.

At the collegiate level, a systematic rip-off begins with the granting of a four-year "athletic scholarship," technically given one year at a time under existing National Collegiate Athletic Association (NCAA) rules. This means that though the athlete is committed to the school for four years, the school is committed to the athlete for only one.

Under circumstances where the grades obtained in many of the courses taken by student athletes are deficient or "automatic" or "fixed" rather than earned, there is little wonder that so many black scholarship student athletes manage to go through four years of college enrollment virtually unscathed by education. Not surprisingly either, studies indicate that as many as 65–75 percent of those black athletes awarded collegiate athletic scholarships may never graduate from college (as opposed to 30–35 percent of white student athletes). Of the 25–35 percent who do eventually graduate from the schools they play for, an estimated 60–65 percent of them graduate either with physical education degrees or in "Mickey Mouse" jock majors specifically created for athletes and generally held in low repute (as compared to approximately 33 percent of white student athletes in such majors).

It was precisely these tragic circumstances that prompted Joe Paterno, 1982 Division I football "Coach of the Year" to quite candidly and succinctly exclaim in January 1983 from the floor of the NCAA convention in San Diego: "For fifteen years we have had a race problem. We have raped a generation and a half of young Black athletes. We have taken kids and sold them on bouncing a ball and running with a football and that being able to do things athletically was going to be an end in itself."

With the end of collegiate athletic eligibility, the former student athlete faces new realities. The black "blue chipper" who completes his eligibility but is not drafted or within reasonable reach of achieving a degree tends no longer to be perceived on campus as a "big gun." Rather, he is frequently seen as a potential embarrassment to the athletic department, his former coaches, and his school. Because of his academic circumstances and his failure to be drafted, he constitutes a "loose canon" on the deck, a potential source of disenchantment and dissension within the ranks of new recruits and student athletes still having sports eligibility. There are no more fast academic fixes, no more fancy fictions, about fame, fortune, and fat city forever. Now the hope all too often is that he will simply go away—the farther, the faster, the better, the more easily forgotten.

Even those student athletes who are drafted by the pros soon learn that the actual realities are quite different from the rumored rewards that have fueled and motivated their athletic development. Approximately 8 percent of the draft-eligible student athletes in collegiate basketball, baseball, and football are actually drafted by professional teams each year. Of the black athletes drafted most are *not* offered professional contracts. Among these, a minority will return to school to complete degrees. But far too many of these former aircraft carriers degenerate into athletic "Flying Dutchmen," season after season drifting pathetically from one professional tryout to another, victims of a dream that has become a perpetual nightmare of futility and disappointment, holding to the hope of professional stardom until age and despair compel them to face the realities of life after sports.

Unlike the white student athlete, the black student athlete tends to have a less economically viable background and tends to come from a more transient community. The latter is also less likely than the former to secure financial support for post-eligibility college matriculation. The result is that there is a much lower social and financial "safety net" under the black collegiate athlete than under the white athlete. When the black collegiate athlete fails to graduate or sign a professional contract, he is therefore much more likely than the white athlete to find himself on the street. This has contributed to the fact that among this group, expressions of "disengagement trauma" sometimes have been severe to the extreme—including antisocial behavior, substance abuse, "nervous breakdowns," and even suicides.

Only 2 percent of the athletes drafted will ever sign a professional contract, and just over 60 percent of these are back on the street within 3–4 years. In the National Football League, where blacks constitute 55 percent of the players and where the average athlete will play only four-and-a-half years, according to NFL figures between 70 and 80 percent of the players have no college degree. Among athletes in the National Basketball Association, where 74 percent of the players are black and where the average playing career lasts only 3.2 years, the graduation figures are equally dismal.

It is simply not understood in black society that despite the fact that 74 percent of the players in professional basketball are black, 55 percent in professional football, and 19 percent in professional baseball, there are still just over 1,400 black people (up from about 1,100 before the establishment of the United States Football League) making a living as professional athletes in these three major sports today. And if one added to this number all the black athletes making a living as professionals in all other American sports, all the blacks making a living in minor and semiprofessional sports leagues, and all the black trainers, coaches, and doctors making a living in professional sports, there would still be less than 2,400 black Americans making a living in professional athletics today.

Fortunately, what we have systematically created we can oftentimes systematically reconstruct in a more productive and humane guise.

What, then, can be done to ameliorate the problems of educational mediocrity and failure among black student athletes? And who has the responsibilities to do it?

One frequently advocated option must be eliminated at the outset. This is the idea of a mass black exodus from American sport. Such a retreat would be ill advised even if it were achievable—which it is not in our sport-saturated society. Sport is simply too important, too influential, and too deeply embedded in American life for blacks to abstain from involvement.

It is also the case that, for all of its drawbacks, sports participation has generated many concrete and intangible benefits for black society. It has provided a portion of the black student athlete population—myself included— a means of achieving an education and of establishing productive careers in both sport and other occupational areas. Sport has also been a powerful source of black spiritual sustenance, a forum where black pride, courage, intelligence, and competitiveness have been exhibited and reaffirmed. Indeed, the athletic field is second only to the battlefield in providing demonstrable proof that what blacks have lacked in America is not the competitiveness, the initiative, the will, the fortitude, or the intelligence to excel. What we have lacked principally are equitable circumstances and opportunities. Blacks, therefore, must be involved in sport because we are inextricably involved with America.

What is called for is not a black retreat from sport but reflection upon the black situation in sport followed by a collective and coordinated offensive aimed, first, at aiding student athletes currently vulnerable to academic victimization and athletic exploitation, and, second, at eliminating or neutralizing the social and institutionalized forces responsible for the systematic creation and accommodation of the black "dumb jock."

One step in that direction was the passage of rule 48 by the NCAA in January 1983. It was perhaps also a somewhat inept step given that the educational standards set by the rule were embarrassingly low and that they have an impact principally upon pre-college academic preparation rather than post-enrollment collegiate matriculation.

Put most simply, rule 48 stipulates that beginning in 1986, freshman athletes who want to participate in sports in any of the nation's 277 Division I colleges and universities must have (1) attained a minimum score of 700 (out of 1600 possible) on the Scholastic Aptitude Test (SAT) or a score of 15 (out of a possible 36) on the American College Test (ACT) as well as have achieved a C average in 11 designated high school courses, that include English, mathematics, social sciences, and physical sciences. Further, as *The NCAA News* bulletin stipulated, rule 48

> does not interfere with the admission policies of any Division I institution. Nonqualifiers under this legislation may be admitted and attend class. Such a student could compete as a sophomore if he or she satisfies the satisfactory-progress rules and would have four varsity seasons starting as a sophomore if he or she continues to make satisfactory progress.
>
> Further, under related Proposal No. 49-B, any student who achieves at least 2.0 in all high school courses but does not meet the new terms of No. 48 can receive athletically related financial aid in his or her first year, but cannot practice or compete in intercollegiate athletics. This student would have three varsity years of participation remaining.

Its shortcomings notwithstanding, I am fundamentally supportive of rule 48 because it communicates to young athletes, beginning with those who are sophomores in high school, *that we expect them to develop academically as well as athletically*. Indeed, this motivational aspect of rule 48 may, in the final analysis, prove most beneficial to that vast majority of high school student athletes who are never going to enroll in college because they will face the realities of life after sports in a "high tech" world immediately upon graduation from high school.

Ironically, rule 48 has been vehemently denounced as racist in its impact, if not its intent, by many black educators. The essential problem is that rule 48 would exacerbate the financial difficulties faced by athletic programs at traditionally black colleges and thereby reduce still further their ability to compete with traditionally white institutions for "blue chip" black athletic talent and the rewards of sports success. Unlike, say, Michigan or Stanford, black colleges—which, for the most part, recruit only black athletes, a majority of whom score less than 700 on the SAT or less than 15 on the ACT—could not financially maintain both a roster of academically ineligible freshman recruits and a roster of active scholarship athletes. A solution proposed by many black college presidents is that black Division I colleges should be exempt from rule 48 or should be allowed to implement their own independent—usually meaning lower—academic standards for athletic eligibility.

It is my view that any exemption of black colleges from the full scope of requirements stipulated under provisions of rules 48 and 49-B would be ill-advised and highly counterproductive so long as all other Division I schools are required to abide by such requirements. Separate or lowered academic standards or both for sports participation at black colleges would constitute nothing less than an officially mandated return—through the locker room door, so to speak—to separate and inherently unequal intellectual expectations and, inevitably, educational aspirations and opportunities for blacks. In the name of accommodating fiscal deficiencies in black college athletic programs, those proposing that black colleges be exempt from specified academic performance standards would barter away the gains of more than a hundred years of struggle for objectivity in this nation's official perceptions of black intellectual and academic capability. To legitimize separate or lowered academic standards or both for blacks at any level—elementary school, secondary school, or college—would be to send a negative signal to citizens of this nation, a signal whose message would reverberate for years as it relates to its impact upon the future of the black community. The message would be, "The 'dumb Negro'—according to *black educators*—is real."

I believe that the fiscal problems in black colleges' athletic programs should be addressed as such and not resolved at the expense of black educational and intellectual integrity. Rule 48 should and must be universally implemented in some guise, at least within the ranks of Division I institutions.

But, it is by no means sufficient for colleges and universities to establish regulations such as rule 48 that essentially have an impact upon student athletes' educational preparation at the high school level. Having passed rule 48, college and university officials must now specify what they are going to do to correct the situation on their own campuses—especially since it is only at the collegiate level that a direct educational obligation is assumed, by implied contract, in exchange for student athlete sports participation.

Over the recent years, I have recurrently proposed the following to colleges and universities as an effective program of action:

1. That each NCAA member institution, upon contacting a prospective student athlete for purposes of athletic recruitment and at the beginning of each academic year once such student athlete is enrolled, provide each student athlete with a statement, by sport, of anonymously listed student athlete academic majors, grade point averages by major and year in college or both, and student athlete graduation rates covering the previous five-year period in each sport. This statement should be compiled, verified, and certified as accurate by the office of the university president or chancellor, with copies made available, upon request, to the public.

2. Replacement of the standard four-year athletic grant-in-aid now given "one year at a time" with a guaranteed five-year grant-in-aid for all scholarship student athletes recruited as freshmen, with proportionate scholarship

support for student athletes transferring from junior colleges (e.g., a scholarship student athlete transferring from a two-year junior college would be guaranteed and granted three years of grant-in-aid support by the university to which he is transferring).

3. The elimination of freshman eligibility for athletic participation, including the elimination of practice and all other athletic obligations at Division I universities for all student athletes in order to give them time to make the social transition from high school to college and to establish a solid academic foundation.

4. Establishment of specific rules defining grounds upon which a student athlete's grant-in-aid may be rescinded, and provisions for independent grievance and due process proceedings should the student athlete desire to challenge such action.

5. Diagnostic testing of each student athlete enrolled in order to determine academic weaknesses and tutorial support and educational development programs targeted specifically for these student athletes, with such support programs accredited and periodically reviewed by an independent, recognized academic accrediting agency.

6. Additional guaranteed financial support for student athletes accruing academic deficiencies as a result of fulfillment of athletic obligations. Where applicable, this provision would make support for summer school as well as for post-eligibility matriculation beyond the guaranteed five years of grant-in-aid support obligatory (through the bachelor's degree).

7. Guaranteed support [beyond the five-year grant-in-aid and support obligation stipulated in (6) above] as a function of the hours per week above 40 spent by student athletes preparing for, traveling to and from, and participating in sports pursuits (through achievement of the bachelor's degree).

8. Establishment of a mandatory, standardized orientation program for incoming and continuing student athletes, alerting them to the realities of collegiate sports participation—especially concerning such issues as their chances of signing a professional contract, topical developments such as drug abuse and disengagement trauma among athletes, the importance of achieving not only a degree but marketable skills, and national statistics reflecting educational and occupational outcomes for athletes.

9. The establishment of specific, professionally acceptable, and enforceable standards of medical service and treatment for collegiate athletes, including regular health checks for all athletes during the season instead of only at the beginning of the season, and provision for injury compensation, therapy, and rehabilitation—including catastrophic injury and travel insurance.

Black communities, black families, and black student athletes themselves also have critically vital roles to play in efforts to remedy the disastrous educational consequence of black sports involvement. The undeniable fact is that through its blind belief in sport as an extraordinary route to social and economic salvation, black society has unwittingly become an accessory to, and a major perpetuator of, the rape, or less figuratively put, the disparate exploitation of the black student athlete. We have in effect *set up our own children* for academic victimization and athletic exploitation by our encouragement of, if not insistence upon, the primacy of sports achievement over all else. We have then sold them to the highest bidders among collegiate athletic recruiters, and literally on the average received nothing in return for either our children or ourselves. It would, therefore, constitute a fraudulent rationalization and a dangerous delusion for blacks to lay total responsibility for correcting this situation upon educational institutions and sports governing bodies.

But even Rip Van Winkle eventually woke up. As a people, we have responsibility to learn about the realities of black sports involvement—its liabilities as well as its opportunities—and to teach our children to deal with these realities intelligently and constructively. As a people, we can no longer permit many among our most competitive and gifted youths to sacrifice a wealth of personal potential on the altar of athletic aspirations, to put playbooks ahead of textbooks. We must also recognize that, in large part, the educational problems of black student athletes will be resolved not on the campus, but *in the home*. Black parents must insist upon the establishment and enforcement of creditable academic standards at all educational levels, and they must instill black youths with values stressing the priority of educational achievement over athletic participation and even proficiency. We must understand that having "graduated" is not synonymous with being "educated." Thus, it is not sufficient to rely upon grades alone. Standards imply testing for skills development. If this tack is taken, I am convinced young black student athletes will rise to the occasion in academics no less than they have in the realm of athletics.

And finally, it must be made unequivocally clear that in the last analysis, it is black student athletes themselves who must shoulder a substantial portion of the responsibility for improving their own circumstances. Education is an activist pursuit and cannot in reality be "given." It must be obtained "the old fashion way"—*one must earn it!* Black student athletes, therefore, must insist upon educational discipline no less than athletic discipline among themselves, and they must insist upon educational integrity in athletic programs rather than, as is all too often the case, merely seeking the most parsimonious academic route to maintaining athletic eligibility. The bottom line here is that if black student athletes fail to take an active role in establishing and legitimizing a priority upon academic achievement, nothing done by any other party to this American sports tragedy will matter—if for no other reason than the fact that *a slave cannot be freed against his will*.

16. *Blaming the Victim: NCAA Responses to Calls for Reform in Major College Sports*

GEORGE H. SAGE

In his insightful volume *Blaming the Victim* (1976), William Ryan describes a scene in which a well-known American actor, impersonating a Southern Senator conducting an investigation into the reasons why the American military was unprepared for the attack by the Japanese on December 7, 1941, and wanting to find a way to exonerate the military, suspiciously booms out, "And what was Pearl Harbor *doing* in the Pacific?" Here is a humorous, but classic, example of blaming the victim. We laugh at the obviously convoluted reasoning that leads to such a question, but I shall argue in this [selection] that the same process is employed by the NCAA and its member universities in their responses to the many outcries for reform in major college athletics; they repeatedly engaged in classic examples of blaming the victim. The victims, in this case, are student-athletes.

Blaming the victim is an ideological process; meaning it is a more or less integrated set of ideas and practices held by a social group about how things should and do work. Social mechanisms for the promotion of an ideology is typically in the hands of the most powerful sector of the group and functions to maintain the existing social order (Mannheim, 1936; Zeitlin, 1968). According to Mannheim (1936), an ideology is formed from the "collective unconscious" of a group and is rooted in the interest of the powerful sector in maintaining the status quo. Similarly, Ryan (1976) says: "Victim blaming is cloaked in kindness and concern, and . . . it is obscured by a perfumed haze of humanitarianism" (p. 6).

This is not the place to describe in detail the numerous scandals that have beset intercollegiate athletics over the past few years (Brooks, 1985; Looney, 1985 a,b,c; Nack, 1986; Ostow, 1985; Shuster, 1985; Sanoff & Johnson, 1986; Wolff & Sullivan, 1985; Underwood, 1980). One outrage is followed by another one of greater proportions. Hardly a week goes by without new revelations about violations of NCAA rules by major university football or basketball programs. Each revelation is followed by righteous promises by university authorities and the NCAA that change is on the way—that collegiate athletics

SOURCE: George H. Sage, "Blaming the Victim: NCAA Responses to Calls for Reform in Major College Sports," *Arena Review* 11 (Fall 1987), pp. 1–11.

167

are going to be "cleaned up." But, as Padilla & Weistart (1986) note: "Scandals develop with a frequency that is astonishing even to the most cynical of observers, and the major regulatory body, the NCAA, seems unable to stop them or the conditions from which they breed." And Cramer (1986), after a thorough study of the NCAA and major college athletics contended: "A glimpse at the workings of college sports programs and at the efforts of the NCAA to reform them is not exactly a pretty sight" (p. 6).

The most recent NCAA effort to do something about the endemic problems of major college sports has been the creation of a university Presidents Commission. It has promised to re-direct the destiny of intercollegiate athletics. But it, too, seems to be floundering; in summarizing its fall 1986 meeting Sullivan (1986a) reported that the Commission "gave no firm evidence of any commitment to reform" (p. 17).

For all of the chest pounding about reform by the NCAA, university athletic departments, and the Presidents Commission, an analysis of changes that have been made or proposed over the past few years clearly shows that the structure of college athletics has been left intact; there have been no substantive changes in the *structure* of college sports—a structure that is largely responsible for the corruption and abuses. Hope for meaningful reform by the NCAA is a chimera.

By structure of college athletic programs I am referring to its rigidly authoritarian organization in which rules and policies affecting student-athletes are enacted and imposed without any input from the largest group in college sports—the student-athletes. I am also referring to the now common practice of keeping athletes involved in one way or another with their sport during the season for 20 to 40 hours per week practicing, watching film, skull sessions, travel from one coast to another for games, and to being away from campus and missing classes.[1] I'm referring to weight training programs, film analysis, and "informal" practice sessions in the "off season" period; indeed, athletes are expected to remain in training year-round. I'm referring to the pressures brought on by mass media attention and the expectations of alumni and boosters who demand championship teams. I'm referring to universities who use athletes as an arm of the public relations department. This is the essential structure of major university athletics, especially in football and basketball.

Instead of addressing structural issues that perpetuate scandals, the NCAA has identified student-athletes as the major cause of the continuing problems suffered by collegiate sports, and various forms of legislation have been passed which are designed to evoke a public image of student-athletes as the real culprits. As rules have been enacted to further control and restrict student-athletes, the NCAA and university authorities claim that they are attempting to solve the problems of college sports. What they have done, instead, is blame the student-athlete for the massive failure of college athletic authorities to address the real causes of corruption, cheating, and unethical behavior that are now well-documented in major college athletics—they have engaged, clearly and directly, in a classic display of "blaming the victim." This has been accomplished with such intensity and persistence that alternative images have been unthinkable.

Proposition 48 (bylaw 5-1-(j) in the NCAA *Manual*) is a good example of focusing the blame for problems in college sports on student-athletes. By requiring that student athletes achieve certain minimum high school grades and standardized test scores to be eligible for participation, the NCAA can publicly proclaim its interest in having qualified students as college athletes, and, of course, no one in his right mind can really quarrel with holding athletes to academic standards. Even many black leaders who recognized the unequal and adverse effects that this legislation would have on black athletes supported the passage of Proposition 48 because to have been against it would have seemed to have implied that they were not for academic standards.[2]

Actually, what all this charade for academic standards has done is deflect attention away from the commercialized structure of major college athletic programs and focused it on the athletes. The only reason that there is an academic standards problem in college sports is that coaches and other university officials have been willing to admit academically unqualified students and, through various ingenious methods, have been able to keep them eligible for one purpose: to help the university athletic teams maintain competitive success in the world of commercialized sport. Moreover, for athletes who are academically qualified and seriously interested in the pursuit of a college degree, the structure of major college sports leads them to become progressively detached from academics and gradually resigned to inferior academic achievement (Adler & Adler, 1985). Proposition 48, then, does nothing to alter the major cause of poor academic performance of many athletes.

Other recent examples of blaming athletes for collegiate sports ills are the imposition of drug testing programs and the punishment of football athletes for improper distribution of complimentary tickets (Latimer, 1986; Looney, 1986; "NCAA authorizes testing for drugs," 1986). In the first case, student-athletes' personal rights are infringed upon and in the second place they are characterized as ungrateful liars because they violated NCAA rules for distributing their game tickets. In both cases, the athletes are defined as the problem and measures are taken to punish them.

It does not take any in-depth investigating into equitable treatment provisions in college sports to see how blatantly athletes are victimized by the drug testing system. While athletes must undergo mandatory, random drug testing, there is no provision for coaches, athletic directors, sports information directors, athletic trainers, athletic secretaries, and various sundry others who are part of the big business of college sports to undergo the same testing. Instead, the public is encouraged to dwell on all the alleged defects of athletes. Moreover, there seems to be no understanding or acknowledgement that the social conditions of big time college sports may actually contribute to drug abuse by athletes. Several recent studies have documented the pressures and the incredible time demands that go with being a major university athlete (Adler & Adler, 1985). It does not seem to be stretching the imagination to think that some of this contributes to drug use by athletes.

As for the distribution of game tickets, NCAA rules forbid athletes from giving their complimentary tickets to anyone except "family members, relatives, and fellow students designated by the student-athlete." At the same time, it is common practice for football and basketball coaches to receive a liberal allotment of complimentary game tickets—LSU football coach Bill Arnsparger receives 26 tickets per game—with no restrictions on their distribution.

But there is an even larger, but related, issue here. Collegiate athletes cannot endorse products or engage in any commercialization of their athletic talent or name recognition. Meanwhile, football and basketball coaches can engage in an incredible variety of commercial activities to supplement their salary. Some of the common perks and benefits of being a major college coach are television and radio shows, worth up to $80,000, free use of a car, university provided housing, and use of university facilities for summer camps. A few coaches have quite lucrative sporting equipment endorsement contracts. For some coaches the perks and benefits push their annual income over $200,000 (USA Today, Special Report, September 24, 1986). It is NCAA rules like this that led Congressman John Moss, during a Congressional investigation of the NCAA, to say: "I have been writing law in this House for 26 years and I've never seen anything approaching the inequality of NCAA procedures" (Good, 1979, p. 35).

The generic process of Blaming the Victim can be seen most clearly in the unwillingness of the NCAA to permit the payment of a salary to college athletes. Here is a reform that has been suggested by a wide spectrum of persons both inside and outside the collegiate sport industry, but it is a reform the NCAA has steadfastly refused to consider.[3] Instead, by a clever manipulation of euphemisms student-athletes are provided a "scholarship" which is said to be a "free ride" to a college education.[4] This clever definition of the situation on the NCAA's terms makes it sound like student-athletes are the beneficiaries of a generous philanthropy by institutions of higher education. In addition, leaders of intercollegiate sport promote an ideology-based doctrine of the adequacy and legitimacy of amateurism, further obviating outright payment.

The college sports establishment uses the acquisition of a highly valued source of human capital—a college education—which, ironically, can be obtained at a relatively low cost (about $5,000 per year at state supported universities) as compensation to athletes. The subtle impression that is conveyed is that athletes are well-rewarded; what is created is an interpretation of reality that serves the interests of the college sports establishment.

The problem is that the total domination of major college athletics by commercial concerns and the undisguised salience of the profit motive make it quite obviously a business enterprise. The athletic director at Michigan accurately summarized the state of major college sports. He said: "This is a business, a big business. Anyone who hasn't figured that out by now is a damned fool" (Denlinger & Shapiro, 1975, p. 252). Today many major universities have athletic budgets over $12 million, football games generate over $33 million for competing teams, and the NCAA has an annual budget in excess of $57 million ("Big Bucks," 1984; McCallum, 1986; "NCAA to spend," 1984).

The main employers in the collegiate sport business are the various colleges and universities, under the control of the NCAA. Employee groups are coaches, athletic directors, athletic trainers, sports information directors, and sundry secretaries and equipment managers, all of whom negotiate in an open market for salaries and wages, and all of whom may be said to make a livable income. As noted above, coaches make a *very good* income, when all the perks and benefits are added to their salary.

The largest single employee group in the big business of college sports—the student-athletes—does not receive a salary or wage, per se. Indeed, NCAA rules prohibit athletes from accepting an offer of a salary or any other money under penalty of permanent debarment from collegiate sports participation. Although athletes are the key in the financial success of big-time college sports through their indispensability in the production process, they are victimized by a system that conceals the deception of extremely low remuneration with references to "scholarships" and "free rides." Thus, while the NCAA preaches the virtues of amateurism and a spartan existence to student-athletes, it lavishly rewards coaches, athletic directors, and some of the other ancillary employees in the college sport enterprise.[5]

In the case of major college sports, enacting legislation that focuses on the control, restrictions, monitoring, and punishment of student-athletes is a brilliant strategy for justifying a perverse system of social action by the NCAA and its member universities. Meanwhile the exploitation of collegiate athletes can continue unabated. Far from desiring to change the basic structure of major college sports, the NCAA and member universities strive for a change in social conditions by means of which existing patterns will be made as tolerable and comfortable as possible.

Blaming the student-athlete, and refusing to change the fundamental structure that perpetuates the continuing series of scandals, is an evasion of the responsibility that collegiate authorities have for either treating athletes as equal members of a commercial enterprise or withdrawing from commodified sports and returning to the promotion of an education model of college sports, where sports are used as a medium for the individual development of the participants.

NOTES

1. An analysis of the time the average BYU football player devoted to football was 2,202 hours per year, or 275 8-hour days, and it has been estimated that college football players devote 60

hours per week and basketball players 55 hours per week during their respective season (Eitzen & Purdy, 1986). A study by Sack & Thiel (1979) found that 68% of the Notre Dame football players who later played NFL football reported that playing at Notre Dame had been as physically and psychologically demanding as professional football.

2. There is a large literature dealing with the pros and cons of Proposition 48; see, for example, Sack (1984) and Edwards (1984).

3. See statement made by Dale Brown, head men's basketball coach at Louisiana State University, on pg. 3 of *The NCAA News*, February 27, 1985; see statement by Don Canham, athletic director at Michigan, on pg. 2 of *The NCAA News*, March 13, 1985; see statements by coaches in "Agents Don't Play By the NCAA Rules," 1984. Nationally reknown philosophers (Weiss, 1986) and economists (Becker, 1985) have called for the payment of major university athletes. Ernie Chambers, Nebraska State Senator, has introduced a bill into the Nebraska legislature to put University of Nebraska football players on the state payroll and pay them an appropriate salary.

4. In lieu of a salary or wage, college athletes are given "scholarships" which are basically coupons redeemable only at a university accounting office for educational expenses incurred by athletes in exchange for playing on an intercollegiate sports team. The scholarship is for a prescribed set of educational expenses and can only be used to pay those expenses. In most cases, the athletes do not actually handle the money themselves. Paper transactions between the athletic department and the university accounting office consummates the financial arrangement.

5. The strong hold of amateurism on the public conscience is a thing of the past. The International Olympic Committee has already dropped the word amateur from its rule book, and it has indicated that it will allow the entry of professionals in the 1980 Olympic Games ("IOC to allow," 1985; Sullivan, 1986b).

REFERENCES

Adler, P. & Adler, P. A. "From idealism to pragmatic detachment: The academic performance of college athletes." *Sociology of Education*. 58: 241–250, 1985.

"Agents don't play by the NCAA rules." *Greeley (Colo.* Tribune). November 2, 1984, p. 81.

Becker, G. S. "College athletes should get paid what they're worth." *Business Week*. September 30, 1985, p. 18.

"Big bucks." *Sports Illustrated*. 61 (September 5): 148, 1984.

Brooks, B. G. "A self-inflicted football injury." *Rocky Mountain News*. August 26, 1985, p. 18-G.

Cramer, J. "Winning or learning? Athletics and academics in America: Kappan special report." *Phi Delta Kappan*. 67: 1–8, 1986.

Denlinger, K. & Shapiro, L. *Athletes for sale*. New York: Thomas Y. Crowell, 1975.

Edwards, H. "The collegiate athletic arms race: Origins and implications of the 'Rule 48' controversy." *Journal of Sport and Social Issues*. 8 (Winter/Spring): 4–22, 1984.

Eitzen, D. S. & Purdy, D. A. "The academic preparation and achievement of black and white collegiate athletes." *Journal of Sport and Social Issues*. 10 (Winter/Spring): 15–27, 1986.

Good, P. "The shocking inequities of the NCAA." *Sport*. 68 (January): 35–38, 1979.

"IOC to allow limited entry of pros in '88." *Rocky Mountain News*. March 1, 1985, p. 96.

Latimer, C. "CU reports 21 misuse tickets." *Rocky Mountain News*. September 26, 1986, p. 113.

Looney, D. S. "Tickets, please." *Sports Illustrated*. 64 (September 15): 65, 1986.

Looney, D. S. "Big trouble at Tulane." *Sports Illustrated*. 62 (April 8): 34–39, 1985a.

Looney, D. A. "Troubled times at Memphis State." *Sports Illustrated*. 62 (June 24): 36–41, 1985b.

Looney, D. S. "Deception in the heart of Texas." *Sports Illustrated*. 63 (September 30): 28–35, 1985c.

McCallum, J. "In the kingdom of the solitary man." *Sports Illustrated*. 65 (October 6): 64–78, 1986.

Mannheim, K. *Ideology and utopia*. New York: Harcourt Brace Jovanovich, 1936.

Nack, W. "This case was one for the books." *Sports Illustrated*. 64 (February 24): 34–42. 1986.

"NCAA authorizes testing for drugs." *Rocky Mountain News*. January 15, 1986, p. 73.

"NCAA to spend $41.6 million this year: Budget balanced by shifting surplus." *The Chronicle of Higher Education*. 29 (September 5): 34, 1984.

Ostow, R. "Sanctions against Florida might be just the beginning." *USA Today*. January 14, 1985, p. 4C.

Padilla, A. & Weistart, J. C. "National commission needed to improve college athletics." *The Washington Post*. July 6, 1986.

Ryan, W. *Blaming the victim*. (Revised edition.) New York: Vintage Books, 1976.

Sack, A. "Proposition 48: A masterpiece in public relations." *Journal of Sport and Social Issues*. 8 (Winter/Spring): 1–3, 1984.

Sack, A. L. & Thiel, R. "College football and social mobility: A case study of Notre Dame football players." *Sociology of Education*. 52: 60–66, 1979.

Sanoff, A. P. & Johnson, K. "College sports' real scandal." *U.S. News & World Report*. September 15, 1986, pp. 62–63.

Shuster, R. "Drug scandal at Clemson linked to 'obsession to win.'" *USA Today*. March 12, 1985, p. 4C.

Sullivan, R. "Barely touching the platter," *Sports Illustrated*. 65 (October 13): 17, 1986a.

Sullivan, R. "Toward an open olympics." *Sports Illustrated*. 65 (October) 60: 15, 1986b.

Underwood, J. "The writing is on the wall." *Sports Illustrated*. 52 (May 19): 36–72, 1980.

USA Today, Special Report, "Money and college athletics." September 24, 1986.

Weiss, P. "Pro sports in college." *U.S. News & World Report*. March 10, 1986.

Wolff, A. & Sullivan, R. "Blowing a fuse over the news." *Sports Illustrated*. 63 (November 11): 52–53, 1985.

Zeitlin, I. M. *Ideology and the development of sociological theory*. Englewood Cliffs, N.J.: Prentice-Hall, 1968.

17. *College Sports Reform: Where Are the Faculty?*

JOHN C. WEISTART

Many surprising things have been revealed in the recent college sports scandals. But one of the most surprising is the historical absence of effective faculty oversight of the educational experiences of student athletes in big-time college programs. Among the revelations that point to a failure of faculty governance in these matters, the most embarrassing must surely be the dismal graduation rates of athletes in several basketball and football programs. Reports in the popular press indicate that 4 percent of black basketball players graduated at the University of Georgia in a recent period. At one Big Ten school, the graduation rate for all basketball players was 9 percent. At Memphis State, the NAACP—and not the faculty, it might be noted—discovered that in a ten-year period, no black basketball player graduated. The list goes on and covers twenty or more schools that should have been embarrassed.

The troublesome question remains: where were the faculties? In almost all instances, the low graduation rates were accumulated over a period of time. While each individual campus yields a different story, available evidence suggests a common and consistent failure on the part of faculties to pick up available signals that things were awry in their revenue-producing sports programs.

A significant commentary on the present state of athletics and higher education can be found in the manner in which improprieties are revealed. The moving force is much more likely to be a newspaper reporter than a concerned faculty member. Indeed, in two of the past three years, Pulitzer Prizes were awarded to reporters who in effect told university communities how their athletic programs were being run.

The faculty, of course, is not the only entity on campus that should be concerned about serious misdirections in the athletic program. The president and, as we have recently seen, the board of trustees often share responsibility. But faculties have a particularly important role to play in shaping a school's academic program and, most importantly, in insuring its integrity. In most universities, the faculty's responsibility for defining the institution's educational mission is explicit. Faculties frequently are quick to indicate the primacy of their role in preserving the rigor and legitimacy of the school's other

SOURCE: John C. Weistart, "College Sports Reform: Where Are the Faculty?" *Academe* 73 (July/August 1987), pp. 12–17.

academic pursuits. Moreover, because it is relatively unaffected by the pragmatic demands of day-to-day administration, the faculty properly serves as the conscience of the university, especially in matters that affect an issue as basic as the institution's academic reputation. As a number of universities have learned, the misdeeds of the athletic department can have a great effect in shaping public perceptions on such matters. Hence, the question remains: where were the faculties?

The recent sports scandals suggest at least two significant issues relating to the faculty's role in athletics. First, why did not faculties assume a greater oversight role over the deteriorating conditions of big-time sports? And second, can we expect a better faculty performance in the future? Virtually every school that has experienced a significant sports controversy has subsequently undertaken a major internal review. Typically, the resulting report promises more careful control for the future, often with significant input from the faculty. But we must ask whether, once the warm winds of scandal have passed, faculties will do better than they historically have.

One view of the role of faculty governance in athletics offers little reason for optimism over the long term. A variety of factors, including the highly commercial nature of athletics, work against an effective governance function by faculty members. There is little evidence that universities are prepared to change this business orientation in athletics. Thus, the persistent tension with the university's educational goals is likely to continue. This raises the prospect of a regulatory role for the faculty that is extremely time consuming and that holds limited prospects of success.

A more fruitful alternative for faculties would be to urge that the basic structure of college sports be reoriented to reduce its conflict with the university's educational goals. Two changes offer particular promise. One involves eliminating the present university monopoly on preprofessional training in football and basketball. By providing the exclusive training for aspiring athletes, universities assume a social role that inevitably places great downward pressures on academic standards. A second change would end the Athletics Arms Race, as Harry Edwards aptly calls it. At present, college athletics operates according to an arrangement in which the rewards of athletic success go to those who spend the most and demand the least academically. Faculties interested in ending this economic and academic pressure would seek to implement changes that rewarded the athletically successful with recognition, but broadly disbursed the revenues from broadcasting, tournaments, and bowl games.

The fact of the faculty's limited oversight of the academic performance of the athletic department is not much in doubt. Less clear are the reasons why faculties choose not to be involved in matters that have turned out to hold such a great capacity for institutional embarrassment.

Faculties at many universities can properly argue that their athletic departments have been organized purposely to operate at great distance from the normal channels of faculty governance. In some instances—the University of Georgia, for example—the athletic association is a legally distinct entity and the faculty has no juridical claim to regulate its affairs. Even when the athletic department is "part of the university," autonomy may be *de facto*. Not infrequently this happens when a powerful coach insists, and a less forceful president agrees, that the supervision of athletes will remain with athletic personnel. Thus, unlike many other issues of academic policy, the special problems of athletes would not normally come before the faculty.

Ultimately, though, explanations based on internal governance structure are only partial ones. It is often unclear whether the autonomy of an athletic program is the cause or the effect of limited faculty oversight. As many of the recent in-house reform efforts confirm, when faculty assert a strong interest in the treatment and achievement of student athletes, structures can be found to accommodate this concern. Thus, it is likely that there are other, more substantive reasons why faculties have tolerated the considerable distance that many athletic programs have put between themselves and their universities' core academic function.

A search for alternative explanations suggests several points that warrant attention.

THE DIFFERENT NATURE OF A MAJOR ATHLETICS ENTERPRISE

Big-time athletics—again mainly football and basketball—have taken on a distinctive characteristic in recent years. At many schools, the athletic department operates as the entertainment division of the university. Largely as a result of the impact of television, big-time programs now produce events that compete with a variety of other offerings in the entertainment market. Increasingly, decisions are made with a view to insuring the suitability of the end product for broadcast purposes.

Most of the large football and basketball programs operate at a substantial profit, largely due to the impact of television. A trip to the Final Four in the NCAA basketball tournament pays each participating school over one million dollars, an amount greatly in excess of the operating expenses of the typical program. When revenues from the conference television package, national telecasts, and ticket sales are added, a three to one ratio of revenues to expenses is not uncommon in basketball. In football, with postseason bowls paying out a total of more than fifty-six million dollars, profits of two to four million dollars in a single program are often attained.

Such levels of profitability are not assured, of course, and continued success requires very astute, very pragmatic decisions about a variety of entertainment-related issues, including how to increase the size of the regular season television audience and how to select opponents so as to attract the attention of the bowls with the most lucrative broadcast contracts. Not surprisingly the entire orienta-tion of the athletic department adjusts to accommodate the demands of produc-ing a successful—that is, profitable—entertainment product. For the people who run the division, a strong business orientation is a necessity. Increasingly success within the profession of athletic administration is judged primarily, although not exclusively, by the dollar results an individual produces.

This athletics-entertainment venture is carried on in an environment that is unusually competitive. College athletics stands in sharp contrast to profes-sional sports in this regard. Revenue-sharing and financial support for weak competitors are the hallmarks of successful sports leagues. The worst NFL team gets as much from the league's lucrative national television contract as does the best. Quite the opposite situation is found at the college level. The greatest rewards from television go only to the most successful programs. These are typically the programs prepared to pay the most for recruiting, facilities, coaches' salaries, and promotion. And the most successful teams have the most to spend. The operative principle seems to be that a school must spend to win and must win to spend. Each new lucrative broadcast arrangement ups the ante and invites an expensive response.

The values important in these ventures are quite different from those that typically come into play in faculty governance decisions. Faculties are not terribly "bottom-line" oriented and have little experience in insuring commer-cial success in highly competitive markets. Indeed, the best of faculty values—deliberateness, a liberal concern for the treatment of individuals, and an openness that encourages the accommodation of differences—are antitheti-cal to the common ingredients of profitable business ventures.

Athletic personnel may thus come to feel that faculties have little to say about athletic policy that will be useful. For their part, faculties may have a natural reluctance to venture into areas where they will be neither welcome nor particularly effective. In the same vein, the trustees and presidents who determine organizational structure often take account of the lack of synergy in this match and develop lines of authority that insure that it does not occur. There is little to suggest to them that the success of the entertainment product will be enhanced by the opposite arrangement.

THE RISK OF BEING CO-OPTED

A second problem is that faculties involved in athletic policy making appear to run a particular risk of being co-opted into a lenient, if not overly favorable, view of the demands of the athletic department. While this is hardly inevita-ble, it does occur with sufficient regularity to suggest that a truly independent faculty governance role in athletics may be very difficult to achieve.

Various devices presently in use are intended to preserve a role for the faculty in athletics matters. Each NCAA school has a "faculty representative," for example. Rarely, though, is this position reflective of carefully gauged faculty sentiment. Direct election of the "faculty representative" by the faculty is rare if not nonexistent in big-time programs. More typical is the situation in which the person is designated by the university president after informal approval by the athletic department. Seldom are NCAA votes subject to systematic faculty review. For all of these reasons the faculty voice in NCAA matters has historically been neither loud nor distinctive.

Many schools have an athletic committee or similar entity that provides the occasion for faculty involvement in deliberations on athletically related issues. Again, at big-time schools, the faculty participation on these bodies has not been noted for its independence. Indeed, such bodies existed at most of the schools that have experienced major scandals in recent years.

The loss of independence by faculty members involved in athletic oversight is difficult to avoid. As already noted, "insuring athletic success" is often the stated goal of committees involved in this work and in the modern environment that means heeding the demands of an external marketplace. Athletic department personnel will consistently speak more authoritatively on these matters.

Other features of work on athletic committees present temptations not found elsewhere in university service. Offers of favorable seating at popular events, school-paid trips to postseason contests, and the opportunity to rub elbows with celebrity coaches and players will inevitably have the effect of reducing criticism and encouraging accommodation. This will be true even when these special rewards for committee service are wholly benign. Combining this bit of human nature with a selection process that favors candidates who have a sympathetic orientation to the athletic department, the mildness of the regulation undertaken by university athletic committees is not surprising.

THE MODEST PROFESSIONAL REWARDS FOR EFFECTIVE OVERSIGHT

Few incentives encourage a faculty member to engage in rigorous examination of athletic department policy. A promising career in English, physics, or geology is not likely to be advanced by correcting the defects of a big-time sports program that enjoys wide support on and off campus. Moreover, the task will seldom be either easy or abbreviated. In short, the absence of professional rewards for university service in the oversight of athletics, the athletic department's coolness to such a role, and the strong incentives to mind one's own business in academia combine to discourage vigorous faculty involvement in reviewing athletic department policy. Indeed, for those who are most promising in their academic endeavors, probing the athletic department may be among the least appealing of administrative assignments.

Almost all of the schools beset by major scandals in recent years have undertaken elaborate self-studies. The end result is typically a thorough report and a list of recommendations addressing a variety of reforms. Increased academic standards for athletes and closer institutional oversight of the athletic policy are commonly urged. The question can reasonably be asked whether these reform efforts provide reason for optimism about the future, either in terms of more effective faculty involvement in athletic matters or in terms of other institutional controls to prevent a recurrence of the problems of the past.

There will certainly be some short-term improvements. Almost every school that has looked at its athletic problems has agreed that standards should be raised for the admission of athletes and that the embarrassing graduation rates of the past should not continue. Moreover, in several schools, the individuals responsible for prior academic misdirections were unmasked and their associations with the university ended. And, in almost all cases, the mechanisms for institutional control were strengthened.

But serious problems are likely to remain. A review of the recent internal reform efforts will reveal that, despite the wide array of matters subjected to reconsideration, little or nothing has been done to address the fundamental cause of the recent scandals—the competitive pressures created by commercialization. Virtually every school that has endured severe academic embarrassment has emerged from its self-study continuing to embrace implicitly, if not explicitly, the notion that its athletic programs will not be "competitive." In the present environment, this means that the cycle of spending to win and winning to spend will continue.

If the evidence of the recent past is taken as a guide, such an orientation will present a considerable threat to the goals of academic rigor and integrity. Even where academic standards for the athletic department have been raised, the new standards are likely to be subjected to considerable downward pressures. As several schools have already learned, there will almost always be competitors willing to admit less-qualified athletes. Thus, a pledge to remain competitive commits a school to a course in which the determinants of success are frequently being influenced by the preferences of the lowest common denominator.

The decision to stay in the athletics arms race also means that the basic entertainment orientation of the athletic department is not likely to change. It can be hoped that personnel antagonistic to the academic function of the university will be eliminated and that more attention will be given to the athletes' classroom endeavors. But at the bottom line is a bottom line. Even allowing for the many good athletic directors who will execute their functions as their universities dictate, we should not be surprised to find that difficulties of the past reappear. With two-million-dollar bowl games and one-million-dollar basketball tournaments at stake, there will be great pressure to shave off the subtle edges of academic preparedness and substantive achievement. Again, over time some athletic departments will likely conclude that academic minimalism enhances their ability to compete.

Just as the basic orientation of the athletic department is unlikely to change, so are incentives for faculties to become involved in a sustained effort at oversight unlikely to increase. The faculty will continue to be ill-equipped to evaluate claims of necessity in a profit-oriented venture. As in the past, the faculty is apt to find itself deferring to the judgments of those who are more knowledgeable and who have more at stake. In addition, the occasions for reducing faculty independence will persist. And ultimately, the same low level of professional reward that has been evident in the past will attend future efforts at oversight, particularly as recent embarrassments fade. Thus, while things have changed, they have in many respects remained the same.

The time has come to reconsider the agenda for college sports reform. To date, the prevailing assumption has been that what is needed is mainly a tightening of the rules. By and large, the basic structure of big-time sports is left unaffected. These features seem inevitably to lead to a more time-consuming regulatory role.

A more positive approach would seek to modify the structural features of big-time sports that create undue pressure for the academic program. Rather than seeking to increase the degree of control that has to be exercised by faculties and others, this different agenda would undertake to reduce the need for intense oversight. Reform would be undertaken with the specific intention of introducing economic forces more naturally complementary to the university's educational goals.

In redirecting the present debate, attention should be given not only to the substance of proposals for change but also to the matter of how change will be achieved. Any internal, single-campus reform is destined to be ineffective in stemming the influences of commercialization in college sports. For a school that plans to operate a visible program, unilateral disarmament simply will not work. As noted, the intensity of the economic competition and the tools necessary to engage in it will in large measure be dictated by forces beyond the individual campus. Thus, if truly effective reform is to occur, it must be in a different forum, specifically one that has authority to impose collective controls. Several alternatives are available.

The NCAA is the logical group to provide the necessary legislative response. However, despite four years of repeated scandals, the NCAA has taken little action. The movement of this body has been so halting as to raise doubts about its basic resolves. While there is no particular reason to assume that the NCAA will take a new direction, the matter of resolve is one that can be affected by the actions of the constituent members. Thus, an appropriate first step for a concerned faculty would be to assert a more active interest in how their institution's votes on NCAA matters are cast.

But the NCAA is not the only forum available. In the event of continued inaction by that group, other outlets for concern will become increasingly attractive. An enhanced role for education accrediting organizations is properly explored. Most of these groups presently have authority to review the academic performance of any component of the university, including the athletic department. Much could be done to increase their role. A clear statement of academic standards, meaningful reporting of academic statistics, and the threat of suspension of accreditation offer the promise of an alternative that avoids the limitations of unilateral action.

Perhaps the ultimate forum for collective action is Congress. While college sports have historically enjoyed something approaching legislative immunity, this situation may be changing. In recent years, various bills have been introduced to address the ills of college sports. A continued failure of self-regulation by the NCAA increases the plausibility of this type of response. And the antimonopoly fervor in Congress in recent years suggests that such legislation might well take a different view of the economic ground rules of preprofessional sports than does the NCAA.

The issue of where further deliberation should occur is a procedural one. On the substantive side, the focus should shift from debates about merely tightening existing rules to a discussion of changing the basic structure of college sports. Two areas in particular offer the prospect of relieving the university's educational venture from much of the pressure that athletics presently creates.

First, the athletics arms race is not inevitable. A range of choices is in fact available that will ameliorate or eliminate it. Revenue sharing would offer the most complete tempering of the inclination toward commercial excess in individual programs, a lesson well learned by professional sports leagues. Schools would still receive the public recognition that attends success in championship events. But there would be no disproportionate financial bonanza for that outcome. Television rights, fees, and the like would be distributed among a wide group of participants, perhaps all who participate at a particular level of play.

The basic objective of a revenue-sharing arrangement would be to eliminate the pressures for bending academic and athletic rules that arise in the present environment. As occasional ups and downs in programs would carry no particular toll, most of the recent by-words—"win at any cost," "eligibility rather than real education," and the like—would lose their justification. Winning would, of course, still be important. But other values would become much more ready competitors because financial outcomes would have been made independent.

While revenue sharing is an anathema to many athletic administrators, those who take a broader view of university budgets may find it quite attractive. The vast majority of schools offering major sports programs would be better off under such an arrangement, for it offers the unavoidably attractive prospect of both enhancing revenues and reducing expenses. In addition, it promises a stability for the future that cannot be assured in the present environment, in which only winners are rewarded.

If control is not exercised over revenues, then the next logical step is the control of expenditures. In this area, further reform could simply involve an undertaking to execute more effectively a regulatory effort that presently receives only half-hearted attention. The NCAA has a number of rules ostensibly intended to equalize the competitive positions of a large range of schools. Thus, there are limits on the size of team rosters, the size of coaching staffs, and the permissible number of athletic scholarships. But to legislate parity only on these matters is almost certain to be ineffective as a control on competition. No spending controls presently exist for many other items that contribute to a school's competitive position. These include training and playing facilities, promotional expenses, salaries, student housing, and a long list of other items. Not surprisingly, with only a part of the expenditure budget subjected to regulation, the pursuit of competitive advantage finds ample alternative avenues through which to express itself. The incompleteness of the present economic regulation invites a corrective response in the form of more extensive budgetary controls.

A second structural issue warrants attention. At the present, a rather unnatural link exists between academics and athletics at the post-high-school level. A promising high school basketball or football player who wishes to secure further training effectively has no choice but to aspire to a four-year degree program. Moreover, the athlete must be a full-time student; part-time status is insufficient for eligibility. Other program options—community college, technical school, corporate sponsored teams, and minor leagues—are unavailable. In what must surely be one of the great non sequiturs of our society, we tell promising athletes in the two most popular high school sports that to get further physical training they must also embrace our most advanced form of post-high-school degree.

Thus, 100 percent of football and basketball players are required to choose an arrangement that only roughly 30 percent of their nonathlete peers select. Moreover, this limitation is not imposed on other aspiring athletes. Those interested in baseball, hockey, golf, and tennis all enjoy sports options not tied to education, let alone a full-time four-year education.

The contrived nature of the present structure should be a particular concern of faculties. A good deal of available evidence—including the experience of baseball players who can choose between college and minor leagues—suggests that perhaps as many as one-half of present college athletes in football and basketball would not choose the college option if good alternatives were available. Thus, educationally it appears that we may be forcing square pegs into round holes. At the minimum, many of the athletes are likely to have their attention focused elsewhere.

Colleges, of course, cannot be expected to bear the full burden of establishing noncollegiate options. But that does not mean that universities and their faculties are powerless to influence the present monopoly. In fact, universities have done much to perpetuate the existing arrangement. Faculties that wished to be relieved of the tensions created by the present compulsory relationships would seek to modify the NCAA rules that sustain them.

A variety of changes could be considered. The mildest alternatives would change existing rules on eligibility. At present, the NCAA embraces an extremely narrow view of amateurism. For the mere receipt of fifty dollars in compensation money, even for an appearance in a perfectly legitimate competition, a young athlete can be denied collegiate eligibility. In a world in which educational values come first, the goal would be quite different: athletes would be encouraged to test their semiprofessional and minor league opportunities before deciding on whether to go to college. An exploratory period of perhaps two years would be allowed. Those who later enrolled in a university presumably would have a more focused interest in the educational opportunity that was available. By the same token, since the university would no longer be the exclusive vehicle for post-high-school athletic training, it could reasonably demand that its athletes approximate the educational achievement of other students.

This [selection] can end where it began, with a reference to the shockingly low graduation rates achieved in several big-time athletic programs. It is difficult to imagine that a faculty at a serious university would tolerate the continuation of an academic program in which, for every student who graduated, nine others did not. Yet, in several athletic programs these levels of failure, and some even worse, were endured.

We would be reassured if we could believe that these institutional lapses were only inadvertent or temporary. However, the frequency of their occurrence and the presence of very powerful economic forces that reward low academic aspiration suggest that the causes are much more basic. Something other than a mere lack of attentiveness appears to be involved. This awareness counsels in favor of a greater boldness in the debate on college athletics than we have seen to date.

Specifically, the time has come to ask whether it is athletic success that is valued or the large dollars that increasingly attend it. The former has a role that can be comfortably accommodated at a university. Profit making, particularly as a part of an intense competitive market, fits much less well. The opportunity to separate athletics from excess does exist. Whether it is pursued is a matter over which the entities with the most at stake—the universities themselves—have considerable control.

■ FOR FURTHER STUDY

Adler, Peter, and Patricia A. Adler. "Role Conflict and Identity Salience: College Athletics and the Academic Role." *The Social Science Journal* 24, No. 4 (1987): 443–455.

Amdur, Neil. *The Fifth Down: Democracy and the Football Revolution*. New York: Delta, 1972.

Baumann, Steven, and Keith Henschen. "A Cross-Validation Study of Selected Performance Measures in Predicting Academic Success among Collegiate Athletes." *Sociology of Sport Journal* 3 (December 1986): 366–371.

Brede, Richard M., and Henry J. Camp. "The Education of College Student-Athletes." *Sociology of Sport Journal* 4 (September 1987): 245–257.

Bryant, James, ed. "Intercollegiate Sports." *Arena Review* 3 (1979): entire issue.

Case, Bob, H. Scott Greer, and James Brown. "Academic Clustering in Athletics: Myth or Reality." *Arena Review* (Fall 1987).

Chu, Donald, Jeffrey O. Segrave, and Beverly J. Becker, eds. *Sport and Higher Education*. Champaign, Ill: Human Kinetics Publishers, 1985.

Corbin, Charles B. *The Athletic Snowball*. Champaign, Ill.: Human Kinetics Publishers, 1977.

Cousins, Norman. "Football and the College." *Saturday Review* (September 28, 1963): 36.

Denlinger, Kenneth, and Leonard Shapiro. *Athletes for Sale: An Investigation into America's Greatest Sports Scandal—Athletic Recruiting*. New York: T. Y. Crowell, 1975.

DeVenzio, Dick. *Rip-Off U*. Charlotte, N.C.: The Fool Court Press, 1986.

Durso, Joseph. *The Sports Factory: An Investigation into College Sports*. Boston: Houghton Mifflin, 1975.

Edwards, Harry. "The Collegiate Athletic Arms Race: Origins and Implications of the 'Rule 48' Controversy." *Journal of Sport and Social Issues* 8 (Winter/Spring 1984): 4–22.

Eitzen, D. Stanley. "How We Can Clean Up Big-Time College Sports." *The Chronicle of Higher Education* (February 12, 1986): p. 96.

Eitzen, D. Stanley, and Dean A. Purdy. "The Academic Preparation and Achievement of Black and White Collegiate Athletes." *Journal of Sport and Social Issues* 10 (Winter/Spring 1986): 15–29.

Feinstein, John. *A Season on the Brink*. New York: Macmillan, 1986.

Frey, James H., ed. *The Governance of Intercollegiate Athletics*. West Point, N.Y.: Leisure Press, 1982.

Gerdy, John R. "No More 'Dumb Jocks.'" *The College Review Board* 143 (Spring 1987): 2–3, 40–41.

Greendorfer, Susan L., and Elaine M. Blinde. "'Retirement' from Intercollegiate Sport: Theoretical and Empirical Considerations." *Sociology of Sport Journal* 2 (June 1985): 101–110.

Haerle, Rudolph K., Jr. "Education, Athletic Scholarships, and the Occupational Career of the Professional Athlete." *Sociology of Work and Occupations* 2 (November 1975): 373–403.

Hammel, Bob. "Student Athletes: Tackling the Problem." *Phi Delta Kappan* 62 (September 1980): 7–13.

Hanford, George H. "Controversies in College Sports." *The Annals* 445 (September 1979): 66–79.

Hart-Nibbrig, Nand, and Clement Cottingham. *The Political Economy of College Sports*. Lexington, Mass.: D. C. Heath, 1986.

Hochfield, George. "The Incompatibility of Athletics and Academic Excellence." *Academe* 73 (July/August 1987): 39–43.

Isaacs, Neil D. *Jock Culture U.S.A*. New York: W. W. Norton, 1978.

Kennedy, Ray. "427: A Case in Point." *Sports Illustrated* (June 10, 1974): 87–100; (June 17, 1974): 24–30.

Kiger, Gary, and Deana Lorentzen. "The Relative Effects of Gender, Race, and Sport on University Academic Performance." *Sociology of Sport Journal* 3 (1986): 160–167.

Knapp, Terry J., and Joseph F. Raney. "Looking at Student-Athletes' Transcripts: Methods and Obstacles." *Arena Review* 11 (Fall 1987): 41–47.

Lapchick, Richard E., with Robert Malekoff. *On the Mark: Putting the Student Back in Student-Athlete*. Lexington, Mass.: D. C. Heath, 1987.

Leonard, Wilbert Marcellus II. "The Sports Experience of the Black College Athlete: Exploitation in the Academy." *International Review for the Sociology of Sport* 21 (1986): 35–49.

Marmion, Harry A., ed. "On Collegiate Athletics." *Educational Record* 60 (Fall 1979): entire issue.

Massengale, John D. "Coaching as an Occupational Subculture." *Phi Delta Kappan* 56 (October 1974): 140–142.

Morris, Willie. *The Courting of Marcus Dupree*. New York: Doubleday, 1983.

Naison, Mark, and Jim Ford. "College Sports—Out of Control." *Left Field* 1 (June 1978): 1, 7.

Nixon, Howard L. III. "Orientations Toward Sports Participation among College Students." *Journal of Sport Behavior* 3 (February 1980): 29–45.

Porto, Brian L. "College Athletics on Trial: The Mark Hall Decision and Its Implications for the Future." *Journal of Sport and Social Issues* 8 (Winter/Spring 1984): 23–34.

Porto, Brian L. "Athletic Scholarships as Contracts of Employment: The Rensing Decisions and the Future of College Sports." *Journal of Sport and Social Issues* 9 (Winter/Spring 1985): 20–36.

Purdy, Dean A., D. Stanley Eitzen, and Rick Hufnagel. "Are Athletes Also Students? The Educational Attainment of College Athletes." *Social Problems* 29 (April 1982): 439–448.

Purdy, Dean A., D. Stanley Eitzen, and Rick Hufnagel. "The Educational Achievement of College Athletes by Gender." *Studies in the Social Sciences* 24 (1985): 19–32.

Raney, Joseph, Terry Knapp, and Mark Small. "Pass One for the Gipper: Student-Athletes and University Coursework." *Arena Review* 7 (November 1983): 53–60.

Sack, Allen. "Proposition 48: A Masterpiece in Public Relations." *Journal of Sport and Social Issues* 8 (Winter/Spring 1984): 1–3.

Sack, Allen, and Robert Thiel. "College Basketball and Role Conflicts." *Sociology of Sport Journal* 2 (1985): 195–209.

Shapiro, Beth J. "Intercollegiate Athletic Participation and Academic Achievement: A Case Study of Michigan State University Student-Athletes, 1950–1980." *Sociology of Sport Journal* 1 (1984): 46–51.

Stevenson, Christopher L. "College Athletics and 'Character': The Decline and Fall of Socialization Research." In *Sport and Higher Education*, edited by Donald Chu, Jeffrey O. Segrave, and Beverly J. Becker. Champaign, Ill.: Human Kinetics Publishers, 1985, pp. 249–266.

Underwood, Clarence. *The Student Athlete: Eligibility and Academic Integrity*. East Lansing, Mich.: Michigan State University Press, 1984.

Underwood, John. "The Desperate Coach." *Sports Illustrated* (August 25, September 1, and September 8, 1969).

Underwood, John. "The Writing Is on the Wall." *Sports Illustrated* (May 19, 1980): 36–72.

Weber, Larry, Thomas M. Sherman, and Carmen Tegano. "Effects of a Transition Program on Student Athletes' Academic Success." *Sociology of Sport Journal* 4 (March 1987): 78–83.

Part Six

The Economics of Sport

A dilemma that characterizes contemporary professional sport and much of what is called amateur sport in the United States has been described by Roger Kahn: "Sport is too much a game to be a business and too much a business to be a game."[1] The evidence indicating a strong relationship between sport and money is overwhelming. Consider the following examples:

item: The Oakland Raiders, although operating at a profit before sellout crowds, moved to Los Angeles in 1982, where the potential profits were much greater. In 1987, the even more profitable Los Angeles Raiders signed a deal to move to Irwindale, twenty miles east of Los Angeles, because the economics were still stronger there.

item: The Meadowlands, a multisport complex in New Jersey, cost almost $400 million to build and costs taxpayers $35 million annually.

item: Herschel Walker left college—where he played for room, board, and tuition—a year early and signed with the New Jersey Generals for $4.5 million covering three years. In the first week after Walker signed, the Generals sold 12,000 season tickets generating $1.25 million in revenue.

item: In 1986, the athletic budget for the University of Michigan exceeded $16 million.

item: In 1985, college sports generated more than $1 billion, more than double the 1978 revenues.

item: In 1986, the Big Ten football teams received $20 million from donors who contributed, in addition to the cost of their tickets, for such perks as preferred seating in the stadium and a prestige place to park a car.[2]

item: CBS pays the NCAA $55.3 million a year through 1990 for the exclusive rights to televise the Division I men's basketball tournament. Each of the Final Four teams in 1988 received $1.15 million from the NCAA.

item: Each school in the 1988 Rose Bowl collected $5,592,578; the Sugar Bowl, $2,279,780; the Orange Bowl, $2,225,387; and the Cotton Bowl, $2,075,387.

item: Just counting base salary, University of Louisville basketball coach Danny Crum makes $110,022, compared to $97,750 for the university president. In addition, Crum receives a minimum of $80,000 annually from television and radio shows and a ten-year annuity worth $1 million.

item: The 1984 Summer Olympics were worth approximately $4 billion to Los Angeles and Southern California.

item: Marvin Hagler received $12 million and Sugar Ray Leonard $11 million for their 1987 fight in Las Vegas. The estimated dollar impact of that fight for Las Vegas was $100 million.

item: In 1987, John Elway, Denver Bronco quarterback, signed a six-year contract worth $12.7 million.

item: According to *Sport* magazine, the top 100 elite athletes in America made $140 million in 1986 (each of them made over $1 million with an average salary of $1,403,441). Michael Spinks led the list with $4 million; Moses Malone was the highest paid basketball player ($2,145,000); Jim Rice the best paid baseball player ($2,412,500); John Madden, the ex-coach turned broadcaster, earned $1 million a year from CBS, another $1 million from endorsements, and $327,500 from a coauthored book. He also receives $30,000 per speech.[3]

item: During 1986, the sporting goods industry grossed about $30.6 billion.[4]

item: Steffi Graf, West German tennis professional, made more than $4 million ($3.3 million in endorsements and $40,000 per appearance, plus winnings)[5] in 1987 when she was only 18 years old. Ivan Lendl, the top male tennis player, made over $6 million in earnings and endorsements.

item: CBS charged advertisers $600,000 per 30 seconds of commercial time for the 1987 Super Bowl. CBS allowed eight minutes for local stations during the game and the Denver affiliate (the Denver Broncos were one of the competing teams) charged $40,000 per 30 seconds to local advertisers.

item: An estimated $600 million was wagered on the 1987 Super Bowl ($500 million illegally).

item: In 1986, the combined network and local television and radio rights for major league baseball exceeded $300 million.

item: Ninety percent of the world's baseballs, including those used in the major leagues, are manufactured in Port-au-Prince, Haiti, by United States owned corporations. The labor cost to produce a baseball that sells for $2.50–$4.50 is nine cents (the workers who hand stitch them are paid $3.10 per day).[6]

Although these examples are diverse, there is a common thread—money. Money is often the motivator of athletes. Players and owners give their primary allegiance to money rather than to play. Playing for high monetary stakes is exciting for fans, too. Television money dictates schedules, the timing of time-outs, and even controls what sportscasters say. Superathletes can become millionaires. Modern sport, whether professional or big-time college, is "corporate sport." The original purpose of sport—pleasure in the activity—has been lost in the process. Sport has become work. Sport has become the product of publicity agents using superhype methods. Money has superseded the content as the ultimate goal. Illicit tactics are commonplace. In short, American sport is a microcosm of the values of American society. Roger Angell has said of baseball what is applicable to all forms of corporate sport: "Professional sports now form a noisy and substantial, if irrelevant and distracting, part of the world, and it seems as if baseball games taken entirely—off the field as well as on it, in the courts and in the front offices as well as down on the diamonds—may now tell us more about ourselves than they ever did before."[7]

The essays in Part Six have been selected to illustrate the problems and issues involving the impact of money on sports. The first selection, by Richard Sandomir, shows just how much money is made through sports—a Gross National Sports Product of $47.2 billion in 1986. The second selection, by Michael Stanton, uses data from a recent report of the Bureau of Labor Statistics to illustrate how few individuals actually make a living from sport. Stanton shows the extremely high odds against the majority of young people realizing their dreams of athletic stardom and affluence. The third essay, from John Underwood's book *Spoiled Sport*, shows how money has changed sport for the worse. In his words: "[Sport] has been transformed into economic snakeoil. From something wonderful, it has been made grotesque by commerce. It has been distorted and polluted by money, and the neverending quest for more."[8] The essay by Murray A. Sperber, English professor at Indiana University, focuses on the financial rewards held out to successful college coaches. This system, the lure of big money, has some potentially negative consequences. Because money flows toward winners, there will be ever greater temptations to cheat. Moreover, there exists the obvious tendency to place athletics far above academics, and the bitter irony of coaches making so much money from the efforts of their "minimum-wage" athletes. The final selection, from Jay J. Coakley's book, *Sport in Society*, provides an important overview of the owners and sponsors of commercial sports at the professional and so-called amateur levels.

NOTES

1. Quoted in CBS Reports, "The Baseball Business," television documentary, narrated by Bill Moyers (1977).
2. Bill Jauss, "Perks Adding Up to Big Bucks for Big 10 Football Programs," *Chicago Tribune* (November 19, 1986), p. 5.
3. Curt Pesman, ed., "5th Annual Sport 100: Salary Survey," *Sport* 78 (June 1987), pp. 23–38.

4. J. Lewandowski, "Sport Nets Big Bucks for Stores," *Fort Collins Coloradoan* (May 25, 1987), p. D6.
5. Mike Zuccarella and Bruce Brauch, "The $4 Million Dollar Woman," *USA Today* (September 4, 1987), p. C2. *See also* Peter Ross Range, "This Little Tennis Star Goes to Market," *U.S. News & World Report* (September 7, 1987), p. 46.
6. Allan Ebert, "Un-Sporting Multinationals," *Multinational Monitor* 6 (December 1985), pp. 11–12.
7. Roger Angell, "The Sporting Scene: In the Counting House," *The New Yorker* (May 10, 1976), p. 107.
8. John Underwood, *Spoiled Sport* (Boston: Little, Brown, 1984), pp. 3–4.

18. *The Gross National Sports Product*

RICHARD SANDOMIR

You're a Sports Consumer. You buy a box seat, a beer, a copy of *Sports Illustrated,* running shoes, Little League registration for your 10-year-old, admission to the Pro Football Hall of Fame, "A Season on the Brink," an exacta ticket, a round at Pebble Beach and a year trying to look like Cher's boyfriend at a health spa.

You're Miami Dolphins owner Joe Robbie—you build a stadium. You're Chrysler—you sponsor the Triple Crown Challenge. You're a skier—you pay for a lift ticket at Aspen. You're Campbell's Soup—you pay Los Angeles Lakers star Kareem Abdul-Jabbar to endorse Chunky Soup.

The money builds. The sports economy percolates. Billions of dollars course through sports, flowing into gate receipts, concessions, sporting goods, books, advertising, licensed products, broadcasting fees and stadium construction—elements of an economic-leisure mosaic built more on psychic gratification than physical need.

For the first time, the sports economy has been quantified, as a portion of the nation's $4.2 trillion Gross National Product—the total value of the nation's output and services.

Last year, the Gross National Sports Product (GNSP) totaled $47.2 billion, up 7% from $44.1 billion in '85, according to research compiled and computed by *Sports Inc. The Sports Business Weekly* and Wharton Econometrics Forecasting Associates. "Gosh, that's a lot of money," said James Miller, director of the federal Office of Management and Budget. "To paraphrase Everett Dirksen, 'A billion here and a billion there, and pretty soon it adds up to real money.'"

Although historic GNSP figures do not exist, sports economists say that rising attendance and participation in leisure sports, among others, make the sports economy grow faster than the overall GNP. Trends like expansion, still-growing interest in sponsorships, increasing stadium and arena construction, and continued growth of participation and leisure sports will keep spurring the GNSP as a diverse measure of economic activity ranging far beyond the white lines.

The GNSP starts in obvious areas like gate receipts, sporting goods, and concessions. It then spreads to gambling, broadcasting and advertising and

SOURCE: Richard Sandomir, "GNSP: The Gross National Sports Product," *Sports Inc.* 1 (November 16, 1987), pp. 14–18.

moves outward to expand into what skiers pay to schuss and what golfers pay to blast out of sand traps. In the process of defining the GNSP, the numbers showed that while spectator sports dwarf participant sports in headlines, participant sports in turn dwarf the spectator segment.

The primary impression of what comprises sports economics is the most obvious one: Gate Receipts. But gate receipts are but one-fifteenth of the overall GNSP. The $3.1 billion in gate revenues last year (which comprises some sports with 1986-87 seasons) included $436 million from college football, $361 million from baseball, $241 million from football, and $179 million from pro basketball.

The gate receipts component of the GNSP also includes a 20% revenue jump to $725,000 for the LaCrosse (Wis.) Catbirds of the Continental Basketball Association last season—the league's most successful as the CBA increased its sponsorships and exposure on ESPN. At Syracuse University, where basketball is close to religion, the football team has climbed into the Top 10—and ticket sales are starting to reach roundballesque frenzy. After averaging 35,000-per-game last year, the team has been playing before crowds of 50,000 this season. That increased attendance can mean as much as $225,000 more in gate revenues per game. "There have been lines every Monday morning for tickets after we've won," said Carrier Dome spokesman Mike Holdridge.

Gate receipts' natural companion is concessions; buy a ticket, you're likely to buy beer, soda, hot dogs, pennants, caps or yearbooks. During a typical sold-out New York Rangers game at Madison Square Garden, concessionaire Harry M. Stevens sells 20,000 hot dogs, 15,000 beers, 10,000 sodas, 2,500 programs, 500 year books and 10,000 pennants, flags and T-shrits. Rangers fans average $5-a-head in concession sales, said souvenir manager Bernie Herman, "but the per capita sales per Knick fan is down to about $3." Stevens' per-game Rangers gross is about $80,000.

Stevens is a major vendor in a $1.9 billion business dominated by concessionaires such as ARA Services, Ogden Allied, Volume Services and Marriott. Experts believe total consumer expenditures on sports concession could be much larger if the contributions of myriad smaller operators are calculated. "I wouldn't be surprised if it were $3 billion or more," said Charles Winans of the National Association of Concessionaires. Concessions feed the fans, but it is television that nourishes sports with at least $1.1 billion paid in television rights fees last year, a year in which the NFL received an estimated $455 million in fees from the three major networks, while baseball picked up $183 million from ABC and NBC. Two other major chunks were paid by NBC and ABC for the 1988 Summer and Winter Olympics.

For the $300 million NBC paid for the Seoul Summer Olympics (for the GNSP, the total was divided by four), NBC carries an elite, multi-day athletic event. But paying the rights fees and the costs of broadcasting is expensive, so it has to feed itself by selling advertising time. The selling is in high gear now,

TABLE 18-1   The Top 50 U.S. Industries by Gross National Product

	1986 Figures in Billions of Dollars	
1.	Real Estate	$483.2
2.	Retail Trade	407.9
3.	State and Local Government	331.1
4.	Health Services	198.6
5.	Construction	197.9
6.	Federal Government	175.6
7.	Business Services	162.8
8.	Electric, Gas and Sanitary Services	132.0
9.	Telephone and Telegraph	102.6
10.	Electric and Electronic Equipment	88.2
11.	Machinery	85.9
12.	Farms	76.4
13.	Oil and Gas Extraction	73.1
14.	Food and Kindred Products	71.1
15.	Miscellaneous Professional Services	70.1
16.	Banking	69.0
17.	Chemicals	64.4
18.	Trucking and Warehousing	60.9
19.	Fabricated Metal Products	56.9
20.	Printing and Publishing	54.4
21.	Other Transportation	54.3
22.	Insurance Carriers	53.6
23.	Legal Services	52.3
24.	Motor Vehicles and Equipment	49.5
25.	SPORTS	47.2
26.	Social Services	40.5
27.	Petroleum and Coal Products	38.9
28.	Paper	35.0
29.	Primary Metals	34.8
30.	Auto Repair	34.3
31.	Security and Commodity Brokers	32.9
32.	Hotel and Lodging Services	31.9
33.	Instruments and Related Products	31.4
34.	Personal Services	31.1
35.	Transportation by Air	29.8
36.	Rubber	27.1
37.	Educational Services	26.7
38.	Insurance Agents, Brokers, Others	25.7
39.	Stone, Clay, Glass Products	25.3
40.	Lumber and Wood Products	24.8
41.	Railroad Transportation	21.6
42.	Amusement and Recreation	21.4
43.	Apparel	20.7
44.	Textile Mill Products	18.5
45.	Agricultural Services, Forestry, Fisheries	16.6

46.	Holding Companies	15.8
47.	Credit Agencies	14.6
48.	Miscellaneous Manufacture	14.0
49.	Coal Mining	13.6
50.	Furniture	13.4
51.	Radio and TV	12.7
52.	Tobacco	12.7
53.	Miscellaneous Repairs	12.6
54.	Transportation Service	10.9
55.	Private Households	9.3
56.	Motion Pictures	8.5
57.	Water Transportation	8.1
58.	Local Passenger and Interurban Transit	8.0

Source: Survey of Current Business; Sports Inc.

as the No. 1 network aims to sell as much as $600 million in advertising. "We're nearly 60-70% sold," Bert Zeldin, NBC vp-Olympics sales and marketing, said early this month.

How the sports economy affects magazine advertising and magazine purchases can be seen in the case of *World Tennis* magazine. When purchased by Family Media from CBS in 1985, the magazine was ailing. But an aggressive sales effort will spike advertising upwards this year by 44%, to about $5.6 million, after a 28% ad revenue tumble last year, said editor-publisher Neil Amdur.

Team and player success nourishes numerous other parts of the GNSP, including endorsements, sponsorships, licensed products and books.

Endorsements (which range in estimated value from $200 million to $500 million annually) come and go. Witness the Chicago Bears' William Perry, whose folksy, porcine appeal two years ago generated millions of dollars in endorsement.

Tyrone "Muggsy" Bogues, the 5'3" Washington Bullets rookie, must "get off to a quick start to show he's not a 5'3" novelty player," said Bogues' agent, Andrew Brandt of ProServ. Bogues' first endorsement last summer was with a Ford dealership to promote "Muggsymobiles"—1988 Ford Festiva minicars with a "Muggsy" decal (a basketball with feet). "He was very affordable," said dealer Don Rogers. "I don't think he's as affordable now."

Rogers is right: Earlier this month, Bogues signed a three-year, $500,000 deal to wear Converse and endorse a line of Converse children's sneakers.

The power of an endorsement: Nike sold $110 million worth of Air Jordan basketball sneakers when Chicago Bull Michael Jordan soared through his first season, in 1984-85. When Jordan sat out most of 1985-86 with an injury, only $5 million in the Jordan-endorsed sneakers were sold.

Sponsorships grew 20% last year to $800 million as post-1984 Olympics interest in sponsoring events surged, said Lesa Ukman, editor of *Special Events Report*. Several major sponsors said that while direct impact isn't always possible to gauge, the attention garnered by putting up money for a major golf tournament or horse race is often worth the expense. That's why John Hancock Insurance Co., a sponsor of the Boston Marathon, added the New York City Marathon on Nov. 1 for a reported $1 million.

The licensing of player, team, and league names for balls, T-shirts, boxer shorts, sneakers, jewelry, mugs, and keychains is booming. "It's been a decade of phenomenal growth," said Arnold Bolka, editor of *The Licensing Letter*. The retail sale of licensed major league baseball products should increase by 40% this year to about $425 million, generating royalties of about $35 million, said Rick White, baseball's exec vp of retail product licensing. Colleges are seeing a major surge in licensed business. Ann Chasser, licensing director of Ohio State, said royalties rose 66% between fiscal 1986 and 1987 to $450,000 (equating to $14 million in retail sales).

A licensing bonanza: In 1984, Charlie Green and Mike Dickerson spied college students wearing boxer shorts—publicly. They acted quickly on the fad. By 1985, they started manufacturing college logo boxers whose sales are often tied to the success of college teams. Now, they've got a $5 million business.

Much like Green and Dickerson's boxer shorts, sports books seem to sell better each year. The past few years have seen blockbusterhood for books capitalizing on the popularity of John Madden, Mickey Mantle, Billy Martin and Jim McMahon. The release late last year of "A Season on the Brink," John Feinstein's chronicle of a season with Indiana basketball coach Bobby Knight made waves: The book unseated Bill Cosby atop the non-fiction best-seller lists and rode Knight's anger over the book to megaselling heights. Of course, "A Season on the Brink" is a rarity, and the books portion of the GNSP may sag without future hits.

On a typical day at Los Angeles' Santa Anita Park, a bettor lays down an average of $178. Back in 1985, Santa Anita was stalked by a mystery gambler dubbed "The Phantom Plunger," a so-called "bridge jumper" who scored on a series of $50,000-$100,000 show bets on heavy favorites. But his demise came in a major filly race when his horse ran next-to-last on odds of 6-5. He hasn't been heard from since.

The bridge jumper is part of the huge legal betting business—from the $2.6 billion net take (total bets minus payouts to winners) at horse and greyhound tracks and OTBs to the $81 million net take at the sports bookmaking operations in Nevada.

Gene Maday is one of the biggest sports bookmakers in Las Vegas. In his operation on the Vegas Strip, he takes in more than $100 million in bets, averaging a net take of between 2% and 3%. "The other sports books [owned mainly by casinos] are like brokerages," said Maday, who will take $500,000 Super Bowl bets, "but we're freewheeling. We're willing to gamble more."

The GNSP spreads further. When it comes to leisure and participant sports, it starts to sprawl. Golfers pay $3.9 billion in greens fees and club

TABLE 18-2 The Anatomy of the Gross National Sports Product

Category (in millions of dollars)	1985	1986
Participant/Leisure Sports	15,750	16,230
Golf Greens Fees and Memberships	3,900	3,900
Golf Lessons/Cart and Equipment Rentals	1,800	1,800
Health/Fitness/Racquet Club Memberships	4,600	4,900
Ski Lift Tickets	1,000	1,130
Ski Lessons/Ski Rentals/Accommodations	450	500
Bowling	4,000	4,000
Sporting Goods	13,400	15,100
Advertising	3,447	3,612
Magazines	497	512
Newspapers	2,600	2,700
Stadium Signage	350	400
Spectator Sports	2,900	3,100
Legal Gambling (Net Take)	2,661	2,681
Nevada: Sports Books		
Horse Racing Books	61	81
Horse and Greyhound		
Parimutuel	2,600	2,600
Concessions, Souvenirs & Novelties	1,820	1,920
Television Rights	1,020	1,080
Corporate Sponsorships	680	800
Athlete Endorsement Fees	425	500
License Fees for Retail Sports Properties	412.5	487.5
Sports Magazine Purchases	405	412
Golf Course Construction	400	400
Sports Book Purchases	255	270
Stadium Construction	146	236
Trading Cards	160	200
Sports Insurance	155	155
Olympic Budgets	23	23
US Olympic Team	36	44
Hall of Fame	1.4	1.8
	$44,096	$47,252

memberships and another $1.8 billion for cart and equipment rentals and lessons. Skiers pay $1.1 billion for lift tickets. Exercise-seekers pay $4.9 billion to work out at health, fitness and racquetball clubs. Runners last year in the major marathons in Boston, New York, Los Angeles and Chicago paid more than $650,000 in entry fees. Among adolescents, an estimated $36.7 million is paid to belong to soccer teams, and $4.3 million to join Babe Ruth League baseball teams. Leisure and participant sports begat almost all the $15.1 billion sporting goods sector of the GNSP last year. It includes $3.9 billion in clothing, $3.2 billion in footwear, and $8 billion in equipment.

The No. 2 footwear manufacturer, behind Reebok, is Nike, based in Portland, Ore. Last year, it sold $800 million worth of footwear in more than 400 styles for running, racquetball, basketball, field sports and fitness. About 500 professional athletes are walking advertisements for Nike, including Michael Jordan, Howie Long and Bert Blyleven.

Across the country, in a suburb of Syracuse, N.Y., Gary Bugenhagen owns The Sporting Foot chain of three specialty athletic footwear stores. He sells more than 350 styles, and is coming off the best of his 13 years in business. "The overall market is leveling off," he said, "with strength now coming from aerobics, soccer and walking." Last month, he opened his The Walking Source to exploit his newest growth niche.

From 1985 to [1987], new stadiums and arenas (as well as improvements, additions and renovations to existing facilities) were being built seemingly everywhere. From Joe Robbie Stadium in Miami to the Cajundome in Lafayette, La., to Pilot Stadium in Buffalo, N.Y., construction is active. A pair of stadiums has been proposed in Baltimore; a stadium is being built without a team to fill it in St. Petersburg; and several spring training facilities are in various stages of construction in Florida and Arizona. The $236 million estimate for stadium construction was based on projected and completed construction costs, which were then pro-rated from one to four years depending on the known or approximate periods of construction.

In the Auburn Hills suburb of Detroit, William Davidson, the owner of the Detroit Pistons, is building his own arena without any public revenues. The $70 million arena, which broke ground in mid-1986, is designed around three levels of luxury suites (cost: $30,000 to $120,000 annually), the closest being 16 rows from courtside to cater to deep-pocketed corporate entertainers.

In Buffalo, an eight-year stadium saga is about to yield $42 million Pilot Stadium, new home of the Triple A Buffalo Bisons baseball team. The Bisons will start next season at the 19,500-seat stadium, where construction began late last year. The city is pursuing major league baseball, and promises the addition of another 23,000 seats in nine months' time if a franchise is landed. "There were few believers in the project at the beginning," said city stadium coordinator Charles Rosenow. "But it became a symbol to the younger people that Buffalo is moving again."

As long as consumers seek psychic and physical relief from everyday pressures by attending, participating in or reading about sports, the GNSP seems poised to continued strong growth. People may back off from buying new cars or washing machines more readily than they would from buying a ticket to a baseball game or a new pair of Reeboks.

And so it seems that when it comes to the Gross National Sports Product, spending isn't everything—it's the only thing.

19. *Playing for a Living: The Dream Comes True for Very Few*

MICHAEL STANTON

Coach Morgan Wootten is talking basketball. His audience is a group of 8-year-olds participating in the annual summer camp run by this man whose teams at DeMatha High School in Hyattsville, Maryland, consistently rank among the Nation's best. Their faces grow intent when he asks, "What's the key to playing good defense?"

A few youngsters raise their hands. "You have to be quick," says one. "Good hands," offers another.

"Those are both important qualities," acknowledges Wootten, "but not exactly what I had in mind, because you have to be in the position to use them. The key is balance. If you're off balance, you'll be beaten every time. That's true in basketball, but, more importantly, it's also true in everything else that you do."

That's the message Coach Wootten has passed to every one of his players for the last 27 years. And it's one of the reasons that every graduating senior on DeMatha's teams, from starter to sub, has received a college scholarship, and nearly all have earned their college degrees.

"We help the kids set priorities," says Wootten. "Faith, family, and academics all come ahead of basketball. If these priorities are out of order, then you won't make it in our program. I always tell my players, 'Dream your dreams, but don't let athletics use you or abuse you. You have to be prepared for the day when they take the ball away. And it will happen sooner than you think.' "

SUCCESS ON THE FIELD

Sports are a national passion in the United States. It's a safe bet that almost everyone who has ever bounced a ball, swung a racket, or caught a pass has also dreamed of a career as an athlete. But sports, the source of fun and fitness for millions, provide a livelihood for very, very few.

SOURCE: Michael Stanton, "Playing for a Living: The Dream Comes True for Very Few," *Occupational Outlook Quarterly* 31 (Spring 1987), pp. 2–15.

A Look at the Stats

The odds against young people realizing their athletic dreams are high. For every player who wears the uniform of a professional team, or sinks a winning putt in a golf tournament, or runs under the checkered flag at Indianapolis, thousands never will. Young athletes who bet their future on professional sports are in for a surprise when they look at the numbers.

Confidence is an asset in any sport, but overconfidence may lead to disappointment and defeat. On a recent broadcast of the "MacNeil/Lehrer NewsHour," a reporter questioned some young athletes about their perception of their chances of playing in the National Basketball Association (NBA). Even the most modest youngster assessed his chances at 50 percent. The real numbers point to much poorer odds. They're not quite a million to one, but they're a long way from 50-50.

The National Federation of State High School Associations and its member State associations coordinate and administer competition in over 30 sports. Football, basketball, and baseball claim the most participants. According to the federation's 1984–85 sports participation survey, 1,006,675 boys played high school football, 494,000 played basketball, and 391,800 were on baseball teams.

These numbers were reduced drastically at the college level. About 111,000 students blocked on the gridiron, dribbled on the court, or shagged flies on the diamond, according to the National Collegiate Athletic Association (NCAA) and the National Association of Intercollegiate Athletics (NAIA). In other words, only one or two players on any high school team are likely to play ball at the college level.

Players who do well in college look forward to the annual drafts conducted by the major leagues. Most of them never feel a breeze. Harry Edwards—a sociologist at the University of California-Berkeley, collegiate track champion, and knowledgeable observer of collegiate and pro sports—says that only about 8 percent of the eligible athletes are drafted by professional teams.

The fortunate few who are drafted still must prove that they can play well enough to make the pros. Not many do. Edwards estimates that only 2 percent of the drafted players ever sign a professional contract. Among college football players, only about 1 percent ever make the National Football League (NFL). The total number of major league players in football, baseball, and basketball is only 2,261—a mere fraction of a fraction of the 1,892,475 who played in high school. The odds of a high school athlete's becoming a pro football, baseball, or basketball player aren't 50-50; they're 837 to 1. According to Edwards, "A youngster has a better chance of becoming a surgeon." And even the one who makes the pros is likely to be out of sports within 4 years.

Making the Pros Isn't Easy

The Saturday sports shows parade an endless variety of athletic events. Many of them are strictly amateur activities, however. Almost nobody makes a living in gymnastics, swimming, or track. For those sports that do have 100 or more professionals, each league or association follows a slightly different procedure in recruiting new players. The differences are greatest between the team sports—football, basketball, baseball, and hockey—and the individual sports— such as golf and tennis.

Team Sports

Team sports trigger strong reactions. Visions of Celtic green and Dodger blue tug at some fans' heartstrings while prompting others to turn red with rage. But in the business of team sports, emotion and loyalty rarely intrude. Who is chosen and who gets to play are carefully calculated decisions.

BASEBALL

Major League Baseball carries 725 players on the 26 club rosters. As with the other major sports, players enter baseball through the draft or free agency. "The number of players drafted each year varies depending upon the year's crop," says Tom Giordano, director of player development for the Baltimore Orioles. "One year, there may be 25 rounds, and the next year as many as 46. The players drafted in the first 10 rounds have the best chance of making it, at least to the minors. But there is no way to predict accurately how well a player will do. Don Mattingly, of the Yankees, was drafted in the 19th round. Look where he is now."

The major league draft takes place every June. To be eligible, a player must be 18 or have completed high school. If he enters a 4-year college, he's eligible after his junior year or when he's 21. "It's very rare that a player goes straight to the majors," says Giordano. "He has to develop his skills first."

Baseball has an extensive minor league system. A player who is drafted will likely spend at least a few years in it, and those years might end up being the player's entire professional career. The minor leagues have 164 teams and about 4,100 players, each of whom believes that he will make the majors, says the Orioles' Giordano. "It usually takes a couple of years at the minor league level to tell whether a player has what it takes to make the big leagues."

BASKETBALL

The National Basketball Association (NBA) has 23 teams; each team carries a 12-man roster, for a total of 276 players. As in baseball, players enter the NBA either through the draft or free agency. The draft is mainly for players currently in college; most are seniors, although a player may declare himself to be a candidate for the draft before his senior year. Larry Fleischer, executive director of the NBA Players Association, says, "Every year, 161 players are drafted. Probably 55 players make the teams; and, by mid-season, this number is reduced to 40 or 45."

The Continental Basketball Association (CBA) might be said to be a minor league for the NBA. Founded in 1946, actually 1 month before the NBA, the CBA comprises 12 teams that are subsidized by the NBA as a whole, although some teams have an individual relationship with an NBA club. The CBA conducts its own draft and selects players that were passed over in the NBA draft.

Jay Ransdall, of the Continental Basketball Association, says, "Players will stick around for 2 or 3 years and hope to make it to the NBA. If they don't, they might try to make one of the European teams. The money is better, but the all-important media exposure is practically nonexistent," says Ransdall.

Derek Wittenberg is a veteran of the European leagues. Now assistant basketball coach at George Mason University in Fairfax County, Virginia, Wittenberg played for Morgan Wootten at DeMatha High and later starred in the backcourt for the 1983 NCAA champion North Carolina State Wolfpack. He was a third round pick of the Phoenix Suns but was released in the final cut. Says Wittenberg, "Many players mistakenly believe that it's easy to make the European leagues. The tryouts were very tough. I went to the tryout camp and found there were 160 players competing, and 120 of them were guards."

Wittenberg caught the eye of one coach, who invited him to LeMans, France, famous for its auto race, where the tryouts continued. He competed against two other guards, both Americans, through a 30-game exhibition season before finally making the team. He played 1 year. Then he returned home to complete his degree in economics and business, saying, "It was time to get on with my life."

FOOTBALL

The NFL has 28 teams; each team carries a roster of 45 players, for a league total of 1,260 players. Players enter the NFL in two ways: the draft and tryout camps. According to Mark Murphy, an NFL Players Association official who was an all-pro with the Washington Redskins, about two-thirds of the players enter the league through the draft conducted each spring. The rest are free agents, who win their way onto a team through individual tryouts. At the beginning of the 1986 season, 161 rookies were listed on team rosters.

Only players who have completed their collegiate eligibility are candidates for the draft. Each of the 28 NFL teams gets 12 picks, or 336 picks in total, from a pool of 15,000 or so eligible players.

HOCKEY

Each of the 21 teams in the National Hockey League (NHL) carries 24 men on its roster, for a total of 504 players. An NHL spokesman says that probably 85 percent of these players enter the league through the draft, which is held annually in June. The remainder win their time on the ice through free agent tryouts.

The clubs pick 252 players during the 12-round draft. To be eligible, a player must be 18 years old or have completed high school. A breakdown of the 1986 draft shows that 120 players came from the Canadian junior leagues; 22 from U.S. colleges; 40 from U.S. high schools; and the others from the various international hockey leagues. Usually, no more than one-fourth of those drafted will make an NHL roster in their first year. Most will skate for at least a few years in one of the minor leagues to refine their skills.

The American Hockey League and the International Hockey League are the two principal minor leagues; although independent of the NHL, each has a direct association with the big league. Mike Meyers, of the International League, says that "a young player is usually signed to a 3-year contract and will hope to be picked up by the NHL." Typically, the odds are against them.

Individual Sports

Athletes in the individual sports—such as golf and tennis—generally have more control over their entry into the professional ranks than do those in team sports, in that there is no draft. An athlete's ability is, obviously, the key determinant. Additionally, each of the associations that govern competition in these sports maintains its own rules of eligibility.

AUTOMOBILE RACING

Several organizations regulate automobile racing, depending on the kind of car or kind of race. One organization, the International Motor Sports Association, authorizes races around the world. IMSA, which licenses about 2,000 drivers—including most of the top drivers in this country—says that probably no more than 20 percent of the total make a living from the sport.

IMSA and most other racing associations require that all drivers attend one of the professional driving schools, which cost at least $1,000. That's only the beginning. Nearly all drivers are members of a racing team that is usually sponsored by a major corporate backer. Sponsors hire only the top drivers. They won't trust a rookie with a million-dollar car.

Hank Ives, of the KRACO Racing Team, which races Indianapolis-style cars, believes that racing is one of the most difficult sports to break into. "Most drivers of Indy cars have worked their way to the top by running the various levels, from gocarts to Formula Fords. No matter the class, the cost is significant." A driver needs financial backing early or, he says half jokingly, "He must grow up in a racing family. In no other sport do you see so many siblings or fathers and sons." Look at the sports pages and you regularly see the Pettys, the Allisons, and the Unsers. Michael Andretti, the son of the Indy winner Mario Andretti, is a driver for KRACO.

BOWLING

One of the most popular sports in America is bowling. The Professional Bowlers Association of America (PBA) has established requirements for becoming a pro. A bowler must average 190 for 2 consecutive years in league play and be 18 years old or a high school graduate. The association has 2,700 members; but, in 1986, only 147 were classified as Touring Pro I or II, which means that they were regular competitors on the PBA National Tour.

BOXING

Professional boxing is legal in 17 States, and each State establishes its own requirements for becoming a professional. Generally, a young boxer works his way through the amateur ranks, beginning at a local boy's club and progressing to Golden Gloves competition. If a fighter shows promise, he may be recruited by a professional boxing manager or trainer, who will help the fighter develop his skills. This professional handling is essential if a boxer wants to turn pro.

But professional boxing is an international sport. According to Herbert Goldman, managing editor of *Ring*, generally recognized as the authoritative magazine for the sport, about 18,000 boxers fought in 1985. But, he cautions, that number includes many thousands who stepped into the ring one time and quit. The number of fighters who actually contend for top prize money is much smaller. "We rank the top 10 fighters in each of the weight classes," says Goldman. "Depending upon how you class them, that's about 150 fighters. You read a lot about multimillion-dollar winnings for a fight. No more than four or five fighters in a generation make that kind of money. I'd say that less than half of the ranked fighters even make a decent living. In the best year of his career, a good fighter is lucky to make $30,000." And a boxer's career doesn't last long. "A 10-year career is several lifetimes for a professional boxer," says Goldman.

GOLF

Competition in professional golf tournaments is regulated by the Professional Golf Association (PGA) and the Ladies Professional Golf Association (LPGA). Only about 350 men were regular players on the PGA Tour in 1984–85, and about 270 women were eligible to compete on the LPGA Tour in the same year.

Numerous golfers try to break into the professional orbit. In fact, the PGA has nearly 9,000 members, but not all of them may compete on the tour. The PGA and the LPGA use similar methods to certify touring players. To compete on the PGA Tour, a player must possess a Tournament Player's Card, which may be earned in two different ways: A player must be among the top finishers in the annual PGA Tour Qualifying Tournament or earn an amount equal to the 150th ranked money winner of the previous year. That sounds like the classic Catch 22: How does a player earn money if he doesn't hold a card? The answer lies in the difference between the Tour and particular tournaments. PGA members who do not hold a card may still participate in tournaments. Two routes are open: Special invitation of a tournament sponsor and competition in a qualifying round held the Monday prior to a tournament. Once in the tournament, players are eligible for the same prize money as the other golfers.

Even players who have earned a card have no guarantee that they will be able to compete regularly for the big money. Only a limited number of slots are available in each tournament. Most of the rest are filled by players who are exempt from qualifying due to previous tournament victories or their rank in the tour.

HORSERACING

According to the *Daily Racing Form,* the newspaper of thoroughbred racing, nearly 3,000 jockeys were in the saddle in 1986, and all of them likely spent years around the track before they got their first mount. Aspiring jockeys usually progress through various stages, "from groom to walker, to exercise boy, to apprentice jockey, and, finally, to jockey," says John Giovanni, an ex-jockey and now an official with the Jockey's Guild. Each position requires a license, which makes horseracing "the most regulated sport in the business," according to Giovanni.

In no other sport is weight so important a factor. "When I was racing, I tried to keep my weight at 113 pounds," says Giovanni. Rarely, if ever, will a jockey weigh more than 120. Despite the weight restrictions and the fact that horseracing is, says Giovanni, "a very dangerous sport," there is no dearth of interested riders.

RODEO

The Professional Rodeo Cowboys Association authorizes more than 600 rodeos around the country. The association has more than 5,000 card-carrying members, but fewer than 200 cowboys ride the circuit full time. Almost every one of these rodeo stars also has another occupation.

To become a professional cowboy, you first have to purchase a permit that allows you to compete, and then you have to win at least $2,500 in a 1-year period.

TENNIS

In many sports, as we have seen, competitors must attain a minimum age, usually 18, before being able to compete professionally. In tennis, there is no minimum age. If a player feels ready to challenge the pros, the key determinant is one's ability, not one's birthday. Still, the opportunity to play for the big money is available to only a few. Men's tournaments are regulated by the Association of Tennis Professionals (ATP); about 1,100 players from the United States and the rest of the world are ranked by it, but probably no more than a third of those ranked play the circuit full time. The governing body of women's professional tennis is the Women's Tennis Association (WTA); about 400 players regularly play its professional tour.

Spots in tournaments are usually afforded to top-ranked players. According to Ron Bookman, the deputy director of the ATP, the rankings are based upon a player's earnings and the tournaments in which the player competed. The results of about 300 tournaments held around the world are used in calculating the ATP rankings, which are recomputed 45 times a year. To be eligible for associate membership in the WTA, a player must either have earned at least $500 in any 1 of the past 2 years, or, if an amateur, have finished sufficiently high in a tournament to have earned an equal sum. Full membership requires that a player have earned $15,000 in competitive tennis in either of the last 2 years or be ranked among the top 100 players by the WTA.

Making Money Isn't Easy Either

Youngsters who imagine their chances of making the pros to be no worse than 50-50 no doubt also believe that, if they do reach them, they'll be driving a Mercedes and eating filet mignon for the rest of their lives. In reality, for every sports millionaire, there is a bench full of people who are just scraping by. Do you find that hard to believe? Read on.

Few people know the business of professional sports better than David Falk, a principal partner in ProServ, Inc., a top international sports management agency. His company counts some of the foremost names in sports as clients. While acknowledging that some athletes are making phenomenal salaries, he asserts that "Using any measure of average earnings in professional sports as a guide to what the average player makes is very deceptive. What we've seen in the last few years has been a very real bifurcation, or split, in pro sports. The stars, and there are very few, are making more and more money. The marginal players in the major leagues, while making a good salary, earn much less." And below the majors, salaries plummet.

Mr. Falk's comments are echoed by Larry Fleischer of the NBA Players Association. "One notion that is absolutely ludicrous is . . . that players are set for life. That can be said of a very small percentage of players, certainly no more than 5 percent. These are the superstars, like Dr. J or Larry Bird, who stand far above the other players. They're also players who have beaten the odds, not only by making it to the pros but by staying far longer than the average."

Mark Murphy of the NFL Players Association concurs. "I hear so many players say that they're going to be set for life, but the odds are against them. Some players are becoming more conservative in how they structure their contracts and in deferring payments until later years. But there's no comparison between the star and the marginal player, either during a player's career or after."

It's difficult to get that message across, particularly to young people who are deluded by the glamour inherent in professional athletics. John Underwood, a senior writer at *Sports Illustrated*, says in his book, *Spoiled Sport,* "The pro myth is fed by an irresistible hype that there is a pot of gold at the end of the rainbow." The pot is smaller than many young people think. And the rainbow fades very quickly.

According to the NFL Players Association, the average player made $193,000 in 1985. In the NBA, the figure was $320,000. Major League Baseball paid the highest average salary, at $371,000. These are certainly high salaries, although they are not as high as those paid to the top managers of America's large corporations. Even the minimum salaries paid in the majors are very, very good: $75,000 in the NBA, and $60,000 in the NFL and Major League Baseball. But remember that not all the pros are in the majors.

Minor league salaries are far lower than those in the majors. Talking of minor league baseball, Tom Giordano says, "A player in the A league usually makes about $700 a month during the season, plus $11 a day for meal money." By comparison, the average typist starts at more than $1,000 a month. Things are not much better in basketball. Jay Ransdall, of the Continental Basketball Association, says that, if a player makes a CBA team, he "stands to make about $450 per week for the 14-week season."

Earnings in the individual sports are even more poorly divided than those in the team sports, because these pros have to pay their own way. A player's expenses are considerable. For the team athlete, expenses such as transportation, room, and board are covered while on the road. It's a different story for a tennis player or a golfer. David Falk says, "A few years ago, it probably cost the player $25,000 or $30,000 a year to play the tour." Ron Bookman of the ATP thinks that the figure is higher now. "It's probably reasonable to assume costs of $1,000 per week to play the tour today," says Bookman, "because players not only must cover travel costs and living expenses but also maintain their own homes. A few players are fabulously wealthy. Many are just breaking even."

On the golf tour in 1985, purses totaled nearly $25 million in official prize money. Its distribution, however, is far from equal. The number 1 player in the PGA earned more than $500,000; the 100th player won about $75,000; and the 200th tallied only $6,000. LPGA sponsors a professional tour that in 1986 offered more than $12 million in prize money. The top 10 players earned more than a third of the total. The number 1 earner garnered more than $400,000. The 100th player, who participated in more tournaments than the number 1 money winner, earned only $15,000.

Tennis tells a similar story. By mid-September 1986, the number 1 ranked player was Ivan Lendl, who had earned more than $900,000 in official prize money. The player in slot number 100 earned less than $40,000, not quite enough to cover expenses for a full season. Prize money totaled more than $12 million in women's tennis during 1985. In that year, 25 players earned more than $100,000. The number 1 player, Martina Navratilova, won nearly $2 million; the 50th captured $50,000; number 100 made $25,000; and number 300 earned $5,000.

Another important factor that aspiring pros have to remember is that even if they do make a team, they won't be around for long. The average length of a typical NBA or NFL career is less than 4 years. It's a little longer in Major League Baseball. Ex-Redskin Murphy says that "competition for positions is intensive; and, except for the superstar, it never ends. There is always a younger player ready to take your job. What this means is that football is becoming a year-round job. If you're a marginal player, you better be in the training room in the off-season, being seen by the coaching staff. Consequently, there's not a lot of time for off-season employment or career preparation. Additionally, the injury rate in the NFL is 100 percent; which means that every player receives at least one injury every season. Any one of those injuries might end your career."

Players who count on adding to their earnings with advertising contracts are also courting disappointment. Some players earn top dollar in endorsement income. But again, says Falk, "The prospects for endorsement income are generally limited to the stars. There are very few players with the national and international appeal that businesses seek." Those who do are principally the stars of individual sports, like tennis. Opportunities for team sport players are smaller because their appeal is basically regional. "There are a few exceptions, like a Michael Jordan, but those are very rare," says Falk.

SUCCESS OFF THE FIELD

John Thompson's classroom is McDonough Gymnasium, a small, drafty, 1920's vintage arena, not the homecourt that you'd expect for the college powerhouse Georgetown Hoyas. But then again, this is the rehearsal hall, not center stage; Georgetown University plays its basketball at the Capital Center, a modern complex on the outskirts of Washington.

Thompson is one of the Nation's premier coaches; but, first and foremost, he is a teacher, always questioning his players, urging them to think. In his office at McDonough, he keeps a prop that he uses to teach his most important lesson. It's a deflated basketball.

"This piece of rubber is absolutely useless unless it's filled with air," Coach Thompson tells his players. "All of you who are planning on going to the NBA better think about that. You're basing your future on 9 pounds of air." He continues, "If you're lucky, you'll play here at Georgetown. If the luck continues, maybe you'll make the pros and stick around for a year or two. But your working life will last about 40 years. What are you going to do with the rest of your life?"

When the Cheering Stops

The single-minded determination necessary to reach the level of performance required to play in the pros sometimes prevents youngsters from thinking about what they will do with the rest of their lives. And the star treatment accorded to many athletes encourages them not to. Coach Thompson's question is one that many young pros avoid.

"I wear several different hats in my relations with my clients," says David Falk. "I'm an agent, a financial manager, and also a career counselor. I urge all my clients to experiment in the off-season, to take an internship and gain some real business experience. One thing most young people fail to realize is that professional athletics is a very cold and a very hard business." How many listen to his advice? "Not very many," he says.

Jim Johnston tried to spread the same message. A former college coach with a doctorate in education, Johnston is president of Educational Advisory Associates, a Philadelphia-based counseling and consulting firm. In the mid-1970s, Johnston worked with both the Philadelphia 76ers of the NBA and the NHL's Philadelphia Flyers to aid players in their postcareer planning. "It was difficult and frustrating. Very few players listened. When you're that young and making that kind of money, it's tough to keep things in perspective. About the only time they were interested was when they were cut or on the trading block."

The PACE Center for Career Development is a San Diego-based organization that is attempting to get athletes, both professional and amateur, to focus on the future. "Although it may not be easy for people outside sports to understand, the problem is real," asserts baseball all-star Steve Garvey, co-founder of PACE. "I've seen many players leave the game faced with a myriad of problems because they're simply not prepared for life outside of sports."

The PACE program is based upon a series of aptitude and vocational assessments that are used to help the athlete plan a career strategy. A trained staff then tries to help the athlete implement it. Nearly 500 athletes have participated in the program.

Ron Stratton, president of PACE, candidly acknowledges that the program is meeting with mixed success. "We want our association with the athlete to be long term; but, frankly, many are not up to the challenge. It can be frustrating." Equally frustrating to Stratton is the fact that many youngsters today are sacrificing their chances at real education in pursuit of an elusive shot at the pros. He recounts his recent experience at a career night at a local school.

"I found that at least 10 young men had listed their career choice as professional athlete. I could list a thousand and one reasons why they'd never make it: Your body shape's not right; you have no foot speed; you're too short. It's difficult to get them to listen."

When he counseled players, Jim Johnston found that, generally, they had an unrealistic idea of what they'd be doing when their playing days were over. Many assumed that success on the field would automatically translate to success off of it.

"Many athletes mentioned going into broadcasting without realizing that it's just as competitive as sports. Another favorite was public relations. I'd ask them what they thought it entailed, and the usual response was making personal appearances and signing autographs. When I mentioned how important writing skills are to the field, most would forget about it."

Another problem that many athletes experience when entering a post-sports career is that they find themselves years behind their peers. In his book, *Spoiled Sport*, John Underwood quotes Ron Johnson, an ex-New York Giant, about the former pro's reentry into the working world: "It was a rude awakening. All those skinny little guys with glasses? Always studying? Well, by the time they're 30, they're doctors or lawyers or businessmen and just beginning to cash in on all those years of struggling. But the football player is almost always through by that age and goes from earning maybe a $100,000 a year to maybe nothing."

Over the Hill at 29

The trauma that athletes experience at the end of their career can be severe. Larry Fleischer of the NBA Players Association says that "for many players, it's the first time they've faced rejection. To be told when you're 28 or 29 years old that you can no longer do what you're best at is painful. I'd say that three-fourths of the players have real trouble adjusting to life out of sports, at least in the first year. After that, it depends upon the individual player." Phil Chenier's experience is a case in point.

"The first year out of the pros was difficult for me, I can tell you that," says Chenier. He was an all-star guard with the Washington Bullets. In a 9-year NBA career, he played with and against some of the greats of the game before a back injury brought his career to a close. "The end wasn't anything like I'd imagined. I always thought I would be able to pick the time," he says. The injury kept him sidelined for a year and a half. He tried a comeback. "Emotionally, I wanted to play more than ever. But my physical skills had grown rusty and that mental toughness, which is so important in the pros, was lacking." He finally realized that it was truly over.

"It was one of the most difficult times of my life," he says. Conservative by nature, he had structured his contracts to afford him and his family financial security. But basketball had been the center of his life from boyhood, and now that was gone. When he entered the pros after his sophomore year at the University of California-Berkeley, he was, at 20, the youngest player in the NBA. He had never really thought about what he wanted to do with his life. When his career ended, he was 29 years old.

For nearly 2 years, he drifted. He tried going back to school, but that didn't last long. And he tried a few jobs, but they didn't satisfy him either. He finally found one that he enjoyed, and through which he could make a contribution. Today, Chenier is Director of Youth Programs at Shiloh Baptist Church in Washington, D.C., where he tries to give kids the benefit of his hard-won experience. Like Coach Wootten, he emphasizes the importance of balance. "Sports have been very good to me and are, in general, a very positive influence. But if you focus too much on sports, you're cutting out other options. You have to be prepared to compete in life as well as in sports. And that preparation starts early."

Preparing for the End
from the Start

"It's difficult to feel sorry for pro athletes who find themselves in a predicament at the end of their career when you consider the money some of them make," says Jim Johnston. "But we have to be concerned about the thousands of kids who never make it to the top."

It's not news that big-time college athletics frequently conflict with academics. Many student athletes have successful academic careers. Many do not. Many are not academically prepared for college, and even those who are sometimes find it difficult to balance their time between the books and the ball. It's estimated that football players at major NCAA division I schools spend between 45 and 49 hours a week preparing, playing, and recovering from football. Basketball players average a little less. Travel time to and from games might add another 10 hours to the schedule.

These demands undoubtedly contribute to the low graduation rate for scholarship athletes. One study by *USA Today* found that only about 27 percent of the basketball players on scholarships during a given year eventually earned their degrees. And for those who did, the question must be asked as to how relevant their degrees were. Mark Murphy says that "many players major in staying eligible."

Back to the Books

One organization is trying to change that and, in the process, get youngsters to realize that a dream career as a professional athlete will likely be just that—a dream.

The Center for the Study of Sport in Society, in Boston, was established at Northeastern University in 1984. The mission of the center, in the words of its founder, Richard Lapchick, is "not only to study sport and its impact on society but also to bring about changes by developing an educated and self-empowered athletic community."

One vehicle that the center has developed to achieve this aim is a university degree completion program, based upon the double premise of scholarship and community service. Tested at Northeastern, the program would give athletes who had failed to earn their degrees the opportunity to continue their studies. In return, they would participate in an "outreach" program designed to spread the word to youngsters that academics should be their number one priority.

The center devised a 2-credit, 4-part course in communications, writing, financial planning, and computers; it then tested it with a number of players from the NFL New England Patriots who had not earned their degrees. The initial effort was a success. Upon completion, 10 players enrolled full time at Northeastern. Soon, other Boston-based pro teams, the Red Sox and the Bruins, were participating.

Lapchick writes, "The program did something that we did not foresee." According to him, most of the players thought that their own academic inadequacy was the reason for their failure to graduate. They believed that they had taken courses in golf and tennis and squash because they weren't up to more academically demanding ones. However, by sharing experiences for the first time, many suddenly recognized that it was the athletic system that prompted them to think about remaining eligible and not about real academic development. This realization lent greater emphasis to the second half of the program—community outreach.

Acknowledging their influence as role models for youth, the athletes realized that they had an important role to play in the program. Keith Lee, formerly a defensive back with the New England Patriots and the Indianapolis

Colts, is the coordinator of the outreach program in the Boston area. "In the last 2 years, we've spoken to more than 60,000 people, and the response has been fantastic." Speaking before assemblies of middle school and high school students and parents' groups like the PTA, the athletes "stress the balance between academics and athletics and emphasize that only 1 high school athlete out of 12,000 will play professionally," says Lee.

For Lee and the other participants in the program, it has been both a rewarding and a humbling experience. "Kids put athletes up on pedestals. From early on, the star treatment of athletes is encouraged. But that treatment evaporates once an athlete's career is over. Many of us let our egos get in the way and allow our self-esteem to be determined by our performance on the field. That's why many athletes have difficulty adjusting," says Lee.

What began at Northeastern University is spreading across the country. The National Consortium of Colleges and Universities was established in 1985. At its founding, the consortium comprised 11 members. According to Tom Sanders, the associate director of the center, the number has risen to 21. He adds that the number of universities expressing interest in the program is growing daily, another indication that people are beginning to recognize the importance of preparing college athletes for a career beyond their playing years.

The members of the consortium have agreed to five basic principles: to set academic standards for their own athletes, to readmit former scholarship athletes to earn their degrees, to develop a degree completion program with the members of professional sports teams in the school's metropolitan area, to create an outreach program using pro athletes to encourage young players to strive for excellence in the classroom, and to provide a counseling program to help current and former pro athletes adjust to the classroom. The cost to the player varies, depending upon the team, the school, and even the player's contract. In general, reduced tuition is offered as long as the athlete completes his studies successfully and participates in the outreach program.

A Final Word from the Coach

In every one of his 27 seasons at DeMatha, Coach Morgan Wootten has had duties in the classroom as well as in the gym, teaching world history to the freshman class. During a recent trip to Greece to provide some pointers to the Greek national basketball team, Wootten had a chance to visit some of the places he had read and taught about for the last quarter century.

"I realized that the message that I and many other coaches try to pass to our players is no different from what the Greeks taught centuries ago—the Golden Mean. You have to keep things in perspective, in balance. The commitment, hard work, and sacrifice that make basketball and all other sports so beautiful are the same qualities that will help you all your life. But you have to remember that basketball is just a game."

20. *A Fan's Lament: The Commercialization of Sport*

JOHN UNDERWOOD

I was about to say that I have lost my taste for sport. Not the sport that I do to satisfy those hidden competitive itches—the erratic tennis, the comic snow skiing—but the sport I watch. The sport that cornered much of my time as a journalist lo these many years, but whose madness, like that of the lovable but eccentric uncle who has finally gone over the line, I no longer find tolerable.

The sport we call "spectator" sport, as though we were detached from it, which could not be farther from the truth. The sport we call "organized" sport, although it is anything but (being packaged and merchandized is not the same as being organized). The sport of the professionals—the "national leagues" of our various pastimes; and the semiprofessionals—the big-time college teams and the aspiring Olympians who are paid, too, but not as much. The sport that drew me into the daily sports pages in my youth to agonize from afar over the ups and downs of teams and athletes who were dumb to my existence (did the Detroit Tigers ever wonder how *I* was doing?), but whom I adored nonetheless. The sport, I admit, that holds me still because in its purest form it is so rousing and conclusive, and therefore so appealing. A place where the enemy is plainly marked and victory is clear-cut, and no (or little) blood need be spilt.

Short of the love of a beautiful woman, I don't know of anything more breathtaking than the recitals of great athletes performing up to snuff before large, admiring audiences; anything more thrilling, say, than a long, broken-field run, or more hair-raising than a last-second goal or a ninth-inning base hit that saves the skin of a favorite team. Such moments plucked from time become treasures as tangible as freeholdings, to cherish and pass down like heirlooms. For no better reason, "my" Tigers become my son's Tigers. It is practically a law.

I was about to say I have lost it, this taste for sport, but I haven't. It was taken from me—from all of us.

It did not fade away naturally, like a blemish on the skin. It was excised, the work of the quack surgeons we call "owners" and "administrators" and "league presidents" and "agents" and "network executives," the modern manipulators of sport.

Where once I would gladly plunk down the price of admission to see a

SOURCE: John Underwood, "A Fan's Lament: The Commercialization of Sport," in *Spoiled Sport* (Boston: Little, Brown, 1984), pp. 3–14.

team of skilled professionals improve on the games we learn in childhood, I am now reluctant, even resentful. I am amazed we have allowed it to happen. I would suspect a conspiracy, but I am not sure the opportunists who run sport are that smart. Duplicity is more their style. And bullying. And greed, of course, is their incentive. I am not sure but what they have taken the heart right out of sport. I *am* sure that it is no longer the same.

It takes no special insight to see that sport is important stuff in America, whatever the manner it is perceived or utilized—as healthy diversion for vast numbers of people, as a refuge from social demons for others, etc. etc. To each his own, and no matter. It is obviously too good to be left to the publicists and bottom-line mentalities who run it (and play it) now.

If it could speak on its own behalf, the real complaining party at the bar would be sport itself. It has been transformed into economic snakeoil. From something wonderful, it has been made grotesque by commerce. It has been distorted and polluted by money, and the never-ending quest for more. It has been appropriated by a growing army of owner-entrepreneurs who made a remarkable discovery after the 1950s: that sport was not sport at all but a tool for extracting incredible riches from the sports-hungry populace.

It is easy to follow the subversions since then. The fingerprints are everywhere. Mainly they can be traced to the two major influences that caught us up in the glamour and beguiled us into believing just the opposite as they suborned sport and altered its face. Grown to full maturity, those two influences now work as an axis, usually with their names on the same gaudy contracts. They are: (1) the rise and spread of professional sport as the *ne plus ultra* and role model (and, conversely, the decline of amateur sport in those capacities), and (2) television.

Sport has become the shill of television. The failure to recognize the contaminating power of television—not in and of itself, because television is no better or worse than we allow it to be, but by permitting it to dominate sport: *that* failure is shocking. Instead of harnessing the good of television for the good of sport, sport has been swept up by it. The irony is that the custodians of sport think it is the other way around. They think they have made television pay (those huge, happy sums) when actually they have just been bought off.

The shameless grafting of Big Sport to Big Television to produce Big Dollars has yielded a harvest of aberrations, from the monstrous brutality and drug abuse infecting the pros to the abysmal disclosures of recruiting bribery and coast-to-coast academic cheating among the major colleges. The former is still being unfolded (but no longer denied) in daily headlines. The true depths are still being plumbed as the emerging stars of the 1980s turned out to be the chemicals athletes use to build themselves up and turn themselves on and tune themselves out. Much of the violence that now saturates Big Sport is little more than that—a form of chemical warfare.

Sport's leadership threw in to this madness by placing such an oppressive burden on winning that it made desperate men out of its coaches and better athletes. Winning pays the bills. Winning assures the television deals, and the outlandish contracts and salaries. The desperate athlete resorts to almost anything—to cheating, to brutality, even to poisoning his body with drugs—to stay in the money.

The desperate coach becomes traumatized by the need to win. He is not blind or deaf to the demands. He knows that by the time he gets his ear to the ground to pick up the negative vibrations he is liable to be out on it. In the Big Sports marketplace, there is no such thing as security for a coach. When he starts out, the one thing he can be certain of is that he will be fired, sooner more often than later. The annual turnover is awesome. The National Football League began the 1983 season with new head coaches for eight of its twenty-six teams—a turnover of almost a third. The National Basketball Association had nine new coaches out of twenty-three—*more* than a third.

The joy is swept from sport when the market relegates everything to the bottom line. "The score" becomes its own reward—and the market doesn't much care how it scores. It glorifies brutes and clowns and brats, and makes heroes of the worst examples of sportsmanship instead of the best. (Having paid to see them once, I would not pay again to watch John McEnroe or Ilie Nastase disgrace the game of tennis. But others do and as long as they do McEnroe and Nastase will continue to act disgracefully.)

The process has debauched sportsmanship to the point where winning at all costs is, indeed, costing too much. The items sacrificed include honor and fair play. To resort to drugs and brutality to gain a competitive edge is a bow to a desperation run amok. To corrupt the educational process, to make a fraud of the student-athlete in order to win, is not to win at all.

We are so anesthetized to this insanity that we do not realize how unsporting our spectator sports have become—how unsportsmanlike it is to cheat, either by illegal, sometimes injurious acts on the field, or the more insidious acts of deception and rules-bending off it.

Cheating corrupts, and inspires greater corruption. Like dry rot, money accelerates the decay. We should admit that we have finally bought enough rope to hang ourselves when we look up to find that illegal gambling is now an accepted resident of the Big Sports community. Illegal gambling on sporting events has grown to a $120 billion mob venture, and the influence is wide-spread and sinister.

College coaches complain that the volume of their hate mail rises and falls not so much with their winning or losing, but whether they "beat the spread." Pro games revolve around point spreads and odds. The shills of gambling now occupy the television booth and get their "lines" printed in the daily paper. That is not just shocking, it is heinous.

Recently, I spoke to a class of law students at the University of Miami. At one point I said the outcome of an athletic contest must never be doubted, because if it is, sport dies. Either that or it becomes pro wrestling. I asked for a show of hands of those who thought what they now see in professional sports is on the up and up. I didn't count the hands, but I would guess no more than sixty percent were raised. A dubious vote of confidence.

Perhaps even worse, the market has taught the young men of sport to accept cheating as part of the process, even as a means to an education, or as a substitute for it. Like zombies they willingly go along as the process hastens their dehumanization. The "pro drafts" are slave auctions that violate every tenet of the free enterprise system. College recruiting is a ritual of bribery that too often rewards cheaters with conference championships and television dates. The threat of getting caught is no deterrent.

The National Collegiate Athletic Association has had to mete out penalties against 176 of its member schools on 264 occasions since it began a rules-enforcement program in 1952. In 1982, the fed-up president of San Francisco University, facing the school's third probation in four years, dropped basketball. It was the only way he knew to stop the cheating.

Both practices—recruiting and drafting—easily create in the athlete's mind a cynicism for the system and a broad distrust of the "superiors" he must deal with. Especially if he wakes up on the other side of his athletic experience to find he has neither money in the bank nor an education to count on. Along this loathsome byway, the black athlete has been especially misused, although it is difficult to tell him that because he has been getting a large share of the pie lately and doesn't want to let go. His own black leaders—most of them—don't tell him. They allow him to believe that salvation is just one more bounce of the basketball away. From the ghetto to the grave he believes that, and the results are often tragic.

It would be funny if it weren't so sad, but the high-salaried athletes of sport have achieved their own Catch 22 in the marketplace. They have become the willing foils of their own alienation. Because they go along with the hype (the one that confuses inflated contracts with achievement), the greatest practitioners of sport have become affluent freaks. They are now almost impossible to identify with, the one quality they cannot afford to lose.

A sports hero is not Frank Sinatra on tour. To reduce his status to "entertainer" and to excuse his misbehavior on that basis is a popular psychology nowadays, but it is not valid. Entertainers do not wear your school's colors and carry them into battle. They do not "represent" your city. The sports hero is a product of the allegiance of his fans, and uniquely tied to it. Sports entrepreneurs extract from loyal fans great commitments in patience and funding (while they "build a winner") because of this relationship, even to getting tax-paid arenas built for their own profitable use.

In turn, the fan wants (and has every right to expect) the athlete to be loyal—to the school or to the town, and especially to him. In order to be beloved the athlete must be able to impart to that fan the illusion of caring. Caring that the name on his shirt inspires more than just a casual commitment. He *cannot* be loved when it inspires no allegiance at all, or is exposed as a fake by the demands he makes (those massive figures) to keep him happy and in town. As often as not, that is the reason he is booed and pilloried, and has himself come to show such contempt for the fans who underwrite him.

Obviously it *is* hard to love an athlete whose celebrated million-dollar salary supports a dollar-ninety-eight batting average. On those occasions, he is more likely to be despised, if only until his next home run. The tolerance level has sunk alarmingly as the fan sees the athlete in a new and bleaker light. Combine the stupid money hype with the well-publicized acrimony between management and athlete—the almost daily reminders that they are now adversaries instead of partners in sport—and you get an image of a sports hero as mercenary, as a grifter.

Baseball managers complain that it is no longer possible to inspire an athlete with traditional team values. Gene Mauch says you can't even threaten them with fines anymore because they make so much money a fine means nothing. Tony LaRussa says you can't get them to lay down sacrifice bunts because they're afraid of losing the chance to drive in a run. Runs-batted-in are worth more than sacrifice bunts at the bargaining table. A pro football coach told me of a veteran second-string player he had who balked at a trade that would have made him a starter. The player liked the money he was getting for riding the bench and did not want to risk injury "so late in his career."

But don't be too hard on the players of our games. They have merely taken their cues from owners and administrators—from those entrepreneurs who *really* know how to jerk sport around, and the loyal fans with it.

The padrones of sport are milking it dry. They have inflated ticket prices to the point where a trip to the ballpark for the average family is now an adventure in high finance. They move their clubs and players from city to city like gypsies, or threaten to if demands for a new stadium or a better lease or a few million dollars' worth of improvements are not met. They cater to the whims of television by playing games at all hours and twisting the seasons around and stretching them out so that they overlap and smother each other in the endless grubbing for money.

Professional football is now being played in the summertime, courtesy of the United States Football League and the American Broadcasting Company, which, with a $14 million contract, subsidized the USFL's first two years of business. The USFL is, in every sense, made-for-TV sport. Anticipating television windfalls of their own, pro basketball and pro hockey expanded their 1984 playoff formats so that sixteen of twenty-three teams in the NBA and sixteen of twenty-one teams in the NHL were assured places in the "championship" tournaments. That meant that hundreds of regular season games would be all but meaningless for the paying customers of thirty-two of forty-four professional teams.

Owners, as a whole, never stop crying poormouth, and as often as not blame players' agents for their fiscal problems, as if contracts were signed at gunpoint in dark alleys. Agents are a relatively new form of coercion, and undoubtedly deserve some of the credit they get for the spoiling of sport. They crawl over the games like lice, promoting conflict and helping inflate player salaries and benefits so that the average bench-rider in professional basketball makes more than the President of the United States and some seventy baseball players make *four times* that. In the process, "labor relations" and "collective bargaining" and the harsh principles they embrace have become prominent words in the lexicon of sport. Truthbending on both sides is epidemic.

But it is a smoke screen that hardly hides the real issue—the issue of who *really* pays for such extravagance. In this, the market has truly made fools of the paying spectators of sport. We have been cuckolded. One wonders if we will ever wake up to our disgrace. That *we* are the real financiers of the whole bloody mess. It is not the owners and the networks who pay those swollen sums, it is the fans who ultimately pay.

It is the fans who pay when collective bargaining ends and fiscal realities take over. We now have unions in professional sport, and strikes and the specter of strikes, and every time a new settlement is reached it is the fans who have to dig a little deeper. It is the poor foolish fans who make millionaires out of the entrepreneurs, and keep the exalted stars in Bill Blass slacks and the uppers and downers of their choice.

It is the fans who pay when the ticket prices go up to support the massive payrolls. It is the fans who pay when the price of a hotdog jumps a buck, a parking spot rents for five, and the county commission votes a tax increase to build the entrepreneur a new stadium, complete with sky boxes and closed-circuit TV. The fans only *think* the television networks pay when the National Football League gets two billion dollars for a new contract and major league baseball gets a billion. The networks simply pass the expense along to the sponsors, who then jack up the price of their razor blades and beer and shovel it on to the fans.

Maybe it is already too late. Maybe, without realizing it, the fans are already fed up. Not long ago I was on a network talk show with a former Philadelphia Eagles linebacker, John Bunting. The subject, loosely speaking (for that is the way the host, Phil Donahue, treated it), was "fan violence." Bunting brought along his two young children to describe the nature of the beasts who attended Eagles home games. His kids said they dreaded Sundays at the ballpark because of the slurs and obscenities the fans hurled at their dad. Bunting said he wished that that was all they hurled. He said he had taken to wearing his helmet going down the tunnel to the field to ward off the flying examples of fan alienation (cups, ice, bottles, etc.).

If sport were a hospital patient it would be in intensive care. Its very form has been altered to accommodate the marketplace, a restructuring that suffocates sport at those important amateur levels, most especially the high schools. While Big Sport and Big Television combine in the glorious quest for one more prime-time date and one more ratings coup, high-school sport is drowning in a sea of red ink. Car washes and streetcorner pretzel sales can't keep it alive forever. No alarm has been sounded, but in recent years youngsters have been quitting organized sports in droves. Many high schools now complain of an inability to field teams because of dwindling numbers and the high costs.

I have notes, pinned to other notes like pilot fish, measuring the withering away. Twenty-five high-school coaches in Moxee City, Washington, are coaching at half-pay. Entire little league programs across the country have caved in. Minor league and semipro sports are all but things of the past. In Miami, high-school football attendance is on a twenty-seven-year decline. Philadelphia, and the entire state of California, came close to giving up school football. Calumet (Michigan) High School, home of George Gipp, *did* give it up. It could no longer afford it. When tryouts were held for the 1984 football season at St. Cecelia's High School in Englewood, N.J., twelve candidates showed up. The school announced it was dropping the sport. St. Cecelia's is where Vince Lombardi started his coaching career in 1939.

The dying off of sport at the grassroots level does not happen all at once. It is not the quick carnage from some kind of economic cyclone. It happens gradually; a steadily squeezing hand on the throat. The reckless proliferation of Big Sport, with its seasons twining together like noodles on a plate, and its endless hype, and its deadly coalition with Big Television, makes us want to believe a myth: that Big Sport is the only sport worth watching.

It may have achieved the opposite of that: it may be the sport we should *stop* watching. At least until we realize that, on its present course, it will not cross us over into Jordan.

As with all matters of the heart, the passion we give to sport is mostly an involuntary thing. It is not required that we fall in love with the local team or its star players or give them our devotion, and the sense in it is not always easy to find. We do it anyway, probably before our powers of ratiocination are developed. But it is fun, and it is done, and as I have done it myself I accept it without always understanding it. I loved the Detroit Tigers years before I ever saw one in the flesh, or even knew for sure where Detroit was, and I didn't even question that love until I was in my thirties. I figured it was something I would outgrow. I had better luck with asthma.

What follows, therefore, are not the bleatings of a detractor, but the honest concern of a lover of sport who just can't stand the unsightliness of it any more. Or, closer to the point, the meanness of it. Sport is such a personal thing and much of the passion for it so personally felt that one would be lacking good judgment to attack on too broad a front, however. So if I miss some of the more popular areas of complaint, or have not proffered solutions for every single example of mismanagement, it is because these *are* personal feelings that do not naturally stretch out to cover the landscape, and because I simply don't have all the answers. I wish I did.

21. *The College Coach as Entrepreneur*

MURRAY A. SPERBER

If the 1980s are the New Age of the Entrepreneur, then many college athletic coaches are at the front of the charge for the dollars.

Leading the wolfpack is North Carolina State men's basketball coach, Jim Valvano, with an annual income estimated at $500,000 to $700,000. In the world of college athletic coaches, Valvano is less the exception than the model for his peers. Almost all NCAA Division I football and men's basketball coaches have university salaries above those of the higher paid full professors at their schools, but, as Valvano's case illustrates, for these entrepreneurs, the salary line is merely the foundation upon which to build the Schedule "C" return.

According to a recent series of articles in *USA Today*,[1] Valvano's base pay from North Carolina State is $85,000 and he has a ten-year contract that ends in 1993. He also receives about $100,000 a year and other perks from Nike Shoes, mainly for making certain that his players wear Nikes, especially on national television. The N.C. State coach gives forty to fifty speeches a year and charges $5,000 for an appearance. In addition, he endorses various commercial products, has three television and radio shows, runs summer basketball camps, earns money from books and videotapes, and receives a number of season's tickets to N.C. State football and basketball games that he is entitled to sell for personal profit. Valvano is a busy man, and, to help him move about, he has the free use of three new cars.

Unlike many of his coaching colleagues, however, the N.C. State coach does not run his private businesses out of his faculty office. He is incorporated as JTV Enterprises, has an off-campus suite of offices, and also employs a New York attorney, Bill Madden, to handle his financial affairs. Madden describes his client as hating to turn down any business opportunity: "And, candidly, the money's good. He's just active in his community, which in his mind is America." Sportswriter Steve Wieberg of *USA Today* calls Valvano "the epitome of a coach who is also a businessman. Or the businessman who happens to be a coach."

Some business activities available to coaches—such as doing television commercials for a local car dealer—may not appear seemly for a university

---

SOURCE: Murray A. Sperber, "The College Coach as Entrepreneur," *Academe* 73 (July–August 1987), pp. 30–33.

employee, but they are separable from most aspects of the employee's relationship to his or her university. However, other practices considered ordinary and legitimate by most coaches—such as selling complimentary season's tickets, running private camps on university property, and accepting huge gratuities from equipment manufacturers—are the kinds of activities usually forbidden to other members of the university community.

The men's basketball coach at the University of Nevada, Las Vegas, Jerry Tarkanian, is a tenured member of his faculty with an annual salary of $155,393. Among his many income supplements, which include a guarantee of 10 percent of the school's profits from NCAA Men's Basketball Tournament appearances (this year's trip to New Orleans earned UNLV well over a million dollars), is the gift from his university of 234 season's basketball tickets ($38,668 value) for the coach to dispose of as he wishes.

Tarkanian's ticket deal is unusual only in its scale. Just about every college football and basketball coach in America receives free season's tickets, although the amount varies from Bobby Knight's four at Indiana to Tarkanian's hoard. In recent years college athletes have gotten into trouble with the NCAA for selling complimentary tickets, but the coaches' regular sale of season "comps" is never questioned. Joe B. Hall, the former men's basketball coach at the University of Kentucky, came closest to trouble when allegations arose that he was selling 300-plus tickets at more than face value. Hall was eventually cleared of the charges but his alleged crime was scalping, not selling complimentary tickets.

The summer camp is probably the greatest potential abuse of the coaches' relationship to the university and is also the least publicized. Not only are football and basketball camps (for women as well as men) very profitable, but soccer, gymnastics, swimming, and even wrestling camps earn good dollars for their coach camp directors. Usually the camp is held on university property with the coach paying a nominal fee or no fee for the use of the facilities— i.e., all those basketball courts, soccer fields, swimming pools, weight rooms, as well as the equipment therein and thereupon. For his summer camp at the University of Arizona, football coach Larry Smith pays $50 rent for the use of the football stadium, practice fields, and weight room. He also pays the $1.88 sales tax on his $50 rental fee.

Depending on the coach's agreement with the university, the campers are housed and fed in the dorms at cost or less. The coach pays the counsellors whatever he or she feels is appropriate (sometimes very little). The camp counsellors are often physical education students, current and former players, and high school coaches with a professional stake in impressing the head coach. Many counsellors are on the current university payroll as graduate assistants or student athletes and, in effect, are being paid by the university for their work at the coach's private camp.

Most camps are run in one-week sessions, with campers who board at the camp paying an average of $200–$300 a week, and day campers paying $150–

$250. Bill Frieder, the men's basketball coach at Michigan, is reported to have grossed over $350,000 for his 1986 summer camps. When Lefty Driesell, the former coach at Maryland, resigned from his coaching duties after the death of Len Bias, he insisted on keeping his camps at the university (camps which grossed $231,000 in 1986).

"A smart college coach," says Mike Lewis, formerly of the *Rochester Democrat & Chronicle,* "can set up and run a camp with very little money laid out. And one of the bonuses for the coach is that these are great recruiting devices, kids flock to them hoping to catch the coach's eye and eventually win an athletic scholarship. All that a coach with a half-decent camp needs to do is sit back, look over the prospects, and count the bucks."

As good entrepreneurs, 1980s' coaches try to connect their various deals. The summer camp deal ties neatly into the shoe deal when the coach receives free equipment and clothing from the sporting goods manufacturer: equipment for the camp, t-shirts for the campers, warm-up suits and shoes for the counsellors, and so on.

Major sporting goods manufacturers, especially those with shoe lines, regularly pay coaches five- and sometimes six-figure annual amounts to insure that the coaches outfit their teams in the companies' shoes and, in the case of soccer and sometimes basketball, uniforms as well. These payments are sometimes called "consulting fees" (the coach is supposed to make various recommendations concerning the equipment), but the company often hands out the money and the freebies directly in return for the coach's guarantee that the players will wear the shoes and/or uniforms for all games.

In 1986, Rollie Massimino of Villanova received an estimated $125,000 from Puma; ten other men's basketball coaches were in the $100,000 range in payments from Nike, Converse, Adidas, and other companies; about seventy-five other NCAA Division I men's basketball coaches had deals averaging $30,000–$40,000 a year, and some women's basketball coaches earned in the $5,000–$10,000 range. The success and fame of a school's basketball program dictates the amount of the payment, but even coaches of very small programs may receive something.

On shoe deals, however, football coaches average less than half of what men's basketball coaches make: during football games, there are fewer television closeups of players' shoes; also football cleats, unlike basketball sneakers, cannot be marketed as daily, walking-around shoes. When a college basketball player, hanging in the air for a rebound—shoes and brand name clearly displayed—is on the cover of *Sports Illustrated,* the company that paid the coach $100,000 has received more than its money's worth.

While coaches indirectly and sometimes directly endorse sporting goods manufacturers, they also promote a wide variety of other products. Penn State's Joe Paterno, a symbol of probity in men's football, charges $25,000 to $100,000 for a television commercial, and $5,000 to $15,000 for a print ad. Among Paterno's recent clients was Panhandle Eastern Corporation, a Texas pipeline company. Endorsements range from the Coca Cola ads by various Southern football coaches to the spots for Mister Bee, a local potato chip, by Don Nehlin, the football coach at West Virginia. A former Indiana University football coach, Lee Corso, even promoted the South African government's *Krugerrands*.

The most common commercial tie-in for an athletic coach is with a local car dealer. For an endorsement that may be direct but is often only indirect and passive, the coach receives a nice return. Last year, Joe Lee Dunn, football coach at the University of New Mexico, drove a new Oldsmobile Cutlass free of charge under an arrangement that his car generally would be replaced by an unused one every 2,000 miles or three months, whichever came first. Almost all football, men's basketball, many women's basketball, and men's soccer coaches at NCAA Division I schools have some sort of car deal with a local agency (the exceptions, like George Welsh, football coach at Virginia, often have their cars provided free of charge by their universities' foundations or alumni groups). The quantity and quality of cars, as well as the inclusion of free insurance, gas, and repairs, is usually directly proportional to the won-loss record and revenue-generating power of the coach's team, but a head man or woman without some sort of car deal is a very unusual character in the world of NCAA Division I coaching.

Automobile agency owners, however, do not donate the use of their cars simply because they are supporters of a university's athletic programs. Car dealers have no trouble reselling what they call "the coach's car," and, through-out the deal, they receive publicity, referrals, and inquiries about the model that the coach uses. Finally, in a neat twist, some dealers claim a tax deduction on "the coach's car" because they donated its use to a nonprofit educational institution.

Many entrepreneurial coaches tie themselves to car dealers for more than the free use of an automobile. Very often, the automobile agency will sponsor the coach's media show(s). These usually boring, oddly scheduled (late at night or early weekend mornings), and lamely produced "Coach's Corner" programs often earn excellent ratings in their local markets. Howard Schnel-lenberger, football coach at Louisville, receives an $80,000 minimum from television and radio shows, plus one-third of the university's net earnings above $160,000. Mike White, football coach at Illinois, makes $125,000 from his shows. Lou Henson, men's basketball coach at Illinois, takes in only $35,000 from his media shows, but Tom Miller, men's basketball coach at Colorado, with a less ambitious program than that at Illinois, makes $30,000.

Since the television shows usually consist of the coach being prompted by a professional announcer to comment on a highlight film of the most recent game, and the radio programs are usually phone-ins, the coach needs almost no preparation to earn the equivalent or more than the salaries of most faculty members at his university (women coaches have not broken into the media-show deal). But most coaches take their media appearances very seriously and many yearn for postcoaching careers as color commentators on local or national TV and the success of an Al McGuire or Dick Vitale.

Like other entertainers—or business executives who are crucial to their enterprises—many coaches persuade their employers to carry large amounts of insurance on them. The University of Louisville pays the premium on Howard Schnellenberger's $500,000 life insurance policy. The University of Florida puts its coaches on a standard athletic department on-duty policy of $250,000 accidental death or dismemberment, $200,000 disability, and $25,000 medical. That most NCAA Division I schools insure their athletic department personnel for more than they do the health and lives of their regular faculty tells a great deal about current university values.

Traditionally, universities have provided some free or low-cost housing for faculty and staff, including athletic coaches. But some of the entrepreneurial modern coaches have broken new ground on traditional housing practices. Clemson provides football coach Danny Ford with a house and makes payments on a 137-acre farm, which has a mortgage of $280,000. If Ford stays at Clemson until 1995, he will assume ownership of the farm. In a more old-fashioned deal, in 1986, Dennis Erickson, football coach at the University of Wyoming, lived in a university-owned and -maintained house with $5,000 available for redecorating.

As befitting their lifestyles, many coaches want to join their local country clubs. The administration at Florida State University thought it appropriate to pick up men's basketball coach Pat Kennedy's Killearn Country Club membership with its $3,000 initiation fee and $1,827 annual dues. The majority of football and mens' basketball coaches at NCAA Division I schools have some sort of country club arrangement and even the smaller programs, like Illinois State's, try to do a little something for their coaches (in 1986, the Illinois institution picked up men's basketball coach Bob Donnewald's $320 annual YMCA membership).

"Your outstanding jock," says former major league baseball pitcher, Jim Bouton, "has been on scholarship since the third grade." Bouton lists the many perks that even grade school athletes receive: special attention from parents and teachers, special attention from male and female friends, the illusion that they are special and a law unto themselves. When the talented athlete attends high school, the perks mount and then culminate in a college athletic scholarship.

Almost every NCAA Division I college football and men's basketball coach is a product of this culture and was the recipient of a college athletic scholarship. Even coaches who were not good enough to be college stars or even scholarship winners still spent most of their undergraduate days in the hermetic world of the Athletic Department. Thus the average college coach's contact with regular faculty and courses is exceedingly limited. As coaches, they are important members of the athletic culture. In their eyes, regular faculty are likely to be viewed as committed fans, at best, or as "nerds," at worst, with no understanding of an athlete's reality and needs.

Reality for college athletic coaches is further defined by the housing units in which they lived as student-athletes (either special dorms and/or athletically oriented fraternities), and the athletically oriented values of the nonathletes with whom they lived and associated. Since the ethos of this campus social world leads its population, upon graduation, toward the business deals and country clubs of America, athletic coaches would be strange animals indeed if they headed instead toward the faculty lounges and coffee houses of the scholars and intellectuals.

The present phenomenon of the entrepreneurial coach is more a result of the coach's social past and present than it is a reflection of the unbridled capitalism of the times. To change or control coaches' entrepreneurial zeal would require the most fundamental changes in the way universities, and especially their intercollegiate athletic programs, are presently constituted.

In the past, on occasion, university administrators and/or faculties exercised some control over the outside business activities of various members of the university community, including coaches. Now, however, increasingly enchanted by their schools' teams and the prospect of media attention, most administrators are reluctant to place any limitations upon the entrepreneurial appetites, ingenuity, and just plain greed of their athletic coaches.

A generation ago, Vince Lombardi turned an antiquated cliché about sportsmanship upside down by saying, "Winning isn't everything—it's the only thing." Unfortunately Lombardi's dictum seems to be the underlying premise in most NCAA Division I football and men's basketball programs.

The proven way to win is to hire a coach who knows how to win. Coaches who know how to win also know how to make money for themselves. Their good luck indicates bad times for American universities.

NOTE

1. Particular information in this article on salaries and associated arrangements is based largely upon articles appearing in USA Today (Sept. 24–25, 1986, and Dec. 9–11, 1986). In a number of articles on college athletic directors and football and basketball coaches, the newspaper used its resources to turn up accurate figures on salaries and perquisites. Often universities, even public ones, opposed USA Today's efforts, but the Gannett Company's lawyers pursued and obtained the data under state freedom of information acts. Since publication, USA Today's figures have not been substantially challenged.

22. *Owners and Sponsors of Commercial Sports*

JAY J. COAKLEY

PROFESSIONAL SPORTS

On the one hand, team owners and event sponsors are praised for putting teams together, staging impressive events, and bringing professional sports to cities across North America. On the other hand, they are criticized for establishing monopolistic and exclusive businesses in the interest of making money, avoiding taxes, manipulating athletes, and creating publicity for themselves. In actuality, most owners and sponsors deserve both praise and criticism.

Those who invest in professional sports are usually successful business people interested in making money. But if they were interested in money alone, most would have chosen other investments. Professional sports are definitely forms of big business, but they are often risky businesses. The risks can be highlighted by remembering that there have been numerous teams, leagues, and events that were financial disasters. Two football leagues, a hockey league, a number of basketball and soccer teams, a volleyball league, a women's basketball league, and a team tennis league all went out of business leaving many owners and sponsors in debt. Another example of a possible business failure is the USFL, which lost a reported $63 million per year in its first 2 years of existence.

So why invest in such a risky business? According to sociologist Jon Brower (1976) investments in sport are attempts to combine business and fun. Owners and sponsors are, for the most part, wealthy superfans. They buy teams and stage events for ego fulfillment, to satisfy lifelong fantasies, and to vicariously experience the public achievements of their athletes. Their investments in sport gain them more prestige than any of their other business ventures. They become instant celebrities in their cities—from the mayor's office and the Chamber of Commerce to neighborhood bars and local elementary schools.

However, Brower (1976) also points out that those who invest in sport do not get so carried away with fun and fantasy that they forget business. They do not enjoy losing money. They may look at their athletes as heroes and may even treat them as their children, but their attachments have not led them to

SOURCE: Jay J. Coakley, "Owners and Sponsors of Commercial Sports," in *Sport in Society: Issues and Controversies,* 3d ed. (St. Louis: Times Mirror/Mosby, 1986), pp. 82–87.

voluntarily give up control over the lives of those athletes. When it comes to the business side of sport, they think alike.

Team Owners and Sport Leagues as Monopolies

The tendency to think alike has been especially strong among the team owners in the major sport leagues: basketball, baseball, football, and hockey. In fact, unity among these owners has led to the formation of some of the most effective monopolies in the history of American business. The reserve system is basically the result of owners agreeing not to compete with one another for players. Owners have also agreed to prevent new teams from forming without their permission, and when permission is given, the new franchise owner is charged a heavy entry fee to become a part of the league. Furthermore, new owners are only allowed to locate teams in cities approved by the old owners. These policies prevent new teams from competing with established teams for players, spectator interest, gate receipts, and local broadcasting rights. The leagues never allow changes that could threaten the collective interests of existing owners.

The owners in each of the major sport leagues have also gotten together and pooled the broadcasting rights to games. This enables them to negotiate with television companies as a group. Along with limiting the number of games available to the viewing public, this tactic has enabled them to get huge sums of money in their media contracts. Amazingly, the U.S. Congress has approved this monopolistic method of doing business. In fact, it even passed an amendment to the U.S. Code in which it was stated that "antitrust laws . . . shall not apply to . . . [the] organized professional team sports of football, baseball, basketball, or hockey." This rule not only guarantees revenues for owners, but also gives them power to influence television companies along with the commentators working for those companies.

The practical implications of this rule are best seen in the case of the NFL. Working as a group, the owners of NFL teams were able to sell the rights to their games for $2.1 billion to the three major U.S. television networks in 1982. That meant that each NFL team was guaranteed $14 million every year from 1982 to 1986. This income was enough to cover every team's payroll expenses without them ever selling tickets to games. When the NFL owners combine their monopolistic media tactics with the exclusive-use clauses they have written in their contracts with the stadiums they "rent," they can make it very difficult for new football leagues to get started. This was discovered by the World Football League in 1975 when it went out of business after its second season. The teams in the WFL had been forced to locate in smaller cities because they could not use the stadiums used by NFL teams—because of the exclusive-use clauses. And none of the television networks bought the rights to WFL games because of the fear they might be frozen out of future negotiations for televising NFL games—a costly consequence because NFL games were played in the biggest television market areas in the United States. Without large gate receipts and without the sale of television rights, the WFL went broke.

In the mid-1980s the USFL ran into a similar situation, even though they chose to play their games in the spring rather than the fall. In a desperate attempt to avoid bankruptcy, the USFL filed a $1.32 billion antitrust suit against the NFL in late 1984. At the time of this writing, the fate of the USFL is still in doubt. The league continues to exist, but it is experiencing serious financial problems.

Being able to ignore antitrust laws does more than just limit competition. It also drives up the values of teams. For example, the Denver Broncos in the NFL were purchased by Edgar Kaiser, Jr. for $35 million in 1981 and sold in early 1984 for $70 million—after Kaiser complained for 2 years that he couldn't make any money because his players' salaries were too high and ticket prices were too low! In fact, over the 3 years he owned the team he increased ticket prices from $12 to $19.25. The Dallas Cowboys were purchased by Clint Murchison in 1960 for $500,000 and sold in 1984 for $80 million (including a $20 million stadium lease). The money made on the sales of these teams does not include the annual profits and tax benefits enjoyed by owners. Of course, these are exceptional cases, but it seems that investors with money realize the benefits of buying a business that is part of a monopoly controlling the most popular spectator sport in the United States. They also realize they can own a team for a number of years without making large annual net profits and still receive large investment returns when they sell the team. In this case, team owners are like the person who buys an apartment building for $2 million, tells the tenants that their rent just covers payments and expenses, and then sells the building for $4.5 million 10 years later. Even though there were 10 years of "breaking even," the owner walks away from the deal with what amounts to a $250,000 annual investment return. With some exceptions, this is what many owners of sport teams have done for years.

Team Owners and Subsidies from Taxpayers

The belief that cities need sport teams and sport events has led to various forms of public support for owners and sponsors. One of the most widespread forms of support is the provision of publicly built and maintained athletic facilities. Of course, owners and sponsors pay rent to use the facilities, but, in the case of the owners, the rent payments usually cover only a fraction of the maintenance and construction costs (Okner, 1974; Surface, 1977). This means local taxpayers make up the difference by subsidizing team owners. According to information gathered in the late 1970s, these subsidies were being used to pay off over $7 billion of debts related to professional sport teams in the United States (Kennedy and Williamson, 1978; Surface, 1977). After looking at this information as a member of a federal commission, one congressman said "a lot of cities would be embarrassed if people knew how much [they] subsidize pro teams."

It is claimed that these subsidies and the operating losses for the facilities are made up by (1) the publicity gained by the cities, (2) the increases in civic pride created by teams, and (3) the spin-off economic benefits experienced by the cities. However, these consequences are difficult to document, and in the case of the spin-off economic benefits, it is certain they are enjoyed primarily by the wealthy business people in the cities; the poor gain little. In fact, many city residents cannot even afford tickets for games in the stadiums they are subsidizing. For example, many of the families in Louisiana would find it tough to afford even the guided tour of the Superdome—although the people of Louisiana subsidize Superdome deficits to the tune of $3 million to $5 million per year. But even in the face of these subsidies and a construction debt of nearly $175 million, the Louisiana state governor recommended in 1984 that the stadium rent charged to the New Orleans Saints football team be cut $800,000 per year. Furthermore, he was hoping to find a piece of land the state could purchase and rent to the Saints for $1 a year as a practice site—all in the name of civic pride.

In many cases it seems as if little caution is exercised by city officials when it comes to supporting professional teams. Such a careless approach is surprising in these days of budget cutbacks. These officials must really believe in the benefits of pro teams for their cities, or they are being influenced by economic self-interests and possibly some inane desires to have season tickets in comfortable box seats, identify with hometown athletes, and second guess coaches— all at the expense of the taxpayers.

In addition to facility subsidies, there are other forms of public support for team owners. For example, the government has allowed the cost of game tickets to be considered as a business expense. This does not sound like a big deal, but a large proportion of season tickets for some teams are purchased by local businesses. This not only means the companies save a few dollars on taxes and company officials see games for nothing, but it also helps teams sell out their stadiums, which allows games to be televised locally. This makes the media rights in the sports leagues more valuable and provides the teams with great local publicity. This makes everyone happy and a few people very wealthy.

Other tax breaks are also received by owners when they buy and sell teams. When teams are bought, the players are defined as usable equipment. This means they can be depreciated over a certain period—usually about 4 to 8 years. This can be a great tax advantage, since owners say that most of the purchase prices for teams are related to the players. Then when teams are sold, the profits are defined as capital gains. This also has advantages for wealthy taxpayers.

In summary, the owners and sponsors of professional sports are successful business people. They invest in sports for a variety of reasons, but they are primarily interested in making money. Although all of them do not make money, those who are fortunate enough to own teams in the NFL, major league baseball, and, for the most part, in the NBA and the NHL have benefited financially. Their success is based on two factors: (1) they have monopolistic control over their specific sports, and (2) they receive public assistance in the form of subsidies, tax breaks, and protection from antitrust suits. However, things are starting to change as the courts around the country begin to see the hypocrisy of businesses using anticompetitive practices to make money selling sport competition as a form of entertainment. What happens through the rest of the 1980s will be interesting to watch and analyze.

AMATEUR SPORTS

In amateur sports there are no owners, but there are sponsors of events and sports organizations that sanction events and control athletes. Generally, the sponsors are large corporations who invest for advertising purposes; they seldom make any money from their sponsorship. The controlling sport organizations operate on a nonprofit basis, although they do use revenues from events to maintain their own organizational structures and their power over amateur sports.

In most countries around the world, amateur sport is administered by a single, centralized organization, which controls events, athletes, and revenues in a consistent fashion. In the United States, however, this is not the case. There are a number of controlling organizations. Each develops its own policies, and each has its own sources of funding. The major organization in intercollegiate sport is the NCAA. However, rules vary in each of the four major membership divisions in the NCAA; each school within the NCAA may also develop its own policies to supplement NCAA policies. Furthermore, schools must finance sport programs on their own. They only receive indirect aid from the NCAA. For sports not connected directly with schools, the major controlling organization is the USOC. However, within the USOC there are 38 separate national governing bodies (NGB), which control each of the amateur sports in the United States. The NGBs raise most of their own funds through their own corporate and individual sponsors, and they each set their own policies to supplement those of the USOC.

If this situation sounds confusing, it is. When people from other countries come to visit me in Colorado Springs and I show them the Olympic Training Center (OTC), it takes a long time to explain who sponsors and controls amateur sports in the United States. My visitors have a hard time understanding that the Training Center is not directly administered by the USOC and that each of the 38 NGBs for the different amateur sports operate independently of the USOC in most situations. I also try to explain that this separation of control leads to numerous political battles between organizations. Each is afraid of giving up its power so they all fight to maintain control over their own rules, revenues, and athletes. As the USOC has been more effective in recruiting money to support amateur athletics, it has also been able to increase its control over various NGBs. And with the windfall profits associated with the 1984 Los Angeles Games, this move toward increasing centralization will continue. In the meantime, my foreign visitors will continue to leave Colorado Springs with many unanswered questions about the administration of amateur sports in the United States.

In my tours of the OTC I never even refer to the fact that amateur sports are also controlled by the NCAA and its approximately 800 member schools. If I did I would then have to say that intercollegiate sports are also controlled by the National Association for Intercollegiate Athletics (NAIA), the College Football Association (CFA), and, up until 1983, the Association of Intercollegiate Athletics for Women (AIAW). I would also have to say that the NCAA has four levels of membership, each with its own rules and regulations, and that the NCAA administers intercollegiate football differently than each of the other sports.

Despite all this confusion in amateur sports, each of the different sport organizations has one thing in common: they are interested in their own *power,* and when it comes to revenue-producing sports, they are interested in *money.* For example, when the popularity of women's sports reached new heights in the early 1980s, the NCAA's interest in power led it to abandon its long-time policy of ignoring women's teams; it started to sponsor championship events for women and quickly forced the AIAW out of existence. The NCAA's interest in money has led it to operate as a monopoly in its control of intercollegiate sports—especially in the case of football and the case of broadcasting rights to football games. However, this monopolistic control was broken in 1984 when a series of court decisions made it possible for individual schools to break away from the NCAA and sell the broadcasting rights to games on their own. This single change will have a dramatic effect on the manner in which intercollegiate sports are controlled through the rest of the 1980s. There is little hope of making any accurate predictions on what will happen. It seems that the power of the NCAA will be decreased and that revenues will be distributed in new ways among schools. However, the implications of these shifts are unknown at this point.

In summary, there are numerous sponsoring and controlling organizations in U.S. amateur sports. In the past these organizations did little to coordinate their governance of athletes and events. In fact, there has been a history of conflict over power and control issues. In intercollegiate sports, the NCAA has been the dominant organization, although its power has been limited by the courts. In other amateur sports, the dominant organizations have been the different NGBs, although the increasing financial resources of the USOC is leading to a more centralized system of control.

REFERENCES

Brower, J. 1976. "Professional Sport Team Ownership: Fun, Profit and Ideology of the Power Elite." *Journal of Sport and Social Issues* 1 (1): 16–51.
Kennedy, R., and N. Williamson. 1978. "Money in Sports." *Sports Illustrated* 49 (3): 28–88.
Okner, B. A. 1974. "Subsidies of Stadiums and Arenas." In R. G. Noll, ed., *Government and the Sports Business*. Washington, D.C.: The Brookings Institute.
Surface, B. 1977. "Get the Rook!" *New York Times Magazine* (January 9): 14–15.

■ FOR FURTHER STUDY

Axthelm, Pete. "The Year of the Cynic: Money is King and the Loss of Innocence is Affirmed," *Newsweek* (January 4, 1982), 43.
Burwell, Bryan. "Super Deals for Superstars." *Black Enterprise* 14 (July 1984): 37–42, 57.
Coakley, Jay J. *Sport in Society: Issues and Controversies*. 3d ed. St. Louis: Times Mirror/Mosby, 1986, pp. 64–89.
Curry, Timothy J., and Robert M. Jiobu. *Sports: A Social Perspective*. Englewood Cliffs, N.J.: Prentice-Hall, 1984, pp. 136–158.
Daymont, Thomas N. "The Effects of Monopsonistic Procedures on Equality of Competition in Professional Sport Leagues." *International Review of Sport Sociology* 10 (1975): 83–99.
Ebert, Allan. "Un-Sporting Multinationals." *Multinational Monitor* 6 (December 1985): 11–12.
Eitzen, D. Stanley, and George H. Sage. *Sociology of North American Sport*. 3d ed. Dubuque, Iowa: Wm. C. Brown, 1986, pp. 191–217.
Flint, William C., and D. Stanley Eitzen. "Professional Sports Team Ownership and Entrepreneurial Capitalism." *Sociology of Sport Journal* 4 (March 1987): 17–27.
Garvey, Edward R. "From Chattel to Employee: The Athlete's Quest for Freedom and Dignity." *The Annals of the American Academy of Political and Social Science* 445 (September 1979): 102–115.
Gilbert, Bil. "Gleanings from a Troubled Time." *Sports Illustrated* (December 25, 1972): 34–46.
Gruneau, Richard S. "Elites, Class and Corporate Power in Canadian Sport." In *Sport, Culture and Society*, edited by John W. Loy, Gerald S. Kenyon, and Barry D. McPherson. Philadelphia: Lea & Febiger, 1981, pp. 348–371.
Harmond, Richard. "Sugar Daddy or Ogre? The Impact of Commercial Television on Professional Sports." In *Screen and Society*, edited by Frank J. Coppa. Chicago: Nelson Hall, 1979, pp. 81–105.
Hughes, Robert, and Jay J. Coakley. "Mass Society and the Commercialization of Sport." *Sociology of Sport Journal* 1 (1984): 57–63.
Johnson, Arthur T., ed. "Political Economy of Sport." *American Behavioral Scientist* 21 (January/February 1978): entire issue.

Johnson, William O., Jr. "You Ain't Seen Nothin' Yet." *Sports Illustrated* (August 10, 1981): 48–64.

Kardong, Don. "Star Wars II." *The Runner* 8 (October 1985): 40–46.

Kennedy, Ray, and Nancy Williamson. "Money: The Monster Threatening Sports." *Sports Illustrated* (July 17, July 24, and July 31, 1978).

Koch, James V. "Intercollegiate Athletics: An Economic Explanation." *Social Sciences Quarterly* 64 (June 1983): 360–374.

Kowet, D. *The Rich Who Own Sports*. New York: Random House, 1977.

Lipsyte, Robert. *Sports World: An American Dreamland*. New York: Quadrangle/New York Times, 1975.

Loy, John W., Barry D. McPherson, and Gerald Kenyon. *Sport and Social Systems*. Reading, Mass.: Addison-Wesley, 1978, pp. 256–283.

McPherson, Barry D. "Sport Consumption and the Economics of Consumerism." In *Sport and Social Order*, edited by Donald W. Ball and John W. Loy. Reading, Mass.: Addison-Wesley, 1975, pp. 243–275.

Millman, Joel. "Miami Blitz." *Mother Jones* 11 (December 1986): 37–50.

Nader, Ralph, and Peter Gruenstein. "Fans: The Sorry Majority." *Playboy* (March 1978): 98–100, 198.

Nisbet, Robert. "Professional Sports: The Decline and Fall of the Sports Empire." *The American Spectator* 15 (December 1982): 42–44.

Noll, Roger G., ed. *Government and the Sports Business*. Washington, D.C.: The Brookings Institution, 1974.

Sewart, John J. "Recent Corporate Involvement in the World of Sport." *Arena Review* 5 (November 1981): 33–35.

Shults, Fredrick. "Freedom Issues in Sport." *Journal of Physical Education, Recreation, and Dance* 53 (February 1982): 57–61.

Taafe, William. "The Other Game in New York." *Sports Illustrated* (September 29, 1986): 32–33.

Welling, Brenton, Jonathan Tasini, and Dan Cook. "Basketball: Business Is Booming." *Business Week* 2918 (October 28, 1985): 73–82.

Part Seven

The Politics of Sport: International Dimensions

International sport is political.[1] Participants represent and show allegiance to their countries in international competitions. The rituals accompanying sporting events (music, colors, uniforms, flags) are aimed at symbolically reaffirming fidelity to one's country. Phillip Goodhart and Christopher Chataway have argued that there are four kinds of sport: sport as exercise, sport as gambling, sport as spectacle, and representative sport.

> [Representative sport] is a limited conflict with clearly defined rules, in which representatives of towns, regions, or nations are pitted against each other. It is primarily an affair for the spectators: they are drawn to it not so much by the mere spectacle, by the ritual, or by an appreciation of the skills involved, but because they identify themselves with their representatives. . . . Most people will watch [the Olympic Games] for one reason only: there will be a competitor who, they feel, is representing them. That figure in the striped singlet will be their man— running, jumping, or boxing for their country. For a matter of minutes at least, their own estimation of themselves will be bound up with his performance. He will be the embodiment of their nation's strength or weakness. Victory for him will be victory for them; defeat for him, defeat for them.[2]

This last point is important. Evidence from international competitions shows that for many nations and their citizens, victory is an indicator of that nation's superiority (in its politico-economic system and its culture).

Sport, then, is a source of national pride, a source of unity, and a mechanism used by ruling elites to impress its citizens and those of other countries as well. This use of sport as a propaganda vehicle is found in developing countries, the Communist bloc countries, and in the United States and its allies.

Sport is also a tool of foreign policy, as the first selection by James A. R. Nafziger, demonstrates. Sport is used as a prelude to formal relations between countries, as has occurred between the United States and China and between the United States and Cuba. Conversely, refusal by one country to compete against another is a way of pressuring that country, as the United States attempted in its boycott of the 1980 Olympics in Moscow and as the Soviet Union tried in its boycott of the 1984 Olympics in Los Angeles.

The second selection, by Richard E. Lapchick, provides a political history of the modern Olympic Games, highlighting the strong political threads running from 1896 to the present. The final essay, by D. Stanley Eitzen, also examines the Olympics, focusing on the political, bureaucratic, and economic problems inherent in their current structure. He proposes concrete ways to minimize these problems.

NOTES

1. Of course, sport at all levels is inherently political. See D. Stanley Eitzen and George H. Sage, *Sociology of North American Sport*, 3d ed. (Dubuque, Iowa: Wm. C. Brown, 1986), pp. 167–168.
2. Phillip Goodhart and Christopher Chataway, *War without Weapons* (London: W. H. Allen, 1968), p. 3.

23. *Foreign Policy in the Sports Arena*

JAMES A. R. NAFZIGER

The international sports arena is also a political arena. The ancient Greeks, Hitler, pro-Palestinian terrorists, Canadian wheat lobbyists, antiapartheid forces, President Carter, and President Chernenko have all known this to be true and have used sport as an instrument of foreign policy. The intervention of governments in the sports arena raises several policy issues. First, what is the proper role of government—promoter or facilitator? Second, what are or should be the political objectives—for example, to establish diplomatic relations? Third, what are the legal constraints on political intervention in the sports arena? Fourth, in order to accomplish political objectives, how much and what kind of power is necessary?

THE PROPER ROLE OF GOVERNMENT

There are three levels of governmental intervention in the sports arena:

- *Level I*. Simple governmental financial assistance by direct appropriations, by the use of revenue from governmental lotteries, or by other means. Such assistance is not only acceptable, but encouraged, as an international practice. Among the few examples of this practice in the United States at the federal level is official support of exchanges or clinics. States and local jurisdictions subsidize athletics in making appropriations to educational institutions.
- *Level II*. Indirect or direct governmental authorization, supervision, or control over the administration of sport is a widespread practice in most countries. The activity of sport is often supervised by a Ministry of Sports, but sometimes, as in the United States, by a chosen instrument of the government, such as a National Olympic Committee.
- *Level III*. Diplomatic exploitation of sports in the external affairs of the government. Boycotts, sports propagandizing, refusal of visas, hosting the Olympics, and sports exchanges are examples of how governments can use or abuse sport to fulfill foreign policy purposes.

SOURCE: James A. R. Nafziger, "Foreign Policy in the Sports Arena," in *Government and Sport: The Public Policy Issues,* edited by Arthur T. Johnson and James H. Frey (Totowa, N.J.: Rowman and Allanheld, 1985), pp. 248–260.

Level III, which stirs up most of the controversy in international sport, will be the primary focus of this essay.

In the United States, a coherent foreign sports policy did not emerge until the 1970s. Since then, sport has become a controversial and very visible part, though only a minor part, of United States foreign policy. The sources of the new attention to sport during the 1970s lay in a gradually accepted awareness that governmental involvement in sports helps promote the national interest and that political adversaries score points in the international sports arena. A more immediate interest in federal sports policy was provoked by public disenchantment with the management and quality of American participation in the 1972 (Munich) Olympic Games and the shock of witnessing terrorism there. The spectacular expansions in media coverage of transnational athletic competition brought all the excitement, glory, humanity, administrative bungles, and ultimate horror of the 1972 Games into living rooms so graphically as to confirm the important role of sports in global affairs. The involvement of this country's athletes in global competition came to be of major public interest, if not concern. The terrorist nightmare in Munich prompted the State Department to introduce a Draft Convention for the Prevention and Punishment of Certain Acts of International Terrorism[1] and generated legislative proposals to govern internationally related aspects of amateur athletics. More generally, it was apparent after the Munich Games that responses to political problems in the sports arena could not arise strictly from the private sector.

The early 1970s brought an articulation of a foreign policy interest "in furthering mutual understanding and communication through sports."[2] Accordingly, the federal government initially strengthened its role in sports by committing further resources to facilitate people-to-people communication and public diplomacy conducted by private individuals and groups.[3] The federal government became more involved in supporting technical athletic assistance abroad and in helping procure athletic equipment for programs in developing countries. The government recognized that transnational athletic exchange could help improve international relations. Even limited athletic exchange could serve to make foreign policy more "human."

A study undertaken for the Department of State in 1971, which is still useful to policy planners, observed that sports had largely been ignored in diplomacy and suggested two policy options besides the existing role of the department as a *facilitator* of international athletic exchange and competition. Alternatively, the department could work (a) as an active *promoter* to increase the stature of United States participation in international sports programs as a primary means of achieving the objectives of the Fulbright-Hays Act; or (b) as a *programmer* of United States participation in international sports—sport would become a foreign affairs resource that, when balanced with other such resources, might be important to the achievement of foreign policy objectives.[4]

The study recommended that the government's choice among these options should be made by balancing the attendant risks and benefits. As to risks, the facilitative role seemed the safest. The promoter role was slightly riskier because it depends on the vagaries of congressional funding. The programmer role seemed even riskier, since foreign affairs officials might not know how to employ sports skillfully as a diplomatic tool and athletes might dislike the political implications. As to benefits, the promoter and programmer roles offered greater assurance of effective and more visible participation in international competition, in which the United States had been poorly represented in the past. The programmer role would recharacterize the government as a partner rather than a handmaiden of sports activities, and it would therefore tend to encourage a more positive role for sports and physical fitness in public life.[5] In considering which option to pursue, the study concluded that "the Department must first decide the objective of its sports activities and have a cogent plan for achieving that objective before very strong feelings, either way, emerge."[6] Clearly, some form of foreign sports policy was an idea whose time had come.

Criteria for judging the efficacy of a foreign sports effort under governmental auspices may vary according to the intensity of governmental involvement. Low-level policies will be concerned with more or less immediate returns on each dollar invested. For example: What works at a clinic in a particular country? What doesn't? Should a government send a basketball coach to Mauretania after his visit in Dakar? If a government sees itself as simply a facilitator at Level I, the exposure it receives abroad and the contacts the activity generates will be critical. If, however, a government's role extends to that of a promoter or programmer, then the success of its athletes in competition abroad, the degree to which a foreign country adopts a newly introduced sport, or the accomplishment of some other major objective will likely dominate an evaluation of governmental performance.

On Level I of governmental intervention, the State Department's former Bureau of Educational and Cultural Affairs, which was absorbed into the United States Information Agency in 1978, established three objectives that have shaped official programs of athletic exchange: (a) to enlarge the circle of those able to serve as influential interpreters between the United States and other nations, (b) to stimulate institutional development in directions that favorably affect mutual comprehension, and (c) to reduce structural and technical impediments to the exchange of ideas and information. Within this framework the government has conducted programs of athletic exchange while often eschewing direct sponsorship.

The Amateur Sports Act of 1978

The relationships between "nationalism and sports" and "politics and sports" often have been viewed as disjunctive or antagonistic. Until recently, for example, any acknowledgment of an official United States intervention into the sports arena was shunned. Now, however, there is a recognition of the inevitability of athletic realpolitik and of governmental involvement in sports.

After years of discussion and preliminary bills, Congress confirmed its commitment to a federal sports policy and to the supremacy of the Olympic Movement by passing the Amateur Sports Act of 1978. That act largely defines the scope and nature of involvement by the federal government in sports, at least on Levels I and II. The act establishes the United States Olympic Committee (USOC) as a chosen instrument to "promote and support amateur athletic activities involving the United States and foreign nations" (§ 374[5]), and to "establish national goals for amateur athletic activities and encourage the attainment of those goals" (§ 374[1]). Among other provisions, the act instructs the USOC to "coordinate and develop amateur athletic activity in the United States directly relating to international amateur athletic competition, so as to foster productive working relationships among sport-related organizations" (§ 374[2]). With specific references to the Olympic and Pan-American Games, the Amateur Sports Act expresses a public determination to "obtain for the United States, either directly or by delegation to the appropriate national governing body, the most competent amateur representation possible in each competition and event" (§ 374[4]).

An "exclusive jurisdiction" provision in the 1978 act is of particular significance in defining options for using sport as an instrument of foreign policy. Accordingly, the USOC shall "exercise exclusive jurisdiction, either directly or through its constituent members of committees, over all matters pertaining to the participation of the United States in the Olympic Games and in the Pan-American Games, including the representation of the United States in such Games, and over the organization of the Olympic Games and the Pan-American Games when held in the United States."[7] Although this provision cannot in itself constrain federal action that is otherwise legitimate, it nevertheless does establish an expectation that the decisions of the USOC, within a larger international framework, will shape the implementation of foreign sports policy.

Soon after the Amateur Sports Act became law, the boycott of the 1980 (Moscow) Olympic Games confirmed the Carter Administration's willingness to politicize the sports arena by raising federal intervention to the highest level of policymaking. The Reagan Administration generally maintained a low profile, limiting its actions to Levels I and II. In sum, the intensity of United States foreign sports policy peaked at Level III (full governmental intervention) in 1980.

POLITICAL OBJECTIVES

What should be the objectives of a foreign sports policy? At which of the three levels of governmental intervention should it operate? Perhaps a government should look upon sport simply as a diplomatic tool to serve immediate purposes, or perhaps it should view sport more ambitiously as a tool to promote world order.[8] If a government acts unilaterally, either perspective may be deficient because of the degree of ambiguity and complexity inherent in unilateral decisions and policy. A government is therefore ill-advised to "go it alone." Rather, governments are well advised to develop comprehensive and coherent foreign sports policies consistent with international sports law. Good policy can mean an end to bad politics. What is important is not the quarantine of governments and politics from the international sports arena, but the channeling of governmental decisions and politics along acknowledged lines of world ordering. A government can best establish constructive policy, not on the basis of bureaucratic interplay, political expediency, ideological constraints, and pluralistic pressures, but on the basis of accepted international practice. Foreign sports policy consistent with international law seems to be the best means of protecting individual athletes from political injury and promoting athletic values in global society.

In considering the policy options, it may be useful first to identify six political uses of international sports competition: international cooperation, national ideology and propaganda, official prestige, diplomatic recognition and nonrecognition, protest, and conflict.[9] Of these, only diplomatic nonrecognition and conflict are improper official uses of sports competition according to international law, although variations on the other uses may constitute unfriendly acts. Within this margin of discretion, it is necessary for governments to clarify their objectives. The Carter Administration's demand for a boycott by the USOC of the Moscow Games was based on what appeared to be unclear policy concerns.[10] The Administration variously argued principles of diplomatic protection of its nationals, deterrence and retribution. The President first justified the boycott on the grounds of a presumed danger to American athletes and spectators, which was the rationale parroted by the Soviet Union to justify its boycott of the 1984 Games.[11] After having advanced this rationale for the compelled boycott, the White House later changed its mind by asserting that the real reason for the boycott was to deter future aggression and to send the Soviets "a signal of world outrage."[12] To add to the confusion, the Secretary of State, however, appeared to disagree by viewing the boycott as retribution for the Soviet violation of what he thought was a principle against contemporaneous involvement by a sovereign host in open warfare.[13] It became clear that the Carter Administration was indecisive in establishing a rationale for the boycott.

In 1984 the Reagan Administration's quiet handling of the Soviet retaliatory boycott of the Los Angeles Games implicitly acknowledged the futility of distinguishing between the 1980 and 1984 cases. President Reagan's response was particularly apt because not only did he acknowledge, quite correctly, that there was no "prudent" action within his discretion, but he correctly pledged to work through "citizens groups and our people," to encourage the Soviet Union and its allies to reverse their decision not to compete in the Los

Angeles Games. By responding carefully within the ambit of its authority under the Amateur Sports Act of 1978, the Reagan Administration deferred at Level II to the authority of the Olympic movement.

United States foreign policy objectives are limited not only by specific law—in particular, the Amateur Sports Act of 1978 and international law—but also by the federal constitutional structure. The federal government could do nothing to override a decision by Colorado voters not to host the 1976 Winter Games. Similarly, the financing structure of the 1984 Games in Los Angeles was beyond direct federal supervision. In 1978 the citizens of Los Angeles overwhelmingly approved an amendment to the city charter that prohibited the city from spending any tax revenue on the Games that would not be reimbursed by binding, legal contract. This meant that the Los Angeles Olympic Organizing Committee (LAOOC) had to break with Olympic tradition. While previous organizing committees had been part of the municipal government of the host city, the LAOOC by necessity was formed as a private, nonprofit corporation under California laws.

Aside from these limitations on policy options, policy failures sometimes result from ineffective implementation. For example, when the Australian government compensated those athletes and sports bodies that had stayed home from the 1980 Games, it did so for the express purpose of financing their involvement in alternative sports events. Later, to the chagrin of the public and the delight of the media, it was determined that Canberra had failed to supervise or at least monitor the use of the payments. Hence, to the embarrassment of the policymakers, the public came to view the compensation payments as a questionable use of tax revenue.

LEGAL CONSTRAINTS

Unfortunately, commentaries about sports policy too often overlook the legal constraints. Sometimes social observers view law not as prescription, but as just another datum. Thus "[t]he cumulated sociological research on the Olympics may broadly be classified into descriptive investigations, studies on the Olympic Movement as a formal organization, examinations of the relationship between the Olympic Games and various societal subsystems, and analyses of the Olympics as a cultural system."[14] A legal framework seems to be missing in much of the empirical inquiry.

Under the United States Constitution the Executive may, under its foreign relations power or under delegated congressional authority,[15] intervene in the arena of international sports. Generally, the Amateur Sports Act of 1978 defines the government's policy options and related private options even to some extent on Level III of governmental intervention. For example, a study of the boycott of the Moscow Games concluded that "the Act did not authorize the USOC to boycott the Games in order to effect national policy objectives."[16] There are, however, gaps and uncertainties in the supervision of amateur sports under the 1978 act. Whenever the act is silent or ambiguous— as, for example, in providing rather cryptically for the "exclusive jurisdiction" of the USOC—the federal legislation has less force.

Foreign sports policy must comply with international law, including that governing nation groups such as the Commonwealth of Nations. Although a full discussion of international legal constraints lies beyond the scope of this essay and has been undertaken elsewhere,[17] a brief summary of some important aspects will at least indicate the framework.

The Olympic Charter best evidences international custom pertaining to sports competition, Olympic or not. The Rules of the Charter are administered by a "supreme authority,"[18] the International Olympic Committee (IOC). The IOC is a corporate body having juridical status and perpetual succession.[19] Rule 9 of the Olympic Charter provides that "[e]very person or organization that plays any part whatsoever in the Olympic movement shall accept the supreme authority of the IOC and shall be bound by its rules and submit to its jurisdiction."[20] Although the IOC is a nongovernmental organization[21] that cannot in itself compel state obedience, its rules best evidence current international practice and therefore have legal significance.[22]

Three of the IOC rules are particularly instructive. Rule 3, one of the cornerstones of international sports law, provides that "[n]o discrimination . . . is allowed against any country or person on grounds of race, religion, or *politics*."[23] Rule 9 states that "[t]he Games are contests between individuals and teams and not between countries."[24] Rule 24 obligates National Olympic Committees (NOCs) to be autonomous, to resist all political pressures, and to enforce the Rules and Bylaws of the IOC; "NOCs shall be the sole authorities responsible for the representation of their respective countries at the Olympic Games."[25] Bylaw 8 to Rule 24 defines the term "representation" to cover a decision to participate or not.[26] Violations of the rules, such as yielding to political pressures, expose NOCs to penalties.[27] Thus governmental intrusion into these rules of custom is abusive. The Draft Declaration Relating to the Protection of the Olympic Games,[28] although still under study, would confirm the binding force of these rules, especially Rules 3 and 24, on members of the United Nations.

In interpreting these and other provisions, a line may be drawn between governmental support of individual athletes, teams, and events on the one hand, and governmental interference in the sports arena on the other. The IOC has long emphasized "the importance and desirability of government aid, and reconfirmed the dangers of government interference of a political nature in the running of sport in any country."[29] Also, as a matter of textual interpretation, the validity of political intervention in the sports arena is generally acceptable when it furthers specific provisions of international law. Thus boycotts to combat apartheid and other forms of official racism are valid, whereas geopolitically motivated boycotts must be evaluated on a case-by-case basis.[30]

Given the weakness of the international legal system, a government's perception of the strength of international norms and institutions may influence its decisions. For example, rightly or wrongly, the Dutch government compelled a boycott of the 1980 Games, but later it drew only passing attention to human rights problems in Uruguay when the issue arose of whether to disallow participation by the Royal Dutch Football Federation in a tournament in politically controversial Uruguay: "It is not for the Government to say in a case like this: you may not go."[31] The Minister of Foreign Affairs justified the distinction between the two situations largely on the basis of the strength and transcendental purposes of the Olympics, "unlike a series of football matches."[32]

Remedies for the rights accorded by international sports law take many forms, including adjudication and diplomacy. The Amateur Sports Act of 1978 prescribes that "the United States Olympic Committee shall 'provide for the swift resolution of conflicts and disputes involving amateur athletes, national governing bodies, and amateur sports organizations, and protect the opportunity of any amateur athlete, coach, trainer, manager, administrator, or official to participate in amateur athletic competition.' "[33] The act requires that the USOC constitution and bylaws establish and maintain provisions for the swift and equitable resolution of disputes involving any of its members and relating to the opportunity of an amateur athlete, coach, trainer, manager, administrator, or official to participate in the Olympic Games, the Pan-American Games, world championship competition, or other such protected competition as defined in such constitution and bylaws. The act also specifies procedures for settling two common types of conflicts: (1) those that arise when an amateur sports organization or eligible person attempts to compel an NGB to comply with the organizational and sanctioning criteria in the act, and (2) those generated when an amateur sports organization seeks to replace an incumbent NGB.[34] Although these procedures may address issues of international consequence, they primarily are concerned with such technical issues as organization, team recruitment, and financing.

A new international institution, the Court of Arbitration for Sport (CAS), is designed to help settle "disputes of a private nature arising out of the practice or development of sport, and in a general way, *all* activities pertaining to sport."[35] Although the CAS may have limited impact in itself, it evidences the gradual institutionalization of international sports law and therefore is relevant to policy planning. Article 4 of its statute provides that "[s]uch disputes may bear on questions of principle relating to sport or on pecuniary or other interests affected on the occasion of the practice or the development of sport, and in a general way, all activities pertaining to sport."[36] The following parties have the standing to submit a case to the CAS "provided they have an interest in so doing":[37] the IOC, National Olympic Committees, Organizing Committees of the Olympic Games, sports association, national federations, "and, in a general way, any natural person or corporate body having the capacity or power to compromise."[38] The statute of the CAS provides for a discretionary procedure of conciliation in addition to arbitration.[39]

ASSESSMENT OF POWER TO EFFECT RESULTS

A foreign sports policy will be unproductive if it is not realistic; power is a driving force of policy. Thus the Carter Administration's failure to assess its limited power to encourage a global boycott of the 1980 Games led to diplomatic embarrassment. The boycott divided athletes, threatened to destabilize the international Olympic movement, aggravated a global public, worried persons with a business stake in the Moscow Games, and threatened to isolate the United States from some of its most important allies. "The boycott policy was long on risks and short on assurances."[40]

Although the deficiencies of the 1980 boycott policy were numerous, the "power failure" was prominent. The Carter Administration incorrectly assessed the power of the International Olympic Committee and the various sports federations to control their members, ward off government intervention, and thereby defy governmental pressures. In addition, the United States could not rely on a total commitment from its allies because sport is really symbolic of relationships and is not worth hard-core persuasive efforts—for example, a denial of economic aid or political support. Vital interests were not at stake in this situation. The president of the IOC emphasized that reality, as did another observer when he wrote:

> In the final analysis, the policy posed too stern a test for the Western alliance over a non-crucial matter. While sports can certainly be used as a political weapon, the Administration was ill-equipped to employ it effectively as a sanction of the Afghanistan invasion. Participation in Moscow would have been less harmful to U.S. interests than the boycott. . . . The Administration gave very little thought to the Olympics prior to Afghanistan. There had been some discussion of the Moscow Games during consideration of the Amateur Sports Act in 1978, but nothing was sustained. Possibly, some Administration members were familiar with amateur sports, but only one or two had had personal contact with amateur sports officials. This lack of knowledge caused the government to underestimate the USOC's independence and to overestimate the USOC's status in international amateur sports.[41]

Most seriously of all, the Administration failed to understand that unilateral boycotts, by and large, are of doubtful legality, do not work very well, and are almost guaranteed not to work in a geopolitical context. Generally, boycotts do not seem to change or eliminate the condition at which they are directed. Examples of the futility of boycotts outside the sports arena are legion. They did not work against Italy in the 1930s (after that country's occupation of Ethiopia), Rhodesia in the 1960s (after the marshaling of global opinion against the segregationist regime of Ian Smith), or Cuba from 1960 on (after the establishment of the Cold War between the new Castro regime and the United States government). In sum, the United States government, and this applies as well to other governments, "must be better equipped to deal with the Olympic movement should the U.S. attempt to make the Games an instrument of U.S. policy again in the future."[42] If sports is to be a meaningful instrument of policy in the geopolitical scene, any government that uses it must be prepared to follow up with strong, decisive measures. It is easier for the Soviets to coerce its allies. The United States, on the other hand, has more of a "partnership" relation with its allies and therefore can seldom resort effectively to anything but persuasive tactics. The Carter Administration was unwilling or unable to use more forceful tactics in order to obtain boycott cooperation. If a foreign sports policy is to work, a government must have sufficient power, including expertise and supervisory personnel, and it must be willing to risk its power. Also, a government's actions must be acceptable under international law and to pertinent international bodies, such as the IOC, to achieve success.

CONCLUSION

Politics is apparently in the sports arena to stay, but playing politics in the sports arena can turn out to be futile. Recent boycotts of the Olympic Games confirm that they generally do not work well and may even work against the implementing governments.

For the future, governments are well advised to develop comprehensive and coherent foreign sports policy, rooted not in geopolitics but in international law, including the accepted rules of the Olympic movement. Good policy can mean an end to bad politics. What is important is the channeling of governmental decisions and politics along acknowledged lines of world ordering rather than on the basis of bureaucratic interplay, political expediency, ideological constraints, and pluralistic pressures. Legitimate foreign sports policies consistent with international norms and rules are the best means of protecting individual athletes from political injury, while guiding governmental and nongovernmental decisionmaking along appropriate lines. At the very least, internationally acceptable policies will help keep governments running on the same track.

NOTES

1. John F. Murphy, *The United Nations and the Control of International Violence: A Legal and Political Analysis* (Totowa, N.J.: Rowman & Allanheld, 1982), p. 181.
2. See transcript of the speech delivered by Alan A. Reich, Deputy Assistant Secretary of State

for Educational and Cultural Affairs, before the General Assembly of International Sports Federations, in 119 *Congressional Record* 95 (daily ed., June 19, 1973); remarks of Walter Boehm, in R. Singer, *Multidisciplinary Symposium on Sport and the Means of Furthering Mutual International Understanding*, U.S. Department of State, Bureau of Educational and Cultural Affairs, December 4, 1973, (1974).

3. See Alan A. Reich, *New Role for Associations in Promoting World Understanding, Association Management* (February 1973), p. 32.

4. Harris/Ragan Management Corporation, International Sports Policies for the Department of State: A Presentation of Options 25, 7, unpublished (September 24, 1971) [hereafter cited as Harris/Ragan Report].

5. Ibid. at 25–26.

6. Ibid. at 28.

7. 36 U.S.C. §§ 371–396 (Supp. IV 1980).

8. The press frequently reported on international policies in sports. See, for example, *New York Times*, October 25, 1974, p. 49, col. 4; *The Washington Post*, October 30, 1974, p. F1, col. 8 (refusal of India to participate against South Africa in Davis Cup competition); *The Washington Post*, February 7, 1975, p. A14, col. 1; and *Sports Illustrated* (February 24, 1975), p. 18 (refusal of India, contrary to its prior commitment, to allow participation by South Africa and Israel in world table-tennis championships held in Calcutta, together with a simultaneous invitation to the Palestinian Liberation Organization). Indian teams in particular appeared to be "guided by the rules and regulations of the State." *The Washington Post*, February 7, 1975, p. A14, cols. 1, 5; *The Washington Post*, March 20, 1975, p. E4, col. 5 (refusal of the Mexican government to grant visas to a South African Davis Cup tennis team to play in Mexico and a directive to Mexicans not to compete with South Africans elsewhere); *Sports Illustrated* (May 12, 1975), p. 15 (same with respect to World Championship Tennis Competition in Mexico); *The Washington Post*, May 7, 1975, p. D2, col. 3 (French exclusion of Rhodesian tennis team). On the politicization of the International Chess Federation, see *The Oregonian*, March 20, 1975, p. A10, col. 1 (on rule-changing proposals by the United States Chess Federation): "The voting Wednesday went generally by blocs, with East and West European and Arab federations siding with the Russians, and Asian and Latin American federations lining up with the United States." Public and professional opinion on this subject was ambiguous. A 1971 sampling of forty-four sports administrators, government administrators, sports commentators, government observers, and sports participants revealed mixed attitudes toward expansions of the government's role in sports, including federal financial support for sports and questions about the efficacy of a sports policy. Most of these surveyed did, however, agree on what they then saw as a need to keep "politics" aloof from sports and to improve the program administered by the Department of State. Harris/Ragan Report. This survey was taken prior to the Munich Olympic Games and the demise of plans for the Denver Winter Games. A Harris sports survey taken after the Munich Games disclosed considerable public disenchantment with both the administration and particularly the enforcement of the Olympic Rules, and it indicated considerable public support for official protection by the government of U.S. interests in the Games. "Sports Fans Assess '72 Olympics," *The Harris Survey* (October 5, 1972).

9. James A. R. Nafziger and Andrew Strenk, "The Political Uses and Abuses of Sports," *Connecticut Law Review* 10 (1978): 280–89.

10. See James A. R. Nafziger, "Diplomatic Fun and the Games: A Commentary on the United States Boycott of the 1980 Summer Olympics," *Willamette Law Review* 17 (1980): 67.

11. *Department of State Bulletin* 80 (January 1980): Special-B.

12. *Department of State Bulletin* 80 (March 1980): 51.

13. Ibid., p. 50.

14. Jeffrey Segrave and Donald Chu, *Olympism* (Champaign, Ill.: Human Kinetics, 1982), p. 201.

15. U.S. Constitution article II, pp. 1–3; United States v. Curtiss-Wright Export Corp., 299 U.S. 304 (1936).

16. Comment, "Political Abuse of Olympic Sport: DeFrantz v. United States Olympic Committee," *New York University Journal International and Politics* 14 (1982): 155, 178.

17. James A. R. Nafziger, "Nonaggressive Sanctions in the International Sports Arena," *Case Western Reserve Journal of International Law* 15 (1983): 329.

18. Olympic Charter (1984), at Rule 4. Rule 23 of the Olympic Charter provides also that "[t]he

IOC is the final authority on all questions concerning the Olympic Games and the Olympic movement."

19. Ibid., at Rule 11.
20. Ibid., Rule 9.
21. Ibid., at Rule 11. The IOC is a permanent organization. It selects such persons as it considers qualified to be members, provided that they speak French or English and are citizens of and reside in a country which possesses an NOC recognized by the IOC. The IOC welcomes them into membership with a brief ceremony during which they accept the required obligations and responsibilities. There shall be only one member in any country except in the largest and most active countries in the Olympic movement, and in those where the Olympic Games have been held, where there may be a maximum of two. Members of the IOC are representatives of the IOC in their countries and not their delegates to the IOC. They may not accept from governments or from any organizations or individuals instructions which shall in any way bind them or interfere with the independence of their vote. [ibid., at Rule 12]
22. A 1977 Belgian court decision, confirming the position of the French courts, the Council of Europe, and the High Court of Justice of the European Communities, ruled that the international rules of sport supersede conflicting national policies and laws. The Second Conference of European Sports Ministers adopted a resolution that explicitly confirmed the authority of the Olympic Charter. Furthermore, leading publicists have established the authority of the Olympic Rules in the international sports arena.
23. Olympic Charter, note 18, Rule 3 (emphasis added).
24. Ibid., Rule 9.
25. Ibid., Rule 24.
26. Ibid., Bylaw 8 to Rule 24.
27. Ibid., Rule 25.
28. *Olympic Review* (1982): 481–82.
29. *Olympic Review* (1974): 490. See also Letter from Lord Killanin to President Gerald Ford in *Sports Illustrated* (September 2, 1974), p. 12.
30. See note 17.
31. The Netherlands participation in the mini-world football championship in Uruguay, *Netherlands Yearbook of International Law* 13 (1982): 268.
32. Ibid.
33. 39 U.S.C. 374(8). On related issues, see James A. R. Nafziger, "The Amateur Sports Act of 1978," *Brigham Young University Law Review* (1983): 86–94.
34. Ibid.
35. Article 1., Statutes [sic] of the Court of Arbitration for Sport, *Olympic Review* (1983): 763 (emphasis added).
36. Ibid., Article 4.
37. Ibid., Article 5.
38. Ibid.
39. Ibid., Article 29, p. 766.
40. Adam Goldstein, "The 1980 Olympic Boycott: The Role of National Olympic Committees and of the International Olympic Committee" (May 19, 1981), unpublished, p. 86.
41. Ibid., p. 84.
42. Ibid., p. 92.

24. A Political History of the Modern Olympic Games

RICHARD E. LAPCHICK

In recent times—as we have been forced to watch a succession of political events associated with the Olympic Games—politicians, sportswriters, editorial writers, and most of the American public have expressed shock at the mixing of politics and sport. The black protest in 1968, the assassination of Israeli athletes in Munich in 1972, and the African boycott of the 1976 Games all heightened the battle cry. However, when President Carter called for the boycott of the 1980 Moscow Olympics, the cry of "Let's keep politics out of sport" was silenced. The same people who had criticized others were suddenly on the patriotic bandwagon and ready to go along with the boycott to protest the Soviet invasion of Afghanistan. By 1984, a subsequent Soviet boycott of the Los Angeles Games was all too predictable.

In fact, the modern Olympic spirit, even from inception in 1896, has never been free of political influence. While the political strings were initially petty, the 1936 Berlin Olympics opened a new era where politics has vied with sport for the spotlight in the Olympic Games.

This essay is an attempt to trace the history of that entanglement and to analyze what this might mean for the future of the international sport.

THE EARLY YEARS: 1896–1933

When Le Baron Pierre de Coubertin helped to rekindle the Olympic flame in 1896, he was largely moved by the noble thought that international sports competition would move men and nations to view each other as peaceful friends. Sports could be the area where a common understanding might be reached. In 1894, de Coubertin stated that: "The aims of the Olympic Movement are to promote the development of those fine physical and moral qualities which are the basis of amateur sport and to bring together the athletes of the world in a great quadrennial festival of sports thereby creating international respect and goodwill and thus helping to construct a better and more peaceful world."[1]

SOURCE: Richard E. Lapchick, "A Political History of the Modern Olympic Games," in *Fractured Focus: Sport as a Reflection of Society*, edited by Richard E. Lapchick (Lexington, Mass.: D.C. Heath, 1986), pp. 329–345.

Years later it was discovered in de Coubertin's personal correspondence that the decline in the French spirit after the Franco-Prussian War was a prime motivating factor in his work to rebuild the Olympic Games. He even worked behind the scenes to keep Germany out of the first Games.

However, there was at least a verbal commitment that international sport must be free from all government pressures. This was incorporated into the Olympic Principles. Participation could never be determined by race, religion or politics. The late Avery Brundage, who dominated international sport for three decades from his post in the International Olympic Committee (IOC), summed up the need for such a principle as the root of the Olympic Movement: "Were this fundamental principle not followed scrupulously, the Olympic Movement would surely founder. It is essential to the success and even to the existence of any truly international body that there are no restrictions of this kind. . . . As it is, the Olympic Movement furnishes a conspicuous example that when fair play and good sportsmanship prevail, men can agree, regardless of race, religion, or political convictions."[2]

Indeed, sportsmen have chosen to believe in these principles ever since de Coubertin. On the level of individual competition, it has long been believed that sport is an area where there was equal opportunity for all, based purely on the ability of the athlete, with no reference to the athlete's personal background and/or beliefs. On the level of international competition, it has long been said that nations compete with each other for the sake of sport only. Avery Brundage said: "We must never forget that the most important thing in the Olympic Games is not to win but to take part."[3] In essence, ". . . sport, like the fine arts, transcends politics."[4]

These are the ideals of sport in general and of the Olympic Movement in particular. The reality has been something less than the ideal.

The first overt act of politics in the Olympics took place in 1908 when the United States team refused to dip the American flag to King Edward VII at the opening ceremonies of the 1908 Olympics in London. For the next 25 years the politics of international sport were played at this low-keyed, almost petty level. But the Hitler regime changed all of that very quickly.

THE GROWTH OF THE OLYMPIC "POLITICAL SPIRIT": 1933–1967

In May of 1933 the German Reichssportfuhrer, Hans Von Tschammer-Osten, announced the Nazi sports policy: "German sports are for Aryans. German Youth Leadership is only for Aryans and not for Jews. Athletes will not be judged by ability alone, but also by their general and moral fitness for representing Germany."[5] The Reichssportfuhrer thus sowed the seeds that inexorably dragged politics into sport.

In June of 1933, Osten approved the anti-Semitic resolutions in German sports clubs, which, taken with the municipalities, controlled most of the sports facilities in Germany.[6] It became impossible for German Jews to train properly.

In November of that year, Osten ruled that Jews could not be members of athletic governing boards, thus effectively cutting them out of sports administration.[7]

In August of 1935, Jews were forbidden to join in the new Nazi consolidated sports clubs.[8] It was ruled that they could not compete abroad and, therefore, could not represent Germany.[9]

Jewish spectators were also frequently prohibited. In August of 1935 Jews were forbidden to attend the Winter Olympic Games in Garmisch as signs on the gates proclaimed. "Jews are not admitted."[10] (These signs were subsequently taken down after international protest.) In October, a United States swimming team swam in Berlin before an all-Aryan audience. A sign over the box office read, "Jews are not wanted."[11] The segregation of sports was complete, encompassing athletes, administrators and spectators.

In the 1930s, protests against staging the Games in Berlin were held in Canada, Britain, Sweden, France, the Netherlands, Poland, Palestine, and, of course, the United States.[12] Despite the protests, these countries all sent teams to Berlin.

It was in the United States that the Berlin boycott movement had the widest base. Led by prominent public figures, the Fair Games Committee was formed.[13] Other groups were involved in the boycott crusade between June of 1933 and January of 1936: twenty Olympic champions; various Catholic and Protestant groups, numerous Jewish groups, six U.S. Senators, seven governors, forty-one university presidents, the American Federation of Labor, the Women's League for Peace, the National Association for the Advancement of Colored People, and other black groups, the American National Society of Mural Painters, which withdrew its Berlin exhibit, and the Amateur Athletic Union (AAU).[14] The last was particularly important: without the AAU's sanction, no American athlete could go to Berlin. In November of 1933, the AAU decided it would boycott the Games unless the Germans changed their policy immediately.[15]

Reichssportfuhrer Osten clearly showed the importance which Germany attached to the American's participation in Berlin: "The protest of the AAU is a complete impossibility and represents the dirty handiwork of conscienceless agitators who want systematically to undermine Germany's position abroad."[16] Osten knew that if the American's withdrew, many others would follow and the Games might collapse in Hitler's face. It was not to be as Avery Brundage, then President of the American Olympic Committee (AOC), stepped to center stage. As the AAU appeared ready to finalize its decision, Brundage said that American athletes must meet this "un-American boycott offensive with historic American action. . . . To those alien agitators and their American stooges who would deny our athletes their birthright as American citizens to represent the United States in the Olympic Games of 1936 in Germany, our athletes reply in the modern vernacular, 'Oh, yeah!' "[17] He went on to say that American athletes must follow "the patterns of the Boston Tea Party, the Minute Men of Concord, and the troops of George Washington at Valley Forge. . . . Regardless of AAU action, we (AOC) are going to send a team abroad."[18]

The American protest against the Berlin Games was clearly not the work of one particular ethnic or religious group; it represented a cross-section of society that spanned religious, economic, and political boundaries. The movement brought together 20,000 people in August of 1935 at Madison Square Garden to ask for the withdrawal of the American team from the 1936 Games.[19] This remains the largest single group ever to come together at one time to protest a sports-related event.

The importance of sport to Hitler was shown in the press (*Der Angriff*) after the German soccer team played in London in December of 1935 amidst widespread British protests: "For Germany, it was an unrestrained political, psychological, and, also, sporting success. . . . It is hardly a secret in well-informed circles that a resumption of closer contact with Great Britain is earnestly desired."[20] The Reichssportfuhrer, as early as 1933, had said: "Sports are something to conjure with in international relations and it is my duty to improve these relations."[21]

Later, when the American Olympic Committee voted to participate in the Berlin Olympics despite the controversy then raging in the United States, Reichssportfuhrer Osten said that the decision marked, "a turn in the international campaign of hate against Germany."[22]

As the opening of the Games neared, the official Nazi party newspaper, *Volkischer Beobachter*, revealed the propaganda value of the Games and the national exhibit 'Germany.' "The exhibition will present a concrete demonstration of the National Socialist principles and program."[23]

Despite Brundage's pledges—made both before and after the Berlin Games—that the Olympics were run solely by the German Olympic Committee and the IOC, the German government actually paid for all the sports facilities and the army paid for the Olympic Village, which later became an army facility.[24]

The use of the Games as blatant propaganda was highlighted by the dedication: "Germany's thousands of years of history find their ultimate meaning in Adolf Hitler. Adolf Hitler fulfills a thousand year old German dream."[25] The official Olympic poster had a map of Europe that included German-speaking sections of Southeast and Central Europe within Germany's borders.[26]

When the Austrian team arrived in Berlin, they were greeted by the German national anthem.[27] The opening ceremonies showcased the British and French teams giving the Nazi salute to Hitler. The 100,000 spectators cheered them wildly; however, the crowd showed tremendous displeasure with the American team when they refused to salute Hitler.[28]

When black American athletes began to roll up victories, *Der Angriff* attacked the AOC for bringing 'black auxiliaries' to the Games.[29] The victories by these blacks caused a huge storm in Berlin. An English report was circulated that the blacks had leg operations to increase their speed. The Germans claimed they were effective because of their peculiar bone structure, while the South Africans openly depreciated their achievements.[30]

The original German plans were to have no Jews associated with their Olympic team. Hitler had even asked Lewald, the head of the German Olympic Committee, to resign because of his Jewish ancestry. However, the Americans made their first threat to withdraw and Lewald was quickly restored in an advisory capacity. It was announced in 1935 that Avery Brundage would personally conduct an investigation into charges of discrimination against Jews in Germany. The Reichssportfuhrer immediately requested that the Jewish federations name 50 Jewish candidates for the German olympic team.[31] *Before* Brundage undertook his investigation, he told American athletes to prepare for the Games.[32] As Brundage left Germany, Rudolf Hess, minister without portfolio in Hitler's cabinet, ordered that Nazis could not fraternize the Jews.[33] Many felt that this meant the end of the Games in Berlin. Brundage expressed great interest in the order as he left.

The American Olympic Committee, which met with Brundage and voted to accept Germany's invitation to participate in the Games, claimed that sport was the wedge that would lead to the end of discrimination in Germany. In a setting that added irony to the situation, the AOC meeting was held in the New York Athletic Club, which barred Jewish membership.[34]

With all the major nations deciding to participate, the Jewish fencing star, Helene Mayer, became the only Jewish member of the 477 person German team. With the threat of isolation gone, the Germans made no real compromise. In 1959, Brundage recalled the situation and analyzed it in the following manner: "In 1936 there was an organized and well financed attack on the Games of the XIth Olympiad, because certain individuals and groups did not approve of the German Government at that time. . . . The outcome, however, was a great victory for Olympic principles and the United States was represented by one of its largest and best teams."[35]

Brundage obviously felt that having one Jewish team member out of 477 was a worthwhile compromise, and all that followed for the Jewish people in Germany did not dampen his enthusiasm for the 1936 Games. It does not take a great deal of insight to see that there were certainly no lasting compromises in terms of an end to discrimination against Jews in Germany. One must decide if the month long journey away from discrimination merited the tremendous propaganda value Hitler enjoyed as a result of the Games.

For the Germans had their sports propaganda success as they rolled to an impressive athletic triumph. Thus, Nazi Germany utilized their sports and sports festivals as tools of propaganda so effectively that they were able to lull sportsmen and diplomats alike into believing that Germany was a fine nation in the family of nations. After the conclusion of the Games, Brundage addressed the pro-Nazi American-German Bund before 20,000 in Madison Square Garden: "We can learn much from Germany. We, too, if we wish to preserve our institutions, must stamp out communism. We, too, must take steps to arrest the decline of patriotism. Germany has progressed as a nation out of her discouragement of five years ago into a new spirit of confidence in herself. Everywhere I found Germans friendly, courteous, and obliging. The question was whether a vociferous minority, highly organized and highly financed, could impose its will on 120,000,000 people."[36] This was a reflection of the effectiveness of the propaganda. Richard D. Mandell, in his study, *The Nazi Olympics*, maintains that this was a major turning point for Hitler, giving him tremendous self-confidence in the international spectrum. The lesson was not lost for other nations have used sports ever since as a vehicle for national prestige or to spotlight political causes.

THE "TWO CHINAS" QUESTION

The question of "Two Chinas" has been addressed in the Olympics since the IOC admitted the People's Republic of China (PRC) in 1954 while retaining the membership of the Republic of China (ROC)—also known as Taiwan or Formosa. The IOC began to maneuver on this question once it became clear that the PRC would not compete *with* the ROC.

When Canada refused to admit Taiwanese athletes as representatives of the Republic of China for the Montreal Games, the question was settled de facto. With the exception of the Socialist nations, Canada was universally condemned for bringing politics into sport. There was no issue in 1980 because of the Western boycott of Moscow. The PRC was alone in 1984 at the Los Angeles Games, and the issue was finally resolved.

The controversy was at its height when the IOC convened in May of 1959 to rule that the "Republic of China no longer represents sports in the entire country of China," and must reapply as Taiwan.[37] It was assumed that Taiwan would not accept this and the PRC would be the only representative of all of China. However, the United States Department of State immediately issued a formal position on the IOC decision: "It is evident that Communist pressures have been directed to obtaining the expulsion of the Chinese Nationalists. . . . We trust that public and sports organs, both here and abroad, will recognize the Communist threats for what they are."[38] On the same day, a resolution condemning the IOC was introduced in the House of Representatives by Francis E. Dorn of New York. Representative Melvin Laird (later to become the Secretary of Defense) introduced an amendment to the bill prohibiting the use of any U.S. Army equipment or personnel in the 1960 Winter Olympic Games, to be held in Squaw Valley, California, if any "free nation" was banned.[39] President Eisenhower himself condemned the IOC action and, suddenly, Avery Brundage became an advocate of readmitting Nationalist

China as the "Republic of China."[40] This represented a complete turnaround position for Mr. Brundage.

When Canada recognized the People's Republic of China in October of 1970, all "Republic of China" passports became unacceptable for entry into Canada. The Canadians informed the IOC of this fact more than a year prior to the Games. The IOC did nothing until Canada reiterated its position on May 28, 1976. Lord Killanin, then head of the IOC, did not call a special meeting of the IOC to discuss the issue but instead waited until IOC delegates gathered in Montreal seven weeks later.

Their compromise offer had no substance: there was no reason to believe that Taiwan would compete under an Olympic banner or as Taiwan. Therefore, the IOC knew what the result would be. The American position was that we were behind the compromise under the guise of a threatened withdrawal on principle. Gold has always been heavier than principle. When the Americans had their threat to withdraw on the table, the American press praised the position for its idealism. To withdraw in this case would be honorable.

EARLY SOVIET-AMERICAN BATTLES IN POLITICAL SPORT

The American view of world communism did not differentiate between the People's Republic of China and the Soviet Union. Therefore, in retaliation for 'communist pressures,' the United States refused visas for East Germans to compete in the modern pentathlon world championships in Harrisburg, Pennsylvania.[41] In February of 1960, the State Department refused visas for the East German press and members of their Olympic staff to attend the Winter Olympics on the grounds that, "admission was not in the best interests of the United States."[42] No one, including major political leaders, wanted to recall the United States had acted in the same way, for more blatantly political reasons, as the Canadians had. Somehow, this condemnation of the Canadians by the United States seems hollow with the knowledge of these past events.

For decades, the Soviet Olympic Committee has fought for the inclusion of communist nations such as East Germany, North Korea and Communist China. The United States Olympic Committee has, dutifully, opposed the same.[43] Both France and the United States refused visas to East Germans as recently as 1962.

Later in that same year, the Fourth Asian Games were marred by President Sukarno's refusal to admit teams from Nationalist China and Israel. When India implied that the Games became 'unofficial' as a result, Indonesian Trade Minister Suharto broke off trade relations and 4,000 Indonesians 'raided' the Indian Embassy in Jakarta. Prime Minister Nehru accused the Chinese Communists of playing up anti-Indian feelings in Indonesia.[44] Demonstrating its pro-Western bias, the IOC chose to ban the Indonesian team from the 1964 Tokyo Games for not admitting Nationalist China and Israel. However, it barely mentioned the actions of France, the United States or the Philippines (which had barred Yugoslavians).[45] The entire Arab League then threatened to boycott the Tokyo Games unless the ban on Indonesia was lifted.[46] President Sukarno left no room for doubt about his intentions for the use of sport, saying, "Indonesia proposes now to mix sports with politics and we are thus establishing 'the Games of the Newly Emerging Forces.' "[47] All of this was in the name of sport.

In the United States, Mr. Edward Herbert, Chairman of the House Armed Services Subcommittee, said that a $2,000,000 bill for athletes was "to make the United States the most powerful nation in the world athletically."[48] In an incredible statement for a man of his position, the then Vice-President, Hubert Humphrey, said: "What the Soviets are doing is a challenge to us, just like Sputnik was a challenge. We are going to be humiliated as a great nation unless we buckle down to the task of giving our young people a chance to compete."[49] This was in reference to the unofficial team defeat (although nations are not supposed to keep a national count of victories, most nations do) of the United States Olympic team at the hands of the Soviet Union in Tokyo. He went on to say that we must conclusively prove that a free society produces better athletes than a socialist society. This is not to say the Soviet Union did not have a similar aim in proving that a socialist society produces better athletes than a free one—all in keeping with the tradition set by Hitler in 1936.

THE RACIAL FACTOR
IN THE GAMES: 1968–1976

"I, therefore, want to make it quite clear that from South Africa's point of view no mixed sport between whites and non-whites will be practiced locally, irrespective of the standard of proficiency of the participants. . . . We do not apply that as a criterion because our policy has nothing to do with proficiency or lack of proficiency."[50] When Prime Minister Vorster of South Africa reaffirmed his government's position on mixing races in sport *during* the IOC investigation of South African sport, many assumed that this statement alone would keep South Africa out of the 1968 Mexico Olympics. The Africans were sure that the IOC would keep South Africa out in 1968 as they had in 1964. They turned out to be poor judges as the IOC, meeting in Grenoble during the Winter Olympics, voted South Africa back into the Games. Although the African nations had threatened a massive boycott of the Olympics if South Africa participated, the IOC apparently felt it to be an idle gesture. It was anything but idle.

The Organization of African Unity (OAU) strongly urged the Supreme Council for Sport in Africa to call for its 32 member nations to boycott the

Games in protest of South Africa's apartheid policy. They did so two weeks after the Grenoble verdict.[51] Most Socialist and Third World countries threatened to join the Africans. By March 10th, four weeks after Grenoble, the *New York Times* reported that only ten nations—all predominantly white—were certain to go to Mexico.[52] Many American athletes began to pick up the idea as the American Committee on Africa (ACOA) tried to enlist support.[53] This, of course, was at the height of the black American boycott. After two months of delay, with their small empire evaporating in the heat of political battle, the IOC reversed its decision. Avery Brundage never admitted that the change was a result of the boycott or because the South Africans violated the Olympic principles. He merely maintained that the Mexicans could not guarantee the safety of the South Africans in Mexico City.[54]

At the end of July, Avery Brundage called Mexico, "the most stable and fastest growing country in Latin America," and claimed that "the Olympic Movement had no little part in making it so."[55] Within days of this statement a student strike began in Mexico City that provoked the worst government crisis in 30 years. As the opening of the Games neared, thirteen were killed and hundreds injured in the three-day riot. It was an ironic scene: Olympic posters saying, "With peace, everything is possible," were plastered everywhere in the city.[56] Brundage, it seems, was slightly premature in his evaluation of the stability of Mexico, but he was not premature in saying that the Olympic Movement had helped to make Mexico what it was. Of the several reasons given by the students for the riots, one was that the incredibly high cost of staging the Games was a national disgrace.

The Olympic-political event best remembered in America was the 1968 black American boycott movement led by Harry Edwards. When that did not materialize to the degree that Edwards hoped, he changed strategies and planned demonstrations at the Games. The best remembered photo of the 1968 Games was the clenched-fist portrait of John Carlos and Tommy Smith during the playing of the Star Spangled Banner after a presentation of medals. Their actions were followed by the gestures of a dozen other black athletes who won medals in track and field events. Sports officials were outraged at the conduct of the black athletes. A survey taken four years later showed that the controversy surrounding these events lingered on: only 32 percent of the whites questioned (8 percent were undecided) felt the athletes' gestures were justified. Even among blacks opinion was divided as only 57 percent approved (9 percent were undecided).[57]

In a press conference at the close of the Games, Avery Brundage was asked what progress the Olympics had made in human relations. He replied: "Right here in Mexico, thanks to the Juegos Deportivos, the Mexicans have proved that boys and girls are able to become better citizens, as they are stronger and healthier and have acquired a sense of discipline and national morale."[58] Mr. Brundage had apparently not noticed the riots of a few days before which took strong police action to stop in time for the Games.

Brundage's most curious statement came in response to a question asking him how the Olympics could survive as long as politics continued to become more and more involved in the Games. His response was, "Who said that politics are becoming more and more involved in the Olympics? In my opinion this is not so. . . . You know very well that politics are not allowed in the Olympic Games."[59] Even as sport became more and more political, the czars of the sports world continued to ignore the trend. Sportswriters and the public seemed very willing to go along with the ruse until the next political-Olympic event when they could condemn the activists for bringing politics into sports as if it were the end of the virginity of a pure and angelic child. They did not have to wait long.

In May of 1970, the IOC met in Amsterdam to consider the expulsion of South Africa from the Olympic Movement in protest of that country's apartheid sports policy. No nation had ever been expelled from the Movement itself and it was thought highly unlikely that the African-led plan would succeed.[60] The difference was that the South Africans had gone too far by refusing a visa to the Black American tennis star, Arthur Ashe, so that he could compete in the 1970 South African Open Tennis Championships. This had the effect of raising American political consciousness about apartheid sport.

The second precipitating event was the insistence on the part of the South Africans on going ahead with plans to send an all-white cricket team to tour Britain in the spring of 1970. There were massive plans for protest in Britain led by the Stop The Seventy Tour (STST) committee. STST had rallied 50,000 demonstrators to various rugby fields in the winter months while a South African rugby team toured Britain. Then Prime Minister Wilson ended up cancelling the tour to avoid the certain conflict.

When the IOC vote was tallied, the South Africans were out. This seemed remarkable in May of 1970, but what really was remarkable was that South Africa, with all the evidence and seemingly the majority of world opinion against them, was able to remain in the Olympic Movement *until* 1970.

The best explanation is that the IOC was dominated by representatives from white member nations who did not oppose South Africa's continued good standing. The IOC, according to its own publication, *OLYMPISM*, was a self-recruiting elite: membership on the committee was the result of election by existing IOC members. The statement, "It is customary to favour nationals of countries with a long Olympic tradition behind them," is reminiscent of the grandfather clause in the post-Reconstruction era of the South in the United States.[61] The custom was a convenient way of excluding representatives from nations that were colonies during the period when "a long Olympic tradition" could have been formed. In fact, the first two representatives from Africa were white men: Reg Alexander of Kenya and Reg Honey of South Africa. De Coubertin commented on the nature of membership in the IOC. "The second characteristic of Olympism is that it is an aristocracy, an elite."[62] He also added, "It is not sufficient to be an elite; it is also necessary for this elite to be a chivalry."[63]

Since 1960, 61 percent of the representatives from non-white nations were admitted to the IOC. However, this meant only a minor change in the racial composition of the IOC as the non-whites had only 33 percent of the voting power on the IOC in 1970. To achieve their 67 percent control, it was necessary for eleven of the white nations to have two or more representatives on the IOC. Moreover, of the national olympic committees (NOCs) without an IOC representative (which, in effect, means they are powerless), only 12.4 percent were from white nations while 87.6 percent were from non-white nations.[64]

To the idealistic sportsman, sportswriter, and fan who might feel that such statistics are meaningless because sport and the Olympic Movement are above politics and race, the results of the following survey should be instructive. The information was gathered in a survey completed in the spring of 1970 in which the NOCs were asked for their position on South Africa's participation in the Olympics. Sixty-eight percent of the white nations were not opposed to South Africa's participation. However, 98 percent of the non-white nations opposed South Africa's participation without complete sports integration in South Africa.

Thus, it can be seen that the South African issue developed along rather strict racial lines. Race and politics had become an integral part of international sport.

The Africans had a firm grasp on their power by 1972. According to Abraham Ordia, President of the Supreme Council for Sport in Africa (SCSA), the new goal was to have South Africa's neighbor, Rhodesia, expelled from the Olympic Movement. The SCSA made the mistake of trying to do this by going through the back door: they made demands on the Rhodesians they were certain would never be agreed to by the Smith regime. Much to their surprise, Smith agreed and the Rhodesian team arrived in Munich ready to participate under the stringent conditions put forth by the Africans. It was at the IOC meeting prior to the Games that the SCSA reversed its stand: the Rhodesians would have to be thrown out of the Movement or there would be another boycott.[65] The IOC complied.

The tragedy of the Israeli athletes in Munich cast a shadow over the Games and their future. The Montreal Olympic Village was an armed camp in an attempt to prevent new terrorist acts. While SportsWorld expressed shock at the Munich terrorism, it is not altogether surprising that such a thing could happen. It has been the theme of this article that the Olympics have become so big and attract so much international attention that they have become the ideal stage for political actors with causes: the French, the Americans, the Nazis, the People's Republic of China, Taiwan, the South Africans, the black Africans, the Socialists and the Capitalists. Why not terrorists?

Even with all this background, many doubted that there was any reason to fear an African boycott in 1976. After all, the threat of an American boycott over the "Two Chinas" issue had been resolved. The Western press condemned the African nations who withdrew. The American press had not even mentioned the real issue involved New Zealand's rugby team being in South Africa. With the election of Prime Minister Muldoon, New Zealand had resumed full sports relations with South Africa. The most controversy, however, had been raised by the rugby tour. While the difference between British and New Zealand teams competing in South Africa may have been lost on the average sports fan, the essence of that difference was not lost on the world's political leaders. Prime Minister Muldoon had made it a policy of his government to compete with South Africa. No other government did this.

It had been known for months that the African nations would withdraw from the Olympics if New Zealand sent its rugby team to South Africa. The Supreme Council for Sport in Africa announced this early in the spring. The Conference of the United Nations Special Committee Against Apartheid supported the Council's resolve at its May Havana meeting. The Organization of African Unity, meeting in Mauritius, also encouraged the African teams to boycott the Games. Therefore, the statements of surprise that 24 African nations did not march in the opening parade were rather unworldly. The fact that other Third World nations joined them is no less surprising if one simply examines the history of the modern Olympics.

Looked at from the point of view of the Africans and their supporters, they took a very strong and idealistic stand in order to keep racial politics out of sport. These countries sacrificed hard training, substantial amounts of money, and the prestige that comes from competing in the global spotlight that accompanies the Olympics. Dennis Brutus, a main moving force behind the boycott, believes that the IOC deliberately dragged out the China issue to divert the attention away from the African threats.[66] It almost worked as it appeared that there would be no boycott. But because the IOC was so involved in the China issue, New Zealand was never put on the agenda and nothing could be worked out prior to the Games. It can be reasonably assumed that the IOC believed that since no nation had ever actually taken itself out of the Games, the Africans would not do so and the issue would go away. As has frequently been the case, the IOC was proven wrong.

THE COLD WAR OLYMPICS: 1980 AND 1984

With the African boycott behind us in 1976, the threats for the future seemed more real. Still, for the American media, the United States was the "good guy"; it was others who had dragged politics into sport. That perception changed very quickly when President Carter announced the United States boycott of the Moscow Games in retaliation for the Soviet invasion of Afghanistan.

The press was on his side, but Carter had to convince two other groups to go along. The first was the athletes. Led by such Olympians as Anita DeFrantz, many athletes resisted the pressure. An informal poll of the USOC

Athletes Advisory Counsel indicated that most athletes wanted to compete. However, confronted by the national wave of patriotism, they ultimately succumbed to the pressure. The president also cajoled U.S. allies into joining the boycott, promising incentives to developing nations, especially in Africa, if they would shun the Games. That was a tough sell, because the United States had never backed the African nations in their protest against the inclusion of South Africa in international sport. In addition, the Russians were offering their own incentives *for* participation.

The boycott had mixed results. Many European and some developing nations joined in the boycott. However, by making his point, Carter forever made it impossible to say that politics and sport are not to be mixed.

The 1980 Games were depicted as a failure in the Western media, yet the contrary is arguable. Thirty-six new world records and seventy-four new Olympic records were set—more than in any previous Olympics. Eighty-one nations participated, more than 60,000 foreign tourists went to Moscow, and an estimated 1.5 billion saw the Games on TV. Moreover, the Soviets are still in Afghanistan more than a half decade later.

Retaliation by the Soviet bloc nations in the 1984 Los Angeles Games was almost guaranteed by the events of 1980. The fact that the Soviet boycott was announced so late was also predictable. Only the rationale was clouded by the "security" issue, although it was a real issue at the time. Reportedly, the Soviet press implied that the Los Angeles Games were a failure because so many of the world's top athletes were not present. However, more nations participated than ever before, more people saw the Games, and they were the first profitable Games. At least in America, they were depicted as the most successful Games ever.

THE FUTURE

It is possible that the political realities that have been forced upon us will make us better able to deal with future problems. The importance of the role of sports in international politics should no longer be overplayed.

While the political involvement has consistently been decried by the sports world, even the idealist, Avery Brundage, must share much of the blame. He, too, had frequently viewed the role of sports in international politics as being far more important than it is in reality. In his own unique historical perspective, Brundage largely attributed the downfall of Ancient Greece and Rome to an improper sports outlook:

> Twenty-five hundred years ago the Greeks made a breach in the city walls to receive their home-coming Olympic champions. A city with such heroes for citizens needed no fortifications. When they began to give large special awards and prizes, however, they created a class of athletic loafers instead of heroes. The Games were finally abolished and the glory of Greece departed.[67]

. . . the Romans did not descend into the arena, which was left to professionals, gladiators, grooms, etc. They were spectators, not participants, and lacked the discipline of sports training. Eventually a victim of her own prosperity, Rome fell to the barbarians, the hard and tough Goths and Vandals, invaders from the North.[68]

The lofty role that Brundage saw fit for modern sport, as led by the IOC, was revealed in his speech to the 62nd IOC Session in Tokyo in 1962: "The Olympic Movement is a 20th Century religion, a religion with universal appeal which incorporates all the basic values of other religions, a modern, exciting, viril, dynamic religion, attractive to Youth, and we of the International Olympic Committee are its disciples."[69]

Even after all of this the sportsworld was ready for a sublime Olympics in Montreal. Naivete is still in its ascendancy in the IOC.

In 1959, George Orwell said of international sport: "It is bound up with hatred, jealousy, boastfulness, disregard for all rules and sadistic pleasure in witnessing violence—in other words, it is war minus the shooting."[70]

While the reality may not be quite that negative, politics is and has always been part of the Olympic Movement. If we want to change that—and many do not—then a complete overhaul must begin. But the time for expressions of astonishment, wonder and shock should have passed many years ago. We have known the reality; now it is ours to face.

NOTES

1. Monique Berlioux, ed., *Olympism* (Lausanne: International Olympic Committee, 1972), p. 1.
2. Speech to the 55th Session of the IOC in Munich (May 23, 1959), from *The Speeches of President Avery Brundage, 1952 to 1968* (Lausanne: International Olympic Committee, 1969), pp. 41–42.
3. Speech to the 53rd Session of the IOC in Sofia, September 22, 1957, in *Speeches of Brundage*, p. 34.
4. Speech to the 60th Session of the IOC in Baden Baden, October 16, 1963, in *Speeches of Brundage*, p. 65.
5. *New York Times*, May 29, 1933.
6. Ibid., June 13, August 27, 1933.
7. Ibid., November 23, 1933.
8. Ibid., August 12, 1935.
9. Richard D. Mandell, *The Nazi Olympics* (New York: Macmillan Co., 1971), p. 59.
10. *New York Times*, October 21, 1935.
11. Ibid.
12. See: *New York Times*, November 5, 22, 1933, August 26, December 8, 1934, March 18, October 4, November 12, 16, 1935, March 9, 13, 31, May 10, 17, June 16, 20, 1936.
13. *New York Times*, October 11, 1935.
14. See: *New York Times*, May 31, June 6, 1933, August 12, September 3, 27, 1934, July 22, 31, August 5, 23, September 1, October 4, 18, 16–27, November 26, 27, December 1–4, 1935, January 4, 25, 1936.
15. Ibid., November 21, 1933.
16. Ibid., November 23, 1933.
17. Ibid., December 4, 1935.

18. Ibid.
19. *The Times* (London), August 12, 1935.
20. Ibid., December 6, 1935.
21. *New York Times*, August 6, 1933.
22. Ibid., September 30, 1934.
23. Ibid., April 23, 1936.
24. Ibid., May 31, 1936.
25. Ibid., July 18, 1936.
26. *The Times* (London), July 18, 1936.
27. Ibid., August 1, 1936.
28. *New York Times*, August 2, 1936; *The Times* (London), August 3, 1936.
29. *New York Times*, August 6, 1936.
30. Ibid., August 7, 1936.
31. Ibid., June 28, 1934.
32. Ibid., August 11, 1934.
33. Ibid., September 19, 1934.
34. Ibid., September 27, 1934.
35. Speech to the 55th Session of the IOC in Munich, May 23, 1959, in *Speeches of Brundage*, p. 41.
36. *New York Times*, October 5, 1935.
37. Ibid., May 29, 1959.
38. Ibid., June 3, 1959.
39. Ibid., June 4, 1959.
40. Ibid., August 1, 1959.
41. Ibid., September 17, 1959.
42. Ibid., February 7, 1960.
43. Ibid., March 17, 1961.
44. Ibid., September 3, 1962.
45. *The Times* (London), February 8, 1963.
46. Ibid., February 21, 1963.
47. Ibid., October 29, 1963.
48. *New York Times*, May 23, 1966.
49. Ibid.
50. Prime Minister John Vorster, address to Parliament, April 11, 1967, from "Report of the IOC Commission on South Africa" (Lausanne: IOC, 1968), p. 68.
51. *The Times* (London), February 27, 1968.
52. *New York Times*, March 10, 1968.
53. ACOA, press release, April 10, 1968. ACOA Collection.
54. IOC *Newsletter* #8, (May 1968), p. 151.
55. *Star* (Johannesburg), July 31, 1968.
56. *The Times* (London), September 26, 1968.
57. Survey conducted in August 1972 in the following cities: New York, Philadelphia, Washington, D.C., Denver, Norfolk and Los Angeles.
58. IOC, *Newsletter* #15, p. 577.
59. Ibid., p. 578.
60. *Star* (Johannesburg), May 14, 1970.
61. Monique Berlioux, *Olympism*, p. 8.
62. Ibid., p. 10.
63. Ibid., p. 2.
64. All figures were compiled from the official *Olympic Directory, 1969* (Lausanne: IOC, 1969).
65. Abraham Ordia, interview, May 26, 1976.
66. Dennis Brutus, interview, July 5, 1976.
67. Speech to the 48th Session of the IOC in Mexico City, April 17, 1953, in *Speeches of Brundage*, p. 10.
68. Speech to the 51st Session of the IOC in Cortinna d'Ampezzo, January 23, 1956, in *Speeches of Brundage*, p. 22.
69. Speech to the 62nd Session of the IOC in Tokyo, October 6, 1964, in *Speeches of Brundage*, p. 80.
70. *New York Times*, October 4, 1959.

25. *The Political-Economic Olympics*

D. STANLEY EITZEN

The motto of the Olympic Games—"Citius, Altius, Fortius" ("Faster, Higher, Stronger")—implies that athletic performance is to supersede all other concerns. Ever since the revival of the Olympics in 1896, however, there has been an erosion of the prominence of athletic accomplishments and a corresponding ascendance of political, economic, and bureaucratic considerations. The move by the United States in 1980 to use the Olympics as a political weapon against an enemy was just one more example of how political the Olympics really are.

The problems with the Olympics are legion. They can be divided into political, economic, and bureaucratic problems, each of which diminishes the importance of athletic competition for its own sake.

POLITICAL PROBLEMS

Politics overshadowing the joy of participation is not a new phenomenon in the Olympics, as a brief history will illustrate:[1]

- 1936—Hitler turned the Games in Berlin into a propaganda show for Nazi Germany. As a concession to the Nazis, the United States team dropped two Jewish sprinters from the 400-meter relay.
- 1940–44—World War II interrupted the Games.
- 1948—Israel was excluded from participation after a threat of an Arab boycott.
- 1952—Taiwan boycotted the Games when Communist China was admitted to the International Olympic Committee (IOC). East Germany was denied admittance because it was not a "recognized state." East Germany refused, in turn, to compete as one team with the West Germans.
- 1956—Egypt, Leganon, and Iraq boycotted the Olympics because of the Anglo-French seizure of the Suez Canal. The Communist Chinese team walked out when the Nationalist Chinese flag was hoisted in the Olympic village. Spain, Switzerland, and the Netherlands withdrew from the Olym-

SOURCE: D. Stanley Eitzen, "The Political-Economic Olympics," in *Sociology of North American Sport,* 3d ed., edited by D. Stanley Eitzen and George H. Sage (Dubuque, Iowa: Wm. C. Brown, 1986), pp. 175–179.

pics in protest after the Soviet Union invaded Hungary. As a direct consequence of Russia's invasion, a riot broke out during their water polo match with Hungary.

- 1960—The IOC decreed that North and South Korea should compete as one team, using the same flag, emblem, and uniform. North Korea refused to participate under these conditions. Nationalist China was forced to compete under the name of Taiwan. As the Chinese placard-bearer passed the reviewing stand in the opening ceremonies, he showed a sign saying "Under Protest."
- 1964—South Africa was banned from the Olympics for its apartheid policies.
- 1968—South Africa was again banned from participation. American black athletes threatened a boycott to protest racism in the United States. Tommie Smith and John Carlos raised a black-power salute during the American national anthem and were banned for life from Olympic competition. The Mexican government shot and killed students protesting the Games in Mexico City.
- 1972—Eleven Israeli athletes were murdered by Palestinian terrorists. Prior to the Games, the IOC ruled that Rhodesia would be allowed to participate. Many African nations were incensed because of the racist policies of the ruling elite in Rhodesia and threatened to boycott the Games unless Rhodesia was barred. The IOC ultimately bowed to this pressure and rescinded its earlier action.
- 1976—Athletes from twenty-eight African nations boycotted the Games because New Zealand, whose rugby team had toured South Africa, was allowed to compete. The host country, Canada, refused to grant visas to athletes from Nationalist China unless they agreed to compete under the designation of Taiwan instead of the Republic of China.
- 1980—Some fifty-four nations—including the United States, West Germany, Canada, and Japan—boycotted the Games to protest Russia's invasion of Afghanistan. Sixteen of the nations that did participate refused to march or show their flags in the opening and closing ceremonies.
- 1984—Nationalist China competed as Taiwan. The People's Republic of China competed as China. Some fourteen nations—most notably Russia, East Germany, Cuba, Bulgaria, and Poland—boycotted the Games.

In addition to these corruptions of the Olympic ideals, the very ways that the Games are organized are political. Nations select the athletes who will perform (no athlete can perform without national sponsorship). The IOC provides ceremonies where athletes march behind their country's flag. The winner's national anthem is played at the award ceremony. The IOC also considers political criteria in the selection of the site of the Olympics and in the choice of judges, ensuring in the latter case a balance between East and West, especially in the judging of events such as boxing, diving, ice-skating, and gymnastics.

ECONOMIC PROBLEMS

Producing the Olympics every four years has become very expensive for the International Olympic Committee, the host nation, and each competing country.[2] These high costs encouraged the United States Olympic Committee, for example, to sell the rights to the Olympic symbol to a variety of advertisers, allowing a corporation to claim that its product is the official beer, chewing tobacco, snow tire, mattress, jeans, tooth paste, or whatever, of the Olympics. The 1984 "Corporate Olympics" were sponsored in the amount of $225 million by ABC Television,[3] $50 million by Levi Strauss & Company, $44 million by Coca-Cola, and $30 million by Anheuser-Busch, among others. IBM provided the computers, McDonald's built the swimming pool, 7-Eleven built the cycling velodrome, and Atlantic Richfield spent $5 million to improve the Coliseum. The problems with corporate sponsorship are many, most notably the reluctance of the socialist nations to legitimize them by participating, and fear that corporate money may lead to corporate control over Olympic rules and regulations.

BUREAUCRATIC PROBLEMS

The IOC, composed of wealthy elite from around the world, has tried unsuccessfully to maintain a standard for amateurs based on the nineteenth-century ideal that sport should be engaged in for enjoyment during leisure time. If strictly applied—and this was the original intent—this ideal would mean that only the affluent could participate. In practice, however, each nation has been allowed to establish its own rules for amateur standing. As a result, fully subsidized Russian athletes have been allowed to compete, as have American college-scholarship athletes, or athletes in the armed services, and those now subsidized by corporations to further their athletic prowess. Moreover, athletes are now able to retain their "amateur" status while receiving money for appearances, endorsements, and performances, provided the money is placed in a trust fund for "training expenses." The logic of "amateurism" is further eroded when, for example, an American basketball player earning $200,000 with an Italian professional league is eligible for Olympic competition, but another who may make $20,000 in a minor professional basketball league in America is ineligible. The inconsistencies, hypocrisies, and inequities involved in who is and who is not an amateur provide ever fuller meaning to the derisive term "shamateurism."[4]

The political problems already mentioned provide further testimony to the impotence of the Olympic hierarchy. Despite the rhetoric of the leadership, those in charge have not been able to transcend national, political, and economic considerations. Obviously, these considerations continually shape and guide their actions.

THE OLYMPIC REVOLUTION: A PROPOSAL

The problems surrounding the Olympics continue to escalate, raising serious questions about the future of the Games. As presently structured, the Olympics are a sham because the athletes' pursuit of excellence has become secondary. The time has come for dismantling the Olympics as we know them and establishing Olympics organized to eliminate or at least drastically minimize the problems endemic in the current system. The following are several proposals that would help to accomplish the aim of neutralizing the crippling political, economic, and bureaucratic problems that presently work to negate the Olympic ideals.

1. *Establish two permanent sites for the Games.* Each permanent site must be neutral; otherwise, the Games would continue to be subject to the influence of power politics. The choices most often mentioned are Greece for the Summer Games and Switzerland for the Winter Games. Greece is a natural choice because the ancient Olympian Games were held there every four years for more than 1,000 years, ending in 393 A.D. Both Greece and Switzerland are preferred sites because they are small, independent countries not considered vital in the political struggles between the East and West. But even these countries are not altogether neutral: Greece, for example, belongs to NATO. A possible solution to the inherent politics of holding the Games within any nation is to have the permanent sites be free zones—land ceded to the International Olympic Committee and therefore land that no nation claims.

2. *Restrict the events to competition among individuals.* All team sports should be eliminated because each team represents a country, which makes political considerations inevitable. Moreover, team sports are inherently unfair: the larger the population base of a nation, the more likely that country will be to field a superior team.

3. *Allow athletes to represent only themselves.* Athletes, in actuality and symbolically, should not represent a country, nor should any nation-state be represented by uniforms, flags, national anthems, or political leaders. When an athlete is awarded his or her medal for winning an event, only the Olympic Hymn should be played. Athletes should also be randomly assigned to housing and eating arrangements at the Games to reduce national identification and to maximize cross-cultural interaction.

4. *Allow all athletes (amateur and professional) of the world to compete.* To avoid encouraging nationalistic feelings, the nation-state should not be involved in the selection process. To ensure that the best athletes of the world are able to compete, a minimum standard for each event should be set by the governing board. Athletes meeting this standard would have all expenses paid to meet in regional competition. At the regionals, another and higher standard of excellence would be set for athletes to qualify for

the Olympics. Again, for qualifying athletes, all expenses for travel and per diem would be paid by the Olympic Committee.

5. *Subsidize the cost of the Olympics by revenues generated from spectators' admissions to the regionals and to the Games and from television.* Establishing permanent sites and eliminating team events would reduce the cost of the Olympics. Yet these would still be considerable, especially during the initial stages of preparing the permanent sites. Revenues from admissions and television should pay expenses after the Games are established; during the building of the permanent sites, though, the Games might need a subsidy from the United Nations. Using television revenues does present a thorny problem because the revenue potential is great, and this threatens overcommercialization, the intrusion of corporations into the decision-making arena, and jingoism by chauvinistic television commentators. To reduce these dangers, the events could be televised and reported by a company strictly controlled by the Olympic Committee. The televising of the Olympics would be provided to each country at a cost determined by the existing number of television sets in that country. Each nation would decide how the fee would be paid, but the important point is that no country would have any control over what would be shown or the commentary emanating from the Games.

6. *Establish an Olympic Committee and a Secretary-General to prepare for and oversee the Games.* The composition of this committee would be crucial. Currently, the members of the IOC are taken from national committees, with an important criterion being the maintenance of a political balance between opposing factions. The concept of a ruling body is important, but the committee should be reorganized to ensure that the intent of the changes suggested here would be implemented. The selection of members is a baffling problem because it will always involve political considerations. One possibility would be to incorporate the procedures used by the United Nations to select its Secretary-General. These procedures have worked, even during the darkest days of the Cold War, toward the choice of a competent, objective, and nonaligned (neither pro-West nor pro-Eastern bloc) arbitrator. In addition to an Olympic Secretary-General, a governing board and a permanent staff would also have to be established.

These proposals are not complete. They are a beginning. As they are amended and others added, the reorganization of the Olympics should be guided by three goals: (1) to encourage individual athletic excellence; (2) to eliminate politics; and (3) to maximize interaction among athletes across national boundaries. The task is challenging but not impossible. The Olympics movement is important—that is why it must be altered radically from its present form if its lofty goals are to be realized.

NOTES

1. For a sample of the sources dealing with the political aspects of the Olympics, *see* Richard D. Mandell, *The Nazi Olympics;* Richard Espy, *The Politics of the Olympic Games* (Berkeley: University of California Press, 1979); James A. Baley, "Suggestions for Removing Politics from the Olympic Games," *JOPER* 39 (March 1978): 73; the entire issue of *Journal of Sport and Social Issues* 2 (Spring/Summer 1978); Roger M. Williams, "Troubled Olympics," *Saturday Review*, 1 September 1979, pp. 12–16; Jonathan Evan Maslow, "Forty Years of Strife," *Saturday Review*, 1 September 1979; WNET/WETA, "The Olympics and Politics," *The Robert MacNeil Report*, show no. 1140, library no. 209, 16 July 1976; John Cheffers, "The Foolishness of Boycott and Exclusion in the Olympic Movement," *JOPER* 40 (February 1979): 44–51; "An Olympic Boycott?" *Newsweek*, 28 January 1980, pp. 20–28; Harry Edwards, *The Revolt of the Black Athlete;* Joel Thirer, "The Olympic Games as a Medium of Black Activism and Protest"; *Arena Review* 6 (December 1982), entire issue; Allen Guttmann, *The Games Must Go On: Avery Brundage and the Olympic Movement* (New York: Columbia University Press, 1984); Harry Edwards, "Sportpolitics: Los Angeles, 1984—The Olympic Tradition Continues," *Sociology of Sport Journal* 1, no. 2 (1984): 172–83; and Robert A. Mechikoff, "The Olympic Games: Sport as International Politics," *Journal of Physical Education, Recreation and Dance* 55 (March 1984): 23–25, 30.
2. For a selection of writings on the economics of the Olympics, *see* Frank Swertlow, "TV Buys the Games," *Saturday Review*, 1 September 1979, pp. 20–21; J. Cicarelli and D. Kowarsky, "The Economics of the Olympic Games," *Business and Economic Dimensions* 9 (1973): 1–5; M. Auf der Maur, *The Billion-Dollar Game: Jean Drapeau and the 1976 Olympics* (Toronto: James, Lorimer, 1976); George Wright, "The Political Economy of the Montreal Olympic Games," *Journal of Sport and Social Issues* 2 (Spring/Summer 1978): 13–18; Paul Good, "The Selling of Our Olympic Teams," *Sport* 69 (July 1979): 30–36; "A Small U.S. Town Takes On a Big Job—the Winter Olympics," *U.S. News & World Report*, 20 November 1978, pp. 89–91; Howard Rudnitsky, "Adam Smith's Olympics," *Forbes*, 8 November 1982, pp. 44–45; Kathy Rebello, "The Games: A Triumph of Capitalism," *USA Today*, 27 September 1984, pp. B1–B2; and Harry Edwards, "The Free Enterprise Olympics," *Journal of Sport and Social Issues* 8 (Summer/Fall 1984): i–iv.
3. ABC-TV was not immune to injecting pro-American sentiments into its broadcasts of the Olympics and received an official reprimand from the president of the International Olympic Committee. *See* Tom Shales, "Jingo Jangle," *Denver Post*, 12 August 1984, p. F4; Harry F. Waters, "Red, White and Blue TV," *Newsweek*, 13 August 1984, pp. 32–33; David Nyhan, "TV Network Wins the Gold Medal for Flag Waving Commercialism," *Des Moines Register*, 7 August 1984, p. 6A; and Lester Rodney, "The Olympics You Didn't See on ABC-TV," *In These Times*, 5–11 September 1984, p. 21.
4. *See* Kathy Rebello, "There's More at Stake than Medals," *USA Today*, 3 August 1984, pp. B1–2; Pete Axthelm, "Money and Hypocrisy," *Newsweek*, 30 July 1984, pp. 68–69; and Jerry Adler, "After the Games, the Cash," *Newsweek*, 20 August 1984, pp. 25–26.

■ FOR FURTHER STUDY

Brutus, Dennis. "South Africa and the 1984 Olympics." *Journal of Sport and Social Issues* 8 (Winter–Spring 1984): i.

Curry, Timothy J., and Robert M. Jiobu. *Sports: A Social Perspective*. Englewood Cliffs, N.J.: Prentice-Hall, 1984, pp. 182–211.

Edwards, Harry. "The Free Enterprise Olympics." *Journal of Sport and Social Issues* 8 (Summer–Fall 1984): i–iv.

Edwards, Harry. "Sportpolitics: Los Angeles, 1984—The Olympic Tradition Continues." *Sociology of Sport Journal* 1, no. 2 (1984): 172–183.

Espy, Richard. *The Politics of the Olympic Games*. Berkeley: University of California Press, 1979.

Greer, Scott, ed. "Olympism: Perspectives on the Olympic Movement." *Arena Review* 6 (December 1982): entire issue.

Guttmann, Allen. *The Games Must Go On: Avery Brundage and the Olympic Movement*. New York: Columbia University Press, 1983.

Heinila, Kalevi. "Sport and International Understanding—A Contradiction in Terms?" *Sociology of Sport Journal* 2 (September 1985): 240–248.

Hoberman, John M. *Sport and Political Ideology*. Austin: University of Texas Press, 1984.

Kanin, David B. "The Olympic Boycott in Diplomatic Context." *Journal of Sport and Social Issues* 4 (Spring–Summer 1980): 1–24.

Lapchick, Richard E. *The Politics of Race and International Sport: The Case of South Africa*. Westport, Conn.: Greenwood Press, 1975.

Mandell, Richard D. *The Nazi Olympics*. New York: Macmillan, 1971.

McIntyre, Thomas D. "Sport in the German Democratic Republic and the People's Republic of China." *Journal of Physical Education, Recreation, and Dance* 56 (January 1985): 108–111.

Pickering, R. J. *Cuba: In Sport under Communism*. London: C. Hurst, 1978.

Redmond, Gerald, ed. *Sport and Politics*. Champaign, Ill.: Human Kinetics, 1986.

Riordan, James, ed. *Sport under Communism*. 2d ed. London: C. Hurst, 1981.

Segrave, Jeffrey, and Donald Chu. *Olympism*. Champaign, Ill.: Human Kinetics, 1981.

Seppanen, Paavo. "The Olympics: A Sociological Perspective." *International Review for the Sociology of Sport* 19 (1984): 113–128.

Strenk, Andrew. "Diplomats in Track Suits: The Role of Sports in the Foreign Policy of the German Democratic Republic." *Journal of Sport and Social Issues* 4 (Spring–Summer 1980): 34–45.

Part Eight

Sport and Religion

There are several facets to the relationship between sport and religion. The first is the strong possibility that sport is the functional equivalent of religion. Some striking similarities exist between the two phenomena that may allow individuals to receive the benefits from sport that are usually associated with religion. Some of these parallels include idols, proverbs, shrines, pilgrimages, fanatic believers, rituals, testimony, miracles, rules, judgment, and mysticism. Let us briefly consider two of these.

Ritual is basic to religion. Through the repetition of particular symbolic acts, worshippers are reminded of the supernatural and unified in a common belief with others sharing in the ceremony. Ritual is also very important to sport. Prior to, during, and after games, the faithful sing songs and recite chants that pledge fidelity to the team and implore the athletes to greater achievements. The national anthem is also part of every athletic event. For the athletes there are rituals such as the interlacing of hands with the coach to express team unity. There are also rituals common to particular sports, such as in baseball's "seventh inning stretch," or in boxing, where the combatants touch gloves at the beginning of the first and last rounds.

Common to all religions is the element of mysticism. Belief in the mystical is to have faith in supernatural forces (powers that transcend normal human experience). The mystical is also found in sport. There is the belief that the individual with the greatest "heart" or "spirit" will win. There is also the intangible quality of team spirit, considered such an important ingredient of success. As a final example of the supernatural forces in sport, there is that elusive factor in a game known as momentum.

Although the parallels between religion and sport should not be overdrawn, the similarities are interesting and provide insight about the similar functions of these two institutions in society. The first two selections, by George H. Sage and Charles S. Prebish, examine the relatively strong ties among sport, religion, and society. The final selection, by Frank Deford, shows the close affinity between Catholic schools of higher education and basketball success. Deford raises the important question of ethical symmetry—Can religious schools "pursue the almighty dollar [of big-time college athletics] and answer to the Almighty at the same time"?

26. Religion, Sport, and Society

GEORGE H. SAGE

RELIGION AND SOCIETY

Religion is the belief that supernatural forces influence human lives. There are many definitions of religion, but the one by French sociologist, Émile Durkheim, has perhaps been cited most. Durkheim said that "religion is a unified system of beliefs and practices relative to sacred things, that is to say, things set apart and forbidden—beliefs and practices which unite into one single moral community called a Church, all those who adhere to them."[1] As a social institution, religion is a system that functions to maintain and transmit beliefs about forces considered to be supernatural and sacred. It provides codified guides for moral conduct and prescribes symbolic practices deemed to be in harmony with beliefs about the supernatural. For all practical purposes, the universality of religious behavior among human beings may be assumed, since ethnologists and anthropologists have not yet discovered a human group without traces of the behavior we call "religious."[2]

Societies have a wide range of forms and activities associated with religion, including special officials (priests), ceremonies, rituals, sacred objects, places of worship, pilgrimages, and so forth. In modern societies, religious leaders have developed elaborate theories or theologies to explain the place of humans in the universe. Moreover, the world religions—Christianity, Hinduism, Buddhism, Confucianism, Judaism, and Muhammadanism—are cores of elaborate cultural systems that have dominated world societies for centuries.[3]

Social Functions of Religion

The term "social functions" as used here refers to the contribution that religion makes to the maintenance of human societies.* The focus is on what

---

* Functionalism as used in the social sciences involves applying to social systems the biological notion that every organism has a structure made up of relatively stable interrelationships of parts. Each of these parts performs a specialized task, or function, that permits the organism to survive and to act. With respect to societies, this notion assumes that they consist of elements each of which performs a specific function contributing to the overall survival and actions of the society.

SOURCE: George H. Sage, "Religion, Sport, and Society," in *Sociology of North American Sport*, 3d ed., edited by D. Stanley Eitzen and George H. Sage (Dubuque, Iowa: Wm. C. Brown, 1986), pp. 136–143.

271

religion does, and what it contributes to the survival and maintenance of societies and groups.

Religions exist because they perform important functions for society and the individual. At the individual level, psychic needs are met by religious experience. The unpredictable and sometimes dangerous world produces personal fears and general anxiety that reverence for the powers of nature or seeking cooperation through religious faith and ritual may alleviate. Fears of death, too, are made bearable by beliefs in a supernatural realm into which a believer passes.

Religion also assigns moral meaning and makes comprehensible human experiences that might seem otherwise a "tale told by an idiot, full of sound and fury, signifying nothing." If one can believe in a God-given scheme of things, the universal quest for ultimate meaning is validated, and human strivings and sufferings seem to make some sense. Finally, the need to proclaim human abilities and achieve a sense of transcendence is met and indeed fostered by many religions through ceremonies and rituals that celebrate humans and their activities.

For society, one function of religion is so crucial that it almost includes all the others—social integration. Religion promotes a binding together, both of the members of a society and of the social obligations that help to unite them. August Comte, considered by many the founder of sociology, believed that a common belief system held people together. Comte summarized the function of religion as an integrative tool in this way: "Our being is thus knit together, within and without, by a complete convergence both of the feelings and of the thoughts towards that Supreme Power which controls our acts. At this point there arises Religion in its true sense, that is, a complete unity, whereby all the motives of conduct within us are reduced to a common object, whilst our conduct as a whole submits with freedom to the necessity imposed by a power without."[4]

Religion is an important integrative force in society because it organizes the individual's experience in terms of ultimate meanings that include but also transcend the individual. When many people share this ordering principle, they can deal with each other in meaningful ways and can transcend themselves and their individual egotisms, sometimes even to the point of self-sacrifice.

Since all human social relationships are dependent on symbols of one kind or another, religion supplies the ultimate symbols, the comprehensive ones, the ones through which all other ones make sense. As sociologist Neil J. Smelser said: "Religion is a symbolic canopy stretched out over the network of social institutions, giving them an appearance of stability and 'rightness' that they would otherwise lack. In this manner, religion functions to maintain and perpetuate social institutions."[5]

Religious ceremonies and rituals also promote integration, since they serve to reaffirm some of the basic customs and values of society. Émile Durkheim, in his classic study of religion, noted that "before all, [religion is] a means by which the social group reaffirms itself periodically."[6] Here, the societal customs, folkways, and observances are symbolically elevated to the realm of the sacred. In Ronald L. Johnstone's words: "In expressing common beliefs about the nature of reality and the supernatural, in engaging in joint ritual and worship activities, in retelling the sagas and myths of the past, the group (society) is brought closer together and linked with the ancestral past."[7]

Another important integrative function that religion performs is to bring persons with diverse backgrounds into meaningful relationships with one another. To the extent that religious groups can reach people who feel isolated and abandoned and are not being relieved of their problems elsewhere, to that extent religion is serving society.

Religion also serves as a vehicle for social control; that is, religious tenets constrain the behavior of the community of believers to keep them in line with the norms, values, and beliefs of society. In all the major religions, there is an intertwining of religion and morals, and schemes of otherworldly rewards or punishments for behavior, such as those found in Christianity, become powerful forces for morality. The fear of hell fire and damnation has been a powerful deterrent in the control of Christian societies. The virtues of honesty, conformity to sexual codes, and all the details of acceptable, moral, behavior in a society become merged with religious beliefs and practices.

A third social function of religion is that it tends to legitimize the secular social structures within a society. There is a strong tendency for religious ideology to become united with the norms and values of secular structures, producing, as a consequence, religious support for the values and institutions of society.[8]

From its earliest existence, religion has provided rationales that serve the needs and actions of a society's leaders. It has legitimized as "God-given" such disparate ideologies as absolute monarchies and democratic forms of government. Particularly when obedience to the social agents of control is interpreted as a religious duty and disobedience is interpreted as sinful, religion performs this social function well.

THE RELATIONSHIP OF RELIGION AND SPORT

Primitive Societies

According to Rudolph Brasch, sport began as a religious rite: "It's roots were in man's desire to gain victory over foes seen and unseen, to influence the forces of nature, and to promote fertility among his crops and cattle."[9] The Zūni Indians of New Mexico played games that they believed would bring rain and thus enable their crops to grow. In southern Nigeria, wrestling matches were held to encourage the growth of crops, and various games were played in the winter to hasten the return of spring and to ensure a bountiful season. One Eskimo tribe, at the end of the harvest season, played a cup-and-ball game to "catch the sun" and thus delay its departure. In his monumental work on the Plains Indians, Stewart Culin wrote: "In general, games appear to be played ceremonially, as pleasing to the gods, with the objective of securing fertility, causing rain, giving and prolonging life, expelling demons, or curing sickness."[10]

Ancient Greece

The ancient Greeks, who worshiped beauty, entwined religious observance with their athletic demonstrations in such a way that it is difficult to define where one left off and the other began. Greek gods were anthropomorphic, and sculptors portrayed the gods as perfect physical specimens who were to be both admired and emulated by their worshipers. The strong anthropomorphic conceptions of gods held by the Greeks led to their belief that the gods took pleasure in the same things as mortals—music, drama, and displays of physical excellence. The gymnasia located in every city-state for all male adults provided facilities and places for sports training as well as for the discussion of intellectual topics. Furthermore, there were facilities for religious worship—an altar and a chapel were located in the center of each gymnasium.

The most important athletic meetings of the Greeks were part of religious festivals. According to one scholar of Greek athletics: "The Olympic Games were sacred games, staged in a sacred place and at a sacred festival; they were a religious act in honor of the deity. Those who took part did so in order to serve god and the prizes which they won came from the god."[11] The Olympic Games were held in honor of Zeus, king of the gods; the Pythian Games took place at a festival in honor of Apollo; the Isthmian Games were dedicated to the god Poseidon; and the Nemean Games were held in honor of Zeus. Victorious athletes presented their gifts of thanks upon the altar of the god or gods whom they thought to be responsible for their victory. The end of the ancient Olympic Games was a result of the religious conviction of Theodosius, the Roman emperor of A.D. 392–95. He was a Christian and decreed the end of the games as part of his suppression of paganism in favor of Christianity.[12]

The Early Christian Church

In Western societies, religious support for sport found no counterpart to that of the Greeks until the beginning of the twentieth century. The Roman

Catholic church came to dominate society in western Europe from A.D. 400 until the Reformation in the sixteenth century, and since then Roman Catholicism has shared religious power with Protestant groups.

At first opposing Roman sport spectacles, such as chariot racing and gladiatorial combat, because of their paganism and brutality, eventually Christians came to regard the human body as an instrument of sin. The early Christians did not view sports as evil per se, for the Apostle Paul wrote approvingly of the benefits of physical activity.[13] But the paganism prominent in the Roman sports events was abhorrent to the Christians. Moreover, early Christianity gradually built a foundation based on asceticism, which is a belief that evil exists in the body and, therefore, the body should be subordinate to the pure spirit. As a result, church dogma and education sought to subordinate all desires and demands of the body in order to exalt the spiritual life. Saint Bernard argued: "Always in a robust and active body the mind lies soft and more lukewarm; and, on the other hand, the spirit flourishes more strongly and more actively in an infirm and weakly body."[14] Nothing could have been more damning for the promotion of active recreation and sport.

Spiritual salvation was the dominant feature of the Christian faith. Accordingly, the cultivation of the body was to be subordinated to the salvation of the spirit, especially since the body, it was believed, could obstruct the realization of this aim. An otherwise enlightened Renaissance scholar, Desiderius Erasmus, while a monk at a monastery (before he became a critic of Roman Catholicism), wrote an essay "On the Contempt of the World," which articulately characterized the Christian attitude of his time toward body and soul:

The monks do not choose to become like cattle; they know that there is something sublime and divine within man which they prefer to develop rather than cater for the body. . . . Our body, except for a few details, differs not from an animal's body but our soul reaches out after things divine and eternal. The body is earthly, wild, slow, mortal, diseased, ignoble; the soul on the other hand is heavenly, subtle, divine, immortal, noble. Who is so blind that he cannot tell the difference between body and soul? And so the happiness of the soul surpasses that of the body.[15]

The Reformation and the Rise of Protestantism

The Reformation of the early sixteenth century signaled the end of the vicelike grip that Roman Catholicism had on the minds and habits of the people of Europe and England. With the Reformation, the pejorative view of sports might have perished where the teachings of Martin Luther and John Calvin prevailed. But Protestantism had within it the seeds of a new asceticism, and the Calvinism imported to England, in its Puritan form, became a greater enemy to sport than Roman Catholicism had been.

Puritan influence grew throughout the sixteenth century, and by the early seventeenth century had come to have considerable influence on English life. Moreover, since Puritans were among the earliest English immigrants to America, they had considerable influence on the social life in the colonies. Perhaps no Christian group exercised a greater opposition to sports than the Puritans. Historian Dennis Brailsford asserted that "the Puritans saw their mission to erase all sport and play from men's lives."[16] They gave England the "English Sunday" and its equivalent in the United States, the blue laws which, until a few decades ago, managed to bar sports on the Sabbath and severely limit the kinds of sports that were considered appropriate for a Christian. As a means of realizing amusement and unrestrained impulses, sport was suspect for the Puritan; as it approached mere pleasure or involved physical harm to participants or to animals (boxing, cockfighting) or promoted gambling, sport was, of course, altogether evil. The English historian Thomas B. Macaulay claimed that the Puritans opposed bearbaiting not so much because it was painful for the bear but because the bear's pain gave pleasure to the spectators.[17]

From the Seventeenth to the Twentieth Century

The principal relationship between the church and sport for the early North American settlers was one of restriction and probation, especially with regard to sports on the Sabbath. Legislation prohibiting sports participation on Sunday began soon after the first English settlement in the American colonies and was enacted by a group of Virginia ministers. But such repressive acts are more commonly associated with the Puritans in New England who enacted similar legislation. Actually, most of the colonies passed laws against play and sport on the Sabbath, and it was not until the mid-twentieth century that industrial and economic conditions brought about the repeal of most of these laws, although most had been annulled by custom.[18]

There were a number of reasons for Protestant prejudice against play and sport among the early settlers. One prominent objection was that participation would divert attention from spiritual matters. There was also the belief that play and its resultant pleasure might become addictive because of the inherent weakness of human nature. There was, of course, the practical matter that survival in the New World required hard work from everyone; thus, time spent in play and games was typically considered time wasted. Finally, the associations formed and the environment in which play and sport occurred conspired to cast these activities in a bad light. The tavern was the center for gambling and table sports; dancing had obvious sexual overtones; and field sports often involved gambling and cruelty to animals.

Churchly opposition to leisure pursuits was firmly maintained in the first few decades of the nineteenth century, and each effort to liberalize attitudes toward leisure pursuits was met with a new attack on sport as "sinful." Sports were still widely regarded by the powerful Protestant religious group as snares of the devil himself. But in the 1830s, social problems became prominent concerns of American social reformers, many of whom were clergy and intellectual leaders. There were crusades against slavery, intemperance, and poor industrial working conditions; widespread support for the emancipation of women, public education, and industrial reform; indeed, every facet of American life came under scrutiny. One aspect of this comprehensive social-reform movement was the concern for human health and physical fitness.

Social conditions had begun to change rapidly under the aegis of industrialization—the population was shifting from rural to urban residence, labor changing from agricultural toil to toil for wages in squalid working and living conditions. The physical health of the population became a major problem, leading a number of reformers to propose that people would be happier, more productive, and healthier if they engaged in vigorous sports activities. Surprisingly, some of the leading advocates of play and sport were clerics, and from their pulpits they presented forceful arguments that physical prowess and sanctity were not incompatible. Intellectual leaders joined the movement. Ralph Waldo Emerson said, "Out upon the scholars . . . with their pale, sickly, etiolated indoor thought! Give me the out-of-door thoughts of sound men, thoughts all fresh and blooming."[19] The esteemed poet and novelist Oliver Wendell Holmes joined the attack on the physical condition of the youth. He wrote: "I am satisfied that such a set of black-coated, stiff-jointed, soft-muscled, paste-complexioned youth as we can boast in our Atlantic cities never before sprang from the loins of Anglo-Saxon lineage."[20] Holmes argued that widespread participation in sports would make for a more physically fit citizenry, as well as create a more exciting environment.

The proposals of support for physical fitness and wholesome leisure had a profound effect on the church. Responding to the temporal needs of the people, the clergy began to shed much of the otherworldly emphasis and seek to alleviate immediate human problems. Recognizing the need for play and the health benefits of leisure amusements, the church began to soften its attitude toward play and sports. Sport historian Donald J. Mrozek summarized the change: "Ministers and religiously enthusiastic laymen showed increasing concern over the behavior of young people . . . and they often turned to sport" to guide them toward the right way of life. "In a broad range of denominations from Baptists to Congregationalists, there arose spokesmen who depicted Christ as primarily a man of action, thus seeking to appeal to the inclinations of the young by drawing out qualities which they believed most closely resembled those valued in their society."[21]

Although the development of a more liberal attitude by church leaders toward sport began to appear by the mid-nineteenth century, not all church authorities subscribed to the trend. A staid Congregationalist magazine, the *New Englander*, vigorously attacked sport: "Let our readers, one and all, remember that we were sent into this world, not for sport and amusement, but for labor; not to enjoy and please ourselves, but to serve and glorify God, and be useful to our fellow men. That is the great object and end in life. In pursuing this end, God has indeed permitted us all needful diversion and recreation. . . . But the great end of life after all is work. . . . It is a true saying . . . 'We come into this world, not for sports.' We were sent here for a higher and nobler object."[22]

In official publications and public speeches, some church leaders fought the encroaching sport and leisure mania throughout the latter nineteenth century. Militant organizations, such as the American Sabbath Union, the Sunday League of America, and the Lord's Day Alliance, were visible proof of the vitality of the strong forces still mobilized in support of this phase of Protestant doctrine.[23] But there was a growing awareness that churches were fighting a losing war. Churchmen gradually began to reconcile play and religion as medical, educational, and political leaders emphasized that physical, mental, and, indeed, moral health was developed through games and sports. City churches began to minister to the social, physical, and economic needs of their members and residents in the neighborhood, extending their role beyond just preaching salvation of the soul. To meet the social needs of rural and city members, churches adopted sports and sponsored recreations to draw people together, and church leadership played an important part in the promotion of community recreation and school physical education in the latter nineteenth century. Many clergy used their church halls and grounds as recreation centers for the neighborhood. The playground movement in America began in 1885, when the sand gardens were opened in the yards of the West End Nursery and the Parmenter Street Chapel in Boston. The New York City Society for Parks and Playgrounds was begun in 1890 with the support of clergymen, who delivered sermons to their congregations on childrens' need for playgrounds.[24]

Support for physical education found its way into denominational journals and meetings, and religious support for physical education helped promote its acceptance by colleges and its eventual adoption by public school boards across the country. The Young Men's Christian College (now Springfield College) at Springfield, Massachusetts, made sport and physical fitness one of the cornerstones of a proper Christian education and life-style.

Increasingly, churches broadened their commitment to play and sport endeavors as means of drawing people together. Bowling leagues, softball leagues, and youth groups, such as the Catholic Youth Organization (CYO), were sponsored by churches for their young members. The church's prejudice against pleasure through play had broken down almost completely by the beginning of the twentieth century.

Twentieth-Century North America

Churches have been confronted with ever-increasing changes in the twentieth century; economic pressures, political tendencies, and social conditions have been the chief forces responsible for the drastically changed relationship between religion and sport. Increased industrialization turned the population into a nation of urban dwellers, while higher wages were responsible for an unprecedented affluence. The gospel of work (the Protestant work ethic) is no longer acceptable to everyone, and increased leisure has enhanced the popularity of sports. The story of changes in the attitudes of religionists in the twentieth century is largely one of accelerating accommodation. Much of Protestant North America has come to view sport as a positive force and even as a useful means of promoting the Lord's work. Sports and leisure activities have become an increasingly conspicuous part of the recreation program of thousands of churches and many church colleges. Richard A. Swanson summarized the new role of the church: "Throughout the twentieth century, the church has moved steadily further into recreation. Camping programs, athletic leagues, organized game periods at various group meetings, and even full-time recreation directors are all evidences of a positive relationship between religion and play."[25]

Roman Catholic and Protestant clergymen who over the centuries have preached that sport is a handmaiden of the devil must be shifting uneasily in their graves at events of the past half-century. Times have certainly changed, the church as well, and reconciliation between sports and organized religion has approached finality.

Sport as Religion

In the past two decades, the powers and influence of sport has increased enormously, while at the same time formalized religion and the institutional church have suffered a decline of interest and commitment. Sport has taken on so many of the characteristics of religion that some have argued that sport has emerged as a new religion, supplementing, and in some cases even supplanting, the traditional religious expressions.[26] Cornish Rogers contended that "sports are rapidly becoming the dominant ritualistic expression of the reification of the established religion in America."[27]

A few examples will illustrate how organized sports have taken on the trappings of religion. Every religion has its idols (or saints or high priests) who are venerated by its members. Likewise, sports fans have persons whom they worship: the saints who are now dead, such as Knute Rockne and Babe Ruth—and, of course, Vince Lombardi, who earned a place among the saints for his fierce discipline and the articulation of the basic commandment of contemporary sport, "Winning is the only thing." The high priests of contemporary sports are the professional, collegiate, and national amateur team coaches who not only direct the destinies of their athletes but also control the emotions of large masses of sports fans.

In addition to the fundamental commandment according to Saint Vince, numerous proverbs fill the world of sport: "Nice guys finish last"; "When the going gets tough, the tough get going"; "Lose is a four-letter word"; and so forth. These proverbs are frequently written on posters and hung in locker rooms for athletes to memorize.

The achievements of athletes and teams are celebrated in numerous shrines built throughout the country to commemorate and glorify sporting figures. These "halls of fame" have been established for virtually every sport played in North America, and some sports have several halls of fame devoted to them. According to Gerald Redmond: "Athletes become "immortal heroes" as they are "enshrined" in a sports hall of fame, when "devoted admirers" gaze at their "revered figures" or read plaques "graven in marble" before departing "often very moved" (or even "teary-eyed") from the many "hushed rooms, filled with nostalgia." This is the jargon of the churches of sport in the twentieth century."[28]

Symbols of fidelity abound in sports. The athletes are expected to give total commitment to the cause, including abstinence from smoking, alcohol, and, in some cases, even sex. The devout followers who witness and invoke traditional and hallowed chants show their devotion to the team and add "spirit" to its cause. It is not unusual for these pilgrims to travel hundreds of miles, sometimes braving terrible weather conditions, to witness a game, thus displaying their fidelity.

Like religious institutions, sport has become a function of communal involvement. An article in the *Christian Century* entitled "The Super Bowl as Religious Festival" commented: "There is a remarkable sense in which the Super Bowl functions as a major religious festival for American culture, for the event signals a convergence of sports, politics and myth. Like festivals in ancient societies, which made no distinctions regarding the religious, political and sporting character of certain events, the Super Bowl succeeds in reuniting these now disparate dimensions of social life."[29] "If Jesus were alive today," said Norman Vincent Peale, "he would be at the Super Bowl."[30]

Perhaps the most salient role that sport-as-religion plays for communal involvement is in the sense of belonging and of community that it evokes. In cheering for the Green Bay Packers, the New York Yankees, or the Montreal Canadiens, one belongs to a "congregation." The emotional attachment of some fans to their teams verges on the religious fanaticism previously seen in holy wars against heretics and pagans. Opposing teams and their fans, as well as officials, are occasionally attacked and brutally beaten.

NOTES

1. Émile Durkheim, *The Elementary Forms of Religious Life,* trans. J. W. Swain (New York: Free Press, 1965), p. 62.
2. John Wilson, *Religion in American Society* (Englewood Cliffs, N.J.: Prentice-Hall, 1978).
3. Bryan Wilson, *Religion in Sociological Perspective* (New York: Oxford University Press, 1982).
4. August Comte, *System of Positive Polity,* trans. Frederick Harrison (New York: Burt Franklin, 1875), pp. 16–17.
5. Neil J. Smelser, ed., *Sociology: An Introduction* (New York: Wiley, 1967), p. 340.
6. Durkheim, *The Elementary Forms of Religious Life,* p. 387.
7. Ronald L. Johnstone, *Religion and Society in Interaction* (Englewood Cliffs, N.J.: Prentice-Hall, 1975), p. 143.
8. J. Victor Baldridge, *Sociology: A Critical Approach to Power, Conflict, and Change,* 2nd ed. (New York: Wiley, 1980), pp. 240–42.
9. Rudolph Brasch, *How Did Sports Begin?* (New York: David McKay, 1970), p. 1.
10. Stewart Culin, *Games of the North American Indian* (Washington, D.C.: U.S. Government Printing Office, 1907), p. 34.
11. Ludwig Deubner, quoted in Ludwig Drees, *Olympia: Gods, Artists, and Athletes,* trans. Gerald Ohn (New York: Praeger, 1968), p. 24.
12. B. Kyrkos, "The Development of Sport in the Hellenistic and Roman Periods," in *The Eternal Olympics,* ed. Nicholaos Yalouris, (New Rochelle, N.Y.: Caratzas Brothers, 1979), pp. 275–85.
13. *See,* for example, I Cor. 9:24–26.
14. Quoted in G. G. Coulton, *Five Centuries of Religion,* vol. 5 (Cambridge: Cambridge University Press, 1923), p. 532.
15. Quoted in Albert Hyma, *The Youth of Erasmus* (Ann Arbor: University of Michigan Press, 1930), p. 178.
16. Dennis Brailsford, *Sport and Society* (London: Routledge and Kegan Paul, 1969), p. 141. For a more sympathetic but not altogether convincing argument about the Puritan attitude toward sport, *see* J. Thomas Jable, "The English Puritans—Suppressors of Sport and Amusement?" *Canadian Journal of the History of Sport and Physical Education* 7 (May 1976): 33–40.
17. Thomas B. Macaulay, *The History of England,* vol. 1 (London: Longman, Green, Longman & Roberts, 1861), p. 162.
18. John A. Lucas and Ronald A. Smith, *Saga of American Sport* (Philadelphia: Lea & Febiger, 1978), pp. 15–39; J. Thomas Jable, "Sunday Sport Comes to Pennsylvania: Professional Baseball and Football Triumph over the Commonwealth's Archaic Blue Laws, 1919–1933," *Research Quarterly* 47 (October 1976): 357–65.
19. Quoted in Van Wyck Brooks, *The Flowering of New England* (New York: Random House, Modern Library, 1936), p. 253.
20. Oliver Wendell Holmes, "The Autocrat of the Breakfast Table," *Atlantic Monthly* 1 (May 1858): 881.
21. Donald J. Mrozek, *Sport and American Mentality, 1880–1910* (Knoxville: University of Tennessee Press, 1983), p. 202; *also see* Roberta Park, "The Attitudes of Leading New England Transcendentalists toward Heathful Exercise, Recreation and Proper Care of the Body, 1830–1850," *Journal of Sport History* 4 (Spring 1977): 34–50.
22. "Amusements," *New Englander* 9 (1851): 358. Cited in Ralph Slovenko and James A. Knight, eds., *Motivation in Play, Games and Sports* (Springfield, Ill.: Charles C. Thomas, 1967), pp. 124–25.
23. Ted Vincent, *Mudville's Revenge: The Rise and Fall of American Sport* (New York: Seaview Books, 1981), pp. 109–22.
24. Stephen Hardy, *How Boston Played* (Boston: Northeastern University Press, 1982), pp. 85–106; Cary Goodman, *Choosing Sides: Playground and Street Life on the Lower East Side* (New York: Schocken Books, 1979), pp. 21–57.
25. Richard A. Swanson, "The Acceptance and Influence of Play in American Protestantism," *Quest* 11 (December 1968): 58.
26. For examples of the widely differing views on *exactly* how sport relates to religion, *see* Novak, *The Joy of Sports;* Allen Guttmann, *From Ritual to Record: The Nature of Modern Sports*

(New York: Columbia University Press, 1978); A. James Rudin, "America's New Religion," *Christian Century* 89 (5 April 1972): 384.

27. Cornish Rogers, "Sports, Religion, and Politics: The Renewal of an Alliance," *Christian Century* 89 (5 April 1972): 392–94.

28. Gerald Redmond, "A Plethora of Shrines: Sport in the Museum and Hall of Fame," *Quest* 19 (January 1973): 41–48; *also see* Guy Lewis and Gerald Redmond, *Sporting Heritage: A Guide to Halls of Fame, Special Collections and Museums in the United States and Canada* (New York: Barnes, 1974).

29. Joseph L. Price, "The Super Bowl as Religious Festival," *Christian Century* 101 (22 February 1984): 190–91.

30. Quoted in Tom Callahan, "Is It Really Only a Game?" *Time* (8 February 1982): 82.

27. "Heavenly Father, Divine Goalie": Sport and Religion

CHARLES S. PREBISH

Arnold Beisser begins his book *The Madness in Sports* with a reference to a famous Japanese World War II battle cry that was meant to demoralize American soldiers: "To hell with Babe Ruth!" Clearly, the attacking Japanese thought they knew what Americans valued most. In his landmark work on religion in sport, *Sports Illustrated* writer Frank Deford picked up on this same theme when he wrote, "The claim that sport has developed into a national faith may be linked to the nagging awareness that something has happened to Sunday." Deford knew just what it was that had happened, too. He correlated the decline in church attendance with the rise of professional football as the new darling of the American sportsman. For 1976, the year in which Deford's articles were published, he was quite correct: "Now, the trip out of the house on Sunday is not to visit a church, but to see a game or to play one. . . . So the churches have ceded Sunday to sports, to games." Later we shall see that, by 1982, sport had not only won the battle for Sunday, but for all other days as well. In sport religion, the sabbath is Everyday.

The response of the churches to the continually increasing American appetite for sport was to be as obliging as possible. On the one hand, the times of traditional worship services were adjusted so as to free the celebrant for his or her immersion in a Sunday of sport. Catholic churches offered Saturday afternoon services while Protestant denominations scheduled their services in harmony with *TV Guide* announcements of the sport specials of the week. For Jewish families it was somewhat easier. All that had to be sacrificed was the Friday Night Fight; Bar Mitzvah services were over on Saturdays long before the sport scene began to heat up for the day. Of course cable TV and ESPN have changed all that. On the other hand, religious groups, regardless of their specific affiliation, sought to cultivate sport as a means of keeping their clientele firmly in the fold. The holy alliance between religion and sport is not without precedent, however. By 1800, America had cast off the Puritan opposition to sport, and collectively began to realize that a life of physical inactivity was a liability rather than an asset. The American YMCA was founded in Boston in 1851, followed in 1858 by a YWCA chapter in New York. Needless to say, in the middle decades of the twentieth century, it was acknowledged

SOURCE: Charles S. Prebish, " 'Heavenly Father, Divine Goalie': Sport and Religion," *The Antioch Review* 42 (1984), pp. 306–318.

by the various religious groups that participation in sport was healthy for their congregants and unifying for the congregations, and this was evidenced by the large number of church- or synagogue-sponsored athletic leagues, usually carrying the title YMCA, YWCA, CYO, JCC, or some similar identifying designation. Yet it was not until quite recently that churches and synagogues went into the sport business with a fury and passion that advertised *big-time* investments.

By the 1970s, religion was learning a valuable lesson from its secular counterpart. If lucrative television contracts were making club owners and athletes into fiscal wizards while providing ample exposure to an adoring public, then perhaps it was time for professional religion to imitate professional sport. In so doing, television evangelism was to become a hot franchise. The point here is twofold. First, religion was seeking new avenues of reaching the public that rivaled its successful sport adversary. Just like the NFL, NHL, or NBA, religion sought to catch John Q. Public's attention while he sat in his easy chair, newspaper or coffee in hand, and *before* he took his usual dose of O. J. Simpson or Walter Payton. Second, it sought to affirm sport, even champion its fundamental emphases, in order to align itself with a proven winner.

Perhaps the most visible and well-known evangelist to utilize sport in his ministry is the Reverend Billy Graham. Following his appearance as grand marshal of the Rose Bowl parade in 1971, *Newsweek* ran an often cited article entitled "Are Sports Good for the Soul?" In citing Graham's use of sport as a basic metaphor in his preaching, the article quotes Graham's understanding of the role of sport in (at least his) religion: "The Bible says leisure and lying around are morally dangerous for us. Sports keeps us busy; athletes, you notice, don't take drugs. There are probably more really committed Christians in sports, both collegiate and professional, than in any other occupation in America." Although less well-known generally than Billy Graham, on the sporting scene, the most conspicuous religious figure is the Reverend Billy Zeoli. A flashy dresser, he is flamboyant in appearance and speech. A sample from Deford's "Reaching for the Stars" demonstrates:

> By his own proud admission, the Zeoli theology is brutally simple. "I am a total liberal when it comes to methods, but very conservative in theology," he says. As he tells the Bills, as he will tell the Jets, as he always says, Jesus was either the Son of God or a cuckoo—take it or leave it. God and man are separated by sin, which is labelled "The Problem." "The Answer" is to employ Jesus as the intermediary. So there is "The Decision," and to avoid confusion Zeoli lays out the choices: "yes," "no," and "maybe." Taken as a whole, that is what Zeoli calls "God's Game Plan."

Perhaps Billy Zeoli is the extreme case in religion's attempt to use sport, but there are others like him in the arena. These so-called jock evangelists are rapidly becoming a fixture in the locker rooms throughout our land, and organizations are emerging through which athletes are able to take their religious message to the people, playing as much on their role as American heroes as on their ministerial acumen.

The attempt on the part of clergymen to deal with the spiritual needs of athletes is not nearly so altruistic as it might seem. By playing on the widespread appeal of well-known amateur and professional athletes, the ministers are able to expand their operations, numerically and financially, many times over. Frank Deford called this new movement "Sportianity," and to aid in this endeavor the athletes are utilized as amateur evangelists or, as *The Wittenberg Door* calls them, "Jocks for Jesus." There are primarily three organizations through which athletes are used to bring new members into the fold. The first of these is the Fellowship of Christian Athletes (FCA), founded in 1954. It intends "to confront athletes and coaches and through them the youth of our nation, with the challenge and adventure of following Christ and serving him through the fellowship of the church. . . ." In order to carry out its goals, the Fellowship of Christian Athletes uses older athletes (and coaches) to recruit younger ones to Christ.

The second group in athletic religion, Athletes in Action (AIA), is a division of the Billy Graham-inspired Campus Crusade for Christ. With special permission from the NCAA, Athletes in Action fields teams of former college athletes that are allowed to compete against current college squads in basketball, wrestling, gymnastics, track, and weight-lifting. During their various competitions against amateur teams, AIA members give religious speeches, often at half-time or after the match, and distribute materials for the parent organization. Although the organization claims that it relies on the "soft-sell," anyone who has ever attended an AIA event knows that the pitch is several steps up from gentle, with feverish a somewhat more accurate description.

As the FCA and AIA came into increasing competition for the "choice" athletes to serve in a missionary capacity, a third organization was founded to act as a buffer or intermediary between the two: Pro Athletes Outreach (PAO). An outgrowth of Sports World Chaplaincy, Inc., it is a prospering group that sends its professional athletes on what it calls "speaking blitzes" across the country. Like the other organizations, its members offer testimony sprinkled with group publicity.

What all of these groups have in common is that they are completely nondenominational, conservative in their theology, and fundamentalist in approach and lifestyle. They take no stands on questionable moral issues, exclude individuals of doubtful temperament, and insist on absolute fidelity. Everything is done for the glory of Christ, and in so doing, Deford claimed, "Jesus has been transformed, emerging anew as a holler guy, a give-it-100-percenter." Michael Novak, scholar-in-residence at the American Enterprise Institute and a noted Catholic theologian, argues against the religious defensiveness of fundamentalism by boldly stating, "Sports is, somehow, a religion." And while he does not see sport as equal or identical to any of the world's religions, he does concede,

". . . sports flow outward into action from a deep natural impulse that is radically religious: an impulse of freedom, respect for ritual limits, a zest for symbolic meaning, and a longing for perfection. The athlete may of course be pagan, but sports are, as it were, natural religions." Further, despite the fact that each religious group boasts big numbers of fans and converts, all may not be so rosy as claimed. Young Christian athletes often seem to be interested in religion primarily as a means to get an edge, so to speak, to get God on their side. Although such an attitude is not sanctioned religiously, it prevails nonetheless, and though some athletes do indeed stop short of asking God for victory, many do not, thus prostituting the real basis for personal and religious growth. What emerges, then, is an unclear picture with the athletes trying to improve their religious and competitive field position.

On the college campuses today, the relationship between religion and sport is equally cloudy. Although college-level sport competition was originally intended to provide recreation for those who were hard at work cultivating the best that education had to offer, these programs of intercollegiate sport rapidly changed in nature and function in the early years of this century. A plethora of church-supported institutions of higher learning began to exploit the growing American interest in sport, first as a means of publicizing the university and later as a means of attracting funding and students. In many cases, sport as a growth industry within the university was a driving force in upgrading the academic reputation of the school as well. Father James Riehle of Notre Dame was unceremoniously blunt when he said: "Of course Catholic schools used athletics for prestige. Notre Dame would not be the great school it is today, the great academic institution, were it not for football. But the emphases have changed here. I think that now we realize the value of sport in more ways than just the financial, whereas I'm afraid once we didn't." Occasionally, the message does not filter down to the athlete on the field, for one recent Brigham Young quarterback remarked that classes were about the only thing he didn't like at BYU. Most recently, Oral Roberts University, founded in 1965, has utilized both sport and the gospel as a means of calling attention to itself. In fact, Roberts himself proclaims, "Athletics is a part of our Christian witness. . . . Nearly every man in America reads the sports pages, and a Christian school cannot ignore these people."

What effect does all this emphasis on winning, in the name of the Lord, have on individuals who are entrenched in the sports establishment? In the first place, if winning is the result of hard work, discipline, and dedication, as most coaches and athletes suppose, then such an emphasis is certainly consistent with the traditional Protestant work ethic that is such a shaping force in our culture. Some sport sociologists even argue that sport values mirror the core values of Protestantism. Over against this, however, is the growing protest of a rapidly expanding group of vocal clergy. Episcopal priest Malcolm Boyd, for example: "This sort of slick, stage-directed prayer alienates people from religion because anybody can see that it is as shoddy as anything else in the world. The gimmick use of prayer before a game for the purpose of getting psyched up, this use of prayer as *deus ex machina*—I find it simply immoral. To use God in this way—it isn't holy. Hell isn't a bunch of fires. I think that hell is when you're using anybody, even when you're trying to use God, as in this case." The last remark suggests that sport has used religion too, just as the reverse was true. Now we need to explore this other side of the coin.

Today, almost every team in professional sport holds chapel services on Sundays, both at home and away. Many college teams do the same. And the pregame prayer is customary even in the youth leagues of America. Why? Religion provides the athlete with a basis for reinforcement, both physical and spiritual. It allays his psychological anxieties. It enables him to face the competition at hand confident and peaceful, fully concentrated. In addition, an overwhelming number of athletes claim that religious conviction has been a profound factor in enhancing the development of their sport skills. Hardly an American boy of the 1950s or 1960s could escape watching the Reverend Bob Richards pole-vault his way out of a Wheaties box. Nor will we forget Sandy Koufax's refusal to pitch on a Jewish High Holy Day.

One researcher actually did a master's thesis at the University of California, Santa Barbara (in 1967) on "The Incidence of Prayer in Athletics by Selected California Collegiate Athletes and Coaches." It is clearly the case that when prayer is not private, or team sponsored, then it is institutionalized as part of the sporting event. Very often now, sport events, particularly if they are significant, employ *both* the playing of the National Anthem *and a religious invocation*. Perhaps the most dramatic of these invocations was delivered by Father Edward Rupp before the 1976 World Hockey Association All-Star game:

> Heavenly Father, Divine Goalie, we come before You this evening to seek Your blessing. . . . We are, thanks to You, All-Stars. We pray tonight for Your guidance. Keep us free from actions that would put us in the Sin Bin of Hell. Inspire us to avoid the pitfalls of our profession. Help us to stay within the blue line of Your commandments and the red line of Your grace. Protect us from being injured by the puck of pride. May we be ever delivered from the high stick of dishonesty. May the wings of Your angels play at the right and left of our teammates. May You always be the Divine Center of our team, and when our summons comes for eternal retirement to the heavenly grandstand, may we find You ready to give us the everlasting bonus of a permanent seat in Your coliseum. Finally, grant us the courage to skate without tripping, to run without icing, and to score the goal that really counts—the one that makes each of us a winner, a champion, an All-Star in the hectic Hockey Game of Life. Amen.

From the above, we can see that sport and religion have been more than extensively related during the last generation of American history. The relationship has been so complete, in fact, that numerous critics, from each side of the fence, have responded to the phenomenon in a variety of ways.

By 1971, though, *Newsweek* was asking, "Are Sports Good for the Soul?" Its conclusion highlights the alarm apparently felt by more than a few Americans at the time: "It may be impossible to separate sports and religion in America. Nonetheless, more and more players and viewers are now asking themselves whether treating God as some kind of supercoach does not demean both faith and football." What this writer and others seemed to be saying, albeit in round-about fashion, is what sport sociologist Harry Edwards said directly in 1973: "If there is a universal popular religion in America it is to be found within the institution of sport." And, unlike his colleagues, Edwards included even the fan, noting that for the spectator, sport is a "quasi religion." In addition, what makes Edwards's treatment so important is that he demonstrated just where the parallels between religion and sport emerge and interpenetrate.

What I find overwhelmingly hard to understand is why Professor Edwards says, "In sum, sport is essentially a secular, quasi-religious institution. It does not, however, constitute an alternative to or substitute for formal sacred religious involvement." It is apparent that Edwards saw, or at least presented, far more material on the subject than his colleagues in any of the sub-disciplines of sport study. Yet he, too, like all other writers, insisted on stopping short of what is becoming notably obvious.

For me, it is not just a parallel that is emerging between sport and religion, but rather a *complete identity*. *Sport is religion* for growing numbers of Americans, and this is no product of simply facile reasoning or wishful thinking. Further, for many, sport religion has become a more appropriate expression of personal religiosity than Christianity, Judaism, or any of the traditional religions.

Many of the authors cited to this point made reference to the similarity of vocabulary in sport and religion. They suggested that sport has appropriated significant religious terminology as a means of expressing the sincerity, fervor, and seriousness of sport. All mentioned at least a few well-chosen examples of parallel nomenclature, resulting in a profusion of references to words like *sacred, faith, ritual,* and so forth. There are two problems obvious in such an approach. In the first place, it is only the surface of mutually shared terminology that is proverbially scratched. Even a cursory continuance of the procedure reveals that other, equally applicable expressions must be mentioned: *ultimate, dedicated, sacrifice, peace, commitment, spirit, suffering, worship, prayer, festival,* and *holiday*. With a little investigation, it would not be unreasonable to suppose that a list of fifty or more terms and phrases could be compiled. Yet it is the second problem that is critical, for we are not simply playing the numbers game here. Most authors presume a shared vocabulary with a *slightly altered meaning* for each enterprise. For Novak and others, words like *sacred, dedicated,* and *sacrifice* mean one thing for religion and another for sport. This bifurcation results from the axiom that religion is sacred while sport is secular. I would maintain, however, that in many cases there is absolutely no difference in the meaning that each term carries for the two traditions in question. Equally, the yearly Super Bowl is no less a religious holiday than Easter. The child's worship of Ted Williams is no less real than his reverential adoration of Christ, and to some, Williams's accomplishments and capabilities in baseball were unquestionably godly. And, judging from the sentiments it evoked, the Gold Medal victory of the U.S. Hockey team in the 1980 Winter Olympics was quite as ultimate as anything that occurs in a traditional house of worship.

The point of ritual is to approach purity through our actions in order that our attained purity brings us closer to the fulfillment of specific goals. Regarding practicality, these rituals are enacted both publicly and privately. Public expression requires attendance at formal, sanctioned, institutional services. In traditional religion, one attends church or synagogue, whereas in sport religion, one attends the gymnasium or arena. There are numerous examples of identity between religious and sport rituals in the public sphere. It would not be going far, I think, to suggest that in Christian services, communion may well be the most significant ritual activity. For sport religion, the ritual act of the game, its religious service, would also not be complete without its respective act of communion. Richard Lipsky points out in straightforward fashion: "During the game, the social euphoria generates a festive communion and sense of solidarity between the players and fans." Finally, the post-game events explicitly replicate the rituals of traditional religion, replete with trying to catch a word with the religious professional, be he priest, rabbi, minister, *or player*. No religious service would be complete without ritual chants and hymns. These vary from tradition to tradition, but are utilized to some degree by all religions. We find the same ritual practice in sport as well, with each denomination in sport religion presenting its own specific assortment. Football, for example, might offer as its hymn, "You've Got to be a Football Hero"; baseball counters with "Take Me Out to the Ball Game." Chants range from the traditional "We want a touchdown" to the hopeless "Let's Go Cubs." Even the stadium organist is modeled on his counterpart in traditional religion. And the result is identical in each case: individuals go beyond their own ego bonds. In so doing, they open to the possibility of experiencing a different, non-ordinary reality.

No less analogous to public ritual expression is the private search for religious meaning through rites, whether the specific activity is the Muslim's daily domestic practices or the runner's solitary ten-miler at dawn. It is important to note that this is the point at which personal prayer, as a ritual activity, converges in sport and religion. The point is this: all of these ritual acts, both traditional and nontraditional, prepare the participant for what is to follow. Without proper ritual preparation, the game would be lost, a close call would be missed, the fan would feel just plain lousy, or religious catastrophe might occur. In other words, these singular, curious-looking acts bring forth the sacred; they are part of the sacraments of religion, the sport variety and otherwise.

Taken together, rituals are welded into festivals, and in sport religion, just as in its traditional counterpart, the festivals are obvious and seasonal. In each of the world's major religious traditions, it is possible to isolate and identify a series of important seasonal rituals that occur periodically throughout the calendar year, binding the devotees on a seasonal, continuing basis. Each major sport functions in quite the same way, culminating in the pinnacle of the tradition, the crowning of its national champion. The result is clear: from a combination of seasonal and personal ritual processes, sport activity provides a continual stream of resacralization and meaning for our everyday world, just as traditional religion offers.

No religious tradition would be complete or functional without a strong legendary basis to underline and accompany the historical data of the faith. It is the legends that reveal an individual in his or her depth and fullness. It is the legends that provide a three-dimensional glimpse of the person in question, generally manifesting all the characteristics considered exemplary in the particular tradition in question. It is the legends that give us a perspective rarely captured by the historical accounts. Thus, the legends offer the faithful what the history books cannot: a leader to emulate, to model themselves after, and, in some cases, to worship. Sport legends are no less imposing and function in just the same way. To be sure, even in modern times, where media gadgets, journalistic morgues, and computer banks offer instant access to accurate historical data, this is not the stuff of which sport legends are made. Sport legend captures the essence of the sporting figure, reporting little-known bits and pieces of the individual that often defy publication or widespread dissemination. It really doesn't matter whether the specific legendary figure is Babe Ruth, Mickey Mantle, Red Grange, Wilt Chamberlain, Roger Bannister, Babe Didrikson Zaharias, or numerous others. What does matter is that each provides for his or her respective sport an archetypal model that holds true and grows for future generations. As for some of the rather unsavory characteristics, one need only be reminded of similar religious circumstances in the papal line or in the lineage of the Dalai Lama in Tibetan Buddhism.

In *How We Play the Game*, Richard Lipsky tells us (of baseball), "The game takes place in an atmosphere of piety. In many ways the ballplayers themselves can be seen as priests who represent us in a liturgy (game) that is part of a sacred tradition." Lipsky's comment reveals that far too little has been said about the role of the player in sport religion. In other words, we need to reflect on the actors in sport religion. It would be incorrect, though, to suggest that it is only the actual players who fulfill the role of religious participants in sport. We must include the coaches and officials as well, in their role as functionaries in the religious process. They are not untrained, either. Sport, no doubt, has its own seminaries and divinity schools in the various minor leagues and training camps that school the participants in all aspects of the tradition, from theology to ritual. The spectators, as video viewers, radio listeners, or game-going die-hards, form the congregation of sport religion. Their attendance is not required for all religious observances, but they do attend at specified times to share in religious rites. And they bear the religious symbols of their faith: the pennants, emblems, hats, coats, gloves, and whatever other objects the media geniuses can promote to signify the glory of sport in general and the home team in particular. The sport symbol may not be the cross, rosary, or mezuzah, but it is no less valuable to the owner, and likely considered to be just as powerful as its traditional counterpart, or more so.

It is necessary to note here that one would be *incorrect in assuming that all sport is religion*. In fact, quite the opposite is true. Utilizing a definition of religion as "a means of ultimate transformation," the whole issue of sport as religion turns on the premise that sport is a religion only insofar as it brings its adherents to an experience of ultimate reality, radically alters their lives as a result of the experience of ultimacy, and then channels their positive gains back into society in a generally viable and useful fashion. This is not so simple as it sounds. In traditional religion, not everyone gets religious experience. That is to say, not everyone experiences God (or some other symbol for the ultimate), irrespective of how pious or devout in worship. Nor is the experience of the ultimate an occasion that repeats itself each time the worshiper attends church or synagogue. For the athlete, religious experience is not simply having a good time, an important win, or being "turned inward" on a run or in a workout. No less than in traditional religion, sport religion is actualized only when an aspirant genuinely experiences that which is considered to be ultimate. And it is no less awe-inspiring. Yet there is no so-called sport religion for the athlete who attains ultimate reality through sport as a means of worship or religious practice in traditional religion. For sport to be considered a religion, it must quite self-consciously attempt to be just that. It must present all the rituals, practices, holidays, myths, legends, shrines, and so forth that all traditional religions provide. The results of ultimate transformation through sport must be socially functional in a way that is consistent with sport and the ethical imperative that derives from its practice.

If the potential for experiencing ultimate reality is so readily available in sport, why is it that athletes have so far been relatively silent in affirming their personal religious encounters? There are two likely answers here. First, I think that athletes, for the most part, simply do not have the equipment to speak comfortably and intelligently about religion *or* sport. One hopes, however, that as people actively involved in sport gain some real measure of intellectual facility in these areas, they will be able to recount numerous occasions in which the case for religious experience in sport is made thoroughly and believably. In other words, we are trying to provide those engaged in all aspects of sport with a new way of looking at themselves and their religious world. The second reason for the relative silence in the sporting world is that athletes are simply afraid of being held up to public ridicule. Many in our culture will find the suggestion that sport has become a genuine and sacred religious tradition to be utterly blasphemous. For the average citizen, the person professing sport religion becomes the object of scorn and derision, but for the professional athlete, the repercussions are worse still. There are endorsements and public appearances to be lost, all of which quickly translates into loss of revenue, and we should not overlook the fact that professional sport is big business. It is both sad and unfortunate that when dollars are at stake, integrity all too often becomes an unprofitable luxury.

There are other problems in sport religion. Just who is it that gets religious experience in sport? Curiously, these experiences seem not to be specific to the athlete-participant, the specialist. Similar responses can be evoked from coaches, officials, and, not so surprisingly, spectators (present or otherwise). After all, each of the above advocates does participate in his or her own way. This latter point is particularly important, I think, because it indicates that *no special athletic talent is required in the quest for salvation in sport*. What is self-evident here, then, is that *religious experience in sport is open to anyone, at any time, anywhere*—just as it is in traditional religion. Consequently, religious experience in sport is no more confined to the participants on the playing field than is traditional experience confined to the priest, minister, or rabbi. Also problematic is the theology of sport religion. A most obvious concern is who this god of sport might be. Is it the God of ancient Israel? Is it consistent with the Trinitarian notion of Christianity? Does sport present us with a primitive polytheism in which we find a god of running, one of tennis, and still another of swimming? Is there some arena in which the pantheon of sport deities might gather? What is the gender of the sport god(s)? How much power and might is wielded? What is important in this rather lighthearted approach is the understanding that sport theology must face the same questions as traditional religious theology, and this is no simple dilemma. Conversations I have had with athletes indicate support for *each* of the above positions, including god as female with little, medium, or great powers. Still another complicating factor is that for some participants, ultimacy is defined in nontheistic terms, usually as a oneness with nature, union with an impersonal absolute.

Earlier, I suggested that if sport is to be considered a religion in the proper sense of that word, it must, in addition to bringing its followers to an experience of ultimacy, radically alter their lives and channel that positive change back into society in a useful way. Does the sport experience change lives? One need only look at the manner in which athletes persevere in increasing their training, sometimes at the expense of all else, and their religious zeal after experiencing the supremacy of union with the Absolute. Is the smile and fulfillment of the Monday-morning quarterback to be doubted when some inordinately significant "Eureka" occurred to him while watching Walter Payton's uncanny ability to succeed despite the ineptitude of the Bears' offensive line? The changes are far too diverse and numerous to document here, but they do occur—and with startling regularity. And as a result, everything changes: attitudes, values, frames of reference, interpersonal relationships, and social involvements. We have tacitly avoided any mention of social ethics to this point. There is no question that some sport figures today have been less than exemplary in their conduct. To be sure, sport religion faces the same series of ethical difficulties as traditional religion. The presumption is that as one's religious faith matures, so does one's ethical behavior. It is no wonder, then, that so many religious groups of all denominations emphasize charitable acts and social involvement in good works for their members. In addition, the leaders of the congregation are expected to be especially consummate in their behavior. Sport religion is no less responsive to social needs in requiring devout participation by its advocates. Well, it's no wonder. Social concern, charitable acts, and personal conduct are all founded on discipline, and it is precisely here that the follower of sport religion excels. It doesn't matter whether this discipline is expressed by a daily twelve-mile run or three hours glued to ESPN. It can be corraled and marshaled for good causes, both personal and collective.

A final problem must be noted. Is it possible to maintain multilateral religious affiliations? Can the proponent of sport religion also retain standing within his or her traditional religious affiliation? Ostensibly not! When one declares that one adheres to sport as a formal religious tradition, this implies a *constant pursuit* that is also the *most important pursuit* and a *religious pursuit*. If such individuals were to then state that they are also Jews or Protestants (or Catholics or whatever), they would be referring to their *cultural heritage only*, to the complex series of factors that are essentially ethnic and locational rather than religious.

What it all boils down to is this: if sport can bring its advocates to an experience of the ultimate, and this (pursuit and) experience is expressed through a formal series of public and private rituals requiring a symbolic language and space deemed sacred by its worshipers, then it is both proper and necessary to call sport itself a religion. It is also reasonable to consider sport the newest and fastest-growing religion, far outdistancing whatever is in second place.

28. *Heavenly Game?*

FRANK DEFORD

Three of the four finalists in the NCAA basketball championship last season were Roman Catholic colleges, and for the second year in a row a Catholic school won. Villanova, that champion, was also in the Final Four in 1939, the first year of the NCAAs, and since then 17 different Catholic institutions have achieved that level. In 1947 Holy Cross became the first Catholic college to win the NCAAs, and five more have also triumphed. Eleven other Catholic colleges won the NIT back in the quarter-century when it was still a genuine national championship. Thirty-nine of this year's 283 Division I basketball schools are Catholic; 12 of the 237 colleges with Phi Beta Kappa chapters are Catholic. . . .

For many Americans college basketball is the outward and visible sign of Catholicism in the United States. And because private schools of any stripe tend to be smaller and more focused than the sprawling public mega-universities that they play games against, basketball has become even more the cynosure on the Catholic campus.

The perception that education has become the token white at the end of the Catholic basketball bench may be all the more damaging because, historically, Catholic universities have never been accepted as intellectual company, neither with the private nondenominational elite nor with the great state schools. Some of this snubbing has come, reflexively, from cynical Protestants, but even many American Catholics themselves have long questioned whether the term *Catholic education* is an oxymoron, like military justice. At many Catholic schools, as one Catholic historian has written, "Original research became original sin."

Moreover, as Catholic school basketball has thrived, it has seemed all the more contradictory—hypocritical?—that the standard-bearers for white Catholic schools are, in the main, black Protestants. Most people who watched a nearly all-black Villanova team upset a totally black Georgetown squad in the championship game last spring would probably be startled to learn that, notwithstanding what appeared on the court, Villanova is so white (98%), so Catholic (86%) and so suburban preppie upper middle class that it is known in its own bailiwick as Vanilla-nova.

Of course, much of this Catholics can't help. Abroad in the land, the image

SOURCE: Frank Deford, "Heavenly Game?" *Sports Illustrated* (March 3, 1986), excerpts from pp. 60–70.

of almost all American universities is related to athletics. Basketball and football—*programs*—attract more attention than chemistry and Romance languages—*departments*. The question is whether religious schools can really afford to strike this deal with . . . well, with the devil, the same as secular institutions. In other words, can the Catholic colleges pursue the almighty dollar and answer to the Almighty at the same time? What price prime time?

In 1971, the last year before 1985 that Villanova made the Final Four, the Wildcats had to forfeit their second-place finish when their star player was found to be a pro. The only fix disqualification in the history of the Final Four was leveled against another Philadelphia-area Catholic school, St. Joseph's, in 1961. Boston College was caught in the fix trap four years ago. In 1982 San Francisco gave up basketball for three years after a succession of tawdry scandals that would have sorely tested even Jesus's inclinations toward forgiveness. The damage done to Creighton when one of its players had to go back to an elementary school to learn how to read after several years at the Omaha school remains incalculable. A scholar-athlete at Providence was charged with assaulting a teammate with a tire iron. Holy Cross's team took to racial skirmishing last year. Georgetown's reputation for fighting—at least half a dozen brawls in the last four years—is well established.

Now none of this is the peculiar province of Catholic higher education. Indeed, anybody even remotely familiar with football at Texas Christian and Southern Methodist can only draw the conclusion that the inherent problem with big-time college sports and religion is that the former is so pervasive, so rotten, so—let's say it—sinful that it is bound to soil any of the latter that lies down with it. Does religion need this? . . .

Religious schools, whatever the denomination, are forever torn about what sort of moral guidance they are mandated to provide. And, of course, there is also the perennial question: Where does house theology become propaganda and squeeze out open inquiry? Villanova's mission statement attempts to draw a line: "Although Villanova functions as an independent institution in the conduct of its own affairs, in matters theological it recognizes its obligation to the Magisterium of the Church."

Thus, last year the editor of *The Villanovan*, John Marusak, was censured for running a paid advertisement for a birth control device. More recently, the Villanova president, Father John Driscoll, rescinded the invitation of a pro-choice speaker who was to appear on campus for a theological symposium. "Within the framework of academic freedom," Driscoll says, drawing on his pipe, "anyone identified with a Catholic university has a right to teach the students the doctrine of its ruling body."

As suggested by the raging debates on many campuses over institutional investment in South Africa, universities must often make moral choices for themselves—and this is especially true if they feel their "explicit reason for existence," as Driscoll says is the case with Catholic schools, "is value orientation." But while big-time basketball is indisputably a rotten borough, Catholic schools have hardly been shy about residing there. When it comes to morality, they often seem to ask more of their students than of themselves. Of course, maybe they believe they haven't got any choice. Maybe they think if they want to compete in basketball, they've got to wink at the sinners. Praise the Lord and pass the ammunition. The one person at a Catholic institution who comes easily to mind for having spoken out courageously against the system is not a cleric, but Digger Phelps, the basketball coach at Notre Dame. And when he was derided, then, by both his coaching colleagues and the press for being a tattletale, who in Catholic education came to his side?

Questions about the direction of big-time intercollegiate athletics are regularly brought up by Catholic school presidents when they gather together, but apart from perfunctory nods toward goodness and light, no strong moral protests ever seem to be publicly ventilated. Driscoll shares what seems to be the benign, majority view. "In this country the tradition of athletics runs deep," he says. "And not only that of participating. Observing sports is also a strong part of our culture. Now we all must concern ourselves with overemphasis, and if abuses take place because of indifference on the part of the coaches or the administration, then it's wrong. But if mistakes are made unintentionally, there's no reason to punish athletics. That's just the way human beings operate."

A championship such as that won by Georgetown or Villanova—or even just a nicely publicized winning season—can enlarge for a university what politicians call "the recognition factor." Villanova's applications rose almost 15% last year—although it's a safe guess that these are just more of the same sort of kids.

Villanova's vanillaness is not altogether of its own choosing, though. Like so many private schools just below the top rank, it is caught in a bind. With tuition and costs totaling in excess of $10,000 a year, it obviously is going to attract a high percentage of well-heeled applicants. Yet because Villanova is not generously endowed, it cannot offer the bountiful scholarship assistance that wealthier schools can. (Villanova's endowment totals $15 million as compared with $300 million for Notre Dame and more than $3 billion for Harvard.) The well-endowed Ivies routinely dip down the scale to accept reasonably well-qualified minority scholarship applicants. This leaves Villanova with, as Capone characterizes them, "second-round draft choices" and poses this dilemma: How do you justify offering aid to kids who don't project as graduates?

Contradictory as this may sound, the better academic schools—such as Georgetown among Catholic institutions—also seem more comfortable in practicing a form of noblesse oblige and granting admission to borderline students. East Cupcake State bends the rules; Harvard provides minority opportunity. Charles Deacon, Georgetown's dean of undergraduate admissions, says flatly, "We have no minimum averages or standards." So long as an applicant is projected as capable of graduating, who is to say that a 7-foot basketball player with a minimal SAT score isn't more deserving than a wimpy poet with an SAT score out of sight?

There was grousing on the Georgetown campus when Patrick Ewing was admitted in 1981, complaints that he was taking the place of some more deserving student. But as Father James Redington, a Georgetown theology professor who also serves as scorekeeper for the Hoya team, says, "After a year it was no longer an issue. The main way I see Georgetown—as a Catholic university, but as one with basketball—is in terms of the increased commitment by Catholic universities, and by Jesuits in particular, in support of social justice. Or, specifically, it's what we Jesuits call an option in favor of the poor." Cynics might suggest that the option is more likely to be exercised in favor of those among the poor who excel at basketball, but the fact is, long before Thompson arrived as a coach at Georgetown, the university had begun a "community scholars program" to help students with special educational needs. . . .

Almost all Catholic schools keep sports in better perspective than do their secular counterparts. At the same time, it is clear that in a period when Catholic universities are struggling for identity, even for justification, they are often mainly visible as accomplices in the big-time basketball mob. Even Georgetown, generally regarded as the finest academic Catholic institution, and with a perception of itself as being in competition with such colleges as Duke and Northwestern, acknowledges that abroad in the land it is viewed as "the Southern California of basketball." The fact is that Catholic colleges are playing somebody else's game, and even when they win, it is not clear that they do.

■ FOR FURTHER STUDY

Brody, M. Kenneth. "Institutionalized Sport as Quasi-Religion." *Journal of Sport and Social Issues* 3 (Fall/Winter 1979), 17–29.

Burhmann, H. G., and M. K. Zaugg. "Religion and Superstition in the Sport of Basketball." *Journal of Sport Behavior* 6 (October 1983), 146–151.

Coakley, Jay J. *Sport in Society: Issues and Controversies.* 3d ed. St. Louis: Times Mirror/Mosby, 1986, pp. 317–330.

Deford, Frank. "Religion in Sport." *Sports Illustrated* (April 19, April 26, and May 3, 1976): 88–100, 55–56, 68, 69, and 43–44, 57–60 respectively.

Eitzen, D. Stanley, and George H. Sage. *Sociology of North American Sport.* 3d ed. Dubuque, Iowa: Wm. C. Brown, 1986, pp. 135–166.

Fagin, R., and P. Brynteson. "The Cohesive Function of Religion and Sport at a Sectarian University." *Sport Sociology Bulletin* 4 (Spring 1975): 33–47.

Fellowship of Christian Athletes. *The Christian Athlete* (any issue).

Frame, Randy. "Christianity Comes of Age in the NFL." *Christianity Today* 28 (January 1984): 36–37.

Gmelch, George. "Baseball Magic." *Trans-action* 8 (June 1971): 39–41, 54.

Kirshenbaum, Jerry. "Reincarnation and 13 Pairs of Socks." *Sports Illustrated* (March 28, 1977): 30–33.

Neil, Graham. "Demystifying Sport Superstition." *International Review of Sport Sociology* 17, no. 1 (1982): 99–126.

Novak, Michael. *The Joy of Sports.* New York: Basic Books, 1976.

Price, Joseph L. "The Super Bowl as Religious Festival." *The Christian Century* (February 22, 1984): 190–191.

Redmond, Gerald. "A Plethora of Shrines: Sport in the Museum and Hall of Fame." *Quest* 19 (January 1973): 41–48.

Rogers, Cornish. "Sports, Religion, and Politics: The Renewal of an Alliance." *The Christian Century* (April 5, 1972): 392–394.

Womack, Mari. "Why Athletes Need Ritual: A Study of Magic among Professional Athletes." In *Sport and the Humanities,* edited by W. J. Morgan. Knoxville: University of Tennessee Press, 1979, pp. 22–38.

Part Nine

Race and Sport

By definition a *minority group* is one that (1) is relatively powerless compared with the majority group, (2) possesses traits that make it stand apart from others, (3) is systematically condemned by negative stereotyped beliefs, and (4) is singled out for differential and unfair treatment (i.e., discrimination). Unquestionably, blacks constitute a minority group in American society.[1] But although the members of this minority have been the objects of discriminatory treatment throughout American history, there is the widespread, persistent— and mistaken—belief that contemporary sport is an island free of racial animosities and tensions. After all, some would argue, blacks are dispropor- tionately represented in sport, constituting approximately three-fourths of all professional basketball players, over half of all professional football players, and more than one-fifth of all professional baseball players while they are but 12 percent of the population. Moreover, blacks are among the highest paid athletes. And, perhaps most important, sport is one area of American life where performance is all that counts.

The selections in Part Nine make the opposite case. The thesis is that sport is a microcosm of society that reflects the biases present in society. The first selection, by D. Stanley Eitzen, traces black participation in American sport, especially since World War II. The second selection, by Lynn Rosellini, presents facts that substantiate the extent of racial discrimination in contempo- rary American sport. The third selection, by sociologists John J. Schneider and D. Stanley Eitzen, details one type of racial discrimination in sport— stacking—and explains how it has actually increased in professional football.

NOTE

1. The discussion in Part Nine is limited to blacks because they are the most prominent minority in American sports.

29. *Black Participation in American Sport since World War II*

D. STANLEY EITZEN

With few exceptions, organized sports in American society prior to 1945 were racially segregated (Chalk, 1975; Govan, 1971; Henderson, 1968; Rust and Rust, 1985; Tygiel, 1983). Prior to the Emancipation Proclamation in 1863, most blacks were unable to participate in organized sports. After the Civil War, blacks made a few inroads as boxers, jockeys, and team players but they were clearly exceptions. Society and sport remained racially segregated by custom and in some places by law (e.g., the Jim Crow laws). The period from World War I to World War II was especially segregated. There were no blacks in major league baseball or basketball, and none in football after 1933, nor did blacks play in integrated tournaments in golf, tennis, or bowling. Many states and municipalities, primarily in the South, had laws prohibiting racially mixed athletic events. High schools and colleges in the North and Midwest rarely had black players and the schools in the South were totally segregated. This exclusion of blacks from white sports generated parallel organizations created for blacks such as teams, leagues, traveling exhibitions, and colleges. Thus, blacks prior to 1945 did have some opportunity for organized athletic participation but in separate and unequal circumstances.

A number of factors occurred around the time of World War II that served to change the racial structure of sport. To begin, Joe Louis, the famous black heavyweight boxing champion, defeated Max Schmeling in 1938. This event was celebrated by American blacks and whites as a triumph over Germany. When Louis enlisted in the military he became a national symbol of American youth's patriotism, despite his minority racial status. Louis also was instrumental in desegregating baseball and football at the Army camp at Fort Riley, Kansas (prior to this change, Jackie Robinson was stationed there but could not compete on the camp teams because of segregation).

Second, during the early 1940s there was a general movement for greater equality of employment opportunity for blacks. President Roosevelt in 1941 issued an Executive Order declaring that *all* citizens be encouraged to participate fully in the defense program. He also appointed a Fair Employment Practices Committee to investigate complaints and hear grievances concerning racial discrimination in the workplace. Third, a major barrier to integration in baseball was the commissioner of baseball, Judge Kenesaw Mountain

SOURCE: This essay was written for the third edition of *Sport in Contemporary Society*.

Landis. Upon his death in 1944, he was replaced by A. B. Chandler, a former senator from Kentucky, who went on record opposing racial segregation in baseball.

Fourth, the inconsistency of waging war against the Nazi theory of the master race abroad while denying racial equality at home was obvious. As *The New York Times* editorialized in 1945: "If we are willing to let Negroes as soldiers fight wars on our team, we should not ask questions about color in the great American game" (quoted in Smith, 1979:14). "Nazism . . . revealed racism as 'an unmitigated evil,' forcing white society to question its own moral integrity" (Capeci and Wilkerson, 1983:10). Similarly, many influential white writers such as Westbrook Pegler, Heywood Broun, and Jimmy Powers wrote and spoke against the racial barrier in baseball. One black newspaper, the *Pittsburgh Courier-Journal,* waged a long and vigorous campaign against segregation in sport (Wiggins, 1983; Simons, 1985).

Fifth, the G.I. Bill of Rights gave large numbers of blacks the chance to attend college, which increased the probability of their trying for athletic teams. Finally, there were economic incentives that promoted desegregation. The prosperity following the war was to a limited extent extended to blacks who now had some money for leisure activities. Many owners began to see the economic advantages of attracting black spectators. Thus, "economic power became social power" (Rust and Rust, 1985:48). During the 1947 baseball season, for example, the attendance of blacks at the home games of Jackie Robinson's Brooklyn Dodgers increased by 400 percent from the previous year and the team set a league attendance record (Lowenfish, 1978). During an early season game in St. Louis, the lure of watching Jackie Robinson play brought so many blacks to the game that the small segregated seating area reserved for blacks would not accommodate them. The St. Louis management quickly realized that their discriminatory treatment of black spectators was costing money. Thus, the restrictive seating policy was eliminated and blacks were able to buy any seat they could afford (Thompson, 1964).

Since World War II, blacks have made tremendous strides in professional sport. The percentages of blacks in professional football went from zero to 57 percent and in professional basketball from zero to almost 80 percent by 1987. All NFL football coaches remain white, however, as are the owners of all professional teams in the major sports. Let us examine the history of black participation, especially since 1945, in several representative sports and at the professional and amateur levels. (See Table 29-1 for a summary of the breakthroughs made by black athletes since 1945.)

PROFESSIONAL BOXING

There were few American black fighters until relatively recently. Tom Molineaux, for example, was an ex-slave who fought around 1810. The most

TABLE 29-1   Black Breakthroughs in American Sports: 1945–1988

1945	Kenny Washington and Woody Strode of the Los Angeles Rams became the first blacks to play in the National Football League (NFL).
1946	Marion Motley of the Cleveland Browns became the first black in the All-American Football Conference.
1947	Jackie Robinson broke the racial barrier in modern major league baseball when he played for the Brooklyn Dodgers.
1948	Satchel Paige at the age of 42 became the first black pitcher in the major leagues. Also, in 1948, he became the first black pitcher to appear in a World Series.
	Don Barksdale of UCLA became the first black to play on the U.S. Olympic basketball team.
1949	Jackie Robinson bacame the first black to win Most Valuable Player honors in the major leagues.
1950	Althea Gibson became the first black to play in the National Tennis Tournament at Forest Hills, Long Island.
	Chuck Cooper became the first black drafted and signed to play in the National Basketball Association (NBA). Earl Lloyd, however, because of a quirk in the schedule, became the first black to play in the NBA (by one day).
1953	Willie Thrower of the Chicago Bears became the first black to play quarterback in the NFL.
1957	Willie O'Ree of the Boston Bruins became the first black to play in the National Hockey League.
1959	Althea Gibson became the first black professional tennis player.
1961	Charlie Sifford became the first black golfer to play on the Professional Golf Association (PGA) tour.
	John McLendon became the first black head coach of a professional basketball team (Cleveland Pipers of the American Basketball Association).
	Ernie Davis, Syracuse University, became the first black recipient of the Heisman Trophy, the highest honor in collegiate football.
	Wilma Rudolph became the first black woman to win the James E. Sullivan award (female amateur athlete of the year).
1962	Jackie Robinson became the first black inducted in the National Baseball Hall of Fame.
1963	The Boston Celtics of the NBA became the first integrated professional team to have an all-black starting lineup.
	Arthur Ashe became the first black named to the American Davis Cup team.

1964 Pete Brown became the first black to win a PGA event.

1965 Burl Toler became the first black game official in the NFL.

1966 Bill Russell became the first black head coach in the NBA (Boston Celtics).

For the first time more than 50 percent of the NBA players were black.

The last major college conference—the Southeastern (SEC)—integrated.

Emmett Ashford became the first black umpire in major league history.

1967 For the first time blacks constitute a numerical majority on the college All-American basketball team.

Emlen Tunnell became the first black elected to the NFL Hall of Fame.

1968 Blacks under the leadership of Harry Edwards organized to use the Olympic Games as a vehicle to dramatize racism in America.

Arthur Ashe became the first black male U.S. Open champion in tennis.

1969 Curt Flood challenged the reserve clause in baseball through a court suit opening up free agency and much higher salaries for players.

1971 Althea Gibson became the first black elected to the International Tennis Hall of Fame.

Wayne Embry became the first black general manager (Milwaukee Bucks of the NBA).

Bill White became the first full-time black radio announcer doing play-by-play (New York Yankees).

1975 Frank Robinson became the first black field manager in baseball (Cleveland Indians).

James Harris of the Los Angeles Rams became the first black starting quarterback for a season in the NFL.

Lee Elder became the first black to play in the Master's Golf Tournament.

All starters for the University of Alabama basketball team were black.

1976 Willie Wood became the first black head coach in modern professional football (Philadelphia Bells of the World Football League).

1979 Two NFL teams with black quarterbacks as starters faced each other for the first time—Doug Williams of Tampa Bay and Vince Evans of Chicago.

1984 John Thompson of Georgetown University became the first black coach to win the National Collegiate Athletic Association (NCAA) Division I basketball championship.

1985 Eddie Robinson of Grambling State University became the all-time leader in career coaching victories in football.

1986	Debi Thomas became the first black to win a national ice skating title— U.S. Women's Champion (she also won the world championship that year).
	Walter Payton, the NFL's all-time rushing leader, became the first black signed by General Mills, Inc. to appear on Wheaties cereal boxes to sell "The Breakfast of Champions."
	John Thompson was selected as the first black head coach of the U.S. Olympic basketball team (for the 1988 Olympics).
	George Branham III became the first black champion in the history of the Professional Bowlers Association.
1988	Doug Williams, of the Washington Redskins, became the first black to start at quarterback in the Super Bowl. He was voted the most valuable player in that game.
	Debi Thomas became the first black from any nation to win a medal at any Winter Olympics when she won the bronze for figure skating.

famous early black boxer was Jack Johnson, who was heavyweight champion from 1908 to 1915. But Johnson was the last champion before Joe Louis, although there were always some black boxers, others dominated. The domination by members of other groups prior to the late 1930s was the result of two factors. First, black fighters were discriminated against by the white boxing establishment. Second, boxers tend to come from the most oppressed strata in cities. The changing racial/ethnic composition of urban slums is reflected in the changing proportion of fighters by race and ethnicity. In the early 1900s, for instance, the Irish dominated boxing. By 1928, Jewish fighters replaced them and they were subsequently succeeded by Italians in 1936. Meanwhile, blacks steadily increased their numbers in boxing. Joe Louis, the great black fighter, became heavyweight champion in 1937 and reigned until 1949. His dominance, popularity, and the success of other blacks such as Sugar Ray Robinson gave black youth role models to emulate. Moreover, by 1948, huge numbers of blacks had migrated to the urban North fueling the numbers of black fighters and black spectators (Weinberg and Arond, 1952). By 1971, more than 70 percent of fighters were black (Hare, 1971).

The most notable black fighter of the post-World War II era was Muhammed Ali (originally named Cassius Clay) who became the heavyweight champion of the world. Unlike previous black fighters who tended to be reticent outside the ring, Ali's behavior was considered outrageous. A product of the disorderly and changing 1960s, Ali was not content to be a docile champion. He converted to the Muslim faith, he was cocky and brash, and he defied the establishment. For many blacks, Ali symbolized the new black hero, one who did not just confine his activities to the athletic arena but used his influence to shake up the political and social arenas as well. These behaviors unified many blacks in a time of societal upheaval. Many whites, on the other hand, found Ali's behaviors troublesome, even frightening (Rust and Rust, 1985:197–98).

PROFESSIONAL FOOTBALL

A few blacks played professional football in the 1920s but the league owners conspired in 1933 to ban blacks from the NFL. The ban was broken in 1945 when Woody Strode and Kenny Washington were signed by the Los Angeles Rams. In 1946, Cleveland, of the All-American Football Conference, signed two blacks, Bill Willis and Marion Motley.

Professional football opened to blacks following World War II for three reasons. First, there were many vacancies since the colleges had not supplied players during the war and 638 NFL players had left for the armed services and were now much older. Second, a rival league, the All-American Football Conference, was formed. The competition for high-calibre players was fierce in this climate. And, third, both leagues expanded to the West Coast following the war. The adding of California teams was significant because blacks were starring in college football there, especially at UCLA.

By 1951, a year after the two leagues merged, six teams employed a total of sixteen black players. By 1975, blacks comprised 43 percent of the league's total and in 1987 they were a majority of 57 percent. The NFL in the modern era, however, still had never had a black as head coach, general manager, or owner. In 1987, only 6.5 percent of the administrative posts in the NFL were held by blacks, only 11 of the 106 (10 percent) game officials were black, and only 14 percent of the assistant coaches were black (Michoces, 1987). As Rick Telander has noted, "Evidently blacks can pull the oars, but they can't crack the whips. Oh, there are black NFL assistants—34 in fact—but that works out to about one black per 10-man staff, perfect tokenism" (1987:80).

PROFESSIONAL BASEBALL

Although blacks broke the segregation practices in other sports first, Jackie Robinson's breakthrough in baseball is commonly viewed as the greatest achievement. Breaking the racial barrier in baseball was considered more significant than in other sports because baseball was *the* national game and, seemingly, the anti-black sentiments were harsher in baseball.

Before 1900, some 30 blacks played in predominantly white leagues and they were subject to considerable harassment. In 1887, the International League's Board of Directors declared in writing that there would be "no more contracts with colored men." This formal declaration along with the unwritten social rules of the time and the infamous Supreme Court decision of *Plessy* v. *Ferguson*, which justified "separate but equal," effectively barred blacks from the major leagues for about fifty years. A few blacks did play after 1900, but as "Cubans" and "Cherokee Indians." Most blacks formed their own teams and leagues during this period, and many of them were exceptional players (e.g., Satchel Paige, "Cool Papa" Bell, Josh Gibson, "Buck" Leonard, and "Pop" Lloyd) who played in the Negro Leagues and occasionally against whites in exhibitions.

Following World War II, baseball made several gestures toward hiring black players. In 1945, the Brooklyn Dodgers had an official tryout for two blacks, the first time this had occurred since 1901. The Boston Red Sox also had a tryout for three blacks. None of these players was signed, however. The owner of the Brooklyn Dodgers, Branch Rickey, signed Jackie Robinson to play for Brooklyn's minor league team in Montreal in 1946. In 1947, Robinson played for Brooklyn, against the objection of most players on his team, the players of other teams, and their owners. He suffered much verbal and physical abuse from players and fans. The management of two National League teams—the Philadelphia Phillies and the St. Louis Cardinals—tried to organize the teams to strike against Brooklyn. Ford Frick, the president of the National League, squelched this effort in writing: "If you do this, you will be suspended from the league. You will find that the friends you think you have in the press box will not support you, that you will be outcasts. I do not care if half the league strikes. Those who do it will encounter quick retribution. They will be suspended, and I don't care if it wrecks the National League for five years. This is the United States of America, and one citizen has as much right to play as another. The National League will go down the line with Robinson whatever the consequence." (Cited in Rust and Rust, 1985:60)

Robinson's pioneering effort was followed by a number of exceptional black players—Larry Doby, Roy Campanella, Don Newcombe, Monte Irvin, Willie Mays, Hank Aaron, Roberto Clemente, Frank Robinson, and Elston Howard, who all signed by 1955. In 1957, 14 clubs had 36 black players. Total major league integration occurred in 1959 when the Boston Red Sox added Elijah "Pumpsie" Green to their club. Since then there have been three black managers—Frank Robinson, Larry Doby, and Maury Wills. In 1987, blacks constituted about 22 percent of the major league rosters, but there were no black managers or general managers. Of the 60 umpires in major league baseball, two were blacks. And, of the 879 top administrative posts in the major leagues, only 17 (1.9 percent) were held by blacks, with 15 of the 26 teams having no minorities in management (Antonen and O'Driscoll, 1987).

PROFESSIONAL BASKETBALL

Basketball originated in 1891 and was quickly received in YMCAs and colleges throughout the country. Blacks were typically excluded from these teams and clearly from white professional leagues. Their only opportunities were at segre-

`gated black schools and on traveling exhibition teams such as the Harlem Globetrotters and the Renaissance Big Five.

In 1950, the Boston Celtics broke the color barrier in the National Basketball Association by drafting Chuck Cooper. Two other blacks—Earl Lloyd and Nat "Sweetwater" Clifton—also played that year. These players encountered various forms of racial hostility and racial segregation as did black players in other sports at that time. In Cooper's words: "Traveling around the league, I encountered all the problems of any black man of that period—be he a diplomat, a porter, or a basketball player. I had to sleep in different hotels than the team in Washington and Baltimore. My teammates and the management acquiesced to this like everybody else at the time. Only later when things had changed somewhat and players with stature—like Bill Russell and Elgin Baylor—came along did conditions change. Being superstars and working in a better environment, they could boycott games if they felt things were unfair." (Cited in Rust and Rust, 1985:313)

By the late 1950s, more and more black stars played in the National Basketball Association (NBA). Players such as Bill Russell who began in 1956, Elgin Baylor in 1958, Wilt Chamberlain in 1959, and Oscar Robertson in 1960 clearly revolutionized professional basketball and gave millions of black youth sports heroes.

Blacks have come to dominate professional basketball. Beginning in 1950 with three black players, by 1966 more than half of the league's players were black, and by 1985, about 80 percent were black. Eighteen of the NBA's 26 teams started at least four blacks in 1986, with six teams usually starting all-black teams. Professional basketball has also been the most progressive of all sports in moving blacks into leadership roles. Bill Russell was the first black head coach in the NBA and he was followed by a number of others. In the 1986 season, there were three black head coaches and two black general managers.

TENNIS

Big-time tennis was at the "amateur" level prior to the 1970s. This was because tennis was a sport played for the most part by the affluent in private club settings. Tennis tournaments in those days were invitational, which excluded blacks in the days of segregation. Thus, prior to 1950 blacks were not invited to play in the United States National championships at Forest Hills, Long Island. Blacks had their own American Tennis Association since 1916 but none of their champions was ever invited to compete in the so-called "national" championship.

In 1950, Althea Gibson was the first black invited to the national championship. Ms. Gibson was also invited to the 1951 English championship at Wimbledon, the most prestigious tournament in all of tennis. These two invitations firmly assured the acceptability of blacks in championship tennis. Gibson won the U.S. championship in 1955 and the Wimbledon crown in 1957. She accomplished another breakthrough when she became the first black professional tennis player in 1959.

The first black male tennis champion was Arthur Ashe, who won at Forest Hills in 1968 and Wimbledon in 1975. With Gibson and Ashe as role models, some black youngsters have taken tennis more seriously. Tennis remains an elite sport, however, dominated by those of privilege who have access to the best facilities and coaching. No American black champions have emerged since the days of Gibson and Ashe.

INTERCOLLEGIATE SPORT

Blacks were absent from big-time college sports for most of this century. A few Ivy League and other eastern schools had black athletes, but they were exceptions. Perhaps the most famous black athlete at a white university in the early years was Paul Robeson, who made Walter Camp's All-American team in 1918 playing for Rutgers. For the most part, though, blacks played at black colleges in black leagues. Although the system was segregated, it did provide many blacks with the opportunity to engage in organized sport. Paralleling the situation in professional sports, college sports remained segregated, except for isolated instances, until after World War II.

Although Northern schools fielded integrated teams after the war, the South remained segregated and even refused to play integrated teams. In 1946, the University of Nevada cancelled a game against Mississippi State because the latter objected to Nevada's two black players. Penn State called off a game with the University of Miami for the same reason. However, the South gradually relented. The original breakthrough occurred when Charles Pierce of Harvard became the first black to play against a Southern college—the University of Virginia at Charlottesville in 1947. But agreeing to play against a racially integrated team and admitting blacks to your own team are quite different behaviors. Southern teams resisted integration until the last. The first black athlete to compete for the University of Texas, for example, was in 1964 (Pennington, 1985). The last major conference to integrate was the Southeastern (SEC). The University of Tennessee broke the SEC racial barrier in 1966 by signing a black defensive back, and Vanderbilt signed a black basketball player in that same year. By 1968, there were eleven blacks on scholarships in that conference, but Alabama, Auburn, Florida, Mississippi, Mississippi State, Louisiana State, and Georgia remained all white (In black and white, 1968; Cornwell, 1984). Two years later, 41 blacks were on scholarships in the SEC (30 of them at three schools—Kentucky, Florida, and Tennessee). Two schools, Louisiana State and Mississippi, remained all white athletically in 1970 (Galliard, 1970). In 1972, there were about 100 blacks in football alone in the SEC, and about 10 percent of the blacks in all sports were on athletic scholarships. Significantly, Tennessee and Mississippi had black sophomores starting and starring as quarterbacks. By 1975, black athletes were common in the SEC and in all the other athletic conferences. The transition from a segregated program to an integrated one is perhaps best illustrated by the University of Alabama: in 1968 there were no blacks on its teams, but its 1975 basketball team had an all-black starting lineup. And by 1983, 44 of the league's 50 starters in basketball were black.

As more and more schools searched for talented blacks to bolster their athletic programs, black schools lost their monopoly on black athletic talent. The best black athletes found it advantageous to play at predominantly white schools because of their greater visibility, especially on television. This visibility meant, for the best athletes, a better chance to sign a lucrative professional contract at the conclusion of their collegiate eligibility. The result was a depleted athletic program at black schools, forcing some to drop their athletic programs and some previously black leagues to disband. Moreover, with a diminishing number of all-black teams, the black schools were no longer playing against teams that were exclusively black (Stuart, 1971; Van Dyne, 1976).

The rapid growth in black participation in college sports is greatest in basketball. In 1948, for example, only 10 percent of college basketball teams had one or more blacks on their rosters. This proportion increased to 45 percent of the teams in 1962 and 95 percent by 1985 (Yetman et al., 1985). Examined another way, in 1948 blacks were but 1 percent of all college basketball players; in 1962 they were 10 percent; and in 1985 they were 49 percent (Yetman et al., 1985). Comparable data are not available for black women collegiate basketball players except for 1985, when they comprised 24 percent of all female basketball players (Yetman et al., 1985).

Although intercollegiate sport has integrated faster than the professional leagues, the record is still damning. In 1987, leadership positions in college sports were rarely held by blacks: (1) of the 105 schools in Division I, only 2 had black athletic directors; (2) only three Division I football teams had black head coaches; (3) 30 of the 273 predominantly white Division I basketball schools had black head coaches; (4) no major college conferences have black commissioners; and (5) of the 73 staff positions in the NCAA, only 5 were held by blacks (Farrell, 1987).

THE CONSEQUENCES OF THE WHITE/BLACK RATIO IN SPORTS

We have seen that in some sports blacks have moved from token representation to a numerical majority in a generation. In other sports such as tennis whites continue to dominate. Figure 29-1 shows selected sports and the ap-

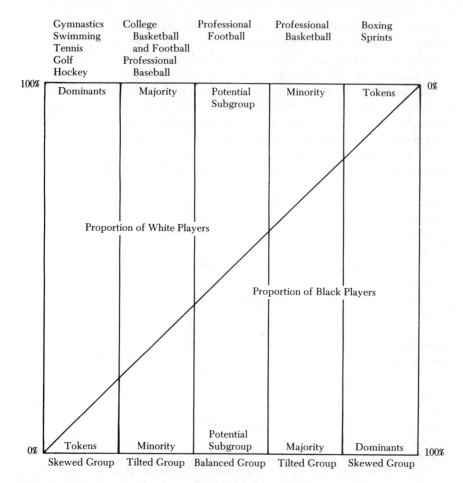

FIGURE 29-1 Proportional Racial Representation in Selected Sports.

* Eldon E. Snyder and Elmer A. Spreitzer, *Social Aspects of Sport,* second edition (Englewood Cliffs, N.J.: Prentice-Hall, 1983), p. 175.

proximate ratio of white and black athletes in American sport. The figure divides sports by racial ratios into those where one race dominates (with 80–100 percent) and where both races are relatively balanced (40–60 percent). This scheme of proportional representation has heuristic value as it allows us to anticipate the behavioral patterns typical at each level. The assumption is that the relative proportion of blacks and whites in a sport (or on a team) makes a difference in interaction. Kanter (1977) has shown this to be the case for the relative number of males and females in industrial contexts, and Yetman (1980) and Snyder and Spreitzer (1983) have speculated on its effects in sport.

When the first members of a racial minority break the "color barrier" in a sport, they are very visible and their behaviors are given unusual symbolic significance. Branch Rickey was well aware of this when he selected Jackie Robinson to be the first black in modern baseball. Robinson's behavior, since it was under intense scrutiny by the media, players, and fans, had to be exemplary if the experiment was to succeed. This heightened visibility of blacks decreases as their proportion increases.

Informal interaction will be restricted across the races when the minority is very small. Blacks in this case are likely to be excluded from off-the-field socializing, in-group humor, and generally treated as outsiders. Meggyesy (1970) has written that this was the case when he was a member of the St. Louis Cardinals' professional football team in the early 1960s.

The typical response of minorities faced with this ostracism is to be subdued and conventional. As their numbers grow, however—and blacks have the social support of their own group—their behaviors tend to become more expressive and assertive (Snyder and Spreitzer, 1983:177). By the late 1960s and early 1970s, for example, blacks became assertive in the struggle for equal rights and in the more general power struggle with owners over player rights. In 1968, Harry Edwards organized a boycott of the Olympics by American blacks (Edwards, 1969). For those blacks who participated in the Olympics, some such as Tommy Smith and John Carlos used the Olympics as a showcase to symbolize black grievances. Baseball player Curt Flood in 1969 brought a suit against organized baseball, which, along with the efforts of others, struck down the reserve clause, giving rise to free agency and much higher salaries for players. Similarly, Oscar Robertson was largely responsible for a significant rise in power by players in professional baseball. Such aggressive behaviors would not have occurred by a black playing in a sport dominated numerically by whites, as was the case of Jackie Robinson in baseball, Marion Motley in football, and Althea Gibson in tennis. Clearly, a critical mass of minority group members must be present for them to be comfortable, and effective, in assertive roles.

REFERENCES

Antonen, Mel, and Patrick O'Driscoll. 1987. "Long, Slow Road: Racism or Nature of Business?"*USA Today* (April 9): 6C.

Capeci, Dominic, J., Jr., and Martha Wilkerson. 1983. "Multifarious Hero: Joe Louis, American Society and Race Relations During World Crisis." *Journal of Sport History* 10 (Winter): 5–25.

Chalk, Ocania. 1975. *Pioneers of Black Sport*. New York: Dodd, Mead.

Cornwell, Mike. 1984. "The Dark Eyes of Dixie." *Denver Post* (December 26): 10D–11D.

Edwards, Harry. 1969. *The Revolt of the Black Athlete*. New York: Free Press.

Farrell, Charles S. 1987. "Scarcity of Blacks in Top Jobs in College Sports Prompts Founding of Group to Monitor Hiring." *Chronicle of Higher Education* (May 6): 40,42.

Galliard, Frye. 1970. "Crumbling Segregation in the Southeastern Conference." *The Black Athlete—1970*. Race Relations Information Center (August): 19–40.

Govan, Michael. 1971. "The Emergence of the Black Athlete in America." *Black Scholar* 3 (November): 16–28.

Hare, Nathan. 1971. "A Study of the Black Fighter." *The Black Scholar* 3 (November): 2–8.

Henderson, Edwin B. 1968. *The Black Athlete: Emergence and Arrival*. New York: Publishers Company.

In Black and White, 1968. *Sports Illustrated* (February 15): 10.

Kanter, Rosabeth. 1977. "Some Effects of Proportion on Group Life: Skewed Sex Ratios and Responses to Token Women." *American Journal of Sociology* 82 (March): 965–990.

Lowenfish, L. E. 1978. "Sport, Race, and the Baseball Business: The Jackie Robinson Story Revisited." *Arena Review* 2:2–16.

Meggyesy, Dave. 1970. "Sex and Racism in the NFL." *Look* (December 1): 65–74.

Michoces, Gary. 1987. "NFL Black Coaches: Still Waiting." *USA Today* (February 17): C1.

Pennington, Richard. 1985. "Orange and White (and Black): The History of University of Texas Football Will Be Forever Colored by the Big Fumble Over Integration." *Third Coast* (September): 39–45.

Rust, Edna, and Art Rust, Jr. 1985. *Art Rust's Illustrated History of the Black Athlete*. Garden City, N.Y.: Doubleday.

Simons, William. 1985. "Jackie Robinson and the American Mind: Journalistic Perceptions of the Reintegration of Baseball." *Journal of Sport History* 12 (Spring): 39–64.

Smith, Ronald A. 1979. "The Paul Robeson–Jackie Robinson Saga and a Political Collision." *Journal of Sport History* 6 (Summer): 5–27.

Snyder, Eldon E., and Elmer A. Spreitzer. 1983. *Social Aspects of Sport*, 2d ed. Englewood Cliffs, N.J.: Prentice-Hall.

Stuart, Reginald. 1971. "All-Black Sports World Changing." *Race Relations Reporter* (April 19): 8–10.

Telander, Rick. 1987. "Shamefully Lily-White." *Sports Illustrated* (February 23): 80.

Thompson, R. 1964. *Race and Sport*. London: Institute of Race Relations and Oxford University Press.

Tygiel, Jules. 1983. *Baseball's Great Experiment: Jackie Robinson and His Legacy*. New York: Oxford University Press.

Van Dyne, Larry. 1976. "The South's Black Colleges Lose a Football Monopoly." *Chronicle of Higher Education* (November 15): 1, 8.

Weinberg, S. Kirson, and Henry Arond. 1952. "The Occupational Culture of the Boxer." *American Journal of Sociology* 57 (March): 460–469.

Wiggins, David K. 1983. "Wendell Smith, the *Pittsburgh Courier-Journal* and the Campaign to Include Blacks in Organized Baseball, 1933–1945." *Journal of Sport History* 10 (Summer): 5–29.

Yetman, Norman R. 1980. "Racial Participation and Integration in Intercollegiate Basketball." Paper presented at the meeting of the North American Society for the Sociology of Sport, Denver (August).

Yetman, Norman R., Forrest J. Berghorn, William E. Hanna, and Brad Demo. 1985. "Continuity and Change in Racial Participation and Integration in Men's and Women's Intercollegiate Basketball, 1958–1985." Paper presented at the meeting of the North American Society for the Sociology of Sport, Boston (November).

30. *Strike One and You're Out*

LYNN ROSELLINI

Scene 1, Riverfront Stadium: It's an hour before game time and black super-star Dave Parker is flipping through mail in the Cincinnati Reds' locker room. Davey Concepcion, the veteran Venezuelan infielder, is reading a Spanish-language newspaper. As underwear and socks fly into a laundry hamper in the middle of the room, Tony Perez, Cuban first-base coach, ambles by and grabs a white coach, Tommy Helms, teasing him about being a "redneck" from North Carolina.

"It never gets tense around here," says white pitcher Rob Murphy, observing the easy jive among black, white and Hispanic players.

Cut to Scene 2, three floors above: The blond kid who runs the elevator points down the curving hallway to the hushed, carpeted sanctuary of the Reds' main offices. Inside, the secretaries are white. So are the public-relations director, the head scout, the general manager and all but one of the 50 front-office personnel.

In her cluttered office, the Reds' amiable owner, Marge Schott, boasts of her good relations with both black and white players. "I'm the only owner who can hug the players," she is saying. "I feel as close to Eric Davis as to Tracy Jones." But when asked about fair employment, she talks of inviting the players' wives and children out to her baronial estate to pet the cows and have a picnic. Affirmative action? "I would never do anything falsely," she says. "I don't want a token."

FRONT-OFFICE FREEZE

Welcome to baseball, 1987, the reverse Time Warp where it's Jackie Robinson vs. the color barrier all over again. Only this time the weapons aren't racist epithets and rotten tomatoes but attitudes so subtle—yet systematized—that it took Al Campanis, with his shot-heard-round-the-sports-world assessment of blacks' fitness for management, to articulate what no whites wanted to believe: Racial stereotypes persist in American sports, barring all but a few blacks from front-office jobs and "thinking" playing positions.

The new-fashioned racism is like a chill breeze that sneaks through the

SOURCE: Lynn Rosellini, "Strike One and You're Out," *U.S. News & World Report* (July 27, 1987), pp. 52–57.

dugout late in the season, creeping among the stands, nosing into stadium offices, wandering unexpected and unwanted across the field. It is there in the way a white catcher keeps looking at the dugout when a black pitcher—there are only about a dozen in the big leagues—argues with him.

It is there in the mutterings of some white coaches, who consider injured blacks who don't play malingerers. It's there in the numbers: No black major-league managers, no general managers, no third-base coaches. "They want my knowledge," says former Cardinal All-Star Lou Brock, who coaches at hitting clinics but can't find a permanent job in baseball. "They ask me to come and teach, but I can't be part of the [permanent] course."

The National Basketball Association does slightly better, with four black coaches out of a total 23 and two black general managers. Yet while Isiah Thomas, Detroit's star guard, was rightly stomped [in June 1987] for suggesting that the success of white NBA stars like Larry Bird was due to race, his observations about stereotypes rang true. Sportscasters described black players as "wondrous to watch" and "acrobatic" during the Boston Celtics–L.A. Lakers playoffs [in June 1987]—while the Celtics' Bird was "smart."

The same assumption—that blacks, in Campanis's memorable words, lack management "necessities"—permeates the National Football League, where there are no black head coaches and few black coordinators. Thirteen years ago, the L.A. Rams' James Harris became the first black starting quarterback in the NFL. Today, black starters in the game's premier leadership position number exactly two. "One hundred years ago, blacks carried cotton balls," says civil-rights activist Jesse Jackson. "Now, they carry footballs and basketballs." And while Jackson conveniently overlooks the million-dollar salaries of today's ball carriers, his complaints about pro sports as the "private game reserve" of white owners have given baseball Commissioner Peter Ueberroth a busy year.

Under threat of a boycott organized by Jackson and other rights leaders [in June of 1987] Ueberroth hired black sociologist Harry Edwards of the University of California at Berkeley and extracted a promise from team owners to increase minority hiring. The NFL and the NBA have taken similar steps. And while nobody expects conditions to improve overnight (in the only firings of major-league managers so far this year, the Philadelphia Phillies and the Cleveland Indians both named white replacements), many agree with Mets' first-base coach Bill Robinson. "This is the first time in anyone's life," says Robinson, "it doesn't hurt being black."

In part, the problem has been economics. No blacks own major-league football, basketball or baseball teams. Indeed, only 0.1 percent of black households have assets of greater than $500,000, and the going price for an NFL team is now more than $70 million.

Yet even in college sports, where ownership isn't an issue, black coaches are few. "If there were more black head coaches in colleges," says NBA

Commissioner David Stern, "that would increase the pool of prospective NBA head coaches"—an observation that applies equally to pro football. As the Lakers' Magic Johnson was quoted recently: "It starts on the levels of boys' clubs, high schools and colleges."

A MIRROR OF THE CULTURE

Indeed, the ultimate barrier for blacks is probably not money or skill but lingering prejudices that are deeply ingrained in American culture—despite a generation of civil-rights reform. "There is racism in sports," says Benjamin Hooks, executive director of the NAACP, "to the same extent that there is racism in the country."

In a way, today's attitudes are more insidious than the old ones—simply because they are often unconscious. White owners who would blanch at being labeled racist nonetheless want coaches who are educated, articulate and well dressed, and they don't necessarily associate those qualities with blacks. "Even if they have the highest regard for blacks on some other level," says sociologist Edwards, "it never crosses their minds to choose a black accountant or to make a black person head of player-personnel development or public-information director."

Consider, for instance, Larry Doby. Forty years ago, a few months after Jackie Robinson became the first black player in the National League, Doby put on a Cleveland Indians uniform and integrated the American League. For much of the next 30 years, Doby made his career in baseball—as a player, coach and eventually as manager of the Chicago White Sox during the second half of the 1978 season. But after the Sox lost 50 games, Doby, one of only three blacks to have managed a major-league team, was replaced with a white.

Doby believes his race played a part in his dismissal—a suggestion disputed by some Sox sources. But what's important is that Doby never got a second chance. Demoted to hitting instructor, he was unable to find another managing spot and finally ended up leaving baseball for a job as director of community affairs for basketball's New Jersey Nets. Now, Doby, 63, still puzzles over the "buddy-buddy" system that allows white managers to fail and rise again, but not blacks.

"[White] managers are hired and fired every day," says Hank Aaron, who as Atlanta Braves vice president is baseball's highest-ranking black. "That manager goes somewhere else and gets the same type job. That's the thing that bothers me."

Cincinnati superstar Pete Rose walked directly from the playing field into his job as Reds manager, without even a warm-up. The Seattle Mariners' Dick Williams has hopscotched among seven major-league teams as manager. Yet the Mets' Bill Robinson and Baltimore's Elrod Hendricks—both viewed as rising stars among black baseball coaches—have never had a shot.

Ueberroth admits that baseball hasn't provided enough opportunities for minorities—a case he made to owners last December, months before the Campanis furor. "Now we're trying to research every single minority who has played in the major leagues," he says, "to find out where they are and who they are."

NBA owners seem to have a better idea of "who they are," as well as a greater willingness to utilize talented black ex-players. And unlike their counterparts in the baseball world, black NBA coaches tend to keep circulating once they get in—a good indication that the system is more open. Perhaps because 75 percent of NBA players are black (compared with 25 percent in baseball and 55 percent in football), men like Sacramento's Bill Russell and Cleveland's Lenny Wilkins have each coached three NBA teams. Still, with just four black NBA coaches, it's clear that getting in can still be a problem. Former Los Angeles Laker Jamaal Wilkes says he considered management after retiring but decided against it. "I saw what the numbers were. I never took it seriously that I could be a general manager in the NBA."

In football, the story is much the same. "People are angry and keeping it down deep because they need what the NFL is offering," says Earnel Durden, San Diego's black former running-backs coach, summing up the feelings of many black assistant coaches. "But it's seething beneath the surface."

With good reason. Despite the illusion that success in American pro sports is based strictly on merit, the system has historically kept blacks down. The NBA didn't have a black player until the Celtics' Chuck Cooper in 1950. In baseball, blacks played and managed in the Negro leagues for a quarter-century, until the major leagues absorbed their stars.

But while blacks increasingly joined the ranks of players, few became fans. Although blacks make up 12.1 percent of the U.S. population, they comprise just 6.8 percent of baseball crowds and 7.5 percent of football audiences. Escalating ticket prices could be a factor, yet 17 percent of NBA fans are black—perhaps because it's a big-city schoolyard sport—and a basketball ticket is more expensive than a baseball ticket. As one baseball executive observed recently, with such limited black attendance, "from a P.R. standpoint, hiring a black manager is not the best thing to do."

Still, the commissioners of all three sports seem determined to make changes. "We all admit there should have been a black coach before now," says Dan Rooney, president of the Pittsburgh Steelers. "At a league meeting, there will be [only] one or two blacks in the room." NFL Commissioner Pete Rozelle himself met last December—four months before the Campanis incident—with seven black assistant coaches and executives in an effort to develop an across-the-board minority-hiring program. He says all clubs will have programs in place by September, and he also boasts of the league's minority-intern program and its annual training program for black college coaches.

WHO'S CALLING THE SIGNALS?

Even Rozelle admits, however, there's little he can do to force teams to hire blacks as head coaches. "Choosing a head coach is like choosing a wife," he once said. "It's a very personal thing."

Choosing a quarterback—the player who directs a team's offense—may be a "personal thing," too. Blacks are still firmly segregated by position, and playing quarterback isn't an option for many. While blacks account for 92 percent of NFL cornerbacks and 88 percent of running backs, they make up just 1 percent of quarterbacks and 13 percent of centers. Gregory Sojka, an expert on American sports culture at Wichita State University, says such positional segregation reflects a "very dangerous racist way of thinking. Coaches think the quarterback has to be a team leader, intelligent," he says, "as if to say a black player hasn't these abilities or attributes."

Often, pro teams draft black college quarterbacks, then switch them to more physical positions like cornerback or wide receiver. As a high-school quarterback, former New England Patriot Keith Lee was widely recruited by college scouts—all of whom wanted to switch him to defensive back. Lee refused and, after a stint at a junior college, wound up in 1979 recruited by Colorado State University, where coaches tried once again—unsuccessfully— to move him from quarterback. But the pros succeeded, and Lee finally played four years for the Patriots—as a defensive back.

Rozelle says that most black college quarterbacks play in run-oriented offenses. "There haven't been too many pure passers," he says. "As we get more and more of them in college, we'll see them in the pros." But coaching veteran Durden believes the problem goes deeper. "I've seen it over and over again," he says. "Quarterback, center, linebackers, safeties—those were the positions where a lot of thinking had to go on, and those were white positions."

DIAMOND BIAS

A similar positional segregation prevails in baseball. Blacks represented 48 percent of outfielders but only 6 percent of pitchers last year. There were no black catchers. The pattern extends to baseball's managing ranks: Blacks tend to be outfield coaches or hitting instructors, but rarely decision-making first or third-base coaches.

Most players maintain that the black pitcher-catcher dearth reflects ability, not racism. They frequently cite the popular belief that blacks can run faster and jump higher than whites. "It's a well-known thing that most of your black players can run and hit," says Cincinnati's Pete Rose. "Why ruin your speed being a catcher? Why be a pitcher?" St. Louis superstar Ozzie Smith, who is black, agrees: "If you are a pitcher, that is being able to do only one thing. Most black athletes are well-rounded."

While scientific evidence for such claims is sketchy, several recent studies do indicate that, compared with whites, black athletes are lower in body fat and higher in muscle mass—qualities that enhance athletic performance. (Reds superstar Eric Davis, for instance, has just 6 percent body fat, while white Reds players average 10 percent or more.)

Yet no amount of scientific data can explain a study by Northeastern University's Richard E. Lapchick, who found that, regardless of playing position, black athletes must be better than whites to keep their jobs. Using 1986 team rosters, Lapchick discovered that twice as many black baseball players as whites had career averages greater than .281, while three times as many whites had averages below .241. Among NBA veterans of five or more years, Lapchick found that the scoring averages of the whites were considerably lower than those of the blacks.

"There are still times when race matters for the borderline player," says Jerry Royster, a black player for the Chicago White Sox. "It is not necessarily for the superstar. It exhibits itself when you are picking the last guy on the team. If there is a choice between a black and a white making the team, the white guy makes it."

Yet that bias apparently doesn't extend to salaries. One recent study showed that the mean salary for black major-league players this year is $488,000—$63,000 more than the average white's salary. "But if everything were fair," says Notre Dame sociologist Kevin Christiano, who developed the study, "would blacks be paid more, given that their performance tends to be better?"

Off the field, black superstars do as well as whites in endorsements and appearances. "Consumers can relate very well to an athlete of any color," says sports agent Leigh Steinberg, "as long as he is a superlative athlete, has charisma and an attractive personality." Basketball megastar Michael Jordan, who endorses products like Nike's Air Jordan shoes, made over $4 million last year off court. Famed running back Walter Payton, the first black to appear on the front of the Wheaties box, has turned down 100 endorsement offers for every 1 he accepted, according to his agent. Still, black nonsuperstars have a harder time than whites getting endorsements. "The decisions made by marketing people are predicated on demographics," says sports agent Tom Reich, "and those demographics are based on white purchasing power."

Attempts to change deeply rooted attitudes about blacks in sports, say Lapchick and others, must begin long before athletes reach the pros. Yet black coaches are sparse in colleges, too. Sociologist Edwards says the National Collegiate Athletic Association runs "a more racist operation than any professional team," and he isn't just talking about the way people in the stands threw banana peels at Georgetown's Patrick Ewing a few years ago. (Ewing, a black player, was once confronted with a sign that said, "Patrick Ewing Can't Read Dis.")

BAD GRADES IN NCAA

In the NCAA, there is not a single black among baseball coaches at the 265 predominantly white Division 1 and 1A schools, and there are only three among the 105 head football coaches. Only 30 of 273 top white basketball schools have teams coached by blacks.

Wayne Nunnely, the black head football coach at the University of Nevada-Las Vegas, says that presidents and athletic directors at predominantly white schools fear that alumni and fans might not support a black head coach—and that white players might refuse to play. "Few have enough confidence to name a black to a major position," he says. Indeed, of the few black coaches at major white universities, many were hired to replace white coaches fired either because of scandals or disastrous seasons. For instance, Georgetown recruited John Thompson as coach after its basketball team had won only three games the previous year.

Jesse Jackson goes one step further, suggesting that the NCAA system often hurts the athletes themselves. Jackson argues that colleges mine the playing skills of black athletes to generate revenue. At the same time, he maintains, the schools neglect the academic preparation that could help blacks get jobs later on—an argument that applies to a lesser degree to some white players as well. Indeed, a recent NCAA survey found that more than 650 athletes in Division I schools failed to meet minimum academic standards. The NCAA now requires entering college freshmen who plan to participate in sports their first year to have a 2.0 high-school grade-point average plus a minimum score of 700 on the Scholastic Aptitude Test. "The concern is that student athletes should be prepared to succeed academically," says NCAA President Wilford Bailey, "rather than be exploited as highly skilled athletes."

But Bailey says the NCAA can do little about black coaches, because hiring decisions rest with its member universities. Not surprisingly, Edwards and other civil-rights leaders plan to target NCAA schools this fall, going campus by campus to more than 2,000 college athletic directors to press for the hiring of minorities.

"If there is no cooperation for programs," warns Edwards, "we are going to ask black athletes in football and basketball to boycott games and let the field look just like the front offices in time for the bowls and tournaments."

An all-white Cotton Bowl? This could be an interesting sports year, indeed. It might be the year of the first black NFL club owner, as well, if Chicago's Payton, entering his last season as a player, gets his wish to land a new franchise if the league expands next spring. Reggie Jackson of the Oakland A's wants to do the same thing in baseball and fantasizes about a front office that would include "qualified people" both black and white—like Bob Gibson, Tommie Reynolds, Jim "Catfish" Hunter and Joe Morgan.

Meanwhile, executives in baseball, the NFL and the NBA are scurrying to organize job pools of top black management prospects. It's still too early to tell exactly where such efforts will lead. But players and executives alike agree that the complexion of pro sports' front offices will change—not overnight, perhaps, but gradually, with a defensive coordinator here, a third-base coach there and, ultimately, a general manager and head coach, perhaps several.

Georgetown's John Thompson suggests that former Dodgers executive Campanis deserves a medal—not a pink slip—for spotlighting racism in sports. "This issue comes in and out of style like clothing," says Thompson. "He brought it back in style."

31. *The Perpetuation of Racial Segregation by Playing Position in Professional Football*

JOHN J. SCHNEIDER AND D. STANLEY EITZEN

The prominence of black athletes in the professional sports of football, basketball, and baseball is proof for most persons that the institution of sport is free of racism. This notion of racism-free sport has been shown to be a myth by a number of social researchers (for summaries, see Eitzen and Sage, 1986; Lapchick, 1984). One of the best documented forms of racial discrimination in sport, and the focus of this paper, is stacking (Loy and McElvogue, 1970; Brower, 1972; Eitzen and Sanford, 1975; Madison and Landers, 1976; Eitzen and Yetman, 1977; Schneider and Eitzen, 1979). The term *stacking* refers to situations in which minority group members are relegated to specific team roles and are excluded from others. The research on team sports has found consistently that blacks are systematically underrepresented at those positions that require thinking and leadership abilities and overrepresented at positions requiring physical skills (for a summary of the research, see Curtis and Loy, 1979).

The intent of this selection is threefold: (1) to discuss why football positions tend to be segregated by race; (2) to show that racial segregation by position in professional football has become more prominent in the past ten years; and (3) to demonstrate that recent changes in the structure of professional football have exacerbated racial segregation by position.

EXPLANATIONS FOR STACKING

The assumption of "stacking" is that the assignment of playing positions by race is not random. The question is, why are whites found disproportionately in control positions while blacks are overwhelmingly in positions where physical attributes are most important?

SOURCE: This selection expands significantly the article by John J. Schneider and D. Stanley Eitzen, "Racial Segregation by Professional Football Positions, 1960–1985," *Sociology and Social Research* 70 (July 1986), pp. 259–262.

Centrality

The original examination of the stacking phenomenon was by Loy and McElvogue (1970). They argued that racial segregation in sports is a function of centrality—that is, spatial location—in a team sports unit. To explain positional racial segregation in sports, they combined organization principles advanced by Hubert M. Blalock and Oscar Grusky. Blalock argued that:

1. The lower the degree of purely social interaction on the job, . . . the lower the degree of (racial) discrimination.
2. To the extent that performance level is relatively independent of skill in interpersonal relations, the lower the degree of (racial) discrimination (Blalock, 1962:246).

Grusky's notions about the formal structure of organizations are similar: All else being equal, the more central one's spatial location: (1) the greater the likelihood dependent or coordinative tasks will be performed; and (2) the greater the rate of interaction with the occupants of other positions. Also, the performance of dependent tasks is positively related to frequency of interaction. (summarized from Grusky, 1963:345–353) Combining these propositions, Loy and McElvogue (1970) predicted that racial segregation in professional team sports is positively related to organizational centrality. Their analysis of football, and subsequent ones by others, found that the central team positions of quarterback, center, and linebacker were overrepresented by whites while the "noncentral" positions were disproportionately held by blacks.

Position Responsibility and Racial Stereotypes

Harry Edwards has argued that the centrality of playing position is an incidental factor in explaining segregation by position: "The factors which should really be considered have to do with the degree of relative outcome control or leadership responsibilities institutionalized into the various positions. The factor of centrality itself is significant only insofar as greater outcome control and leadership responsibilities are typically vested in centrally located positions since actors holding these positions have a better perspective on the total field of activity." (Edwards, 1973:209)

What accounts for the relative lack of blacks at "central" positions, then, is not the interaction potential of the playing position but the leadership and degree of responsibility for the game's outcome built into the position. This interpretation is consonant with the stereotype hypothesis advanced by Jonathan Brower: "The combined function of centrality in terms of responsibility and interaction provides a frame for exclusion of Blacks and constitutes a definition of the situation for coaches and management. People in the world of professional football believe that various football positions require specific types of physically- and intellectually-endowed athletes. When these beliefs are combined with the stereotypes of Blacks and whites, Blacks are excluded from certain positions. Normal organizational processes when interlaced with racist conceptions of the world spell out an important consequence, namely, the racial basis of the division of labor in professional football." (Brower, 1972:27; see also Williams and Youssef, 1975)

From this perspective, then, the racial stereotypes of blacks' abilities lead to the view that they are more ideally suited for positions requiring athletes with speed, quickness, strength, aggressiveness, "good hands," and "instinct" (i.e., defensive lineman, wide receiver, running back, and defensive back). Whites, on the other hand, are more likely to hold the "central" positions that require leadership, thinking ability, stability under pressure, and responsibility for the game's outcome (i.e., quarterback, interior offensive lineman, linebacker, safety, and kicker).

Black-Initiated Position Segregation

Another possible explanation for stacking is that blacks, themselves, may switch from "central" to "noncentral" positions, since they perceive their chances for playing as much greater in "safe" positions. This is a rational response to a system perceived by blacks to be biased against them. Knowing, for example, that black college quarterbacks rarely play that position as professionals but are switched by coaches to either wide receiver or defensive back, black quarterbacks may change to the position where they have the greatest probability of success. The earlier they make such a change the better their chances, in that they will have more time to learn the sophisticated techniques required at the professional level.

Related to this, black youths may segregate themselves into specific sport roles because they wish to emulate black stars (McPherson, 1975). Instead of discriminatory acts by members of the majority being the cause of racial "stacking," blacks learn and subsequently occupy specific roles played by blacks who currently have attained a high level of achievement. Since the first positions to be occupied by blacks were offensive and defensive backs and defensive linemen, the imitation of these role models may have resulted in blacks being overrepresented in those positions today. Although this process does not explain the initial discriminatory position placements, it helps to explain why, once operative, the pattern of discrimination-by-player position tends to be maintained.

THE CONTINUITY OF STACKING

Is stacking in professional football becoming less prominent? Table 31-1 presents the proportion of blacks at each position in the National Football League for 1960, 1975, and 1985. These data show clearly that the pace of stacking has actually increased. This has occurred despite the increased numbers of blacks in professional football. Historical comparisons in basketball have shown that

Table 31-1 Percentage of Black Professional Football Players, by Position: 1960, 1975, 1985

Playing Position	1960[a] % Black	1975[b] % Black	1985[c] % Black
Kicker/Punter	0	1.3	3.4
Quarterback	0	3.5	2.9
Offensive line	14.1	24.0	10.8
Linebacker	4.2	26.0	57.4
Defensive front four	15.4	47.6	54.0
Receiver	2.2	55.3	61.5
Running back	17.5	65.2	86.4
Defensive back	27.5	67.3	84.5
Totals	13.5[d](27)	41.6[d](620)	51.3[d](647)

[a]Adapted from Brower (1972). These data were obtained from the media guides published annually by each team.
[b]Taken from Eitzen and Yetman (1977). These data are from the 1975 Football Register, by The Sporting News.
[c]These data were obtained from the official rosters of the 28 National Football League teams at the beginning of the 1985 season.
[d]This percentage provides the dividing line for establishing whether blacks are overrepresented or underrepresented at a given position for the year in question.

"stacking" is diminishing in that sport. As college and professional basketball have become disproportionately black, the stacking relationship has weakened and virtually disappeared (Yetman, Berghorn, and Thomas, 1982). This trend has led Curtis and Loy to speculate that "Trend studies may eventually show that stacking relationships in baseball and football [will] weaken and disappear" (1979:310). This prediction may occur when professional football approaches 80 percent black, as is the case in professional basketball, but there are differences in the sports that tend to make the probability of stacking in football greater. Positions in football are much more specialized, requiring quite specific tasks, whereas basketball is a more fluid game, requiring more generalized tasks. Moreover, and this is the thesis of this selection, the structure of professional football has changed in recent years, directly and indirectly perpetuating the stacking phenomenon.

THE CHANGING STRUCTURE OF PROFESSIONAL FOOTBALL

Although the forward pass has long been an important offensive weapon in professional football, its importance has become even more pronounced recently. After the 1977 season and in subsequent years, a number of rules were enacted or changed to open up passing attacks. One rule moved the hashmarks inward, giving passers more space than before in which to direct their attack. Two new rules neutralized the effect of defensive linemen rushing the passer. A major weapon of defensive linemen was taken away by the prohibition of the head slap. But more important, new pass block rules allowed offensive linemen freer use of their hands and arms. As one defensive player said, "It's not football anymore. They tackle you, they throw their arms out, the game has been ruined for the sake of passing. All the rules are on their side" (quoted in Zimmerman, 1984:47). Another major change reduced the effectiveness of defensive backs by limiting them to bump potential pass receivers only once and then within the first five yards beyond the line of scrimmage. Under the previous rule, defensive backs were allowed to bump pass receivers anywhere on the field as long as the ball had not been released by the quarterback. As Table 31-2 shows, these rules have resulted in an increase in passing efficiency.

The Consequences of Rule Changes for the Offense

Most teams have, as a consequence of the post-1977 rule changes, emphasized the passing game. There is more pressure than ever on the quarterback to produce. In the past the quarterback did some passing, handed the ball off to the runners, and exhibited leadership. Now he does all these things, with an added emphasis on passing effectiveness, and the ability to read ever more complex defenses. "The way the game is played today, a quarterback had better be sharp, because the guy on the other side will probably be on target. Defense can't carry the offense like it did in the old days. Football's like tennis now. Hold your service and you'll win the set. You score on your possessions, they score on theirs. Break service, stop the other team on its possessions, and you've got an edge. . . . You outscore people these days, you rarely stop them. And if you don't have a quarterback who's capable of a 300-yard, four touchdown game every now and then, you're in trouble." (Zimmerman, 1984:64)

This emphasis on passing should work to increase racial stacking for offensive positions. Quarterbacks, as we have seen, must be especially reliable and productive. So, too, must be their primary protectors, the offensive center, guards, and tackles. The emphasis on the passing game over the past few years also places greater emphasis on the "good hands," quickness, and reactive moves of the "black" positions of running backs who have now also become primary receivers as well as runners.

So, we expect that racial stacking on the offensive unit in 1985 will be greater than in 1975. Moreover, since offensive positions are more control-oriented and less reactive, we expect whites to be disproportionately found in offensive positions and blacks in defensive positions. Perhaps this is also a consequence of the greater visibility of the offense, and as Richard Lapchick has suggested, "clubs do this for fans who want to recognize more white faces" (1984:229). Or, perhaps, the offense is believed by coaches, players, and fans to be more important than the defense. "The defensive troops are football's counterpunchers. They can score knockouts, but they don't lead. When

Table 31-2 Passing and Rushing Statistics in Professional Football for Selected Years

Year[a]	Average Rushing Yardage per Game	Average Passing Yardage per Game	Difference in Pass vs. Rush	Percentage of Total Yards from Passing
1975	145.5	183.0	+35.5	55.7
1980	127.5	196.0	+68.5	60.6
1985	124.9	204.5	+79.6	62.1

[a]In the 1975 season there were 26 teams playing a 14-game schedule. In 1980 and 1985 there were 28 teams playing a 16-game schedule.
Source: Neft, Cohen, and Deutsch (1982); and U.S.A. Today (December 26, 1985), p. 5C.

they've stunned the enemy, when they've got him on the ropes, the offense takes over." (Zimmerman, 1984:119) But more important for our purposes is that defenses, as we will see shortly, have changed. And, so have the requirements for people who play defense. Now more than ever defensive players must have the physical tools. "[Defenses have] never been as sorely tested as they are now, thanks to the new, liberalized passing rules of 1978. Defensive people are sleeker now, built more for speed, to counter the quick, flashy offense." (Zimmerman, 1984:119)

The Consequences of Rule Changes for the Defense

To offset the advantages given the offenses, defenses have had to adapt. When running was the preferred offensive strategy, defenses were employed primarily to stop the run using the 4–3 alignment (four "down linemen," one middle linebacker, and two outside linebackers). This formation dominated defenses from the early 1950s through the late 1970s. In response to the new emphasis on passing, more and more teams have shifted to a 3–4 defense (three "down linemen," two inside linebackers, and two outside linebackers). Whereas the 4–3 alignment was designed for containment, the 3–4 was made for attacking (rushing one of the linebackers), and pass defending with the outside linebackers having primary pass coverage responsibilities. Not surprisingly, then, by 1981, twenty-three of the twenty-eight teams had changed from a 4–3 to a 3–4 alignment.

The responsibilities of the linebackers in a 4–3 alignment differ considerably from those in a 3–4. In a 3–4 alignment, the two "outside" linebackers have become more like defensive backs because they need to have the speed and quickness to cover wide receivers and running backs on deep pass coverages as well as be strong and fast enough to fill "gaps" and stop the run. This is a new development. In the old 4–3 alignment, each linebacker was primarily responsible to stop the run. The three linebackers in the 4–3 defense of old most closely resemble the two "inside" linebackers in the 3–4 defense of today with responsibilities geared to stopping the run and short passes.

Because of the requirements of the new defenses to stop the pass, the qualities required of outside linebackers have shifted from the ones of leadership and knowledge to a much greater emphasis on physical qualities. "The only reason the defense survives nowadays is because of the emergence of the great outside linebackers, bigger for the most part than the inside [linebackers] . . . and certainly faster. . . . In the old days a guy could fall back on technique, but some of these guys, well, when they start losing a step, or they're not as strong, they'll find themselves replaced by a new guy faster and stronger." (Zimmerman, 1984:162)

Because of the change in structure of defenses caused by the emergence of the passing game, a reversal in the racial composition for one of the "central" or "control" positions on defense—the position of linebacker—is predicted. More specifically, we hypothesize that (1) the proportion of black outside linebackers will exceed the proportion of white outside linebackers because of the need for greater speed, quickness, and reactive ability required of that position; and (2) because of this hypothesized increase in black outside linebackers, the linebacker position will be disproportionately black in 1985, unlike the situation in 1975. All other positions on defense should be consistent with the "central" versus "noncentral" predictions of the stacking phenomenon. Defensive linemen and defensive backs should be predominantly black. However, with the contemporary emphasis on the passing game, it is hypothesized that the *proportion* of black defensive backs and defensive linemen should be higher in 1985 than in 1975.

THE FINDINGS

Table 31-1 presents the proportion of black football players by position in 1960, 1975, and 1985, respectively. The initial finding of this study is that in 1985, blacks became the numerical majority, increasing from 41.6 percent in 1975 to 51.3 percent in 1985.

A second finding concerns segregation by offensive position. As predicted, there are no dramatic changes in "segregation by position" on offense. Kickers, quarterbacks, and offensive linemen are still predominantly white while wide receivers and running backs are still mostly black. But perhaps more important, predicted changes in the *proportion* of blacks or whites by position have occurred. Among the findings are that (1) the proportion of white quarterbacks has increased; (2) the proportion of white offensive linemen has increased; (3) the proportion of black running backs has dramatically increased; and (4) the proportion of black wide receivers has increased.

Most significant, the racial segregation related to "centrality" remains intact for offensive positions. The positions requiring leadership and thinking ability have become even more "white" and the positions necessitating speed, quickness, and "instinct" have become even more "black." Also as hypothesized, whites are more likely to be found on offense, while blacks are more likely to be found on defense. Table 31-3 shows that over 60 percent of the

Table 31-3   The Distribution of Whites on Offense and
Blacks on Defense, 1975 and 1985

	OFFENSE	
Position	1975 Percent White	1985 Percent White
Kicker/punter	98.7	96.6
Quarterback	95.5	97.1
Offensive line	76.0	89.3
Receiver	44.7	38.5
Running back	34.8	13.6
Totals	62.4(542)	61.1(417)

	DEFENSE	
Position	1975 Percent Black	1985 Percent Black
Linebackers	26.0	57.4
Defensive line	47.6	54.0
Defensive backs	67.3	84.5
Totals	47.3(294)	66.1(382)

players on offense were white in both 1975 and 1985, while over 66 percent of defensive players were black in 1985, compared to only 47 percent in 1975. The apparent explanation is found in the added requirements for control on offense and physical attributes on defense brought about by the increased emphasis on passing in recent years.

For defense, the 1975 to 1985 comparison of the racial distribution for each position shows that the stacking pattern occurs as found in earlier studies but with one interesting difference. Previous research has found consistently that linebacker is a "white" position. This is particularly true for middle linebackers because they typically captain the defense, thus exhibiting leadership and thinking ability. But in the past ten years, as a consequence of the heightened emphasis on passing and the subsequent shift to a 3–4 defense, the linebacker position in the aggregate has become a "black" position—57.4 percent of linebackers were black in 1985 compared to only 26 percent in 1975. This finding, however, does not negate the existence of racial stacking at the linebacker position. When linebackers are classified as either "outside" or "inside," we find that 71.2 percent of all outside linebackers are black and 60.5 percent of all inside linebackers are white.

This reflects clearly the differing responsibilities of these two types of linebackers. Outside linebackers must have the physical attributes of speed, strength, and quick reactions, similar to defensive backs. Inside linebackers, on the other hand, are expected to have more leadership and savvy. This propensity to assume thinking and leadership skills for whites and physical

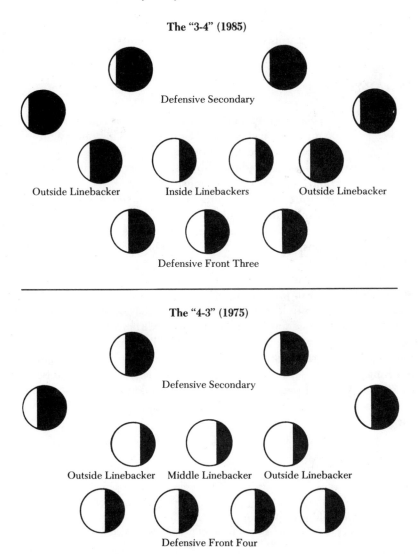

FIGURE 31-1 Percent of black players by position on defense: the "3–4" of 1985 versus the "4–3" of 1975

skills for blacks is seen in the racial composition of linebackers for the five teams in 1985—Atlanta, Chicago, Dallas, St. Louis, and Washington—that continued to play a predominantly 4–3 defense. For those teams, seven of the ten players (70 percent) listed as middle linebackers were white while twelve of the nineteen (63.2 percent) listed as outside linebackers were black. These findings show that while the position of linebacker has become disproportionately black, white linebackers still tend to occupy the positions requiring leadership and thinking ability—the middle linebacker(s).

SUMMARY

The continuity of racial segregation by position in professional football from 1960 to 1985 is documented in this study. Contrary to what one might expect, we found that the sport has become even more racially segregated, particularly in the past ten years, as evidenced by the greater disparity of whites and blacks at "central" and "noncentral" positions.

The unique contribution of this study involves the change in the structure of the professional game and its influence on "segregation by position" (see Figure 31-1). In effect, rule changes intended to make football more exciting by encouraging the passing game have had the latent consequence of perpetuating racial stacking.

The research reported here raises some interesting questions. As blacks increase their numerical proportion in football, will the "racial qualifications" for each position become less and less relevant as has occurred in basketball? Or will the structure of football directly and indirectly contribute to racial imbalances by position as is the current case? Will future changes in the sport inhibit or promote racial stacking? These intriguing questions, along with establishing whether there is a link between the racist attitudes and behaviors of decision makers and positional segregation, should guide future research as we continue to monitor how sport manifests the same social problems found in the larger society.

REFERENCES

Blalock, H. M., Jr. 1962. "Occupational Discrimination: Some Theoretical Propositions." *Social Problems* 9 (Winter): 240–247.

Brower, Jonathan J. 1972. "The Racial Basis of the Division of Labor among Players in the National Football League as a Function of Stereotypes." Paper presented at the annual meeting of the Pacific Sociological Association, Portland.

Curtis, James E., and John W. Loy, Jr. 1979. "Race/Ethnicity and Relative Centrality of Playing Positions in Team Sports." *Exercise and Sport Sciences Review* 6: 285–313.

Edwards, Harry. 1973. *Sociology of Sport*. Homewood, Ill.: Dorsey.

Eitzen, D. Stanley, and George H. Sage. 1986. *Sociology of North American Sport*. 3d ed. Dubuque, Iowa: Wm. C. Brown.

Eitzen, D. Stanley, and David C. Sanford. 1975. "The Segregation of Blacks by Playing Position in Football: Accident or Design?" *Social Science Quarterly* 55 (March): 948–959.

Eitzen, D. Stanley, and Norman R. Yetman. 1977. "Immune from Racism?" *Civil Rights Digest* 9 (Winter): 2–13.

Grusky, Oscar. 1963. "The Effect of Formal Structure on Managerial Recruitment: A Study of Baseball Organization." *Sociometry* 26 (September): 345–353.

Lapchick, Richard. 1984. *Broken Promises: Racism in American Sports*. New York: St. Martin's.

Loy, John W., and Joseph F. McElvogue. 1970. "Racial Segregation in American Sport." *International Review of Sport Sociology* 5: 5–24.

Madison, Donna R., and Daniel M. Landers. 1976. "Racial Discrimination in Football: A Test of 'Stacking' of Playing Positions Hypothesis." In *Social Problems in Athletics*, ed. Daniel M. Landers, pp. 151–156. Urbana: University of Illinois Press.

McPherson, Barry D. 1975. "The Segregation by Playing Position in Sport: An Alternative Hypothesis." *Social Science Quarterly* 55 (March): 960–966.

Neft, David S., Richard M. Cohen, and Jordan A. Deutsch. 1982. *The Sports Encyclopedia: Pro Football, The Modern Era, 1960 to the Present*. Rev. ed. New York: Simon & Schuster.

Schneider, John J., and D. Stanley Eitzen. 1979. "Racial Discrimination in American Sport: Continuity or Change?" *Journal of Sport Behavior* 2 (August): 136–142.

Schneider, John J. and D. Stanley Eitzen. 1986. "Racial Segregation by Professional Football Positions, 1960–1985." *Sociology and Social Research* 70 (July): 259–262.

Williams, R. L., and Z. I. Youssef. 1975. "Division of Labor in College Football along Racial Lines." *International Journal of Sport Psychology* 6: 3–13.

Yetman, Norman R., Forrest J. Berghorn, and Floyd R. Thomas, Jr. 1982. "Racial Participation and Integration in Intercollegiate Basketball, 1958–1980." *Journal of Sport Behavior* 5 (March): 44–56.

Zimmerman, Paul. 1984. *The New Thinking Man's Guide to Pro Football*. New York: Simon & Schuster.

■ FOR FURTHER STUDY

Aikens, Charles. "The Struggle of Curt Flood." *The Black Scholar* 3 (November 1971): 10–15.

Allen, Maury. *Jackie Robinson: A Life Remembered*. New York: Franklin Watts, 1987.

Ashe, Arthur. "An Open Letter to Black Parents: Send Your Children to the Libraries." *New York Times* (February 6, 1977): section 5, p. 2.

Axthelm, Pete. *The City Game*. New York: Simon & Schuster Pocketbooks, 1971.

Behee, John. *Hail to the Victors: Black Athletes at the University of Michigan*. Ann Arbor, Mich.: Ulrich's Books, 1974.

Bennett, Bruce. "Bibliography on the Negro in Sports." *JOPER* 41 (January 1970): 77–78; and (September 1970): 71.

"Black Dominance." *Time* (May 9, 1977): 57–60.

Bledsoe, Terry. "Black Dominance of Sports: Strictly from Hunger." *The Progressive* 37 (June 1973): 16–19.

Braddock, J. H., "Race, Sports and Social Mobility." *Sociological Symposium* 30 (Spring 1980): 18–38.

Brower, Jonathan J. "The Racial Basis of the Division of Labor Among Players in the National Football League as a Function of Stereotypes." Paper presented at the meeting, of the Pacific Sociological Association. Portland, April 1972.

Brower, Jonathan J. "The Quota System: The White Gatekeeper's Regulation of Professional Football's Black Community." Paper presented at the meetings of the American Sociological Association, New York, August 1973.

Brown, Roscoe C., Jr. "A Commentary on Racial Myths and the Black Athlete." In *Social Problems in Athletics*, edited by Daniel M. Landers. Urbana: University of Illinois Press, 1976, pp. 168–173.

Brown, Roscoe C., Jr. "The Jock-Trap—How the Black Athlete Gets Caught!" In *Sport Psychology: An Analysis of Athlete Behavior*, edited by William F. Straub. Ithaca, N.Y.: Movement Publications, 1978, pp. 195–198.

Chalk, Ocania. *Pioneers of Black Sport*. New York: Dodd, Mead, 1975.

Cheska, Alyce Taylor. "Sport as Ethnic Boundary Maintenance: A Case of the American Indian." *International Review for Sociology of Sport* 19, no. 3/4 (1984): 241–258.

Chu, Donald, and David Griffey. "The Contact Theory of Racial Integration: The Case of Sport." *Sociology of Sport Journal* 2 (December 1985): 323–333.

Chu, Donald, and Jeffrey O. Segrave. "Leadership Recruitment and Ethnic Stratification in Basketball." *Journal of Sport and Social Issues* 5 (Spring–Summer 1981): 13–22.

Curry, Timothy J., and Robert M. Jiobu. *Sports: A Social Perspective*. Englewood Cliffs, N.J.: Prentice-Hall, 1984, pp. 87–114.

Davis, John P. "The Negro in Professional Football." *The American Negro Reference Book*. Englewood Cliffs, N.J.: Prentice-Hall, 1966.

Dickey, Glenn. *The Jock Empire*. Radnor, Penn: Chilton, 1974, chap. 19.

Dodson, D. "The Integration of Negroes in Baseball." *Journal of Educational Sociology* 28 (October 1954): 73–82.

Dommisse, John. "The Psychology of Apartheid Sport." *Journal of Sport and Social Issues* 1 (Summer/Fall 1977): 32–53.

Duda, Joan Lynne. "Achievement Motivation in Sport: Minority Considerations for the Coach." *Journal of Sport Behavior* 4 (February 1981): 25–32.

Edwards, Harry. "The Myth of the Racially Superior Athlete." *Intellectual Digest* 2 (March 1972): 58–60.

Edwards, Harry. "The Black Athlete on the College Campus." In *Sport and Society*, edited by John Talaminż and Charles Page. Boston: Little, Brown, 1973, pp. 202–219.

Edwards, Harry. *The Revolt of the Black Athlete*. New York: Free Press, 1969.

Edwards, Harry. *Sociology of Sport*. Homewood, Ill.: Dorsey, 1973.

Edwards, Harry. "Sport Within the Veil: The Triumphs, Tragedies and Challenges of Afro-American Involvement." *The Annals* 445 (September 1979): 116–127.

Edwards, Harry. *The Struggle That Must Be*. New York: Macmillan, 1980.

Edwards, Harry. "Authority, Power, and Intergroup Stratification by Race and Sex in American Sport and Society." In *Handbook of Social Science of Sport*, edited by Gunther Luschen and George H. Sage. Champaign, Ill.: Stipes, 1981, pp. 383–399.

Edwards, Harry. "Beyond Symptoms: Unethical Behaviors in American Collegiate Sport and the Problem of the Color Line." *Journal of Sport and Social Issues* 9 (Fall 1985): 3–22.

Eitzen, D. Stanley, and Norman R. Yetman. "Immune from Racism? Blacks Still Suffer from Discrimination in Sports." *Civil Rights Digest* 9 (Winter 1977): 3–13.

Eitzen, D. Stanley, and David C. Sanford. "The Segregation of Blacks by Playing Position in Football: Accident or Design?" *Social Science Quarterly* 55 (March 1977): 948–959.

Eitzen, D. Stanley, and Irl Tessendorf. "Racial Segregation by Position in Sports: The Special Case of Basketball." *Review of Sport and Leisure* (June 1978): 109–128.

Evans, Arthur S. "Differences in the Recruitment of Black and White Football Players at a Big Eight University." *Journal of Sport and Social Issues* 3 (Fall/Winter 1979): 1–10.

Fabianic, David. "Minority Managers in Professional Baseball." *Sociology of Sport Journal* 1, no. 2 (1984): 163–171.

Galliard, Frye. "Crumbling Segregation in the Southeastern Conference." *The Black Athlete—1970*. Race Relations Information Center, August 1970, pp. 19–40.

Govan, Michael. "The Emergence of the Black Athlete in America." *The Black Scholar* 3 (November 1971): 16–28.

Hare, Nathan. "A Study of the Black Fighter." *The Black Scholar* 3 (November 1971): 2–8.

Henderson, E. B. *The Black Athlete—Emergence and Arrival*. New York: Publishers Company, 1968.

Henderson, E. B. *The Negro in Sports*. Washington, D.C.: Associated Pubishers, 1969.

Henry, Grant G. "A Bibliography Concerning Negroes in Physical Education, Athletics, and Related Fields." *JOPER* 44 (May 1973): 65–66.

Johnson, Norris R., and David P. Marple. "Racial Discrimination in Professional Basketball." *Sociological Focus* 6 (Fall 1973): 6–18.

Jordan, James. "Physiological and Anthropometrical Comparisons of Negroes and Whites." *JOPER* 40 (November/December 1969): 93–99.

Kane, Martin. "An Assessment of 'Black is Best'." *Sports Illustrated* (January 18, 1971): 72–83.

Kjeldsen, Erik K. "Integration of Minorities into Olympic Sport in Canada and the USA." *Journal of Sport and Social Issues* 8 (Summer–Fall 1984): 30–44.

Lapchick, R. E. *The Politics of Race and International Sport: The Case of South Africa*. Westport, Conn.: Greenwood Press, 1975.

Loy, John W., and Joseph F. McElvogue. "Racial Segregation in American Sport." *International Review of Sport Sociology* 5 (1970): 5–24.

McClendon, McKee, and D. Stanley Eitzen. "Interracial Contact on Collegiate Basketball Teams." *Social Science Quarterly* 55 (March 1975): 926–938.

McPherson, Barry D. "Minority Group Involvement in Sport: The Black Athlete." *Exercise and Sport Sciences Review* 2 (1974): 71–101.

McPherson, Barry D. "The Segregation by Playing Position Hypothesis in Sport: An Alternative Hypothesis." *Social Science Quarterly* 55 (March 1975): 960–966.

McPherson, Barry D. "The Black Athlete: An Overview and Analysis." In *Social Problems in Athletics*, edited by Daniel M. Landers. Urbana: University of Illinois Press, 1976, pp. 122–150.

Madison, Donna R., and Daniel M. Landers, "Racial Discrimination in Football: A Test of the 'Stacking' of Playing Positions Hypothesis." In *Social Problems in Athletics*, edited by Daniel M. Landers. Urbana: University of Illinois Press, 1976, pp. 151–156.

Marsh, Richard L., and Richard J. Heitman. "The Centrality Phenomenon in Football." *Journal of Sport Behavior* 4 (September 1981): 111–118.

Medoff, Marshall H. "Positional Segregation and the Economic Hypothesis." *Sociology of Sport Journal* 3 (December 1986): 297–304.

Mogull, Robert G. "Discrimination in Baseball Revisted." *Atlantic Economic Journal* 7, no. 2 (1979): 66–74.

Mogull, Robert G. "Racial Discrimination in Professional Sports." *Arena Review* 5 (September 1981): 12–15.

Pascal, Anthony M., and Leonard A. Rapping. *Racial Discrimination in Organized Baseball*. Santa Monica, Calif.: The Rand Corporation, 1970.

Peterson, Robert. *Only the Ball was White*. Englewood Cliffs, N.J.: Prentice-Hall, 1970.

Phillips, John C. "Toward an Explanation of Racial Variations in Top-Level Sports Participation." *International Review of Sport Sociology* (1976): 39–55.

Rainville, Raymond E., and Edward McCormick. "Extent of Covert Racial Prejudice in Pro Football Announcers' Speech." *Journalism Quarterly* 54 (Spring 1977): 20–26.

Robinson, Frank, with Roy Blount, Jr. "I'll Always Be Outspoken." *Sports Illustrated* (October 21, 1974): 31–38.

Rosenblatt, Aaron. "Negroes in Baseball: The Failure of Success." *Transaction* 4 (September 1977): 51–53.

Ruck, Rob. *Sandlot Seasons: Sport in Black Pittsburgh*. Urbana: University of Illinois Press, 1987.

Russell, William F. "Success Is a Journey." *Sports Illustrated* (June 8, 1970): 81–93.

Rust, Art, Jr. *Get That Nigger Off the Field!* New York: Delacorte Press, 1976.

Schneider, John, and D. Stanley Eitzen. "Racial Discrimination in American Sport: Continuity or Change?" *Journal of Sport Behavior* 2, no. 3 (1979): 136–142.

Scully, Gerald W. "Discrimination: The Case of Baseball." In *Government and the Sports Business*, edited by Roger G. Noll. Washington, D.C.: Brookings, 1974, pp. 221–247.

Smith, Marshall. "Giving the Olympics an Anthropological Once-Over." *Life* (October 23, 1964): 81–84.

Spirey, Donald, and Thomas A. Jones. "Intercollegiate Athletic Servitude: A Case Study of the Black Illini Student-Athletes, 1931–1967." *Social Science Quarterly* 55 (March 1975): 939–947.

Stuart, Reginald. "All-Black Sports World Changing." *Race Relations Reporter* 2 (April 19, 1971): 8–10.

Thirer, Joel. "The Olympic Games as a Medium for Black Activism and Protest." *Review of Sport & Leisure* 1 (Fall 1976): 15–31.

Tygiel, Jules. *Baseball's Great Experiment: Jackie Robinson and His Legacy*. New York: Oxford University Press, 1983.

Van Dyne, Larry. "The South's Black Colleges Lose a Football Monopoly." *The Chronicle of Higher Education* (November 15, 1976): 1, 8.

Wolf, David. *Foul! The Connie Hawkins Story*. New York: Warner Brooks, 1972.

Yetman, Norman R., Forrest J. Berghorn, and Floyd R. Thomas, Jr. "Racial Participation and Integration in Intercollegiate Basketball, 1958–1980." *Journal of Sport Behavior* 5 (March 1981): 44–56.

Yetman, Norman R. "Positional Segregation and the Economic Hypothesis: A Critique." *Sociology of Sport Journal* 4 (September 1987): 274–277; and the reply by Medoff (1986), pp. 278–279.

Part Ten

Gender and Sport

Traditionally, gender role expectations have encouraged girls and women to be passive, gentle, delicate, and submissive. These cultural expectations clashed with those traits often associated with sport, such as assertiveness, competitiveness, physical endurance, ruggedness, and dominance. Thus, young women past puberty were encouraged to bypass sports unless the sport retained the femininity of the participants. These "allowable" sports had three characteristics: (1) they were aesthetically pleasing (e.g., ice skating, diving, and gymnastics); (2) they did not involve bodily contact with opponents (e.g., bowling, archery, badminton, volleyball, tennis, golf, swimming, and running); and (3) the action was controlled to protect the athletes from overexertion (e.g., running short races, basketball where the offense and defense did not cross half-court).

In effect these traditional expectations for the sexes denied women equal access to opportunities, not only to sports participation but also to college and to various occupations. Obviously, girls were discriminated against in schools by woefully inadequate facilities—compare the "girls' gym" with the "boys' gym" in any school—and in budgets. The consequences of sexual discrimination in sport were that: (1) the femininity of those who defied the cultural expectations was often questioned giving them marginal status; (2) approximately one-half of the population was denied the benefits of sports participation; (3) young women learned their "proper" societal role (i.e., to be on the sidelines supporting men who do the actual achieving); and (4) women were denied a major source of college scholarships.

Currently, quite rapid changes are occurring. Unquestionably, the greatest change in contemporary sport is the dramatic increase in and general acceptance of sports participation by women. These swift changes have occurred for several related reasons. Most prominent is the societal-wide women's movement that has gained increasing momentum since the mid-1960s. Because of the consciousness-raising resulting from this movement and the organized efforts to break down the cultural tyranny of sex roles, court cases were initiated to break down sexual discrimination in a number of areas. In athletics, legal suits were successfully brought against various school districts, universities, and even the Little League.

In 1972, Congress passed Title IX of the Education Amendments Act. The essence of this law, which has had the greatest single impact on the move toward sexual equality in all aspects of schools, is: "No person in the United States shall, on the basis of sex, be excluded from taking part in, be denied the benefits of, or be subjected to discrimination in any educational program or activity receiving federal financial assistance."

Although the passage of Title IX and other pressures have led to massive changes, discrimination continues. The selections in this part show the progress and the difficulties that remain in achieving equality.

The first selection, by historians William H. Beezley and Joseph P. Hobbs, documents the history of women in sport in American society. Their historical overview provides an excellent description of the persistence of obstacles to women's equal participation in sport despite the recent significant changes.

The second selection, by G. Ann Uhlir, documents the continued inequities faced by women and women's athletic programs at the college level. She argues, with solid documentation, that opportunities for women have leveled off and that, in the case of coaches and administrators, opportunities have actually declined. The next essay, by Mary E. Duquin, shows that within sport women become aware of the structural and cultural boundaries that shape their lives. Duquin also argues that sportswomen must become aware of and join in opposition to their oppression.

While sport has been limiting to females in so many ways, it presents problems of a different sort to males. Boys and men are expected to be successful in sports. They are expected to develop "masculine" traits from sports. But what are the effects of sports failure on the identities of boys and men? What are the consequences of developing the traits of traditional masculinity in intimate relationships? What happens to the identity of male athletes after they have left sport? These questions and issues are discussed perceptively by sociologist Michael Messner in the final selection.

32. "Nice Girls Don't Sweat": Women in American Sport[1]

WILLIAM H. BEEZLEY AND JOSEPH P. HOBBS

Why do women want to participate in organized sport? The literature grows daily on the unsavory aspects of sport—winning at all costs, cheating, gambling, recruiting violations, injuries, drugs, exploitation of athletes, the increasing resemblance of sport to the larger society where the individual is unrecognizable and unimportant. But the literature also grows on the value of sport for teaching discipline, competitiveness and teamwork, and bringing relaxation and healthful exercise to participants and entertainment for spectators.[2] For women, as for other excluded groups such as immigrants, sport seems an important avenue to full citzenship, and an escape from the status of house slave on an isolated "plantation."

To begin with, let us consider the efforts to provide participation in sport for college women. Lydia Huntley Sigourney in some 2000 articles and 60 books exhorted women toward emancipation.[3] Organized physical training and sports in higher education was still some 20 years away, yet some educators in the antebellum period acted on their belief that women in school needed exercise. For example, Mary Lyon, the founder of Mount Holyoke College, was not alone in including physical education as part of women's education. Although southern female education continued to be centered in the home during the antebellum period, over 200 private schools were founded and some school curricula required physical activities. Wesleyan Female College, along with others, even provided indoor recreation rooms for use during inclement weather.[4] These physical educators would provide a mixed, indeed controversial, legacy. They did not urge that young women compete with men in sport or anything else. They accepted and encouraged the notion of women's place—mother and housekeeper. They prescribed exercise that would not make young women "ungraceful" and "unlady-like" but instead would make and keep them healthy enough to fulfill their given role in society. Catherine Beecher's *Course of Calisthenics for Young Ladies* set out activities that for many became a model.[5] And so educated young women participated in calisthenics, walks, dancing, horseback riding and other activities, but they were not to enter the man's world.

Nevertheless, as collegiate sport organized in the last half of the 19th

SOURCE: William H. Beezley and Joseph P. Hobbs, " 'Nice Girls Don't Sweat': Women in American Sport," *Journal of Popular Culture* 16 (Spring 1983), pp. 42–53.

century, women began to compete, as did men, in intercollegiate basketball, volleyball and field hockey.[6] The pioneers had their difficulties: Lynne Emery, at the 1979 meeting of the NASSH, in a paper entitled "The First Intercollegiate Contest for Women: Basketball, April 4, 1896," recounted how it was.[7] The game was between the University of California-Berkeley and Stanford University. No men were allowed to attend. The young women were, after all, playing in bloomers and might even be sweating, sights not to be witnessed by men who were not blood relatives. All went well until one of the baskets needed to be repaired. Because only men could use tools, two male laborers were called in to make the repairs. At the sight of the men, the Berkeley team screamed and hid in a corner. But Stanford, according to Emery, "paid scant attention to the men and moved indifferently to a convenient area where they assumed becoming postures of ease." The Berkeley team behaved more conventionally; newspaper accounts dealt primarily not with the athletic abilities of the players, but with their "pleasing appearance and becoming actions."

As the skill of college women in sport increased, so did competition. This development, coupled with the growing accomplishments and publicity of other women's sports figures in the early 20th century, caused a reaction of alarm among many, including the intellectual heirs of those female physical educators of the early 19th century. They did not want women to enter this man's world of competition. As these physical educators looked around in the 1920s, they saw other disquieting signs: the suffragette who talked of women voting as a bloc since they had now acquired the franchise, and the flapper who not only indulged in but actually talked about sex, drank in public with men and showed her legs. The next thing one knew, women would want to take off their bulky sport clothes and show most of their bodies to be able to run better, swim better or shoot baskets better. And so began what Barbara Jane Walder has called "Mrs. Hoover's Holy War on Athletics." Mrs. Hoover was Lou Henry Hoover, wife of then Secretary of Commerce Herbert Hoover. Mrs. Hoover and others succeeded in reducing intercollegiate competition as we know it today from a still small percentage of colleges to nearly none by 1930. What competition remained occurred on play days and sports days and through telegraphic meets. High level competition was discouraged.[8]

By the end of World War II, however, about one-third of eastern colleges had intercollegiate athletics for women. But although practice changed, principle remained intact until the late 1960s, when, as part of the second feminist wave of the 20th century, a new generation of physical educators insisted that women's place was wherever she wanted to be. Intercollegiate competition among women increased dramatically.

Today's students of college physical education for women do not simply write off the founding mothers as Aunt Janes. Instead, they point out the dangers of being too present-minded when looking at the past. Ellen Gerber reminds us that the perceived mission at that time was to provide physical activity for all women instead of today's emphasis on equality of opportunity, especially in quality programs.[9] If such women had flown the ideological flag of equality, they might well have not made the gains they did.

From the myriad of organizations overseeing college women's athletics came a National Commission on Intercollegiate Sports. This commission established national Intercollegiate Championships in the late 1960s in Gymnastics, Golf, Track and Field, Swimming, Volleyball and Badminton. This proliferation of championships demanded a strong, unified body to give direction and governance to women's athletic programs, and in 1972 the AIAW (Association for Intercollegiate Athletics for Women) was founded.

The AIAW hoped to bring about more intense and higher level competition while avoiding the abuses threatening men's college athletics. The AIAW placed strong restrictions on recruiting and took other steps to avoid cheating on transcripts and recruiting, exploitation of students and too much emphasis on commercialism.[10] The AIAW's hope for a separate but equal and purer existence than the governing body of male college athletics, the NCAA (National Collegiate Athletic Association), received a rude reception from the sister body. The NCAA fought the growth of women's programs, but the number of women participating in collegiate competition continued to grow. This pressure, intensified by aid from the federal government, resulted in the NCAA's decision: If you can't lick them, take them over. In January 1980 the NCAA established women's championships in five sports for Divisions II and III, the smaller colleges, and in January 1981 the NCAA established women's championships in twelve sports for Division I, the major colleges.[11] Where the NCAA will take women's athletics, only Walter Byers knows.

Of perhaps even greater impact on women's sports in educational institutions is something known as Title IX. Section 901(a) of Title IX of the Education Amendments Act of 1972 brought women's education under the protection of the Civil Rights Act of 1964. It reads: "No person in the United States shall on the basis of sex, be excluded from participation in, be denied the benefits of, or be subjected to discrimination under any education program or activity receiving federal financial assistance."[12]

Sports was obviously an area in which education discriminated by gender. Funding for competitive sports for women was estimated to be less than one percent of that provided for men's programs. Some women opposed certain aspects of the act, fearing that athletic scholarships and related things would pervert women's athletics. Men, however, acting through the NCAA, provided the major opposition. Father Edmund M. Joyce, executive vice president of Notre Dame, condemned the bill's guidelines on equal spending for men and women as "asinine." Small wonder: in 1978, Notre Dame had a total scholarship budget of just under one million dollars for male athletes, and nothing for women athletes.[13] The federal government has been slow in formulating policy to implement the act and to this date passive in its actual implementation. Even now, the NCAA has a class action suit which argues that athletic departments are self-sufficient and therefore the federal government cannot decide how they must spend their self-generated funds. In a recent separate case a federal district judge in Michigan ruled that colleges and public schools do not have to provide equal expenditures for men and women if a particular sport in question does not receive federal assistance.[14]

Despite resistance by the NCAA and confusion from the federal government, participation by high school and college women in sport continues to grow. For example, in 1971–72 there were 95 AIAW college track teams; in 1977–78, 424. In 1973, 7,292 high schools had girls' track teams with 178,209 participants; in 1977–78, 13,789 high schools sponsored over 466,000 participants.[15] These statistics and others reflect the efforts of educators and government officials as well as the determination of a generation of more confident young women not to surrender the world of sport simply because of gender. Shortly after Fr. Joyce of Notre Dame denounced Title IX, NEW Secretary Joseph Califano was Notre Dame's graduation speaker. He was greeted by a silent protest against Title IX by the seniors, some of whom had "IX" taped to their graduation caps. It is rumored that Califano then talked to the President of Notre Dame. In any event, the very next semester Notre Dame produced $80,000 for women's athletic scholarships—only a start, but a beginning.[16]

The experience of women in collegiate sport is mirrored in the larger history of women in sport—a start from near zero, some change amidst great opposition, a way yet to go. Women's growing involvement was influenced by factors that were changing a rural agrarian nation—a nation seen as homogenous, governed by an unchanging orthodoxy—into a dynamic modern nation which, in acknowledging its diversity, made more difficult the imposition of an orthodoxy.

Developments in transportation and communication, along with continuing technological break-throughs, brought from mid-19th century on a new America and along with it, new and modern sports.[17]

Women's place and possibilities were affected by all aspects of the New America, but developments such as labor-saving home appliances and better birth control devices would give women more leisure time. Conceivably, women would both need exercise and have time for it. Industrial might brought a new kind of total war. The factories needed workers, and women were increasingly an available and always cheap source of labor. Wars against the bad guys raised questions about bad practices at home.

Within this context, then, women inched into the man's world of sport. John A. Lucas and Ronald A. Smith, in *Saga of American Sport* (probably to date the best overall history), maintain that three questions summarize women's place in sport. In the 1890s, the question most frequently asked was, "Should a lady ride a bicycle?" In the 1920s it was, "Shall women compete in highly competitive athletics?" In the 1960s and '70s we asked, "Shall women have equal opportunity with men to compete in athletics at all levels?"[18]

"Should a lady ride a bicycle?" In order to ride a bicycle without killing herself, a woman had to hike a skirt. Rising hemlines could lead to just about anything. We know now it did.[19] Women and men now played together at croquet, proving correct those good souls who had opposed women playing croquet at all, on the grounds that such activity would debase women and society.[20] Mary E. Outerbridge of Staten Island introduced tennis to the United States in 1874. Angela Lumpkin of UNC-Chapel Hill has shown the consequences.[21] Women played daintily for a while but eventually adopted "male" tactics. They dressed in an appropriately modest manner at first but then—simply to play better—wore fewer clothes. Despite all these efforts and subsequent gains, women remained second class citizens during the 19th century.

Yet things were moving the way of those who were not white Anglo-Saxon males. In a burgeoning economy, jobs had to be filled. At the start of the 20th century millions of immigrants arrived, and they were coming, not from north and west Europe, but from south and east Europe. New and different immigrants meant new and different ways of living, and a new, necessarily more egalitarian ethic could have to be adopted in an economy that depended for growth on everyone—not just WASPs—buying things.

Despite strong opposition, women began to compete in the Olympics, beginning in 1900 with golf and tennis.[22] The New York Female Giants played softball. Even more amazingly, a woman, Helene Britton, in 1911 inherited ownership of baseball's St. Louis Cardinals and, despite intense opposition, remained owner for 6 years.[23] The changing status of women in the first two decades of the century culminated in the passage of the 19th Amendment, bringing national suffrage to women in 1920. And so Eleanora Sears—who, bred in Boston's upper class, played sports with an attitude and vigor thought at the time to be only masculine, and who at age 44 was still good enough to win the 1928 National Women's Singles Championship in squash[24]—had company early in the century.

In the 1920s technological innovations and scientific management doubled productivity.[25] Workers benefited both at home and in the factory. Leisure time and more money meant that people could go out to be entertained by, among other things, sporting events. George E. Mowry, in *The Twenties*, acknowledges that among the reasons for the spectacular rise of professional sports in the 1920s were the new leisure time of the masses, increased living standards, and the new means of creating reputations through ballyhoo:

But perhaps as important as all of these other factors was the instinctive need of a rapidly growing collectivized society for individual expression. On the battlefield, in the factory production line, at home in a city apartment, and increasingly even in the business world the individual was becoming lost in a welter in the hive. The sporting field was one of the few remaining areas of pure individual expression where success or failure depended precisely upon individual physical and intellectual prowess. And if the masses themselves could not or would not participate directly, they could at least, by a process of identification, salute the old virtues.[26]

The decade of the 1920s was indeed the Golden Age of American Sports, and women were part of it. Glenna Collett was the first woman to break 80 for a round of 18 holes of golf. Gertrude Ederle in 1926 became the first woman to swim the English Channel and her time of 14 hours and 23 minutes bettered the existing male record by two hours. Helen Wills, Little Miss Poker Face, dominated tennis. Margaret Gisolo even broke the gender barrier in American Legion Junior Baseball before the Legion changed its rules. But Gisolo's brief career at least raised questions about the prevailing belief that females could not compete equally with male peers.[27] Floretta McCutcheon in 1922, at age 39, defeated the long reigning male bowling champion, Jimmy Smith, in a 3 game set,. 704–687.[28] Women's play in the 1920s became more intense: losers got angry.

Yet the 1920s proved not to be the liberation of workers or women. Worker's wages did not rise nearly so much as corporate profits, and women were still clustered in individual or dual sports such as swimming, golf and tennis. Team sports were not really acceptable—thus the triumph of Mrs. Hoover and the anticompetitive movement. The feminine mystique, aided by the sudden and dramatic Great Depression of the 1930s, persisted despite the vote and despite the flapper. A woman's place was in the home and not in the job market competing with those who were the breadwinners.

And so, despite the efforts of women like Babe Zaharias—who set world records in the 1932 Olympics and changed the style of play in women's golf[29]—a woman's world on the eve of World War II was still a very small one. The 1940 census showed twenty five percent of women gainfully employed— nearly the same percentage as in 1910. In addition, most women who entered the labor force in the 1920s and '30s went into areas traditionally defined as women's work. Middle-class women still had to choose between a career and marriage.

World War II changed nearly everything and nearly everyone, including women.[30] Economic prosperity, spurred by technological innovation, solved the Great Depression. It brought full employment, even more massive government intervention in our lives, and America the self-appointed responsibility of leadership of the free world. Women went to work—*married* women went to work and performed jobs requiring skills and/or physical strengths. There was hardly a job they did not fill. All of this was accepted because it was necessary to defeat the Axis. After the war, however, women continued to work. The economy was prospering and there was room for women. Jobs opened up, not in the manufacturing sector, where resistance to women's participation was strongest, but in the service area. Two incomes became increasingly necessary for a family to keep up with the middle-class Joneses, and women went into the labor force under the traditional banner of helping out, not a flag that demanded equality. Attitudes changed more slowly. It would be unrealistic to believe that as soon as numbers of married women began to work they would demand equal treatment. And yet the fact that they were working would become an essential condition in women's lives. In the 1950s, the country rested after the turbulence of the 1930s and '40s. By the 1960s, the country was ready for a new period of activism.

The civil rights movement was the catalyst for all groups tired of seeing a good life on TV which they could not share. Thus, in the 1960s, when Betty Friedan and others raised again an ideological alternative to "a woman's place is in the home," the appeal made sense, because there was now a huge gap between the reality of women's lives and the rhetoric of women's place.

And so the feminist movement surged again in many forms. Organizationally there were moderates such as NOW (The National Organization of Women) and there were radicals such as cell groups in SDS (Students for A Democratic Society) and independent organizations such as WITCH (Women's International Terrorist Conspiracy from Hell). Tactics varied as well: direct action such as boycotts, naming a sheep as a counter Miss America in 1968, establishing day-care centers and abortion clinics, and providing alternatives to children's books that contained sexual stereotypes. Congress responded with the Equal Pay Act of 1963, Title VII of the Civil Rights Act of 1964, and Title IX in 1972. Finally, the movement came together in support of a proposal to amend the Constitution, a proposal that had first been introduced in Congress in 1923. In March, 1972, the Congress passed and sent to the states the proposed Equal Rights Amendment, the substantial part of which reads: "Equality of rights under the law shall not be denied or abridged by the United States or by any State on account of sex." The proposed amendment swept through a couple of dozen of the required 38 states almost immediately,[31] before finally failing to receive the required number of state approvals before the extended time period ran out.

The Supreme Court also moved. Until 1971, every legislatively drawn gender line was accepted by the Court.[32] For example, the Court as recently as 1961 had upheld a state law that placed women on juries only if they volunteered (that decision was not overturned by the Court until 1974).[33] Beginning in 1971 the court began to question the legitimacy of distinction by gender in many areas.[34]

Individual women also forced change by entering male preserves. The female percentage of lawyers, bank managers, physicians, accountants, and bus drivers increased dramatically, although in no instance to majority status. Female workers rose from thirty-four percent of the labor force in 1950 to over fifty percent in 1980.[35] 1980 alone saw the first women graduates of the military academies, the first female military test parachutist, the first female head of a Hollywood motion picture studio, the first woman elected to the policy making council of the AFL-CIO, and the first woman to receive the highest award of the Radio-Television News Directors' Association. In 1980 women received some twenty-eight percent of the 31,200 doctorates awarded in the U.S. as compared to some ten percent in 1965.[36] A woman or a man could now drive a truck or cry.

And yet, problems remained in all these areas. The ERA stalled because of opposition from women and men. The Supreme Court continued to uphold some distinctions by gender. Traditionally female jobs continued to be dominated by women. The gap between the median earnings of men and women remained as great as ever; as in 1960, women's earnings continued to be about sixty percent of those of men.[37] Sociologists began talking of the feminization of poverty. The lack of child-care centers and means for collecting child support payments, and the lack of access to good jobs are bringing poverty among female-headed families to the point where the majority of all poor families is now headed by a woman. Some experts contend that the proportion of the poor who are in female-headed families may comprise one hundred percent within twenty years.[38]

The story of women in American sport since World War II is similar to the story of other women.[39] Participation increased dramatically, but not until the late 1960s did women begin to demand such things as equal prize money in tennis tournaments or equal PE facilities. But, as in other areas, the pioneers in participation must be given due credit.

Some competed against other women. In the Olympics, track and field stars like Wilma Rudolph and Wyomia Tyus continued to lower women's times so dramatically that even the most diehard male chauvinist could no longer be certain that women could never run as fast as men. Women's times in the marathon became so close to men's that the Olympics finally decided to add the event for women in 1984. Basketball continued to be an area of competition for women. UCLA signalled one effect of Title IX by becoming the first major college to win the women's collegiate championship. The success of collegians such as Nancy Leiberman led in 1978 to the formation of the Women's Professional Basketball League. Tennis and golf continued to be the most prominent sports. Golfers Mickey Wright and Kathy Withworth dominated the tour in the 1960s, and Nancy Lopez won purses in the 1970s that were actually respectable. In tennis, Maureen Connally and Doris Hart were great players, and Althea Gibson smashed tennis' color barrier. But it took Billie Jean King to demand successfully that women's prize monies be of the magnitude that players of the 1970s such as Chris Evert and Tracy Austin won. Small wonder that in 1980 when the inaugural dinner of the Women's Sports Hall of Fame was held, King was among the first nine women inducted into the hall.[40]

Alongside traditional activities, women moved into new areas of sport. The All-American Girls Baseball League was formed in 1943 and continued through the early 1950s, albeit with chaperones and an emphasis on decorum.[41] Little girls played baseball in Little League. Kathy Kusner in 1961 became the first woman in 10 years to join the U.S. Equestrian team—

champion in the only Olympic sport where men and women competed against each other. In 1968 she became the first woman in the U.S. to be granted a jockey license. Soon both Mary Bacon and Robyn Smith were riding horses and winning against men. Suzy Chaffee skied to victory in open competition in the world championships, hot dog or freestyle. Others drove cars to victories against men: Donna Mae Mims in 1964 won the Class II (Imported 2 seater) sports car club of America championship in a bright pink Austin-Healey Sprite. Shirley (Cha-Cha) Muldowney in 1977 won the Top Fuel title in the Summer nationals drag racing championships. Janet Guthrie drove in the Indianapolis 500. On the golf tour, a tournament was established in which man/woman duos competed. Bronwin Russell in 1980 became the first female caddy in the U.S. Open Men's tournament. Betsy Rawls in that same tournament became the first female to serve as a rules official. Leonore Modell in 1964, at age 14, became the youngest person ever to swim the English Channel. And the list is growing.

Some women enlarged their area of sport by competing against other women but in areas reserved for men. National championships were established for women in rodeo and weightlifting. Other women formed rugby teams. And not only are women in their own locker room, but some women journalists are demanding entrance to male locker rooms. [42] Where will it end?

Where indeed! Women in sport have come a long way. Not long ago dictionaries defined biography as the history of the lives of men. Women, in challenging this definition, have called into question an attribute—gender—which, along with race and class, has served as a key reference point for individual identity and American society's organization. As such, the movement is by definition controversial.

Some worry whether women should be imprisoned in what Robert Lipsyte calls *SportsWorld*,[43] where the emphasis on winning causes a perversion of what sport should be and where the athlete is exploited almost beyond belief. Some studies argue that a clear majority of professional basketball and football players do not have college degrees, even though they went to college four years. Why should women's athletics imitate the depersonalization, drugs, violence, cheating and the rest that seems to pervade men's sports? Already there are prominent cases of cheating. [44]

The response to this criticism is that sports can be fun, a release of tension, a source of self-confidence and health, and provide the satisfaction of challenge, discipline and accountability. In any event, by allowing athletes to be women, we have allowed athletes to be other things as well; some athletes are male, some female, some tall, some short, some heterosexual, some homosexual. And all are capitalists like the rest of us.

Women have at best advanced from the back of the bus only to the middle. Their second-class citizenship is apparent in many ways. For example, last year Tom Watson, the leading male golfer, won $530,800; Beth Daniel, the leading female golfer, won $231,000, less than fifty percent of Watson's earnings, and golf and tennis are the nearest to parity for male and female athletes.[45] College athletic budgets remain much lower for women than men. Media coverage of women's sport is but a tiny fraction of coverage for men. The same disparity occurs in the academic study of sport.[46]

So for both scholars and journalists, the term "athlete" continues to mean male. Do you read of the Wolfpack men's basketball team? No, but you do read of the Wolfpack women's basketball team. At least they are not called Wolfpackettes, as our female colleagues are not called historianettes. Where is it written that athletes are supposed to be male? The Dallas Cowboy Cheerleaders have gotten more exposure—if you will pardon the term—on national television, including prime time, than all of women's sports put together. We don't object to the Dallas Cheerleaders, but we do wonder why we cannot be given a chance to learn to appreciate other examples of the athletic skills of women. *Sport Illustrated,* founded in 1954, put out its first bathing suit issue (this means pictures of women) shortly thereafter. The bathing suit issues are among the most popular. Recently a magazine funded by *Newsweek* arose to challenge *Sports Illustrated: Inside Sports*. Sure enough, it was a bathing suit issue—and it was this cover, jokingly but openly challenging *Sports Illustrated*'s bathing suits—that *Newsweek* ran as a full page ad for the magazine.[47]

Why must women's accomplishments in sport be measured by definitions concocted by men, even as noted in the title of this paper? Can you imagine a paper on "men in sport"? Why not try to have the best of both worlds? Despite setbacks, the direction of women's involvement in our society is clear; they'll not go back to the bedroom and the kitchen alone. Let's make the best of it and develop a new *zeitgeist*. Perhaps, for example, college women could show college men what basketball is: a game of joy, of movement toward the basket, of rigorous exercise, of incredible displays of individual skills and coordinated team efforts. The task will be difficult because the men play a game called keepaway in which the coaches "strategize"ways to keep the young men from getting tired, having fun or even sweating. But women could give it a try.

The notion of "everybody knows" is a chimerical one. In *Sports Illustrated*'s review of 1954, the only women depicted were cheerleaders. Now there is nothing wrong with being a cheerleader or a housewife or a secretary. But in 1954 "everybody knew" those jobs and a few others were the only ones women were capable of performing. But we believe now that the world of women ought to be a choice not a mandate. What everybody knows, in short, has changed. Fundamental economic and technological developments, coupled with the courage and skill of human beings, have enlarged woman's world. Women have more options now. This has made the world more uncertain; it was nice to know that a person defined by gender had to get the cup of coffee. On the other hand, if whoever gets a cup of coffee does so by choice, then maybe the other person won't have coffee accidentally spilled in his or her lap. Each may realize that the simple act of getting someone a cup of coffee can be an act of love. Then, perhaps all of us can accept the notion that, while some girls glow, some women sweat.

NOTES

1. The statement that "Nice Girls Don't Sweat" is not original to the authors. The authors first saw it as the title of a senior history undergraduate thesis submitted to North Carolina State University, April 16, 1974 by Sally Williamson. Others attest that they have known the expression for at least fifty years. John A. Lucas and Ronald A. Smith, in *Saga of American Sport* (Philadelphia: Lea & Febiger, 1978, especially in chapters 15 and 20) provide an excellent narrative summary and analysis of women in sport. For a multidisciplinary perspective on women in sport, see Ellen W. Gerber, et al., *The American Woman in Sport* (Reading, Mass.: Addison-Wesley, 1974). The latter work contains an excellent historical account by Ellen Gerber, which complements nicely the work by Lucas and Smith. Both historical accounts place the development of women's sport in the broader context of social, political and economic events. See also Mary L. Remley, *Women in Sport. A Guide to Information Sources* (Detroit: Gale Research Co., 1980).
2. John Underwood assesses the current debate in "A Game Plan for America," *Sports Illustrated*, 54, No. 9 (Feb. 23, 1981), 65–80.
3. Lydia Huntley Sigourney devoted much of her life to the emancipation of women, which to her included sound physical and mental health.
4. Roxanne Albertson, "School Physical Activity Programs for Antebellum Southern Belles," North American Society for Sport History *Proceedings* (1979), p. 15.
5. Patricia Vertinsky, "Sexual Equality and the Legacy of Catherine Beecher," *Journal of Sport History*, 6, No. 1 (Spring 1979), 38–49.
6. Guy Lewis, "The Beginning of Organized Collegiate Sport," *American Quarterly*, 22, No. 2, Pt. 1 (Summer 1970), 222–29; June A. Kennard, "Review Essay, The History of Physical Education," *Signs: Journal of Women in Culture and Society*, 2, No. 4 (Summer 1977), 835–42; Margaret A. Coffey, "The Sportswoman—Then and Now," *Journal of Health, Physical Education and Recreation*, 36 (Feb. 1965), 38–41, 50; Judith A. Davidson, "The Homosocial World of Intercollegiate Athletics," North American Society for Sport History *Proceedings* (1978), p. 32; Dewar, "The Beginnings and Directions of Ms. Basketball in North America," North American Society for Sport History *Proceedings* (1977), pp. 33–34.
7. North American Society for Sport History *Proceedings* (1979), pp. 19–20.
8. Barbara Jane Walder, "Mrs. Hoover's Holy War on Athletics," *Women Sports*, 1, No. 4 (Sept. 1974), 23–24.
9. Ellen Gerber, "The Controlled Development of Collegiate Sport for Women, 1923–1936," *Journal of Sport History*, 2, No. 1 (Spring 1979), 1–28.
10. For the birth of the AIAW, see Joanna Davenport, "The Historical Development of AIAW," North American Society for Sport History *Proceedings* (1979), pp. 35–36.
11. "NCAA 'Takeover' and Inevitable Power Play," *Raleigh News and Observer*, Jan. 16, 1981, p. 21. On the past and present NCAA, see Skip Applin, "The Recent Historical Development of the NCAA," and Niels Thompson, "The Present Status of the NCAA," North American Society for Sport History *Proceedings* (1979), 35–37.
12. "How HEW Will Measure Campus Compliance with Title IX," *Chronicle of Higher Education* (Dec. 10, 1979), Vol. XIX, No. 15, 13–16.
13. Lisa Gubernick, "Catching Up With the Pack," *The Runner*, 3, No. 2 (Nov. 1980), 72–77.
14. Doug Tucker, "Title IX Issue Appears Headed for High Court," *Raleigh News and Observer*, Feb. 28, 1981, p. 15.
15. Gubernick, "Catching Up," *Runner*, 75.
16. Gubernick, "Catching Up," *Runner*, 72.
17. Allen Guttman, in *From Ritual to Record: The Nature of Modern Sports* (New York: Columbia University Press, 1978), assigns to modern sports seven distinct characteristics that scholars such as Max Weber and Talcott Parsons have used to describe modern society: secularism, equality of opportunity to compete and in the conditions of competition, special-

ization of roles, rationalization, bureaucratic organization, quantification and the quest for records. See also John R. Betts, "The Technological Revolution and the Rise of Sport, 1850–1900," *Mississippi Valley Historical Review*, XL (Sept. 1953), pp. 231–256.

18. Lucas and Smith, *Saga of American Sport*, p. 342.
19. Lucas and Smith, *Saga of American Sport*, pp. 257–61. See also D. Margaret Toohey and Betty V. Edmondson, "An Historical Perspective on Beliefs about Women's Health Issues which had an Impact on Attitudes Toward Women's Sport Participation in the Nineteenth Century," North American Society for Sports History *Proceedings* (1980), p. 40.
20. John Durant and Otto Bettman, *Pictorial History of American Sports—From Colonial Times to the Present* (Cranbury, N.J.: A.S. Barnes, 1952, 1956, 1973), pp. 46–47.
21. Angela Lumpkin, *Women's Tennis: A Historical Documentary* (Troy, N.Y.: Whitson Publishing Co., 1980).
22. Sheila Mitchell, "Women's Participation in the Olympic Games, 1900–1926," *Journal of Sport History*, 4, No. 2 (Summer 1977), 208–28.
23. Bill Borst, "The Matron Magnate," *Baseball Research Journal* (1977), 25–30; See also David Voigt, "Sex in Baseball: Reflections on Changing Taboos," *Journal of Popular Culture*, XII, No. 3 (Winter 1978), 389–403.
24. Joanna Davenport, "Eleanora Randolph Sears, Pioneer in Women's Sports," North American Society for Sport History *Proceedings* (1976), p. 17 and Cleveland Amory "Boston Unique— Miss Sears," 141, *Vogue* (Feb. 15, 1963), 81–83; and Lucas and Smith, *Saga of American Sport*, pp. 342–43.
25. William E. Leuchtenburg, *The Perils of Prosperity* (Chicago: University of Chicago Press, 1958).
26. George E. Mowry, *The Twenties: Fords, Flappers & Fanatics* (Englewood Cliffs, N.J.: Prentice-Hall, 1963).
27. Tony Ladd, "The Girl Who Broke and Set the Gender Barrier in Baseball," North American Society for Sport History *Proceedings* (1978), p. 31.
28. Phyllis Ryant Ement, "Foremothers: Floretta McCutcheon," *Women Sports*, 3, No. 10 (Oct. 1976), 60–62.
29. Babe Didrikson Zaharias, *This Life I've Led* (New York: Barnes, 1955); *Current Biography* (1956), 663; *New York Times*, Sept. 28, 1956; Betty Hicks, "Foremothers: Babe Didrikson Zaharias," *Sports World*, 2, Nos. 11 and 12 (Nov.–Dec. 1975), 24–28, 18–25; and William Oscar Johnson and Nancy Williamson, "Babe," *Sports Illustrated*, Vol. 43, No. 14, 112–33; Vol. 43, No. 15, 48–57; Vol. 43, No. 16, 48–62.
30. William H. Chafe, *The American Woman: Her Changing Social, Economic and Political Roles, 1920–1970* (New York: Oxford, 1972). See also June Sochen, *Herstory* (Sherman Oaks, Ca.: Alfred Pub. Co., 1974, 1981); Lois W. Banner, *Women in Modern America—A Brief History* (New York: Harcourt Brace Jovanovich, 1974); and Peter G. Filene, *Him/Her/Self—Sex Roles in Modern America* (New York: Harcourt Brace Jovanovich, 1974).
31. For a discussion of the legal context and implications, see Ginsburg, "Gender," *Cincinnati Law Review*, 44 No. 1 (1975), p. 1042.
32. Ginsburg, "Gender," p. 4.
33. *Hoyt v. Florida*, 368 U.S. 57 (1961).
34. *Reed v. Reed* 404 U.S..71 (1971).
35. "Battle of the Sexes—Men Fight Back," *U.S. News & World Report*, XXIX No. 23 (Dec. 8, 1980), 50–52.
36. Associated Press, "1980 Has Been a Landmark Year for Women," Savannah *Morning News*, Dec. 22, 1980, p. 6B.
37. "Battle of the Sexes—Men Fight Back," *U.S. News & World Report*, XXIX No. 23 (Dec. 8, 1980), 50–52.
38. Dianne Dumanoski, The Boston *Globe*, "Poverty Takes on a Feminine Look," in the *Raleigh News and Observer*, March 8, 1981, III, pp. 1, 6.
39. Joanna Bunker Rohrbaugh assesses the "joyous" impact on women of their growing involvement in sport in "Femininity on the Line," *Psychology Today*, 13, No. 3 (August 1979), 30–42. Letty Cottin Pogrebin assesses the impact of boys and girls playing together and concludes that both sexes would benefit by seeing females "who are not only lovers and friends, but leaders, heroes, high-scorers and champions." *Next* (Jan.–Feb. 1981), 96–101. Shelly Armitage, in "The Lady as Jock: A Popular Culture Perspective on the Woman Athlete,"

Journal of Popular Culture, 10, No. 1 (Summer 1976), 122–132, traces the changing role models for women. Phyllis Hollander, *100 Greatest Women in Sports* (New York: Grosset & Dunlap, 1976), summarizes the career of many modern women athletes. Harry Edwards, in "Desegregating Sexist Sport," *Intellectual Digest*, III, No. 3 (Nov. 1972), 82–83, contends that American women cannot obtain equality "until they have succeeded in overthrowing male domination of sport."

40. *Raleigh News and Observer*, Sept. 17, 1980, p. 16.
41. Merrie A. Fidler, "The All-American Girls' Baseball League, 1943–1954," North American Society for Sport History *Proceedings* (1977), pp. 35–36; W. G. Nicholson, "Women's Pro Baseball Packed the Stands," *Women Sports*, 3, No. 4 (April 1976), 22–24.
42. Bob St. John, *Landry* (Waco, TX: Word Books, 1979), 167.
43. Robert Lipsyte, *Sports World: An American Dream Land* (New York: Quadrangle, 1975).
44. See, for example, Jane Leavy, "The Saga of Rosie Ruiz," *The Washington Post*, April 27, 1980, p. N1.
45. *Sports Illustrated*, 54, No. 7 (Feb. 12, 1981), 112.
46. An NCSU undergraduate history major, Robert Levin, did a survey of the *Proceedings* of the meetings of the North American Society for Sport History. He discovered that, since 1974, of the 40–50 or so papers given each year, usually only 5 or so dealt with women; of books displayed at the convention—varying year to year from below 20 to over 60—only 1 or 2 are about women. Levin found similar results in the *Journal of Sport History*, both as to articles printed and articles cited from other journals in the section "Journal Surveys." *The Journal of Sport History*, 6 No. 1 (Spring 1979)—lists only 8 books about women. Lists of recommended books by prominent scholars and journalists yield similar results. Obviously much monographic work needs to be done in the field.
47. The first issue of *Sports Illustrated* to have a bathing suit feature was Vol. 1 No. 19 of Dec. 20, 1954. *Newsweek's* ad for *Inside Sports* was in *Newsweek* (March 28, 1981).

33. *Athletics and the University: The Post-Woman's Era*

G. ANN UHLIR

A number of related events of the early 1970s, including the passage of Title IX, the founding of the Association for Intercollegiate Athletics for Women (AIAW), and rising expectations for women's rights, launched an auspicious era for women in college sport. The end of the era came only a decade after its beginning. Failure to ratify the ERA, the negative impact of the Grove City decision on Title IX, and the death in 1982 of the AIAW combined to terminate the movement. We are in a lag between the end of an age and the discovery of that end, a time of "parenthesis." It is the beginning of the post-woman's era.

Despite the widespread belief that women have arrived in the sacrosanct bastions of athletic power and privilege within the university, the reality is otherwise. In no area of higher education are women so noticeably absent from the most prestigious positions of decision making. A woman may even aspire more realistically to become chief executive officer or a member of a governing board, than to become a director of athletics of an NCAA Division I institution.

Opportunities for elite women athletes have improved, but total participation slots available for women have declined. As the economic crunch facing athletics is confronted, women are expected to share equally in the cuts. Since women never achieved anything close to parity (participation is less than a 1:2 ratio), participation would still be less than equitable even if all cuts came from men's athletics.

Part of the inequity rises from the very fact that more sports are offered for men than for women. In 1987–88, NCAA sponsored seventy-six national championships: forty-one for men, thirty-three for women, and two for both, with fourteen sports available for women and two more (riflery and skiing) available for both men and women. In 1980–81, AIAW sponsored thirty-nine national championships for women in seventeen different sports. If a Division I institution offered the maximum scholarship limits in the maximum number of sports available for women, it would award 135 full awards in thirteen sports. Football alone permits ninety-five awards, and other Division I men's sports allow an additional 150 awards.[1]

SOURCE: G. Ann Uhlir, "Athletics and the University: The Post-Woman's Era," *Academe* 73 (July–August 1987), pp. 25–29.

While NAIA also offers championships for women in ten sports, these ten sports represent no additional opportunities beyond those already available through the NCAA. Sports that have been strong interest areas for women in the past (badminton, slow-pitch softball, and synchronized swimming, sports that men have not pursued at the collegiate competitive level) have gone by the board altogether. The popular woman's sport of gymnastics is declining at such a rate that the NCAA Division II championship has already been eliminated.[2]

But I am ahead of my story. During the decade between the early 1970s and the early 1980s, the governance of women's athletics under the Association for Intercollegiate Athletics for Women had assured a "different voice" for the world of collegiate sport. It was the voice of women who had as their goal an educational model for college sport. The focus was on the values derived from competitive sport that contributed to the education of the student athlete.

Before the early 1970s, higher education had known but one version of athletics—i.e., men's athletics. During the woman's era of college sport, an attempt was made to establish a viable alternative to the existing model for intercollegiate athletics. With creativity and imagination, an organization was founded that developed a championship program for women comparable to that of the long-established men's programs. Of greater significance is the fact that the governance system regulating the championships offered prudent alternatives long advocated by college presidents.

From the outset, AIAW recognized its dual obligation to institutions of higher education and to student athletes. Both students and chief executives were involved in the decision-making processes. Student rights rules provided protection against the possibility of arbitrary actions by administrators. Fundamental due process was afforded students before they could be deprived of eligibility or athletic aid. Plans incorporated distribution of assets from television and championship income to benefit all members, not just winners. The belief that balanced competition could result from efforts to distribute the wealth was fundamental to policy making.

The AIAW enforcement system for rules compliance based on self-policing and self-reporting caused constant scrutiny of not only one's own behavior but also the behavior of competitors. And the mistakes of coaches and administrators were not visited upon the athletes. AIAW penalized only those students who knowingly and consciously violated the rules.

The motivation that drove women leaders to create an organization to govern college athletics was twofold. First, it was believed that college women had been seriously deprived of the lessons of one of the most highly valued extracurricular learning experiences within higher education. Men had long enjoyed the benefits of competitive experience and leveraged these benefits to great gains in the marketplace of life. Second, it was believed that there were approaches to providing competitive experiences other than those that had become institutionalized throughout higher education. The woman's era was both an attempt to enrich the lives of college women through sport and a movement to afford higher education and the American public an alternative option for delivering programs of sport. The scheme was designed by women with no experience in athletic governance. As a result, it was not bound by lessons teaching that the ideal cannot work. The experiment was a radical departure from institutionalized athletics with little hope for acceptance by the public or higher education.

As early as 1975, opposition to the governance experiment began. Initially the opposition came via NCAA proposals to gain control of women's national championships. The concern was that the development of women's sports might dilute resources available for men. Supporters of high visibility sports like football and basketball as well as so-called "minor" sports like tennis and golf were equally vocal. The meteoric rise of women could mean a reduction in funds needed for men's growth or continuance. When the NCAA legislative effort failed, a new strategy to control growth of women's sports was concocted. A coalition of colleges and universities raised funds to lobby against Title IX regulations, seeking exemption for "revenue producing" sports. The final regulations were released in November 1979, with provisions assuring equality for women in the total array of services. Even so, more new dollars went to men's collegiate sports in the seventies than were made available for women.

At the beginning of the woman's era, women's collegiate athletics were typically administered by physical education departments; men's athletics, by contrast, were generally administered by athletic departments. Chief executives, faced with separate athletic structures for women and men and differing rules governing participation of women and men, were pressured by "old boy" networks to consolidate programs. Consolidation on the campuses was expected to bring about athletic conference consolidation and, ultimately, unified athletic governance. In their infinite wisdom, reflected in the "everybody's doing it" model, campus administrators throughout the country moved to unify athletic programs for men and women under the director of the men's program. Many were convinced that equal opportunities for women could occur only in merged administrations.

In 1972, virtually all athletic programs for women were directed by women, with only 6 percent of Division I programs merged into single athletic departments. By 1979–80, over 80 percent of all collegiate athletic administrations were merged,[3] and 90 percent of the merged administrations had men at the helm.[4] Frequently, the woman displaced was more qualified—with more experience, a higher degree, academic rank, and tenure.

Studies in progress are attempting to assess the lives of both those women who survived mergers and those who departed from the primary administrative position in their institutions. Departures include those who were reassigned within the university and those who left the institution altogether.

Disselkoen has identified over 300 women who disappeared from women's athletic decision-making positions during the period between 1975 and 1985.

She interviewed thirty-one of these people in twenty-seven states and found twenty-one involuntarily gave up their positions in the process of mergers. Sixteen left athletics entirely. None of the thirty-one had budget control after merger.[5] In 1986, Rosenbrock interviewed seventeen women who survived these mergers within Division I–A football and men's basketball schools. She found that these women felt powerless. Their previous sources of power— Title IX, AIAW, and gender solidarity afforded by the networks and meetings associated with women's governance—were all gone.[6]

Common findings of both these studies reveal the incredible frustration of women throughout the United States as their lifetimes of work came to naught. Those who remain on the periphery of athletics reflect varying degrees of the exist-persist-resist syndrome. Their motives to continue in their lower status positions relate to the belief that if they resign somehow things will get even worse. A few still hope to change the system and to save their programs. Others have no place to go and feel they have no options at this stage of their careers.

The absence of women in administrative roles is only part of the picture. Declining numbers of women in leadership are observed throughout college sport. Only half of the head coaches of women's sports are now women.[7] The number of women assistant coaches in training for head jobs is also declining. Freshman and junior varsity squads for women have been eliminated. These talent-development programs of the past were lost when financial cutbacks were required, even though opportunities for women had not approached equality. With their demise went leadership-training positions. Women officials, noticeably absent from the high visibility sports, tend to fare better in those sports where men have limited experience. Women basketball officials are rare. Women officials of field hockey and gymnastics tend to be more common. Opportunities for women seem best when there are few qualified males.

Women role models and mentors of female collegiate athletes are few and far between. Coaches and junior administrators who are selected or have survived invariably reach the invisible ceiling in the athletic echelon. Only in institutions that have maintained separate structures for athletics do women reach the top and head their own programs. Most of these situations exist, not incidentally, where former AIAW leaders have maintained autonomy for women. It is no surprise that a Miller Lite study in 1985 of public attitudes toward sport found that 51 percent of all females choose male public figures as role models. Choice is limited.

And so the post-woman's era is upon us. When you turn to the sport pages of the best newspapers you must search the fine print and the back pages for any references to college women. Column inches devoted to collegiate women are but a trifle of the total devoted to collegiate sports. Women tend to be ignored in debates focusing on sports issues.

The invisibility of women is reflected in a May 1987 story in the *Chronicle of Higher Education*. Athletes who failed to meet minimum NCAA standards for participation in 1986–87 were described. Six hundred and fifty of these students enrolled as freshmen in Division I institutions to attempt to qualify to play in their sophomore year. The entire account ignored the existence of women within the group. Whatever the explanation for the omission of women, the treatment of the story gives cause for concern. If women were present in the group, their omission illustrates the blindness of the press to the situation of the woman athlete. If no woman was among the 650 athletes for whom institutions made these special arrangements, then the evidence of discrimination would be more striking still.

Television coverage for collegiate women's sports continues to be all but nonexistent on network stations. Only those events with similar appeal to men's televised events are offered. In 1986–87, spectators were treated to coverage of only the semifinal and final games of the NCAA Division I women's basketball championship.

In this new era, opportunities for women as leaders have diminished, sport options for women athletes have been reduced, and development programs for women athletes have been dismissed as beyond the role of college departments of athletics. The era is characterized by the following:

1. Approximately one dollar in five of financial aid based on athletic ability is awarded to a woman.[8]
2. Fifty percent of the coaches of women's teams are men.[9]
3. Only 15 percent of women's intercollegiate programs are under the supervision of a woman athletic director.[10]
4. Only one of the NCAA Division I merged athletic programs in the United States has a woman as the athletic director.
5. The top-salaried college women's basketball coach in 1986–87 earns thirty-nine cents on the dollar of the top-salaried men's basketball coach.[11]
6. Four of the top ten salaried coaches of women's basketball, 1986–87, are men.[12]
7. Only thirty of the ninety postgraduate scholarships offered by NCAA are available for women.[13]
8. Only 31 percent of the 1985–86 NCAA participants were female, although college enrollments are 52 percent female.[14]
9. Only 30 percent of the NJCAA athletes were women in 1985–86.[15]
10. Median salaries for directors of athletics (1986–87) are $10,783 more for men than for women.[16]
11. Fewer national championships—in fewer sports and in fewer divisions—are available to women than were available in 1981–82, the last year of AIAW.

The annual meetings of the national governing bodies of collegiate sport continue to be dominated by men. And the deliberations continue to follow the standard course, with little if any substantive change as the result of the participation of women. Athletic issues that are the focus of attention include reducing the costs of programs and institutional integrity. Never mentioned is the continuing minority status of women as participants and leaders despite the majority enrollments of women in higher education.

The institutionalized system of sport in higher education accommodated women with virtually no change in the basic pre-woman structure. The different voice of women in this post-woman's era is not heard. Occasionally the words of a woman speaking from the perspective of the system are audible. This is the voice of the indoctrinated, amalgamated, and homogenized, with the speaker measuring program success by the same yardsticks that have long stood as the standards—titles won, seats filled, and dollars raised. These standards rarely consider the individual gains of students, how they benefit from the competitive experience, and the value of these lessons to the society at large. The investment in the education of athletes—an investment in the building of the social order—is not a priority.

But, as Tom Paxton once said, "It's okay to look at the past, just don't stare at it." This time of "parenthesis" may be the dawn of a new age of collegiate sport. In this time of public outrage fomented by scandals of all sorts within the higher education sport establishment, a national dialogue on the compatibility of intercollegiate athletics with the aims and values of colleges and universities has been inaugurated by the Presidents' Commission of the NCAA. The commission has proposed a series of studies on "effects of participation in intercollegiate sports on both the student athlete and the collegiate institution." The studies are expected to evaluate the lives of graduates, assess graduation rates, and assess the impact of athletics on institutional "morale, prestige, and integrity."

Perhaps the forum provided by this national dialogue is an unforeseen opportunity to revitalize and reestablish the role of women. Perhaps the isolation of those who speak "in a different voice" will soon be ameliorated by the earnest desire for serious answers about the difficult questions of athletics in the university. The consequences of decisions made about athletics affect the entire academic community, as is evident on campuses that have had major problems as well as those that have benefited by increased public awareness and prestige. The university, after all, is a community of scholars. Any and all academic or auxiliary enterprises must enhance the role and mission of the institution. The delegation of decisions about "bats and balls" only to those who direct the locker rooms will inevitably lead to episodes that move from the sports page to the front page of our newspapers.

Faculty throughout the university, in their shared governance responsibility, owe it to themselves to enter the coming dialogue. The athletic council might well be placed within faculty governance in order to assure full review of all policies that have a direct impact on the institution's academic environment. The faculty governance body might even establish a task force to augment and supplement official statements of the college or university. Faculty representatives to athletic governing bodies should be expected to transmit the views of the faculty and be held accountable to the faculty as well as the administration.

Athletics as an integrated part of the academic enterprise continues to be an evasive reality. That a women's organization or women in the organization could save the world of college sport from sin was a dream. The mere existence of persons of the female gender has not, can not, and will not alter the deeply entrenched and institutionalized world of college sports. Reform will require the best efforts of all persons in higher education. Our hope is that men and women—faculty and students—will rise to the challenge.

NOTES

1. National Collegiate Athletic Association, *NCAA Manual* (Mission, Kansas: NCAA, 1987), 113.
2. See, Candace Lyle Hogan, "What's in the Future for Women's Sports," *Women's Sports and Fitness* (June 1987):43–48.
3. Vivian Acosta and Linda Carpenter, unpublished paper, Brooklyn College CUNY, 1980.
4. Resa Nelson, "The Impact of Women's Athletic Programs When Athletic Departments Merge," unpublished paper, University of Massachusetts, 1980.
5. Jackie Disselkoen, "The Departing Experience: A Qualitative Study of Personal Accounts by Women Former Athletic Directors of Intercollegiate Athletic Programs for Women," unpublished paper, North Texas State University, 1987.
6. Pat Rosenbrock, "Realities Experienced by Women Athletic Administrators Who Have Persisted in their Roles since the Mid-1970's," unpublished paper, Bemidji State University, 1987.
7. Less than 1 percent of all head coaching positions for men's sports are held by women.
8. See G. Ann Uhlir, "For Whom the Dollars Toll," *Journal of the National Association of Deans, Administrators, and Counselors* 47(Winter 1984):13–22.
9. Vivian Acosta and Linda Carpenter, unpublished paper, Brooklyn College CUNY, 1986.
10. Acosta and Carpenter, 1986.
11. *USA Today*, December 8, 1986, p. 1.
12. Ibid.
13. *NCAA General Information*, brochure, p. 17, 1986–87.
14. *NCAA News*, March 4, 1987, p. 1.
15. *JUCO Review* (February 1987):10–14.
16. *Chronicle of Higher Education*, March 11, 1987, p. 18.

34. *The Importance of Sport in Building Women's Potential*

MARY E. DUQUIN

Relations between the sexes are changing as a result of the technological, economic, and political realities of twentieth century life. According to anthropologist Marvin Harris, the "demise of the marital and procreative imperative has contributed to a rapid and irreversible restructuring of American domestic life and of the American way of love and sex."[1] As parts of the American package, sport and play are also being restructured. Now that life-long reproduction is no longer a cultural mandate, women are expressing their physical and social freedom in many ways, one of them being greater sport participation.[2] As they actively engage in a wide variety of sports, girls and women also develop the skills needed to successfully fulfill personally chosen life goals and lifestyles.

Sport and play provide immediate lessons on living. Women learn about themselves, society, and men. Within the sport environment women become aware of the cultural boundaries which shape their lives and learn to restructure those boundaries or themselves. Through the intellectual and physical exercise involved in sport women discover their physical potentials, test their ambitions, and realize their ability to create their own destiny.

The knowledge women have gained through sport will be explored through five areas: women's sport boundaries, sex-specific sport behavior, definition and designation of sport roles, recognition of injustice, and resistence to exploitation.

BALLPLAYING BOUNDARIES

Social institutions define social reality. The cultural boundaries of female participation in sport are established by *science,* which identifies what females can and cannot do, by the *legal system,* which mandates what they may and may not do, and by the *value shapers,* which stipulate what they should and should not do. Throughout history some women have ignored these boundaries, pursuing their interest in participation, defying fashion, breaking records, and breaking laws. Nevertheless, female sport participation has been limited by the often

SOURCE: Mary E. Duquin, "The Importance of Sport in Building Women's Potential," *Journal of Physical Education, Recreation, and Dance* 53 (March 1982), pp. 18–20, 36.

unsporting standards set by social institutions. Not only the sports which women play, but also the skills they do and do not develop, are a function of cultural codes of conduct. The answer to the mystery of why women perform on the unevens and put the shot, but do not pole vault or throw the hammer, lies less in biology than in the history of cultural institutions.

Experience in sport and other societal areas has taught women that to be self-determined and autonomous, *they* must produce science, write laws, and be sources, as well as transmitters, of society's values. That is, women must exercise greater control over the institutions which create and govern their social and physical reality.

THE PUSH-UP PRINCIPLE

In sport, as in other spheres of activity, women's boundaries often are determined by cultural patterns which label certain behaviors and responsibilities sex-specific. Gerber, however, notes that ". . . being embodied female or male does not necessitate a particular or sex differentiated experience. . . . No inherent or inevitable sensations or understandings or reactions will arise because one experiences the world embodied female or male."[3] Anthropological evidence also reveals that, apart from childbearing, sex-specific behavior has little to do with the biological differences between the sexes. In describing the hard physical life of primitive groups, Harris observes that, ". . . women are physically and mentally capable of performing all the basic tasks of production and subsistence . . . they can hunt with bows and arrows, fish, set traps, and cut down trees . . . they can and do carry heavy burdens . . . work in gardens and fields throughout the world . . . and among many groups . . . are the main food producers."[4] Thus, female-designated behaviors vary from culture to culture. They are further mediated by factors such as race, religion, socioeconomic status, education, occupation, and geographic location. In our culture, the stereotype of male athletic competence and female incompetence wanes when females, through interaction with males, discover that skills and abilities among women and men overlap to a large extent. Through participation women have found that there are greater differences *within* each sex than *between* the sexes.

Like behavior, sex stereotypic images of the aesthetic ideal are culturally relative and vary with time. Such images can be professionally counterproductive particularly when the "feminine ideal" is pictured as a pale, weak, sedentary ectomorph. Although sportswomen are no longer required to curl their hair and wear makeup, dresses, and heels to project the socially defined image of *proper* femininity, they still recognize and feel discriminated against by unprofessional prejudice and ridicule directed toward the mesomorphic female softball player who moves boldly and the ectomorphic male dancer who moves gently.

In sport, women are beginning to examine the foundations of sex-specific behavior, of sex-specific sports and events, of sex-specific rules, of sex-stereotypic sport style, and of the restrictions placed on women in such sports as running, swimming, archery, and sledding. Physiological evidence for the female athletic capability shows such arbitrary limitations on women's sport behavior to be inappropriate and artificial. In determining the basis for sex-differentiated behavior and practice in sport, women are seriously trying to sort out sport practices which genuinely reflect a philosophical commitment to an alternative sport model for all from sport practices which, like the teaching of "girls' push-ups," mainly serve to keep women on their knees.

DESIGNATED DUTIES

Responsibility, like behavior, is often viewed as sex-specific. While knowledge of one's *ability* to perform a role (e.g., mother, athlete) does not necessitate a desire to engage in that behavior, belief in one's *inability* to perform a role is usually accompanied by a lack of desire. Desire to perform depends upon personal belief and perception of the costs and benefits which accrue.

The practice of specifying roles and responsibilities by sex not only ignores information about individual critical strengths, weaknesses, and inclinations, but also tends to accord differential status to the roles played by females and males. Lerner comments:

American women have always shared in the economic life of the nation. . . . Although the majority of women have always worked for the same reason as men—self-support and the support of dependents—their work has been characterized by marginality, temporariness and low status. . . . Typically they have moved into the male-defined work world as outsiders, often treated as intruders. Thus, after each of the major wars in which the nation engaged, women who, during wartime, did all essential work and services, were at war's end shunted back to their traditional jobs.[5]

A similar pattern has taken place in sport. Many women who efficiently organized and administered sport programs during the days of sex segregation found themselves out of jobs when departments merged. In sport, as in the rest of society, leadership is often defined as a male duty.

Legitimate criteria in assigning responsibility are a person's ability and desire to fulfill the roles associated with the task. Both in and out of sport, judgments based on inaccurate perceptions of women's capabilties and interests result in unequal distribution of responsibilities and rewards.

Women have found that the roles played in sport, just as in other spheres of life, are within their ability. Not surprisingly, discovering these abilities has stimulated women's desire to use them.

DOUBLE FAULTING

The fact that one group occupies a lower social position or plays an inferior social role in relation to another group does not necessarily result in the first group feeling oppressed or deprived. Specific knowledges and feelings are prerequisite for personal or group awareness. A group (or person) will feel deprived if they (1) see something others have that they have not, (2) decide they want it, (3) feel they deserve it, (4) think it is possible to get, and (5) believe it is not their fault for not having it.[6]

Oppression is insidious when the oppressed group is socialized to believe they are inferior. The oppressed group comes to believe either that they do not deserve the benefits enjoyed by others or that they are responsible for not achieving them. Thus the failure of equal rights legislation such as Title IX to effect social equity is partially explained by Torney, who states that ". . . 'equal opportunities' will not and cannot lead to social justice where the existence of oppression affects the beliefs and attitudes of some persons to the extent that they are rendered incapable of taking advantage of the supposed opportunities."[7]

In sport, women have learned that if they are to take advantage of equal opportunities, they must be wary of those who would restrict their knowledge, of those who would tell them what they "should" want, of those who would question their deservedness, of those who would claim it is not possible or legal, and of those who would blame women for the inequities which lie within the system.

RESISTENCE RULE

People have a moral responsibility to oppose their own exploitation. To be exploited is to be "used by another person (or group) for his (or their) benefit or gain in a relation where your own interests are either ignored or accorded less than fair consideration."[8]

One technique used in gaining a person's (or group's) consent to exploitation is to encourage the morality of self-sacrifice. The morality of womanly self-sacrifice promotes the view that women have a duty to give the interests of others greater consideration than their own and to assume more than their fair share of burdens and/or take less than their fair share of benefits. Women in sport have long been expected to practice the virtue of self-sacrifice, to coach for no or low pay, to accept unequal job responsibilities and, in addition, to promote among their students a loyalty toward and support of a sport establishment which gives women's athletic interests less than fair consideration. Women have come to understand the relationship between their self-sacrifice and their exploitation and they have witnessed how an exploitive relationship affects everyone negatively. Torney notes the moral imperative to resist exploitation:

> For someone to act without due regard for the interests of others is (at least *prima facie*) wrong. . . . Thus, to consent to exploitation, is either to concur in or to create an opportunity for someone to do something wrong . . . the exploitee is in effect contributing to the moral corruption of the other person in the relation by condoning or encouraging an unfair balance of benefits and burdens. If this relationship continues (and exploitation is ordinarily a long term relation) habits of expectation or traits of character may arise which will carry over into the exploiter's relations with others. They will be expected to acquiesce in the same unfair balance of benefits and burdens the exploiter has come to take for granted from the willing submission to exploitation experienced in the relation in question.[9]

The beginning of the end to this cycle comes when one changes the structure of the relationship. Change in sport happens when individuals challenge old patterns of behavior. As a result of the changing relations between the sexes, both in and out of sport, a myriad of new structural relationships and behavior patterns are emerging.

Sportswomen have a long history of opposition to certain sport roles and practices, such as boxing, athlete exploitation, and sport violence. This opposition has been made on religious, philosophical, moral, and political grounds. While the principle of *equal rights* affirms women's right to be considered for role participation in the sport system as it now exists, *emancipation* requires women's freedom to reject the status quo in favor of an alternative system. The right to participate equally in a male-defined sport system may be a legislative mandate, but it falls far short of the goal of women's defining and administrating all sport.

Those who attempt to change present realities are often accused of "going too far"; they are viewed as radicals, either mad, bad, or both. Women's attempts to exercise control of their physical being often have been met with outrage. As Morgan observes, "An end to foot binding? . . . learning karate . . . abolishing slavery, wife-buying and -selling and -beating, rape, clitoridectomies, butcher-abortions, suttee—attacks on such issues were all radical, 'extremist' notions in their time (in some parts of the world, radical and extreme to this day)."[10] Regardless of the success of such efforts, individuals who try eventually serve as models for others. They create new realities.

For women, to participate in sport is to learn about physical freedom and control. It is to learn about giving the body (self) the freedom to move, to experience, to develop, to risk, to choose. It is to learn about creating a sense of personal control, of joy in self-mastery, of confidence in physical competence, of power in self-determination, of strength in communion with others. Through sport women are learning to expand their freedom and assert their control. Women are becoming aware of the cultural reality which shapes their lives and of their capacity to change it. According to Lerner, "Autonomy for women means moving out from a world in which one is born to marginality, bound to a past without meaning, and prepared for a future determined by others. It means moving into a world in which one acts and chooses, aware of a meaningful past and free to shape one's future."[11] In a complex and heterogeneous culture such as ours, the degree to which a society can cope with change and accommodate diverse beliefs, values, and lifestyles is a measure of its freedom. The degree to which a woman is aware of and able to choose among these alternatives is a measure of her freedom. It is here, now, at this moment that the roles of sport and the sport educator are vital: ". . . to stretch out a hand and whisper, yes, here, step out over the edge. . . ."[12]

REFERENCES

1. Harris, M. "Why It's Not the Same Old America," *Psychology Today,* August 1981, p. 36.
2. Sport is understood to mean any form of physical play, recreation and dance, as well as participation in organized competitive activities.
3. Gerber, E. "My Body, My Self," in *Sport and the Body: A Philosophical Symposium,* Gerber and W. Morgan, eds. Philadelphia: Lea & Febiger, 1979, p. 184.
4. Harris, M. *Cows, Pigs, Wars, and Witches: The Riddles of Culture.* New York: Random House, 1974.
5. Lerner, G. *The Majority Finds Its Past: Placing Women in History.* New York: Oxford University Press, 1979, p. 64.
6. Crosby, F. A. "A Model of Egoistical Deprivation," *Psychological Review* 83, 1976, pp. 85–113.
7. Torney, J. "Exploitation, Oppression, and Self-Sacrifice," in *Women and Philosophy: Toward a Theory of Liberation,* C. C. Gould & M. W. Nartofsky, eds. New York: G. P. Putnam's Sons, 1976, p. 217.
8. Ibid., p. 215.
9. Ibid.
10. Morgan, R. "Metaphysical Feminism," in *Going Too Far,* R. Morgan, ed. New York: Random House, 1978, p. 8.
11. Lerner, op cit., p. 162.
12. Morgan, op cit.

35. *The Meaning of Success: The Athletic Experience and the Development of Male Identity*

MICHAEL MESSNER

Vince Lombardi supposedly said, "Winning isn't everything; it's the only thing," and I couldn't agree more. There's nothing like being number one.

Joe Montana

The big-name athletes will get considerable financial and social remuneration for their athletic efforts. But what of the others, the 99% who fail? Most will fall short of their dreams of a lucrative professional contract. The great majority of athletes, then, will likely suffer disappointment, underemployment, anxiety, or perhaps even serious mental disorders.

Donald Harris and D. Stanley Eitzen

What is the relationship between participation in organized sports and a young male's developing sense of himself as a success or a failure? And what is the consequent impact on his self-image and his ability to engage in intimate relationships with others? Through the late 1960s, it was almost universally accepted that "sports builds character" and that "a winner in sports will be a winner in life." Consequently, some liberal feminists argued that since participation in organized competitive sports has served as a major source of socialization for males' successful participation in the public world, girls and young women should have equal access to sports. Lever, for instance, concluded that if women were ever going to be able to develop the proper competitive values and orientations toward work and success, it was incumbent on them to participate in sports.[1]

In the 1970s and 1980s, these uncritical orientations toward sports have

SOURCE: Michael Messner, "The Meaning of Success: The Athletic Experience and the Development of Male Identity," in *The Making of Masculinities: The New Men's Studies*, edited by Harry Brod (Winchester, Mass.: Allen & Unwin, 1987), pp. 193–209.

been questioned, and the "sports builds character" formula has been found wanting. Sabo points out that the vast majority of research does *not* support the contention that success in sports translates into "work success" or "happiness" in one's personal life.[2] In fact, a great deal of evidence suggests that the contrary is true. Recent critical analyses of success and failure in sports have usually started from assumptions similar to those of Sennett and Cobb and of Rubin:[3] the disjuncture between the *ideology* of success (the Lombardian Ethic) and the socially structured *reality* that most do not "succeed" brings about widespread feelings of failure, lowered self-images, and problems with interpersonal relationships.[4] The most common argument seems to be that the highly competitive world of sports is an exaggerated reflection of advanced industrial capitalism. Within any hierarchy, one can actually work very hard and achieve a lot, yet still be defined (and perceive oneself) as less than successful. Very few people ever reach the mythical "top," but those who do are made ultravisible through the media.[5] It is tempting to view this system as a "structure of failure" because, given the definition of *success*, the system is virtually rigged to bring about the failure of the vast majority of participants. Furthermore, given the dominant values, the participants are apt to blame themselves for their "failure." Schafer argues that the result of this discontinuity between sports values–ideology and reality is a "widespread conditional self-worth" for young athletes.[6] And as Edwards has pointed out, this problem can be even more acute for black athletes, who are disproportionately channeled into sports, yet have no "social safety net" to fall back on after "failure" in sports.

Both the traditional "sports builds character" and the more recent "sports breeds failures" formulas have a common pitfall: Each employs socialization theory in an often simplistic and mechanistic way. Boys are viewed largely as "blank slates" onto which the sports experience imprints values, appropriate "sex-role scripts," and orientations toward self and world. What is usually not taken into account is the fact that boys (and girls) come to the sports experience with an *already gendered* identity that colors their early motivations and perceptions of the meaning of games and sports. As Gilligan points out, observations of young children's game-playing show that girls bring to the activity a more pragmatic and flexible orientation toward the rules—they are more prone to make exceptions and innovations in the middle of the game in order to make the game more "fair" and maintain relationships with others.[7] Boys tend to have a more firm, even inflexible orientation to the rules of a game— they are less willing to change or alter rules in the middle of the game; to them, the rules are what protects any "fairness." This observation has profound implications for sociological research on sports and gender: The question should not be *simply* "how does sports participation affect boys [or girls]?" but should add "what is it about a developing sense of male identity that *attracts* males to sports in the first place? And how does this socially constructed male identity develop and change as it interacts with the structure and values of the sports world?" In addition to being a social–psychological question, this is also a *historical* question: Since men have not at all times and places related to sports the way they at present do, it is important to explore just what kinds of men exist today. What are their needs, problems, and dreams? How do these men relate to the society they live in? And how do organized sports fit into this picture?

THE "PROBLEM OF MASCULINITY" AND ORGANIZED SPORTS

In the first two decades of this century, men feared that the closing of the frontier, along with changes in the workplace, the family, and the schools, was having a "feminizing" influence on society.[8] One result of the anxiety men felt was the creation of the Boy Scouts of America as a separate sphere of social life where "true manliness" could be instilled in boys *by men*.[9] The rapid rise of organized sports in roughly the same era can be attributed largely to the same phenomenon. As socioeconomic and familial changes continued to erode the traditional bases of male identity and privilege, sports became an increasingly important cultural expression of traditional male values—organized sports became a "primary masculinity-validating experience."[10]

In the post-World War II era, the bureaucratization and rationalization of work, along with the decline of the family wage and women's gradual movement into the labor force, have further undermined the "breadwinner role" as a basis for male identity, thus resulting in a "problem of masculinity" and a "defensive insecurity" among men.[11] As Mills put it, the ethic of success in postwar America "has become less widespread as fact, more confused as image, often dubious as motive, and soured as a way of life [Yet] there are still compulsions to struggle, to 'amount to something'."[12]

How have men expressed this need to "amount to something" within a social context that seems to deny them the opportunities to do so? Again, organized sports play an important role. Both on a personal–existential level for athletes and on a symbolic–ideological level for spectators and fans, sports have become one of the "last bastions" of traditional male ideas of success, of male power and superiority over—and separation from—the perceived "feminization" of society. It is likely that the rise of football as "America's number-one game" is largely the result of the comforting *clarity* it provides between the polarities of traditional male power, strength, and violence and the contemporary fears of social feminization.

But these historical explanations for the increased importance of sports, despite their validity, beg some important questions: Why do men fear the (real or imagined) "feminization" of their world? Why do men appear to need a separate male sphere of life? Why do organized sports appear to be such an attractive means of expressing these needs? Are males simply "socialized" to dominate women and to compete with other men for status, or are they seeking (perhaps unconsciously) something more fundamental? Just what is it that men really *want?* To begin to answer these questions, it is necessary to listen to athletes' voices and examine their lives within a social–psychological perspective.

Daniel Levinson's concept of the "individual life structure" is a useful place to begin to construct a gestalt of the life of the athlete.[13] Levinson demonstrates that as males develop and interact with their world, they continue to change throughout their lives. A common theme during developmental periods is the process of individuation, the struggle to separate, to "decide where he stops and where the world begins." "In successive periods of development, as this process goes on, the person forms a clearer boundary between self and world. . . . Greater individuation allows him to be more separate from the world, to be more independent and self-generating. But it also gives him the confidence and understanding to have more intense attachments in the world and to feel more fully a part of it."[14]

This dynamic of separation and attachment provides a valuable social–psychological framework for examining the experiences and problems faced by the athlete as he gropes for and redefines success throughout his life course. In what follows, Levinson's framework is utilized to analyze the lives of 30 former athletes interviewed between 1983 and 1984. Their *interactions* with sports are examined in terms of their initial boyhood attraction to sports; how notions of success in sports connect with a developing sense of male identity; and how self-images, relationships to work and other people, change and develop after the sports career ends.

BOYHOOD: THE PROMISE OF SPORTS

Given how very few athletes actually "make it" through sports, how can the intensity with which millions of boys and young men throw themselves into athletics be explained? Are they simply pushed, socialized, or even *duped* into putting so much emphasis on athletic success? It is important here to examine just what it is that young males hope to get out of the athletic experience. And in terms of *identity*, it is crucial to examine the ways in which the structure and experience of sports activity meets the developmental needs of young males. The story of Willy Rios sheds light on what these needs are. Rios was born in Mexico and moved to the United States at a fairly young age. He never knew his father, and his mother died when he was only 9 years old. Suddenly he felt rootless, and at this time he threw himself into sports, but his initial motivations do not appear to be based upon a need to compete and win. "Actually, what I think sports did for me is it brought me into kind of an instant family. By being on a Little League team, or even just playing with all kinds of different kids in the neighborhood, it brought what I really wanted, which was some kind of closeness."

Similar statements from other men suggest that a fundamental motivational factor behind many young males' sports strivings is a need for connection, "closeness" with others. But why do so many boys see *sports* as an attractive means of establishing connection with others? Chodorow argues that the process of developing a gender identity yields insecurity and ambivalence in males.[15] Males develop "rigid ego boundaries" that ensure separation from others, yet they retain a basic human need for closeness and intimacy with others. The young male, who both seeks and fears attachment with others, thus finds the rulebound structure of games and sports to be a psychologically "safe" place in which he can get (nonintimate) connection with others within a context that maintains clear boundaries, distance, and separation from others. At least for the boy who has some early successes in sports, some of these ambivalent needs can be met, for a time. But there is a catch: For Willy Rios, it was only after he learned that he would get attention (a certain kind of connection) from other people for being a good athlete—indeed, that this attention was *contingent* on his *being good*—that narrow definitions of success, based on performance and winning, became important to him. It was years before he realized that no matter how well he performed, how successful he became, he would not get the closeness that he craved through sports. "It got to be a product in high school. Before, it was just fun, and having acceptance, you know. Yet I had to work for my acceptance in high school that way, just being a jock. So it wasn't fun any more. But it was my self-identity, being a good ballplayer. I was realizing that whatever you excel in, you put out in front of you. Bring it out. Show it. And that's what I did. That was my protection. . . . It was rotten in high school, really."

This conscious striving for successful achievement becomes the primary means through which the young athlete seeks connections with other people. But the irony of the situation, for so many boys and young men like Willy Rios, is that the athletes are seeking to get something from their success in sports that sports usually cannot deliver—and the *pressure* that they end up putting on themselves to achieve that success ends up stripping them of the ability to receive the one major thing that sports really *does* have to offer: fun.

ADOLESCENCE: YOU'RE ONLY AS GOOD AS YOUR LAST GAME

Adolescence is probably the period of greatest insecurity in the life course, the time when the young male becomes most vulnerable to peer expectations, pressures, and judgments. None of the men interviewed for this study, regardless of their social class or ethnicity, seemed fully able to "turn a deaf ear to the crowd" during their athletic careers. The crowd, which may include immediate family, friends, peers, teammates, as well as the more anonymous fans and media, appears to be a crucially important part of the process of establishing and maintaining the self-images of young athletes. By the time they were in high school, most of the men interviewed for this study had found sports to be a primary means through which to establish a sense of manhood in the world. Especially if they were good athletes, the expectations of the crowd became very powerful and were internalized (and often *magnified*) within the young man's own expectations. As one man stated, by the time he was in high school, "it was *expected* of me to do well in all of my contests—I mean by my coach and my peers, and my family. So I in turn expected to do well, and if I didn't do well, then I'd be very disappointed."

When so much is tied to your performance, the dictum that "you are only as good as your last game" is a powerful judgment. It means that the young man must continually prove, achieve, and then *re*prove, and *re*achieve his status. As a result, many young athletes learn to seek and *need* the appreciation of the crowd to feel that they are worthy human beings. But the internalized values of masculinity along with the insecure nature of the sports world mean that the young man does *not* need the crowd to feel *bad* about himself. In fact, if one is insecure enough, even "success" and the compliments and attention of other people can come to feel hollow and meaningless. For instance, 48-year-old Russ Ellis in his youth shared the basic sense of insecurity common to all young males, and in his case it was probably compounded by his status as a poor black male and an insecure family life. Athletics emerged early in his life as the primary arena in which he and his male peers competed to establish a sense of self in the world. For Ellis, his small physical stature made it difficult to compete successfully in most sports, thus feeding his insecurity—he just never felt as though he belonged with "the big boys." Eventually, though, he became a top middle-distance runner. In high school, however: "Something began to happen there that later plagued me quite a bit. I started doing very well and winning lots of races and by the time the year was over, it was no longer a question for me of *placing*, but *winning*. That attitude really destroyed me ultimately. I would get into the blocks with worries that I wouldn't do well—the regular stomach problems—so I'd often run much less well than my abilities—that is, say, I'd take second or third."

Interestingly, his nervousness, fears, and anxieties did not seem to be visible to "the crowd": "I know in high school, certainly, they saw me as confident and ready to run. No one assumed I could be beaten, which fascinated me, because I had never been good at understanding how I was taken in other people's minds—maybe because I spent so much time inventing myself in their regard in my own mind. I was projecting my fear fantasies on them and taking them for reality."

In 1956 Ellis surprised everyone by taking second place in a world-class field of quarter-milers. But the fact that they ran the fastest time in the world,

46.5, seemed only to "up the ante," to increase the pressures on Ellis, then in college at UCLA.

Up to that point I had been a nice zippy kid who did good, got into the *Daily Bruin* a lot, and was well-known on campus. But now an event would come up and the papers would say, "Ellis to face so-and-so." So rather than my being *in* the race, I *was* the race, as far as the press was concerned. And that put a lot of pressure on me that I never learned to handle. What I did was to internalize it, and then I'd sit there and fret and lose sleep, and focus more on not winning than on how I was doing. And in general, I didn't do badly—like one year in the NCAA's I took fourth—you know, in the *national finals*. But I was focused on winning. You know, later on, people would say, "Oh wow, you took fourth in the NCAA?—you were *that good*?" Whereas I thought of these things as *failures*, you know?

Finally, Ellis's years of training, hopes, and fears came to a head at the 1956 Olympic trials, where he failed to qualify, finishing fifth. A rival whom he used to defeat routinely won the event in the Melbourne Olympics as Ellis watched on television. "That killed me. Destroyed me . . . I had the experience many times after that of digging down and finding that there was infinitely more down there than I ever got—I mean, I know that more than I know anything else. Sometimes I would really feel like an eagle, running. Sometimes in practice at UCLA running was just exactly like flying—and if I could have carried that attitude into events, I would have done much better. But instead, I'd worry. Yeah, I'd worry myself sick."

As suggested earlier, young males like Russ Ellis are "set up" for disappointment, or worse, by the disjuncture between the narrow Lombardian definition of success in the sports world and the reality that very few ever actually reach the top. The athlete's sense of identity established through sports is therefore insecure and problematic, *not simply* because of the high probability of "failure," but also because *success* in the sports world involves the development of a personality that *amplifies* many of the most ambivalent and destructive traits of traditional masculinity. Within the hierarchical world of sports, which in many ways mirrors the capitalist economy, one learns that if he is to survive and avoid being pushed off the ever-narrowing pyramid of success, he must develop certain kinds of relationships—to himself, to his body, to other people, and to the sport itself. In short, the successful athlete must develop a highly goal-oriented personality that encourages him to view his body as a tool, a machine, or even a weapon utilized to defeat an objectified opponent. He is likely to have difficulty establishing intimate and lasting friendships with other males because of low self-disclosure, homophobia, and cut-throat competition. And he is likely to view his public image as a "success" as far more basic and fundamental than any of his interpersonal relationships.

For most of the men interviewed, the quest for success was not the grim task it was for Russ Ellis. Most men did seem to get, at least for a time, a sense of identity (and even some happiness) out of their athletic accomplishments. The attention of the crowd, for many, affirmed their existence as males and was thus a clear motivating force. Gary Affonso, now 42 years old and a high school coach, explained that when he was in high school, he had an "intense desire to practice and compete." "I used to practice the high jump by myself for hours at a time—only got up to 5'3"—scissor! [*Laughs*] but I think part of it was, the track itself was in view of some of the classrooms, and so as I think back now, maybe I did it for the attention, to be seen. In my freshman year, I chipped my two front teeth in a football game, and after that I always had a gold tooth, and I was always self-conscious about that. Plus I had my glasses, you know. I felt a little conspicuous." This simultaneous shyness, self-consciousness, and conspicuousness *along with* the strongly felt need for attention and external validation (attachment) so often characterize athletes' descriptions of themselves in boyhood and adolescence. The crowd, in this context, can act as a distant, and thus nonthreatening, source of attention and validation of self for the insecure male. Russ Ellis's story typifies that what sports seem to *promise* the young male—affirmation of self and connection with others—is likely to be *undermined* by the youth's actual experience in the sports world. The athetic experience also "sets men up" for another serious problem: the end of a career at a very young age.

DISENGAGEMENT TRAUMA: A CRISIS OF MALE IDENTITY

For some, the end of the athletic career approaches gradually like the un-wanted houseguest whose eventual arrival is at least *known* and can be planned for, thus limiting the inevitable inconvenience. For others, the ath-letic career ends with the shocking suddenness of a violent thunderclap that rudely awakens one from a pleasant dream. But whether it comes gradually or suddenly, the end of the playing career represents the termination of what has often become the *central aspect* of a young male's individual life structure, thus initiating change and transition in the life course.

Previous research on the disengagement crises faced by many retiring athletes has focused on the health, occupational, and financial problems fre-quently faced by retiring professionals.[16] These problems are especially severe for retiring black athletes, who often have inadequate educational back-grounds and few opportunities within the sports world for media or coaching jobs.[17] But even for those retiring athletes who avoid the pitfalls of financial and occupational crises, substance abuse, obesity, and ill health, the end of the playing career usually involves a crisis of identity. This identity crisis is probably most acute for retiring *professional* athletes, whose careers are com-ing to an end right at an age when most men's careers are beginning to take off. As retired professional football player Marvin Upshaw stated, "You find yourself just scrambled. You don't know which way to go. Your light, as far as you're concerned, has been turned out. You miss the roar of the crowd. Once you're heard it, you can't get away from it. There's an empty feeling—you feel everything you wanted is gone. All of a sudden you wake up and you find yourself 29, 35 years old, you know, and the one thing that has been the major part of your life is gone. It's gone."

High school and college athletes also face serious and often painful adjustment periods when their career ends. Twenty-six-year-old Dave Joki had been a good high school basketball player, and had played a lot of ball in college. When interviewed, he was right in the middle of a confusing crisis of identity, closely related to his recent disengagement from viewing himself as an athlete. "These past few months I've been trying a lot of different things, thinking about different careers, things to do. There's been quite a bit of stumbling—and I think that part of my tenuousness about committing myself to any one thing is I'm not sure I'm gonna get strokes if I go that way. [*Embarrassed, nervous laugh.*] It's scary for me and I stay away from searching for those reasons . . . I guess you could say that I'm stumbling in my relationships too—stumbling in all parts of life. [*Laughs.*] I feel like I'm doing a lot but not knowing what I want."

Surely there is nothing unusual about a man in his mid 20s "stumbling" around and looking for direction in his work and his relationships. That is common for men of this age. But for the former athlete, this stumbling is often more confusing and problematic than for other men precisely because he has lost the one activity through which he had built his sense of identity, however tenuous it may have been. The "strokes" he received from being a good athlete were his major psychological foundation. The interaction between self and other through which the athlete attempts to solidify his identity is akin to what Cooley called "the looking-glass self." If the athletic activity and the crowd can be viewed as a *mirror* into which the athlete gazes and, in Russ Ellis's words, "invents himself," we can begin to appreciate how devastating it can be when that looking-glass is suddenly and permanently *shattered*, leaving the young man alone, isolated, and disconnected. And since young men often feel comfortable exploring close friendships and intimate relationships only *after* they have established their separate work-related (or sports-related) positional identity, relationships with other people are likely to become more problematic than ever during disengagement.

WORK, LOVE, AND MALE IDENTITY
AFTER DISENGAGEMENT

Eventually, the former athlete must face reality: At a relatively young age, he has to start over. In the words of retired major league baseball player Ray Fosse, "Now I gotta get on with the rest of it." How is "the rest of it" likely to take shape for the athlete after his career as a player is over? How do men who are "out of the limelight" for a few years come to define themselves as men? How do they define and redefine success? How do the values and attitudes they learned through sports affect their lives? How do their relationships with friends and family change over time?

Many retired athletes retain a powerful drive to reestablish the important relationship with the crowd that served as the primary basis for their identity for so long. Many men throw themselves wholeheartedly into a new vocation—or a confusing *series* of vocations—in a sometimes pathetic attempt to recapture the "high" of athletic competition as well as the status of the successful athlete in the community. For instance, 35-year-old Jackie Ridgle is experiencing what Daniel Levinson calls a "surge of masculine strivings" common to men in their mid 30s.[18] Once a professional basketball player, Ridgle seems motivated now by a powerful drive to be seen once again as "somebody" in the eyes of the public. When interviewed, he had recently been hired as an assistant college basketball coach, which made him feel like he again had a chance to "be somebody."

> When I say "successful," that means somebody that the public looks up to just as a basketball player. Yet you don't have to be playing basketball. You can be anybody: You can be a senator or a mayor, or any number of things. That's what I call successful. Success is recognition. Sure, I'm always proud of myself. But there's that little goal there that until people respect you, then—[*Snaps fingers.*] Anybody can say, "Oh, I know I'm the greatest thing in the world," but *people* run the world, and when *they* say you're successful, then you *know* you're successful.

Indeed, men, especially men in early adulthood, usually define themselves primarily in terms of their position in the public world of work. Feminist literature often criticizes this establishment of male identity in terms of work–success as an expression of male privilege and ego satisfaction that comes at the expense of women and children. There is a great deal of truth to the feminist critique: A man's socially defined need to establish himself as "somebody" in the (mostly) male world of work is often accompanied by his frequent physical absence from home and his emotional distance from the family. Thus, while the man is "out there" establishing his "name" in public, the woman is usually home caring for the day-to-day and moment-to-moment needs of her family (regardless of whether or not she also has a job in the paid labor force). Tragically, only in midlife, when the children have already "left the nest" and the woman is often ready to go out into the public world, do some men discover the importance of connection and intimacy.

Yet the interviews indicate that there is not always such a clean and clear "before–after" polarity in the lives of men between work–success and care–intimacy. The "breadwinner ethic" as a male role *has* most definitely contributed to the perpetuation of male privilege and the subordination and economic dependence of women as mothers and housekeepers. But given the reality of the labor market, where women still make only 62 cents to the male dollar, many men feel very responsible for providing the majority of the income and financial security for their families. For instance, 36-year-old Ray Fosse, whose father left his family when he was quite young, has a very strong sense of commitment and responsibility as a provider of income and stability in his own family.

> I'm working an awful lot these days, and trying not to take time away from my family. A lot of times I'm putting the family to sleep, and working late hours and going to bed and getting up early and so forth. I've tried to tell my family this a lot of times: The work that I'm doing now is gonna make it easier in a few years. That's the reason I'm working now, to get that financial security, and I feel like it's coming very soon . . . but, uh, you know, you go a long day and you come home, and it's just not the quality time you'd like to have. And I think when that financial security comes in, then I'm gonna be able to forget about everything.

Jackie Ridgle's words mirror Fosse's. His two jobs and strivings to be successful in the public world mean that he has little time to spend with his wife and three children. "I plan to someday. Very seldom do you have enough time to spend with your kids, especially nowadays, so I don't get hung up on that. The wife do sometimes, but as long as I keep a roof over their heads and let 'em know who's who, well, one day they'll respect me. But I can't just get bogged down and take any old job, you know, a filling station job or something. Ah, hell, they'll get more respect, my kids for me, right now, than they would if I was somewhere just a regular worker."

Especially for men who have been highly successful athletes (and never have had to learn to "lose gracefully"), the move from sports to work–career as a means of establishing connection and identity in the world is a "natural" transition. Breadwinning becomes a man's socially learned means of seeking attachment, both with his family and, more abstractly, with "society." What is salient (and sometimes tragic) is that the care that a woman gives her family usually puts her into direct daily contact with her family's physical, psychological, and emotional needs. A man's care is usually expressed more abstractly, often in his absence, as his work removes him from day-to-day, moment-to-moment contact with his family.

A man may want, even *crave*, more direct connection with his family, but that connection, and the *time* it takes to establish and maintain it, may cause him to lose the competitive edge he needs to win in the world of work—and that is the arena in which he feels he will ultimately be judged in terms of his success or failure as a man. But it is not simply a matter of *time* spent away from the family which is at issue here. As Dizard's research shows clearly, the more "success oriented" a man is, the more "instrumental" his personality will tend to be, thus increasing the psychological and emotional distance between himself and his family.[19]

CHANGING MEANINGS OF SUCCESS IN MIDLIFE

The intense, sometimes obsessive, early adulthood period of striving for work and career success that we see in the lives of Jackie Ridgle and Ray Fosse often begins to change in midlife, when many men experience what Levinson calls "detribalization." Here, the man "becomes more critical of the tribe—the particular groups, institutions, and traditions that have the greatest significance for him, the social matrix to which he is most attached. He is less dependent upon tribal rewards, more questioning of tribal values. . . . The result of this shift is normally not a marked disengagement from the external world but a greater integration of attachment and separateness."[20]

Detribalization—putting less emphasis on how one is defined by others and becoming more self-motivated and self-generating—is often accompanied by a growing sense of *flawed* or *qualified* success. A man's early adulthood dream of success begins to tarnish, appearing more and more as an illusion. Or, the success that a man *has* achieved begins to appear hollow and meaningless, possibly because it has not delivered the closeness he truly craves. The fading, or the loss, of the dream involves a process of mourning, but, as Levinson points out, it can also be a very liberating process in opening the man up for new experiences, new kinds of relationships, and new dreams.

For instance, Russ Ellis states that a few years ago he experienced a midlife crisis when he came to the realization that "I was never going to be on the cover of *Time*." His wife had a T-shirt made for him with the message *Dare to Be Average* emblazoned on it.

> And it doesn't really *mean* dare to be average—it means dare to take the pressure off yourself, you know? Dare to be a normal person. It gets a funny reaction from people. I think it hits at that place where somehow we all think that we're going to wind up on the cover of *Time* or something, you know? Do you have that? That some day, somewhere, you're gonna be *great*, and everyone will know, everyone will recognize it? Now, I'd rather be great because I'm *good*—and maybe that'll turn into something that's acknowledged, but not at the headline level. I'm not racing so much; I'm concerned that my feet are planted on the ground and that I'm good.
>
> [It sounds like you're running now, as opposed to racing?]
>
> I guess—but running and racing have the same goals. [*Laughs, pauses, then speaks more thoughtfully.*] But maybe you're right—that's a wonderful analogy. Pacing myself. Running is more intelligent—more familiarity with your abilities, your patterns of workouts, who you're running against, the nature of the track, your position, alertness. You have more of an internal clock.

Russ Ellis's midlife detribalization—his transition from a "racer" to a "runner"—has left him more comfortable with himself, with his abilities and limitations. He has also experienced an expansion of his ability to experience intimacy with a woman. He had never been comfortable with the "typical jock attitude" toward sex and women,

> but I generally maintained a performance attitude about sex for a long time, which was not as enjoyable as it became after I learned to be more like what I thought a woman was like. In other words, when I let myself experience my own body, in a delicious and receptive way rather than in a power, overwhelming way. That was wonderful! [*Laughs*.] To experience my body as someone desired and given to. That's one of the better things. I think I only achieved that very profound intimacy that's found between people, really quite extraordinary, quite recently. [*Long pause*.] It's quite something, quite something. And I feel more fully inducted into the human race by knowing about that.

TOWARD A REDEFINITION OF SUCCESS AND MASCULINITY

"A man in America is a failed boy," wrote John Updike in 1960. Indeed, Updike's ex-athlete Rabbit Angstrom's struggles to achieve meaning and identity in midlife reflect a common theme in modern literature. Social scientific research has suggested that the contemporary sense of failure and inadequacy felt by many American males is largely the result of unrealistic and unachievable social definitions of masculinity and success.[21] This research has suggested that there is more to it than that. Contemporary males often feel empty, alienated, isolated, and as failures because the socially learned means through which they seek validation and identity (achievement in the public worlds of sports and work) do not deliver what is actually craved and needed: intimate connection and unity with other human beings. In fact, the lure of sports becomes a sort of trap. For boys who experience early success in sports, the resulting attention they receive becomes a convenient and attractive means of experiencing attachment with other people within a social context that allows the young male to maintain his "firm ego boundaries" and thus his separation from others. But it appears that, more often than not, athletic participation serves only to exacerbate the already problematic, insecure, and ambivalent nature of males' self-images, and thus their ability to establish and maintain close and intimate relationships with other people. Some men, as they reach midlife, eventually achieve a level of individuation—often through a midlife crisis—that leads to a redefinition of success and an expansion of their ability to experience attachment and intimacy.

Men's personal definitions of success often change in midlife, but this research, as well as that done by Farrell and Rosenberg,[22] suggests that only a *portion* of males experience a midlife crisis that results in the man's transcending his instrumental personality in favor of a more affective generativity. The midlife discovery that the achievement game is an unfulfilling rat race can as easily lead to cynical detachment and greater alienation as it can to detribalization and expanded relational capacities. In other words, there is no assurance that Jackie Ridgle, as he ages, will transform himself from a "racer" to a "runner," as Russ Ellis has. Even if he does change in this way, it is likely that he will have missed participating in the formative years of his children's lives.

Thus the fundamental questions facing future examinations of men's lives should focus on building an understanding of just what are the keys to such a shift at midlife? How are individual men's changes, crises, and relationships affected, shaped, and sometimes contradicted by the social, cultural, and political contexts in which they find themselves? And what *social* changes might make it more likely that boys and men might have more balanced personalities and needs at an *early* age?

An analysis of men's lives that simply describes personal changes while taking social structure as a given cannot adequately *ask* these questions. But an analysis that not only describes changes in male identity throughout the life course but also critically examines the socially structured and defined meaning of "masculinity" can and must ask these questions.

If many of the problems faced by all men (not just athletes) today are to be dealt with, class, ethnic, and sexual preference divisions must be confronted. This would necessarily involve the development of a more cooperative and nurturant ethic among men, as well as a more egalitarian and democratically organized economic system. And since the sports world is an important cultural process that serves partly to socialize boys and young men to hierarchical, competitive and aggressive values, the sporting arena is an important context in which to begin to confront the need for a humanization of men.

Yet, if the analysis presented here is correct, the developing psychology of young boys is predisposed to be attracted to the present structure and values of the sports world, so any attempt *simply* to infuse cooperative and egalitarian values into sports is likely to be an exercise in futility. The need for equality between men and women, in the public realm as well as in the home, is a fundamental prerequisite for the humanization of men, sports, and society. One of the most important changes that men could make would be to become more equally involved in parenting. The development of early bonding between fathers and infants (in addition to that between mothers and infants), along with nonsexist childrearing in the family, schools, and sports would have far-reaching effects on society: Boys and men could grow up more psychologically secure, more able to develop balance between separation and attachment, more able at an earlier age to appreciate intimate relationships with other men without destructive and crippling competition and homophobia. A young male with a more secure and balanced personality might also be able to *enjoy* athletic activities for what they really have to offer: the opportunity to engage in healthy exercise, to push oneself toward excellence, and to bond together with others in a challenging and fun activity.

NOTES

1. J. Lever, "Sex Differences in the Games Children Play," *Social Problems* 23 (1976).
2. D. Sabo, "Sport Patriarchy and Male Identity: New Questions about Men and Sport,"*Arena Review*, 9, no. 2, 1985.
3. R. Sennett and J. Cobb, *The Hidden Injuries of Class* (New York: Random House, 1973); and L. B. Rubin, *Worlds of Pain: Life in the Working Class Family* (New York: Basic Books, 1976).
4. D. W. Ball, "Failure in Sport," *American Sociological Review* 41 (1976); J. J. Coakley, *Sports in Society* (St. Louis: Mosby, 1978); D. S. Harris and D. S. Eitzen, "The Consequences of Failure in Sport," *Urban Life* 7 (July 1978): 2; G. B. Leonard, "Winning Isn't Everything: It's Nothing," in *Jock: Sports and Male Identity*, ed. D. Sabo and R. Runfola (Englewood Cliffs, N.J.: Prentice-Hall, 1980); W. E. Schafer, "Sport and Male Sex Role Socialization," *Sport Sociology Bulletin* 4 (Fall 1975); R. C. Townsend, "The Competitive Male as Loser," in Sabo and Runfola, eds., *Jock;* and T. Tutko and W. Bruns, *Winning Is Everything and Other American Myths* (New York: Macmillan, 1976).
5. In contrast with the importance put on success by millions of boys, the number who "make it" is incredibly small. There are approximately 600 players in major-league baseball, with an average career span of 7 years. Approximately 6–7% of all high school football players ever play in college. Roughly 8% of all draft-eligible college football and basketball athletes are drafted by the pros, and only 2% ever sign a professional contract. The average career for NFL athletes is now 4 years, and for the NBA it is only 3.4 years. Thus the odds of getting anywhere *near* the top are very thin—and if one is talented and lucky enough to get there, his stay will be brief. See H. Edwards, "The Collegiate Athletic Arms Race: Origins and Implications of the 'Rule 48' Controversy," *Journal of Sport and Social Issues* 8, no. 1 (Winter–Spring 1984); Harris and Eitzen, "Consequences of Failure," and P. Hill and B. Lowe, "The Inevitable Metathesis of the Retiring Athlete," *International Review of Sport Sociology* 9, nos. 3–4 (1978).
6. Schafer, "Sport and Male Sex Role," p. 50.
7. C. Gilligan, *In a Different Voice: Psychological Theory and Women's Development* (Cambridge: Harvard University Press, 1982); J. Piaget, *The Moral Judgment of the Child* (New York: Free Press, 1965); and Lever, "Games Children Play."
8. P. G. Filene, *Him/Her/Self: Sex Roles in Modern America* (New York: Harcourt Brace Jovanovich, 1975).
9. J. Hantover, "The Boy Scouts and the Validation of Masculinity," *Journal of Social Issues* 34 (1978): 1.
10. J. L. Dubbert, *A Man's Place: Masculinity in Transition* (Englewood Cliffs, N.J.: Prentice-Hall, 1979).
11. A. Tolson, *The Limits of Masculinity* (New York: Harper & Row, 1977).
12. C. W. Mills, *White Collar* (London: Oxford University Press, 1951).
13. D. J. Levinson, *The Seasons of a Man's Life* (New York: Ballantine, 1978).
14. Ibid., p. 195.
15. N. Chodorow, *The Reproduction of Mothering* (Berkeley: University of California Press, 1978).
16. Hill and Lowe, "Metathesis of Retiring Athlete," pp. 3–4; and B. D. McPherson, "Former Professional Athletes' Adjustment to Retirement," *Physician and Sports Medicine*, August 1978.
17. Edwards, "Collegiate Athletic Arms Race."
18. Levinson, *Seasons of a Man's Life*.
19. J. E. Dizard, "The Price of Success," in *Social Change in the Family*, ed. J. E. Dizard (Chicago: Community and Family Study Center, University of Chicago, 1968).
20. Levinson, *Seasons of a Man's Life*, p. 242.
21. J. H. Pleck, *The Myth of Masculinity* (Cambridge: MIT Press, 1982); Sennett and Cobb, *The Hidden Injuries of Class;* Rubin, *Worlds of Pain;* and Tolson, *Limits of Masculinity*.
22. M. P. Farrell and S. D. Rosenberg, *Men at Midlife* (Boston: Auburn House, 1981).

■ FOR FURTHER STUDY

Allison, Maria T., and Beverly Butler. "Role Conflict and the Elite Female Athlete." *International Review for the Sociology of Sport* 19, no. 2 (1984): 157–168.

Boutilier, Mary A., and Lucinda SanGiovanni. *The Sporting Woman*. Champaign, Ill.: Human Kinetics, 1983.

Carpenter, Linda Jean. "The Impact of Title IX on Women's Intercollegiate Sports." In *Government and Sport*, edited by Arthur T. Johnson and James H. Frey. Totowa, N.J.: Rowman and Allanheld, 1985, 62–78.

Cheska, Alyce Taylor, ed. "Women's Sports: A Paradox of Equality?" *Arena Review* 4 (May 1980): entire issue.

Chorbajian, Leon. "The Social Psychology of American Males and Spectator Sports." *International Journal of Sport Psychology* 9, no. 3 (1978): 165–175.

Clement, Annie. "Professional Female Athletes: Financial Opportunities." *Journal of Physical Education, Recreation, and Dance* 58 (March 1987): 37–40.

"Comes the Revolution: Joining the Game at Last, Women are Transforming American Athletics." *Time* (June 26, 1978): 54–60.

Curry, Timothy J., and Robert M. Jiobu. *Sports: A Social Perspective*. Englewood Cliffs, N.J.: Prentice-Hall, 1984, pp. 159–195.

Davenport, Joanna. "The Women's Movement into the Olympic Games." *JOPER* 39 (March 1978): 58–60.

De Beauvoir, Simone. *The Second Sex*. New York: Alfred A. Knopf, 1952.

De Crow, Karen. "Hardlining Title IX." *Civil Rights Quarterly Perspectives* 12 (Summer 1980): 16–23.

Duquin, Mary E. "The Androgynous Advantage." In *Women and Sport: From Myth to Reality*, edited by Carole A. Oglesby. Philadelphia: Lea & Febiger, 1978, pp. 471–483.

Felshin, Jan, and Carole A. Oglesby. "Transcending Tradition: Females and Males in Open Competition." *Journal of Physical Education, Recreation, and Dance* 57 (March 1986): 44–47, 64.

Hall, M. Ann. *Sport and Gender: A Feminist Perspective on the Sociology of Sport*. CAHPER monograph (no date).

Hall, M. Ann. "Knowledge and Gender: Epistemological Questions in the Social Analysis of Sport." *Sociology of Sport Journal* 2 (March 1985): 25–42.

Hall, M. Ann, and Dorothy A. Richardson. *Fair Ball: Toward Sex Equality in Canadian Sport*. Ottawa: Canadian Advisory Council on the Status of Women, 1984.

Hannon, Kent. "Too Far, Too Fast." *Sports Illustrated* (March 20, 1978): 34–45.

Harris, Dorothy V. "Femininity and Athleticism." In *Handbook of Social Science of Sport*, edited by Gunther Luschen and George H. Sage. Champaign, Ill.: Stipes, 1981, pp. 274–294.

Hilliard, Dan C. "Media Images of Male and Female Professional Athletes." *Sociology of Sport Journal* 1, no. 3 (1984): 251–262.

Holland, Judith R., and Carole Oglesby. "Women in Sport: The Synthesis Begins." *The Annals* 445 (September 1979): 81–90.

Howell, Reet, ed. *Her Story in Sport: A Historical Anthology of Women in Sports*. Champaign, Ill.: Human Kinetics, 1982.

Johnsen, Kathryn P. "The Development and Maintenance of Gender Differences Through Sports." In *Social Approaches to Sport*, edited by Robert M. Pankin. London: Associated University Presses, 1982, pp. 90–103.

Krotee, March L. "The Battle of the Sexes: A Brawl in the Locker Room." *Journal of Sport and Social Issues* 5 (Fall/Winter 1982): 15–23.

Lenskyi, Helen. *Out of Bounds: Women, Sport and Sexuality*. Toronto: Women's Press, 1986.

Lever, Janet. "Sex Differences in the Complexity of Children's Play and Games." *American Sociological Review* 43 (August 1978): 471–483.

Lopiano, Donna A. "A Political Analysis of the Possibility of Impact Alternatives for the Accomplishment of Feminist Objectives within American Intercollegiate Sport." *Arena Review* 8 (July 1984): 49–61.

Mechekoff, Robert A., with Virginia Evans. *Sport Psychology for Women*. New York: Harper & Row, 1987.

Messner, Michael. "The Changing Meaning of Male Identity in the Lifecourse of the Athlete." *Arena Review* 9 (November 1985): 31–60.

Rintala, Jan, and Susan Birrell. "Fair Treatment for the Active Female: A Content Analysis of *Young Athlete Magazine*." *Sociology of Sport Journal* 1, no. 2 (1984): 231–250.

Rohrbaugh, Joanna Bunker. "Femininity on the Line." *Psychology Today* (August 1979): 30–42.

Sabo, Donald F., Jr., and Ross Runfola, eds. *Jock: Sports and Male Identity*. Englewood Cliffs, N.J.: Prentice-Hall, 1980.

Sage, George H., and Sheryl Loudermilk. "The Female Athlete and Role Conflict." *Research Quarterly* 50, (no. 1, 1979): 88–96.

Schafer, Walter E. "Sport and Male Sex-Role Socialization." *Sport Sociology Bulletin*, 4 (Fall 1975): 47–54.

Selden, Gary. "Frailty, Thy Name's Been Changed: What Sports Medicine Is Discovering About Women's Bodies." *Ms.* 10 (July 1981): 51–53, 96.

Slatton, Bonnie, and Susan Birrell. "The Politics of Women's Sport." *Arena Review* 8 (July 1984): entire issue.

Snyder, Eldon E., and Joseph E. Kivlin. "Women Athletes and Aspects of Psychological Well-Being and Body Image." *Research Quarterly* 46 (May 1975): 191–199.

Snyder, Eldon E., and Joseph E. Kivlin. "Perceptions of the Sex Role Among Female Athletes and Nonathletes." *Adolescence* 12 (Spring 1977): 23–29.

Snyder, Eldon E., Joseph E. Kivlin, and Elmer Spreitzer. "The Female Athlete: An Analysis of Objective and Subjective Role Conflict." In *Psychology of Sport and Motor Behavior*, edited by Daniel M. Landers. University Park: Pennsylvania State University Press, 1975, pp. 165–180.

Snyder, Eldon E., and Elmer Spreitzer. "Correlates of Sport Participation Among Adolescent Girls." *Research Quarterly* 47 (December 1976): 804–809.

Snyder, Eldon E., and Elmer Spreitzer. "Participation in Sport as Related to Educational Expectations among High School Girls." *Sociology of Education* 50 (January 1977): 47–55.

Spears, Betty. "The Transformation of Women's Collegiate Sport." *National Forum* 62 (Winter 1982): 24–25.

Theberge, Nancy. "Some Evidence on the Existence of a Sexual Double Standard in Mobility to Leadership Positions in Sport." *International Review for the Sociology of Sport* 19 (1984): 185–197.

Theberge, Nancy, and Alan Crook. "Work Routines in Newspaper Sports Departments and the Coverage of Women's Sports." *Sociology of Sport Journal* 3 (September 1986): 195–203.

Acknowledgments (continued from p. iv)

Peter Adler and Patricia A. Adler, "From Idealism to Pragmatic Detachment: The Academic Performance of College Athletes," *Sociology of Education*, 1985, Vol. 58, pp. 241–250. Reprinted by permission of the authors.

Harry Edwards, "The Black 'Dumb Jock': An American Sports Tragedy." Reprinted with permission from *The College Board Review*, No. 131, Spring 1984, copyright 1984 © by College Entrance Examination Board, New York.

George H. Sage, "Blaming the Victim: NCAA Responses to Calls for Reform in Major College Sports." Reprinted with permission from *Arena Review*, Vol. 11, 1987. Copyright © The Center for the Study of Sport and Society.

John C. Weistart, "College Sports Reform: Where Are the Faculty?" *Academe* 73 (July–August 1987), pp. 12–17. Reprinted by permission.

Richard Sandomir, "The Gross National Sports Product." Reprinted by permission of *Sports inc. The Sports Business Weekly*. Permission to reproduce may be obtained only from the president of *Sports inc. The Sports Business Weekly*, 3 Park Avenue, New York, New York 10016. 1-800-255-6286 for subscriptions.

Murray A. Sperber, "The College Coach as Entrepreneur," *Academe* 73 (July–August 1987), pp. 30–33. Reprinted by permission.

Jay J. Coakley, "Owners and Sponsors of Commercial Sports." Reproduced by permission from Jay J. Coakley, *Sport in Society*, third edition, St. Louis: Times Mirror/Mosby College Publishing, 1986.

James A. R. Nafziger, "Foreign Policy in the Sports Arena," reprinted from Arthur T. Johnson and James H. Frey, eds., *Government and Sport*. Totowa, New Jersey: Rowman & Allanheld, 1985. Reprinted with permission.

Richard E. Lapchick, "A Political History of the Modern Olympic Games." Reprinted by permission of the publisher, from *Fractured Focus: Sport as a Reflection of Society*, edited by Richard E. Lapchick. Lexington, Mass.: Lexington Books, D.C. Heath and Company; Copyright © 1986 by D.C. Heath and Company.

D. Stanley Eitzen, "The Political-Economic Olympics," reprinted from D. Stanley Eitzen and George H. Sage, *Sociology of North American Sport*, third edition. Wm. C. Brown: Dubuque, Iowa, 1986. Reprinted by permission of the publisher.

George H. Sage, "Religion, Sport, and Society," from *Sociology of North American Sport*, third edition. Wm. C. Brown: Dubuque, Iowa, 1986. Reprinted by permission of the publisher.

Charles S. Prebish, " 'Heavenly Father, Divine Goalie': Sport and Religion." Copyright © 1984 by The Antioch Review, Inc. First appeared in the *Antioch Review*, Vol. 42, No. 3 (Summer 1984). Reprinted by permission of the Editors.

Frank Deford, "A Heavenly Game?" Excerpts are reprinted courtesy of *Sports Illustrated* from the March 3, 1986 issue. Copyright © 1986 Time Inc. ALL RIGHTS RESERVED.

Lynn Rosellini, "Strike One and You're Out," Copyright, 1987, U.S. *News & World Report*. Reprinted with permission from the July 27, 1987 issue.

John J. Schneider and D. Stanley Eitzen, "The Perpetuation of Racial Segregation by Playing Position in Professional Football." *Sociology and Social Research* 70 (July 1986), pp. 259–262. Reprinted with permission.

G. Ann Uhlir, "Athletics and the University: The Post-Woman's Era." First published in *Academe* 73 (July–August 1987), pp. 25–29. Reprinted by permission.

Mary E. Duquin, "The Importance of Sport in Building Women's Potential." This article is reprinted with permission from the *Journal of Physical Education, Recreation & Dance* 53 (March 1982), pp. 18–20, 36. The *Journal* is a publication of the American Alliance for Health, Physical Education, Recreation and Dance, 1900 Association Drive, Reston, Virginia 22091.

Michael Messner, "The Meaning of Success: The Athletic Experience and the Development of Male Identity," in Harry Brod (ed.), *The Making of Masculinities: The New Men's Studies* (Boston, MA: Allen & Unwin, 1987), pp. 193–209. Copyright © 1987 by Allen & Unwin, Inc. Reprinted by permission.